D1601601

Political Participation in Rural China

This volume is sponsored by the
Center for Chinese Studies
University of California, Berkeley

POLITICAL PARTICIPATION
IN RURAL CHINA

JOHN P. BURNS

UNIVERSITY OF CALIFORNIA PRESS
Berkeley · Los Angeles · London

University of California Press
Berkeley and Los Angeles, California

University of California Press, Ltd.
London, England

© 1988 by
The Regents of the University of California

Library of Congress Cataloging-in-Publication Data
Burns, John P.
  Political participation in rural China.
  Bibliography: p.
  Includes index.
  1. Local government—China—History—20th
century.   2. Villages—China—History—20th century.
3. Political participation—China—History—20th
century.   I. Title.
JS7357.A15B87   1988   324.951′05
87–12463
ISBN 0–520–06005–9 (alk. paper)
Printed in the United States of America
1   2   3   4   5   6   7   8   9

To my parents
Harold Deane Burns and
Helen Pond Burns

CONTENTS

TABLES

ACKNOWLEDGMENTS

This manuscript began its life as a dissertation on Chinese peasant interest articulation, completed at Columbia University in 1979. I owe particular debts of gratitude to my advisers at Columbia, Michel Oksenberg, Andrew J. Nathan, and Thomas Bernstein for their help, support, encouragement, and suggestions over the years. I am grateful to Michel Oksenberg for pointing me in the direction of peasant interest articulation and for his intellectual guidance and support. Andrew Nathan, ever patient, read through various drafts of the manuscript and made many valuable suggestions. Thomas Bernstein shared with me his understanding of Chinese peasant politics and suggested revisions, both to the first manuscript and to later versions.

When I decided to redirect the focus of the manuscript from interest articulation to political participation, James Townsend and Victor Falkenheim patiently read through several drafts, provided detailed comments and recommendations, and saved me from many errors. I undertook the revisions in 1982–1983 at the Center for Chinese Studies at Berkeley, supported by a Center postdoctoral fellowship, and benefitted from the critical intellectual environment that the Center fosters. I learned much from Lowell Dittmer and Joyce Kallgren during those years, and I am grateful to the Center's Librarian C. P. Chen, for his help and support. At a later stage, Lenore Barkan, Jean Oi, Ian Scott, Andrew Walder, and David Zweig made many helpful suggestions for revision. I also benefitted from the advice of Ming K. Chan, David Chu, Leo Goodstadt, Peter N. S. Lee, and K. K. Leung.

I undertook much of the research for this study at the Universities Service Centre in Hong Kong, and I am especially indebted to the Centre's director John Dolfin, the librarian Lau Yee Fui, and Jean Xiong for their help and support. I am grateful for the financial assistance that the Social Science Research Council provided from 1974 to 1976, which enabled me to undertake the initial study. In 1982 and 1984 the University of Hong Kong and its Centre of Asian Studies also supported the project financially.

Finally, I wish to thank the many others who have tutored me in Chinese politics and who have provided invaluable assistance over the years: Yang Shichang, Suen Hsiao-man, Chen Zhijin, Yung Ching Ho, Cheung Siu Hing, Chow Siu Nam, and, of course, Ho Wai Kit.

1

Introduction:
Village Politics in China

In spite of collectivization and one-party rule, so-
cialist states have a significant and lively local politics. In any society, local
interests are more clearly defined and local personalities more familiar than
are the issues and the leaders in the capital. Under socialism, however, the
local arena is restricted by the centralized power of the state and by the
Communist party's penetration of local institutions—the family, school,
and workplace. Even with these constraints, however, local interests strive
for power.

An important dimension of local politics is the interaction between
leaders and the masses. Although the direction of influence is mostly
downward with leaders guiding the people, the masses also influence leaders and their policies. Grassroots influence, while rarely initiating policy,
can substantially affect policy implementation.[1] Contemporary local Chinese politics is no exception.

Despite the domination of political leaders in rural China, villagers have
exerted some influence on them. Even during the decade of the Cultural
Revolution, when radical officials touted the personality cult, demanded

and achieved high levels of mobilization, suppressed dissent and opposition, and attacked traditional forms and practices, peasants still attempted to influence public affairs in their localities.[2] During the 1960s and 1970s, peasants used the institutions provided by the state: local assemblies and mass organizations, elections, visiting officials, and the written media. When these failed, they occasionally turned, as they had many times before, to passive resistance and collective violence.[3] Although their influence on public affairs, usually mobilized by the local elites, was generally weak and intermittent, peasants were sometimes effective. They were effective, first, when they were able to ally themselves with leaders to oppose the policies of other leaders and, second, when group solidarity, based on such factors as kinship, community, or village interests, permitted them to take a common position vis-à-vis the authorities.

In contemporary China, then, even a so-called "nonstrategic" group— the peasantry—has initiated action to influence public affairs.[4] Workers and intellectuals, the groups usually identified by modernization theorists who have written about the evolution of socialist one-party states, have not had a monopoly on attempts to participate in politics.[5]

Official China has vastly overstated the extent and effectiveness of peasant participation. In the official view, peasants are allied to China's proletariat and jointly exercise "mastery" over the state and mass participation is both desirable and necessary for policy implementation. Officials have substantially qualified this participation, however. For the Communist party, the conformity of any particular policy to the party's current general line (the policy's "correctness") is more important than majority support. Officials reserve for themselves the authority to determine the scope of participation (who are "the people"?) and to fix the terms of participation. For official China, then, participation means mobilizing its citizens to carry out its policies.

Most local politics in China is, at least in part, issue-oriented. Real interests were at stake when the authorities attempted to restrict free markets, private plots, and family commercial undertakings—all moves that peasants protested. When authorities encroached on village land or requisitioned village laborers, they focused peasant attention on the distribution of benefits. Local politics also involves struggles to protect the prestige of lineages and neighborhoods, formed over many generations, and the status of more recently formed factions and other political groups.

This picture of the contemporary Chinese peasantry does not resolve its often-noted dual character. As Hsiao Kung-chuan notes (and many others point out), peasants in nineteenth-century China, "being long accustomed to despotic rule and very largely illiterate, displayed a decidedly passive mentality." When faced with economic and political crises, however, villagers "might out of desperation take part in riots, banditry, or outright rebellions. An insurrectionary potential lurked behind the normally placid villagers."[6] In contemporary China, the capability of the state has increased tremendously: It can to a much greater extent than previously prevent or moderate economic crises, but it also has greater means at its disposal to control antistate behavior. The peasantry's response has been reserved: It will try to use official channels to communicate to the elite, but, when these fail, it may resort to more direct and violent means.

Political Participation in Republican Villages

The Nationalist rule of China's countryside, especially during the Nanjing decade (1927–1937), was characterized by tensions within the Guomindang (which had been particularly severe before the "leftists" were expelled in 1927) and by conflict between the Nationalist party and local county governments.[7] The early attempts of the party to wrest control of subcounty institutions from local elites, on whom the resource-starved county governments depended, had given way by the early and mid-1930s to accommodation and to an "uneasy or limited alliance."[8]

Nationalist policy during this period can be summarized under the slogans of "self-government" and "democracy." In the Nationalist view, implementing self-government would widen the scope of political participation, which was essential for national integration.[9] Because the masses lacked civic awareness and were incapable of self-government, they required training in civic affairs under the supervision of the Guomindang. During the period of "tutelage," the party would exercise control, leading the nation to constitutional government and full popular sovereignty. Beginning at the county (*xian*) level, officials would set up local self-government, complete with elected officials. Only when this process was complete could constitutional government be implemented.[10]

Under this plan, starting in 1928–1929, authorities would appoint local leaders to newly created subcounty units, and local assemblies would elect (or nominate) the headmen for villages and towns.[11] These plans to implement democratic self-government throughout the countryside were to culminate in 1934. By 1933, however, in the face of mounting communist insurgency and opposition from entrenched local elites, the program was abandoned.[12]

In practice, political power in China's rural pre-1949 communities was wielded by the landowning "local elite."[13] Their power stemmed from access to education, their control of private militias, and their wealth. Their wealth they derived from rents, usury, commerce, and the "fees" extorted from the general populace as they collected taxes and other government revenues. The local elite, widely referred to at the time as "local bullies and evil gentry" (*tuhao lieshen*), staffed the subcounty bureaucracies.[14]

Before 1949 landowning families often filled positions in the ward and village offices. Bradley K. Geisert reports that "many—if not most—ward headmen in Kiangsu [Jiangsu Province] were landlords, or sons of landlords," a situation also found in Shaanxi and Henan provinces.[15] In Jiangsu, village and town headmen also came overwhelmingly from landlord backgrounds.[16] Other scholars report that throughout the period power increasingly lay in the hands of merchants, large landlords, and local politicos, who, according to Philip Huang, were qualified to influence village affairs by virtue of their age, wealth, learning, kin status, or personal prestige.[17]

In 1929, Nationalist reforms called for annual elections of village leaders by universal suffrage, using secret ballots.[18] It is unclear whether these regulations were carried out in practice.[19] Still, Sidney D. Gamble's North China study, conducted during the reform's high tide (1929–1933), concludes that "most" villages had "elected" village officials.[20] The ambiguities of the election process, however, are well illustrated by Martin Yang's account of elections in Taitou, Shandong, in the 1930s:

> At the beginning of every year a meeting is held to elect a *hsiang-chang* [*xiang-zhang*; headman], his chief assistant, and other subordinate officers. Those who attend are the senior members of the families. . . . Ordinarily . . . some representatives of each of the four clans must be present or the election is not considered valid.
>
> The election is conducted very informally. There is no ballot casting, no hand raising, and no campaign for candidates. The meeting is held in the village school or in some other customary meeting place. When several members of each clan have arrived, the person who presides over the meeting will stand up

and say, "Uncles and brothers, now we are all here to discuss the public affairs of our village. As you all know, our *chwang-chang* [*zhuangzhang,* same as *xiangzhang*], Uncle P'an Chi [the P'an lineage was the largest of the four in the village] has served us very well in the past year. He has worked hard and honestly to pacify disputes, to defend our village, to help families which have been involved in unfortunate controversies, to represent our interests in dealing with the government, and so on. As you know, to be a public servant in these days is really a headache. . . . Now is the time to conduct a new election of our *chwang-chang* and other officers. Uncle P'an Chi has recently said that he feels his age, that he is too tired to bear the heavy burden any longer and would like to be relieved. I want to know whether we should let Uncle P'an Chi retire and elect another person to be our *chwang-chang,* or should we ask him to continue. Since this is a matter of importance to our whole village, you are requested to express your ideas and let us know what your opinions are."

This opening address is followed by a moment of silence. Then one of the electors, usually a partially recognized village leader, will say, "Since, as Uncle Heng Li has just said, Uncle P'an Chi has served us well in the past, I cannot see why we should let him retire. I myself, and, I believe, many other fellow villagers, really appreciate Uncle P'an Chi's service, and I do not see any other person among us that is better for the office than he."

"Brother Heng Chun is right," says another representative. . . . A small farmer who does not have much social position in the village might add, "I believe that any person who can be an official, great or small, must be born with an official star. . . . [Uncle P'an Chi] has his official star. Then, why should we bother to say yes or no." At this everybody laughs. After a while, the chairman says again, "Now we have heard the opinions, which are for our *chwang-chang* to continue in office. But is there anyone who has different ideas?" Nobody speaks, but the chairman wants to make sure that there will be no complaints later, so he addresses a member of the Yang clan: "What would you say, Lao San?" "I agree with the others. . . ." When several others have been asked and given an assenting answer, the election is decided, and the village's *chwang-chang* is again in office. Other officers . . . are elected at the same meeting, but in a still less dignified manner.[21]

According to Yang, had Pan Ji [P'an Chi] genuinely wanted to retire, he would have said so to the chairman of the election, who in turn would have indicated that another person be chosen. Yang concludes: "The result of the election is therefore to some extent prearranged and the meeting is a routine matter. The real authority lies in the hands of the laymen leaders. Most villagers understand this and do not attribute too much importance to the office of *chwang-chang*."[22] Writing of the period from 1912 to 1940 in rural Shandong, Huang arrives at much the same conclusions: "These men [village headmen] were clearly not democratically elected representatives presiding over communities of equals. Though commoners, the village leaders generally formed a distinct political and economic elite, whose positions, like landed property, usually passed from generation to generation."[23] Thus, although elections were sometimes held, local elites manipulated them to put their favorites in power.[24] The results of the Nationalist reforms in practice, then, were little different from the experience of the preceding decades.

Links between ordinary peasants and the county government were provided through the local elite. Peasants with some social standing, such as owner-cultivators, probably used their connections to local influentials in their dealings with county authorities.[25] In areas where kinship groups were strong, the lineage elders probably served this "middleman" role.[26]

Villagers during the Nationalist period may also have used written communications to contact higher-level leaders. Contrary to earlier assumptions that commoners in China's villages were "rarely literate,"[27] a relatively high degree of functional literacy existed in rural China, well before the Republican period.[28] Although many peasants learned to read simple books, write letters, and keep accounts (the goals of the Nationalists' Mass Education Movement),[29] I have found few reports of their use of these skills to participate in politics.[30]

In spite of the widespread view that litigation was to be avoided at all costs,[31] by the early twentieth century villagers occasionally pressed claims against their leaders through the courts. In 1929 families in North China's Village D sued their village head for "extravagance in his handling of civic affairs" when he tried to increase a special assessment on the land. Although the magistrate persuaded the parties to settle out of court, the village head resigned as a result.[32] Such cases must have been rare, however.

When more formal channels failed, peasants sometimes turned to passive resistance, such as bribery, or acts of collective violence. Elizabeth Perry shows that, during times of scarcity and weak central government control, peasants have adopted aggressive strategies, both predatory and protective.[33] These acts of collective violence, often led by a disgruntled local elite,[34] were directed at political authority when government imposed, for example, heavier tax burdens. Tax and rent riots were not unknown during this period. In one case, several tens of thousands of peasants laid siege to Yangzhou in October 1932, protesting the results of a government land survey.[35]

The increasing power of the Chinese Communist party (CCP) also con-

tributed to a widening of the scope of political participation, particularly
after the 1927 split with the Guomindang. CCP officials mobilized peasants
to join the party and associations of poor peasants and hired laborers.[36] In
its base areas, the CCP set up local governments and supervised elections
of local leaders.[37] In other parts of the country, the party, in its bid for
power, encouraged peasants to attack local Nationalist authorities.

The ability of peasants to participate effectively in politics during the
Republican period rested in large part on their ability to mobilize community solidarity. Some factors tended to increase community solidarity: the
practice of cultivating in groups; irrigating (which required the cooperation of neighbors); living together in villages or hamlets rather than individually; and maintaining strong kinship groups.[38] The conditions for
community solidarity varied from village to village, however. As Philip
Huang shows for North China, some villages, faced with economic crisis,
simply disintegrated under the weight of outside pressure. Other villages
(composed mostly of owner-cultivators, according to Huang) were able to
mobilize the community to resist the incursions of the state and other
outsiders.[39]

Kinship ties played an important role in binding together communities
or sections of communities. There is little doubt that lineage groups in
South and Central China were much stronger than in the North.[40] In
Guangdong Province, for example, 80 percent of the peasants were estimated to live in lineage groups.[41] Single-surname villages in the North
were reported to be rare.[42] According to Jack Potter, the "necessary and
primary factor" for strong lineage groups was collectively owned land.[43]
Of secondary importance were such factors as mutual aid and protection,
prestige, and sentiment. South and Central China possessed characteristics
that favored strong lineage groups: rich land and natural factors of production to support the organizations; wealth derived from commerce to
maintain them; weak government control; and frontier conditions that required organizations to provide mutual protection and self-help.[44]

Nonetheless, lineage organizations were also an important feature of
North China villages. As Potter points out: "Strong lineages were by no
means absent from the area."[45] Huang and others observe that lineage relations penetrated the political structure of many North China villages.[46] In
some multi-surname villages in the North, where lineages were well developed, leadership positions were rotated among lineage group heads.[47] In
others, authorities felt obliged to consult minority lineages before making

decisions.[48] In North China's Ten Mile Inn, for example, Isabel and David Crook report that "factionalism had flourished for centuries as a tradition fostered by the landlords and rooted in the clans: the Fus, the Wangs, and the Lis."[49] Although single-surname villages were rare, lineage-based politics characterized the North as well as the South to varying degrees.

To summarize, political participation in Republican China was dominated by a strong, entrenched informal elite, whose position rested in large part on their wealth. Their exercise of power was relatively unchecked by outsiders. Although Nationalist authorities attempted to institutionalize village self-government, they were unsuccessful, both because local leaders resisted the implementation of the program and because they had to suspend it in their struggle with the Communist party and in the face of Japanese aggression. In any case, most peasants apparently preferred more informal means of communicating with their leaders, such as contacting, relying on personal relations (*guanxi*), and kinship ties. Other methods, such as written communications, lawsuits, and collective violence also existed, however.

Political Participation in Contemporary Villages

Agreeing with the Nationalists, the Chinese Communist party recognized the principle of popular sovereignty.[50] To implement the principle, the CCP argued that leaders should consult the peasants, like other citizens, on public affairs. The party should carefully control the process of consultation, however, and it reserved for itself the role of making policy. For CCP authorities, then, participation meant mobilizing the peasantry to implement party policies. They encouraged peasants to improve the efficiency of policy implementation through various channels of participation.

Compared to the Republican period, the most significant change in the practice of political participation has occurred in the nature of village leadership and its links to authorities outside the village. Recruiting from among disadvantaged elements in the village, the Communist party put "poor and lower-middle" peasants in positions of leadership. The character of the informal leadership changed as well. Political activists and the heads of labor-strong households took on this role.

By mobilizing China's villages, the party substantially reduced the autonomy of village leaders to handle village affairs. At the same time, it increased the power of national leaders to intervene in village affairs and to shape the character of institutions for participating in politics. From the local perspective, national CCP leaders controlled the formal institutions of participation: they initiated campaigns, propagated official value systems, and set and enforced narrow limits of permissible political behavior. They had a relatively free hand, not constrained by the exercise of popular sovereignty, but by the power of competing elites, some measure of self-discipline, and the low level of resources available to them.

There are significant continuities with the Republican period, however. In the mid-1950s and early 1960s and again since 1979, the Communist party has attempted to institutionalize local government in the countryside, continuing in some sense the policies of the Nationalists. Although the peasants continued to prefer strong, stable, and paternalistic leadership to contentious, more procedurally "democratic" arrangements, they occasionally articulated demands for change in these formal institutions, such as local assemblies and local elections. Most of the formal institutions, however, served other functions, such as legitimizing official policy, communicating policy goals, and mobilizing peasants to implement policies.

It is likely that written communications, such as letter writing and big-character posters, were not any more used by peasants than before to make demands of their leaders. Peasants may have felt that the process was too tightly controlled by political leaders and, thus, ineffective. They continued to prefer informal means, such as contacting, to pursue their interests, and, when these means failed, they sometimes resorted, as they had in the past, to passive resistance and collective violence.

The effectiveness of peasant participation depended in large part on the ability of villagers to unite the community to challenge political authority. In all probability, an important basis for this solidarity continues to be lineage relationships. Although CCP authorities tried to destroy the power of kinship groups in the 1950s by taking away their land, their later attempts to reorganize Chinese agriculture probably inadvertently reinstated kinship group power in many areas. Local politics in socialist China, then, continues to be deeply rooted in the past.

Definitions and Scope

Political participation is defined as activity by private citizens designed to influence public affairs.[51] The concept includes attempts to influence both the formulation and the implementation of policy. The politics of policy implementation is a significant arena, particularly in such systems as China's, where access to the policy formulation process is tightly controlled.

Political participation includes a range of activities, from the legal, legitimate, or formal to the quasi-legal, illegal, illegitimate, or informal.[52] Studying the full range of participatory behavior will help us to assess the strength of legitimate, elite-sponsored institutions. Clearly, China's leaders must themselves take into account all political activity, regardless of its legitimacy, even if only because they wish to suppress it.

Although private citizens are the principal actors, political participation can be mobilized by elites ("support" or "ceremonial") or initiated spontaneously by private citizens ("autonomous").

The definition identifies "public affairs" as the focus of citizen influencing. James R. Townsend defines "public" affairs as "affairs that are seen to have an impact on the entire community even when they deal specifically with only a part of it."[53] This formulation has the advantage of including quasi-governmental matters, which, nonetheless, affect a substantial number of people. Still, in his study of political participation in China, Townsend questions whether much of the individual interest articulation that he found at the grassroots level was really "political."[54]

This view is unnecessarily restrictive. Much of the interest articulation in the Chinese countryside is from individuals or small groups who hope to gain particular benefits; this is a strategy of political participation that characterizes the poor in many other countries.[55] These activities are "political" because peasants attempt to obtain advantages from state and party officials or their agents (who distribute benefits in the course of their official duties) and because these activities have an impact beyond individual concerns on the wider community.

The definition identifies participation as an activity, not as a feeling or an attitude.[56] Although feelings of political efficacy are relevant to the study of political participation, they do not by themselves constitute having participated.

Participation is "influencing," rather than "involvement."[57] To be sure, the same activities, such as voting and speaking out at meetings, often serve other functions. Through elections, for example, China's citizens may be socialized into official norms, the regime may gain legitimacy, and local communities may be integrated into the larger, more comprehensive units that make up electoral districts.[58] These activities only become "political participation," however, when they are designed to influence public affairs. Finally, following conventional usage, political participation is an activity engaged in by private citizens, not by government officials or other full-time functionaries.

A word needs to be said about the "voluntary" nature of participation. By definition, political participation is voluntary, and not coerced.[59] However, determining the precise mix of incentives used by elites to gain citizen compliance is difficult. As Thomas P. Bernstein points out, in the 1950s Chinese authorities applied measures that relied mostly on persuasion and social pressure to mobilize the peasantry into politics, but they also sometimes resorted to coercion.[60] Further, in the 1970s, authorities in Guangdong and Fujian often paid peasants to attend village meetings to compensate them for lost income. If villagers continued to be absent, then leaders persuaded them to attend. While not coercive, this activity was certainly not "spontaneous" or "autonomous" as defined by most Western social scientists. Attending meetings was nonetheless potentially significant behavior and should not be excluded a priori from my investigation.

The scope of my book is limited in a number of ways. First, I take the individual peasant as the unit of analysis and attempt to discover whether peasants individually or as members of groups influenced public affairs. Second, I assume that peasants are self-interested. When villagers decide to participate in politics, they do so because they judge that participation will be in their own or their family's interests.[61] Peasants are not only self-interested, however. As Popkin notes, "It is clearly the case that, at different times, peasants care about themselves, their families, their friends, and their villages. However . . . a peasant is primarily concerned with the welfare and security of self and family."[62]

Nor are peasants suspended in an amoral void, free of ideas of justice, propriety, rights, and obligations. The publicly expressed indignation of some peasants when they denounced landlords who exploited them or foreign invaders during the 1940s and early 1950s was indicative of the depth of their moral feeling. So too was the perplexity that some peasants felt in the mid-1960s when representatives of the Communist party arrived in the villages to root out petty corruption and favoritism, replacing the "traditional way of doing things" with a new Maoist orthodoxy.[63] I assume here that peasants perceive themselves as belonging to a moral order, which may influence their decision to participate in politics. However, most peasants participate to maximize expected benefits.

The picture of village life painted by Thomas P. Bernstein and Vivienne

Shue for the early 1950s conforms to these assumptions. First, following the redistribution of land to poor peasants, many peasants withdrew from politics and "settled down to become rich."[64] They had acquired land— the most coveted possession of peasants everywhere. In the land reform and throughout the subsequent stages of collectivization, party authorities appealed to peasant self-interest and cajoled villagers into joining mutual aid teams and cooperatives. But peasant anxieties remained. According to Shue, they "were simply loath to turn over their property for use by someone else," and they feared that pay in the new collectives would not be distributed according to work.[65] These fears justified the party's gradual approach to collectivization, which emphasized persuasion.[66] Second, even if peasants sometimes cooperated with one another, village politics remained conflictual. The conflicting interests of lowlanders and highlanders, insiders and outsiders, kin and non-kin, rich and poor, to name but a few of the antagonists, were real and played a significant part in village life.

My discussion of Chinese village politics is limited to the period from 1962 to 1982–1984, which can be characterized as the period of the "people's commune" (*renmin gongshe*). Although rural communes were set up in 1958 as a part of the Great Leap Forward, they had undergone significant changes by 1962. Only in 1962 did officials transfer land ownership and income accounting from commune administrations to subvillage administrative units, called production teams. Village leaders took on new functions in 1962, duties they retained throughout most of the period. The study concludes with 1982 to 1984, the years during which authorities stripped political and administrative functions from China's communes and brigades and transferred them to new township and village governments. My analysis, then, is confined to the period of the prereform commune and excludes the new local governments. Although the period from 1962 to 1984 saw policy and personnel changes, especially at the national level during the Cultural Revolution, it was a time of relative institutional stability at the village level.

My primary focus is on the politics of villages (*cun*), which in 1958 were renamed brigades (*shengchan dadui*), and their constituent units, production teams (*shengchan xiaodui*). Although I have focused on the dynamics of politics within villages, I have tried not to ignore the impact of higher levels, such as commune and county administration. By taking the village as my research focus, I have highlighted a significant political unit of several thousand people. Because village administration was the only unit in daily contact with the peasants, if the peasantry acted to influence public authority in China, I expected to find the evidence at this level.

I will explore the activities of "peasants," people living in China's villages, both suburban and rural, whose primary occupation is cultivating the land or engaging in subsidiary occupations, such as brickmaking, handicrafts, trading, or livestock breeding. The definition includes as peasants, however, the part-time nonsubsidized officials of production teams, who spend the majority of their time in production but, in their capacity as officials, are no longer private citizens.

Although most peasants in the early 1960s could be described as rural cultivators, the occupation of China's 176 million rural households has changed during the past twenty years. By 1982, 100 million of China's 800 million peasants were no longer cultivating the land but were employed in "industry, animal breeding, commerce, and service trades." Of these, one-third worked in rural factories.[67] Peasants continued, however, to be tied to the land, through household registration procedures. It is the political behavior of this group that forms the focus of this book.

Data for the study include the provincial and national press in Chinese and in English translation,[68] collections of official documents available outside of China,[69] my own observations made on trips to China since 1978, the results of fieldwork in China conducted by Western scholars,[70] and two series of interviews with former residents of rural China, which I carried out in Hong Kong in 1975–1976 and 1982. (For details see the appendix.)

2

Political Participation: Elite Views and Peasant Culture

Although China's leaders valued mass participation in politics, they have not treated the concept of "participation" coherently or systematically. Instead, they have focused on the general concept of democracy, the relationship between individual and state interests, and the theory of the mass line. Chinese authorities have identified "democratic" systems as those that govern in the interests of the people. The interests of the people collectively were determined by the needs of the state as interpreted by party leaders. The leaders formulated policy based on their understanding of the situation at any particular time, taking into account the desires of the people.

In addition to this idea of democracy, which focuses on outcomes, Chinese authorities sometimes argued that the further development of democracy depended on the institutionalization of certain procedures, such as elections, to enable the people to supervise the process of government. This procedural view dominated official thinking in the 1950s and early 1960s and again after 1978. It did not replace the view that focused on outcomes but rather supplemented it. Since 1978 officials have viewed democracy as both rule in the interests of the people and rule supervised by the people through regular procedures.

These views have implications for political participation. The outcomes view sees participation as a mobilizational problem: How can leaders mobilize the masses to carry out policies that are in their interest? The procedural view, though not denying the importance of mobilization, sees participation as a problem of designing and maintaining procedures to permit people to supervise their leaders. These procedures could permit citizens to initiate attempts to influence public affairs by electing officials who support their views or by dismissing those who do not. This result, however, depends on whether citizens are given choices in the elections and whether the system recognizes the legitimacy of the articulation of individual or sectional interests.

Chinese authorities viewed individual interests as subordinate to collective and state interests. Officials sometimes tended to equate these interests, in both the short and long term. During more liberal periods, such as the 1950s and after 1978, however, officials acknowledged the existence of conflicts of interest between individuals and collectives and attempted to protect individual interests without undermining the interests of the state. Insofar as pursuing individual or sectional interests was legitimate in China, the emphasis on procedural democracy permitted citizens to initiate attempts to influence government policy.

The party expected its officials to rely on the theory of the mass line in their dealings with the people. Both the outcomes and the procedural notions of democracy stressed the importance of soliciting mass opinion. However, leaders controlled the process of solicitation, and they alone determined policy.

Peasants perceived China's elite to include not only officials and party members, but also intellectuals, workers, and other urbanites, some of whom articulated their own unorthodox views on these issues. Dissident city dwellers, for example, questioned the view that democracy was merely a means to other ends and demanded that authorities implement a "genuinely" democratic political system. China's leaders reacted to these challenges both by suppressing the dissidents and by adopting some of their demands as official policy.

Although elites may have held a variety of views on political participation, it is likely that ordinary peasants did not share them, at least completely. Officially China's peasants were allied to the working class in the leadership of the state, but in practice the peasantry has been relatively deprived of the good life in China. Elites have been reluctant to share power with the peasants, and most peasants have not seen the value of organizing to influence public affairs in their favor.

Democracy

The modern meaning of the Chinese characters for "democracy" (*minzhu*) contains the notion of "the people" as "host" or "master," a content given to the word long before the advent of the Chinese Communist movement.[1] The meaning implies that in democracy the people have the right to manage their own affairs. Indeed, the notion that the people are the "masters of the Chinese state" is the central focus of the contemporary meaning of democracy in the elite perspective.[2]

China is a democracy, in the official view, because the country is ruled in the interests of the overwhelming majority of the population by a party that leads the only truly progressive class in Chinese society—the proletariat. Democracy always exists in a particular historical context, which for post-1949 China has required that the people adhere to "Marxism–Leninism–Mao Zedong Thought"; socialism; the dictatorship of the proletariat; and the leadership of the Chinese Communist party.[3]

In the Chinese official view, socialist democracy is different from and superior to the bourgeois democracy that is practiced in capitalist countries because socialism is based on prior political, social, and economic equality. Under socialism, the means of production are owned collectively and cannot be used by private individuals for private ends.[4] Although some recent writers acknowledge that the masses in China are "subordinate" to the leaders in some ways, leaders and masses under socialism enjoy equal economic, legal, and political rights: "Every citizen shares equality in the basic rights and duties conferred by the state constitution." Leaders are servants of the people.[5]

Among the overwhelming majority of the population, relations between the leaders and the masses should be democratic. Democracy is necessary to prevent the alienation of the leaders from the masses, a development that would destroy the unity of the state and prevent the possibility of effective action. As Mao Zedong observed in 1962:

Without democracy, without ideas coming from the masses, it is impossible to formulate good lines, principles, policies, or methods. . . . If there is no democracy, if there is no knowledge of what is going on down below and no clear idea about it, if there is no adequate canvassing of the opinions of all concerned and no communication between higher and lower levels, and if instead issues are decided solely by the leading organs of the higher levels on the strength of one-sided or inaccurate material, then such decisions can hardly avoid being subjective and it will be impossible to achieve unity in understanding and action or achieve true centralism.[6]

Democracy is a necessary means to implement policies. In Mao's words, "Democracy as such sometimes seems to be an end, but it is in fact only a means."[7]

In the official view, though relations among the people should be democratic, the state ought to exercise dictatorship over its enemies. The survival of a newly created socialist state was so threatened that the authorities had to put their enemies under strict supervision—a dictatorship of the proletariat—to prevent a capitalist restoration.[8] The dual character of the Chinese state is reflected in its official designation as a "people's democratic dictatorship."[9]

Finally, authorities always linked democracy to centralism as an organizational principle. Once the majority has reached a decision, all organization members must unite to implement it. Democracy and centralism cannot be separated, for to do so would lead to anarchy.

If elites have generally agreed on the nature of democracy in China, they have not agreed on the nature of procedures for its institutionalization. During the 1950s and early 1960s and after 1978, officials recognized the importance of developing democratic institutions and moved to hold elections and convene people's congresses.[10] During the intervening Cultural Revolution years, however, officials in power did not particularly value procedural democracy. Mao, for example, attacked these institutions for being unresponsive to his will, and efforts to further institutionalize China's democracy atrophied. Mao's "Sixteen Points," issued at the height of the Cultural Revolution, gave birth to an ultra-leftist perspective that demanded the ouster of "capitalist roaders within the party" (enemies attempting a capitalist restoration).[11] To establish a true democracy,[12] the ultra-leftists advocated direct worker management of the state through mass organizations, such as a "people's commune of China."[13]

This view did not acknowledge individual interests outside of those of the collective. The ultra-leftists recognized "the true interests of the peasants" as indistinguishable from the long-term interests of the masses. They saw the conflict between the bureaucratic-capitalist class of rulers and the masses as the major division in Chinese society.[14] The ruling class, composed of most senior officials in China, "has already come to form a decaying class with its own particular interests."[15] New leaders were required, who would embody the authority of the proletariat. In the ultra-left view, the revolutionary people, in the course of overthrowing the bureaucratic ruling class, would spontaneously produce new leaders. Special procedures for selecting them were unnecessary.[16] The leaders would be members of the people's commune on the same footing as the masses.[17]

Although most of those in authority during the Cultural Revolution did not hold these views in their extreme form, they tended to see democracy as an outcome and ignored procedures for achieving it. Since the purge of the Gang of Four, new groups, including dissidents and intellectuals, have shown a keen interest in institutionalizing democratic procedures. Although China's leaders followed along behind, since 1979 they have also emphasized procedural democracy. Authorities have come to define democracy in large part in terms of the procedures required for its realization, acknowledging it as an end in itself, not just a means of driving the economic development machine.

Chinese intellectuals and workers have also sometimes articulated dissident views, which can be divided into two general tendencies—moderate and liberal. The moderates were essentially reformers who accepted the elite definition of the Chinese state as a socialist dictatorship of the proletariat and who subscribed to Marxism–Leninism–Mao Zedong Thought and CCP leadership (the "four principles"). Although including among the "moderates" everyone from the Li Yizhe poster writers[18] to most of the contributors to the unofficial journals that appeared from 1978 to 1981 obscures many significant variations, it is nonetheless a useful classification. The moderate group advocated certain common positions, such as the reformist demand for democracy and the rule of law, which distinguished it from more liberal dissidents.

In the moderate view, democracy meant giving the people a decisive influence on the destiny of society:[19] The people should influence, control, and supervise government decisions.[20] In their view, elections, an important procedure for realizing this kind of democracy,[21] ought to be "conducted from the bottom up" and "modeled on the Paris Commune."[22] They also defended the people's right to use less institutional channels, such as big-character posters—"the weapon of extensive democracy."[23] In addition, the moderates saw democracy as a means of achieving the "four modernizations." As *April 5 Forum* points out: "The purpose of democracy is to concentrate various forces to serve the four modernizations. Democracy is a prerequisite for their realization."[24]

Although the moderates believed that collective interests should predominate, they also stressed the need for authorities to permit the people greater latitude for the pursuit of individual interests, foreshadowing new policies adopted by political authorities in 1980. Why, asked one writer, should we believe in the popular saying, "When the river is high, the streams are full?" (implying priority for collective interests). Is it not also true that the river's water comes from the streams in the first place? Collective prosperity depends on satisfying the interests of individuals.[25]

As early as 1974, Li Yizhe had called for establishing legal processes to enable the people to exercise supervision over party and state leaders. There must be processes, tested by time, for deciding which behavior was correct or erroneous and which was revolutionary or counterrevolutionary.[26] This concern for regulating leader-mass relations by law surfaced again during the 1978 to 1979 democracy movement. In this view, democracy depended on a strong legal system. Democratic rights "should be clarified by a series of legal provisions and insured by a strict judicial system and proceedings for rights to be legally exercised."[27] The moderates, then, called for the institutionalization of democracy. In a sense, they acted as the precursors of official policy, because after 1978 elite orthodoxy largely shared their view.

The liberal group, a small heterodox minority of the 1978 to 1979 democracy movement, centering around Wei Jingshen and his *Exploration,* agreed with the moderate definition of democracy and the need for the rule of law. It also shared the official view, which increasingly saw democracy as an end in itself. Democracy was the only system that could guarantee "the equal rights of all": "Democracy recognizes the equal rights of all human beings. . . . It provides all with an equal opportunity to realize human rights because it is founded on the recognition of everyone's equal right to live."[28]

Unlike the moderates, however, the liberals openly attacked the "four principles" and demanded an end to Communist party dictatorship. They characterized Marxism–Leninism–Mao Zedong Thought as a "single ideology pushed through by force"[29] and deplored Marxist dogma: "Let every Chinese think freely."

The liberals denounced one-party rule in China, arguing that it would lead to future cultural revolutions.[30] Dictatorship by any organization or group is antithetical to democracy, because it "negates the fact that different members of society have the right to satisfy their different desires."[31] In this view, dictatorship ignores the basic pluralism of society.

According to the liberals, society is made up of diverse interests, each of which, under democracy, may legitimately be pursued. Man has a right to carry out political activity to satisfy his personal desires in life and to fight for survival.[32] Because society depends on the interests of individuals, "people's individuality enjoys priority over their sociality." By implication China's single-party state should be replaced with a new multiparty system. The most serious challenge to the elite came from the liberals: They openly attacked the foundations of elite orthodoxy, and, for this, the state crushed them.[33]

China's leaders adopted the moderate position in large part in the post-1978 reforms. The new policies, among other things, emphasized the importance of institutionalizing and legalizing democracy at the grassroots. In an August 1980 speech to the Politburo, Deng Xiaoping pointed out that facilitating democratic management of the state, "especially basic-level and local political power," was not only a means to the realization of the four modernizations, but a desirable goal. "We aim," he said, "to create a higher and better democracy than the capitalist countries."[34] Reflecting this point of view, Liao Gailong, in his October 1980 report to a seminar on party history, highlighted the need for democracy in China's factories and villages. Liao explicitly included rural communes and production teams, which, like other local units, must have the "power to discuss and make decisions on important matters . . . the power to recommend to higher levels the dismissal of incompetent leading personnel," and the power to elect their own leaders.[35]

> In the government and the social life of the grassroots levels, direct democracy must be fully implemented in every residential district, so that every citizen will really be able to participate in discussing and making decisions on various public affairs which are directly related to their livelihood and interests.[36]

The central mechanism for realizing democracy lay in the popular election of leaders and delegates to the nation's people's congresses.[37]

> Universal suffrage, equal rights, direct voting and secret ballot are *the* four basic principles of the electoral system of a socialist state. These principles are being gradually put into practice in China's election, and a realization of them all means the complete democratization of the electoral system. Democratization of the electoral system reflects and embodies the democratization of our political life.[38]

Pressure to adopt these policies came from several quarters. China's intellectuals, on whom Deng and the party depended to implement their ambitious modernization program, demanded that the arbitrariness of the Cultural Revolution be curbed. They sought protection in a strengthened legal system. Cultural Revolution victims within the party also demanded the restoration of the democratic traditions of inner-party life developed in the 1950s and destroyed by Mao during the 1960s and 1970s. These forces together are sufficient to explain the new policies, independent of China's weak dissident movement. The dissidents simply reflected a concern that was taken up by China's elite for its own reasons.

The new emphasis on procedures signaled an abrupt change of policy from the Cultural Revolution. In theory, citizens were to be more than the passive objects of mobilizational politics and now were to exercise their rights to supervise public affairs. Whether or not they could do this, however, depended in part on whether citizens could legitimately pursue individual or sectional interests.

Legitimate Interests

For most of the past thirty years, Chinese authorities have distinguished different levels of interests in Chinese society (state, collective, and individual interests) and have recognized that they may not always coincide. Authorities have acknowledged the need to protect the interests of individuals, a policy especially evident during cooperativization in the mid-1950s and after 1978. A 1953 policy statement, for example, directed that "the individual interests of co-op members should receive first attention and a guarantee should be given to members that their actual incomes will not be lower than the levels they attained before joining the co-ops."[39]

Authorities strictly forbade discrimination against the interests of indi-

vidual peasants by mutual aid teams and coops during the mid-1950s.[40]
During subsequent periods, however, officials ignored the interests of individuals and units, a policy that leaders now acknowledge did serious
damage to the development of the economy.[41] Local authorities encouraged peasants to see their interests in terms of the interests of their collective. Popular rural sayings, such as "If the big river has water, the streams
are sure to be full,"[42] and "As the river rises, the boats go up,"[43] clearly
identified the individual interests of peasants with those of the collective.
Officials taught peasants that their welfare, particularly their income, was
dependent on collective effort. As the propaganda office of the Fujian provincial party committee stated in 1962: "Our emphasis on the collective is
for the purpose of further assuring and satisfying the good of each individual."[44] Only healthy, vigorous collectives can protect individual interests.

Since 1978 with the introduction of household contracting, officials
have attacked these views for being too one-sided. Authorities criticized
the saying that streams derive their water from big rivers as "contrary to
reason" and pointed out that wealth and power came from the people, and
did not "fall from the sky." Only if the state protected the interests of individuals could collective interests flourish.[45]

The party's answer to the problem of conflict between individual and
collective interests has been to deny it, at least in the long term. As Deng
Xiaoping reiterated in 1980: "We have always advocated that in socialist
society the interests of the state, the collective, and the individual are fundamentally identical, and if there are contradictions among them, the interests of the individual must be subordinated to those of the state and the
collective."[46] Conflicts between individual and collective interests were
likely, in the official view, when individuals ignored their long-term per-
manent interests. Authorities, therefore, often justified unpopular policies
by appealing to the long term.[47]

Chinese leaders have also recognized conflicts of interest between collective units. Maximizing the interest of one's production unit to the detri-
ment of collective and state interests has been a serious problem in rural
China. In 1963 authorities denounced officials in Henan, for example, for
their localism: "A few cadres only care about their own particular locality
and not about the overall situation."[48] Officials required that local production units not just look after their own interests, but that they take into
account the needs and interests of the whole.

The official view also recognized that peasants as a group had their own peculiar interests[49] and that within the peasantry there were conflicts of interest. Indeed, for much of the period, authorities encouraged peasants to see themselves in class terms.[50] During the mid-1950s, authorities allowed the different strata within the peasantry, except for landlords and rich peasants, to pursue their own interests. *Renmin Ribao* in 1955, for example, criticized "poor peasant" cadres for retaliating against middle peasants who had excluded poor peasants from their cooperative: "In the leading organs of the agricultural producers' cooperative, there must be upper-middle peasant cadres representing the interests of the upper-middle peasants."[51] By implication, upper-middle peasants had interests of their own, which they could legitimately pursue, and, moreover, cadres from upper-middle class backgrounds could best protect their interests. Since 1982, in the wake of household contracting, class divisions have re-emerged as a significant characteristic of rural society. As a part of their rural reform package, authorities have once again protected the interests of a "new rich" peasantry (those whom officials have encouraged to "become rich first").[52]

During the intervening years, and especially from 1968 to 1978, when authorities implemented more egalitarian policies in rural China, the importance of class distinctions as indicators of behavior declined in the countryside. Class divisions within the peasantry were replaced by a new conflict of interest between labor-rich and labor-poor households and production units—a conflict that received scant recognition in official sources.[53]

To summarize, the Chinese leadership recognized that society was composed of complex interests. During some periods, authorities encouraged citizens to pursue their short-term, largely economic interests, as long as they did not damage collective or state interests. Although officials permitted citizens to express their opinions on various issues, they reserved for the party the role of soliciting expressions of interest and transforming them into policy. The process of solicitation was contained in the theory of the "mass line."

Leader-Mass Relations

In an important essay written in 1943, Mao Zedong identifies the correct leadership method as that which goes "from the masses, to the masses."[54] According to Mao, leaders should take the scattered and unsystematic ideas of the masses and, through study, turn them into concentrated and systematic ideas, methods, and policies. Leaders, then, should return to the masses and propagate these policies among the people until they accept the policies as their own, hold fast to them, and act on them. The process is then repeated, in an unending cycle of "from the masses, to the masses."[55] Leaders as a result are in close contact with their followers, a relationship that is necessary to implement democracy, prevent bureaucratic abuses, and achieve effective action.

The theory of the mass line does not mean that leaders should simply follow the dictates of the masses. Although obtaining mass support for policies is important, the popularity of a policy is not sufficient for leaders to adopt it, because this would result in "following the main flow and letting things drift." Following along behind majorities could undermine socialism and "deviate from the interests and aspirations of the overwhelming majority of party members and people."[56]

The masses cannot veto policies that the party has determined to be correct and in the masses' interests. The party interprets the opinions and demands of the masses based on the party's own experience and on its own world view. In the mid-1960s officials related the case of a commune party secretary in Hubei, to teach the people that majorities could be wrong. The secretary attended a village mass meeting called to discuss whether the villagers should prepare wasteland for cultivation, an arduous and generally unpopular task. After a short discussion, villagers voted not to prepare the land, whereupon the village leader turned to the secretary and said: "Look, that's a majority, isn't it?" The secretary glanced at the peasants' faces and said: "Probably not, if you look into their hearts." The following day the secretary met with a group of village activists and convinced them that they were wrong. "After repeated comparison and summing up," all the villagers agreed to open up the new land: "After this affair, the secretary has often said: 'When seeking the views of the masses, we should not rigidly mouth "majority" and "minority." We must listen to and analyze the views of both sides. All correct views should be supported.'"[57]

The mass line requires that leaders solicit the views of the masses, but party authority is not bound to implement their wishes. In the above case, party authority found the peasants' views wanting and persuaded them to change their minds.

Although the mass line requires leaders to solicit the opinions of Chinese citizens, still it is the party, based on its ideology and program, that makes policy. Mao rather misleadingly likens the role of the party and the state in turning the ideas of the masses into policy to that of a processing factory:

> As far as formulation of lines, principles, policies, and methods is concerned, our leading organs merely play the role of a processing plant. Everyone knows that a factory cannot do any processing without raw material. It cannot produce good finished products unless the raw material is sufficient in quantity and suitable in quality.[58]

The party determines what product will be produced and which raw materials will be used or discarded. The theory is ambiguous, however, because it does not set out clearly how policy is to be formulated. What procedures are appropriate or necessary? What criteria are appropriate for setting priorities? Because the theory does not tie itself to any procedures, China's elites have disagreed on both the formulation and implementation of policy.

Having formulated the policy, leaders are bound by the theory of the mass line to persuade the masses to accept the policy as their own. An important part of the mass line is its emphasis on educating and persuading followers, not coercing them, to accept party policy. The scope of legitimate persuasion can be clarified by comparing it with illegitimate leadership styles, identified by Mao Zedong as including both "commandism" and "arbitrary action," and "ultra-democracy" and "absolute egalitarianism." The former relied on force and the issuing of arbitrary orders, both ineffective means of gaining compliance in the long term. Ultrademocracy was characterized by a lack of discipline, a situation where cadres made policy by themselves, without reference to higher authority. Mao also condemned absolute egalitarianism, the practice of treating everything equally, regardless of differing needs or conditions. Mao proposed that the party use education and persuasion to eliminate these abuses, which, if not corrected, would lead the party to bureaucratism, subjectivism, and the ultimate failure of the policy.[59]

The theory of the mass line assumes, first, that leaders and followers share the same interests: "Other than the interests of the people, our party does not have any special interests of its own."[60] The mass line, therefore, denies the possibility of the elite as a group with their own interests, such as preserving their position or power.[61] Developed for a social movement out of power, the theory is less appropriate when applied to state-society relations.

Second, the theory assumes that the leaders are already in office (the CCP is identified as the leader in Mao's 1943 article), and ignores the possibility that the ways in which the leadership replaces itself or is recruited may affect leader-mass relations. In the theory, leaders are assumed to be "others," outsiders, different from followers. The theory prescribes a method for attempting to bridge this gap. The mass line does not address the question of the origins of leaders ("Where do good communists come from?") or how ordinary people become leaders. But the ease with which the ordinary people can penetrate the leadership ("the ladder of success"), influences the nature of leader-mass relations.

Third, the theory of the mass line is procedurally vague and ambiguous. The procedures for solicitation, policy formulation, mass persuasion, and subsequent evaluation of policy are unstated. How should leaders solicit the views of the masses? Based on what criteria should leaders accept or reject mass views? What are the acceptable boundaries of permissible persuasion? And based on what criteria should implementation of the policy be evaluated? Ambiguity on these issues lay at the base of subsequent elite conflict.[62]

Fourth, the theory assumes that activism is vested in the leadership, not in the masses. Leaders solicit the views of the common people, a process that is leader initiated. It is, therefore, initially "downward." In the theory, leaders solicit at their discretion, because the timing of the solicitation is also leader initiated. The leadership determines when work teams are sent out, and cadres are sent down. The theory assumes that the masses are incapable of initiating action to express their views or concerns (or that such citizen-initiated action is undesirable). In this sense, then, the theory of the mass line presumes that mass participation must be mobilized.

Because of the procedural ambiguities surrounding the implementation of the mass line, China's leaders have been able to interpret the theory in various ways during the past twenty years. From 1962 to 1984, at least two different interpretations of the mass line were evident. From 1962 to 1965 and after 1978, leaders have emphasized the institutionalization of political participation. During the intervening period, a more situational approach prevailed, characterized by an interpretation of the mass line that relied on charismatic leadership, but that did not particularly value regular, predictable participation through legally created institutions. Both trends, however, have strongly emphasized mobilized participation over citizen-initiated attempts to influence public affairs.

Although in theory the mass line provides a fairly coherent concept of leader-mass relations, in practice China's leaders have disagreed on two key issues: Who should have the right to participate? and What form should participation take? On the first issue, China's leaders agreed that participation was the right of "the people," but disagreed on definitions of "the people." In general, Cultural Revolution authorities restricted participation to those with politically acceptable (or "revolutionary") class backgrounds, excluding those who owned property before the 1949 revolution (especially landlords and rich peasants and their descendants in the countryside) and those whose attitudes or behavior the regime deemed threatening. Among the latter category were "rightists," "counterrevolutionaries" (labels applied administratively by public security and party authorities), and "bad elements" or common criminals.[63] Authorities have denied these groups, numbering perhaps 5 percent of the population,[64] political rights in various state constitutions, regulations, and legal codes.[65] Cultural Revolution leaders interpreted the exclusion relatively broadly and extended it to include such intellectuals and professionals as teachers, writers, doctors, scientists, and engineers.

Before and after the Cultural Revolution, however, authorities have, in practice, been less restrictive. Although they have retained the concept of "the people" as a category of the Chinese population, they have sought to limit the use of class labels to restrict participation. Since 1978 in the countryside, for example, most peasants with "landlord" or "rich peasant" class labels have become "commune members" (*sheyuan*), thus entitling them to the same political rights enjoyed by their poor and middle peasant neighbors.[66] Since 1978 the regime has also reduced the number of people (mainly intellectuals) labeled "rightist." Authorities have continued to label some Chinese as "counterrevolutionaries" and "bad elements," labels that they were supposed to apply through the legal system. Thus, though authorities still excluded some Chinese from participation, the current leadership has included many more of China's population within their definition of "the people."

A second area of elite conflict has focused on how China's citizens ought to participate in politics. Through which channels and institutions should people participate? In theory, the regime provides a range of channels for its citizens to communicate to the leadership. The various state constitutions, for example, provide for indirect representation through the people's congress system, with citizens voting for delegates (or electing them "through democratic consultation" in 1975).[67] These congresses have the right to supervise government officials and to recall their deputies.[68] In theory, the law protects the rights of the people,[69] and for much of the period citizens have had the freedoms of speech, press, assembly, association, procession, demonstration, and making written or oral complaints.[70] In spite of the variety of state-sponsored institutions, China's leaders have differed among themselves on which were the appropriate forms for political action.

During the early 1960s and, especially after 1978, China's moderate leaders attempted to institutionalize political participation. Citizens should exercise their right of supervision of government affairs, in this view, through "legal, disciplined, and orderly" channels.[71] This means both "exercising state power as stipulated in the constitution" through the people's congress system and "giving suggestions and making criticisms" through mass organizations, such as the peasants' associations.[72]

During the Cultural Revolution, however, China's radicals restricted (but did not abolish) the use of these channels. They were suspicious of the reliability of existing institutionalized participation, which, in their view, had become routinized, bureaucratic, and served mainly the interests of the leadership. Elections should be less opportunities for competition to choose leaders or to decide on policies than popular referenda to demonstrate support for party policies. Meetings and demonstrations should serve the purpose of mass education. The "four great freedoms,"[73] incorporated in the 1975 and 1978 constitutions, best represented the view that additional noninstitutionalized channels were necessary to supplement the new institutions set up in the Cultural Revolution.[74]

Whether peasants used these institutions to participate in politics has depended, at least in part, on the value they have placed on participation.

Peasants and Participation

Thus far, we have examined the views of China's elite on political participation, without considering the possibility that these views are not wholly accepted by ordinary Chinese people. Do peasants, for example, believe that it is legitimate for them to pursue their own interests? If so, in their view, how ought this be done? Making general statements about the attitudes of 800 million people without survey data is risky, but some attempt to speculate on the issue is required.

Although the 1949 revolution was a "peasant" revolution, it was not led by the peasants, nor have they played a leading role in post-1949 China. In spite of the fact that the People's Republic officially describes itself as a "socialist state . . . led by the working class and based on the alliance of workers and peasants,"[75] leadership and political power belong to the urban working class and its vanguard, the CCP. Although Mao believed that the peasants could be mobilized to make revolution, he, like other Marxists, saw the peasantry by itself as incapable of organizing to take state power.

In the 1949 revolution, the party recruited peasants into newly created positions of power. Officially, China's leaders accorded peasants high status and access to the goods and services provided by the state. Peasants as a group, however, have been relatively deprived in contemporary Chinese society.[76] During most of the period, rural incomes were substantially lower than urban incomes, a gap that, although narrowing now, in the 1970s was still approximately 3 to 1.[77] China's development policies have sought to force high levels of rural savings and to limit consumption. Although the 1978 reforms increased the peasants' standard of living, the income of China's peasants continues to lag behind that of urban dwellers.

Further, government services to rural areas have lagged far behind their urban counterparts. Proportionately many more urban than rural youth, for example, have received higher education.[78] The 1978 reforms may have exacerbated the differences because some peasant families pulled their children out of school to work on the land. Authorities have also limited the opportunities for peasant youth to receive nontechnical higher education by turning rural secondary schools into agricultural technical institutions. Rural medical care and other welfare benefits, such as the provision of old-age pensions, have lagged far behind urban standards as well.[79]

Poverty in the countryside attracted peasants to the cities. However, during the 1960s and 1970s, authorities successfully controlled rural to urban migration through administrative measures, including the household registration system and the rationing of necessities, such as grain, cotton cloth, and cooking oil. Ration tickets were available from work units and usually were only redeemable locally.[80] The opportunity to leave the villages was restricted to those who could obtain places in the army, the party, the government, or higher education. Since 1978 urbanites have filled these places in increasing numbers. In 1983, for example, peasants accounted for only 10 percent of new party recruits.[81]

Urbanites shared these views about the superiority of life in the city. They resisted the attempts of authorities to "send down" to the countryside millions of youths, intellectuals, and cadres, both to learn peasant ways and needs and as a form of punishment. Many of them faced hardship, inadequate housing and medical care, sexual abuse, ridicule, ostracism, and, occasionally, malnutrition.[82] Most urban youth would not even consider marriage to a villager or living permanently in the countryside.[83]

Recent surveys carried out in urban and rural primary and secondary schools indicate that few of the respondents would choose farming as an occupation. In a survey of primary school students in the city of Wuxi, conducted in November 1979, for example, only 4 out of 839 (0.47 percent) of the respondents answered "peasant/farmer" when asked what work they would like to do when they grew up.[84] In another survey of 1,122 urban and rural middle school students, carried out in 1980 in Liaoning Province, only 2 youths (0.18 percent) listed "peasant" as their "ideal future occupation."[85] The social status of the peasantry in contemporary China is very low.

The peasants' lower social and economic status is complemented by their lower political status. Since the 1950s peasants have been underrepresented in China's intermediate- and higher-level people's congresses. More recently, the 1979 Election Law required that each rural deputy to the National People's Congress represent eight times as many constituents as an urban deputy.[86] Officials argued that "this gives expression to the leading role of the working class in our country and the need to realize the four modernizations."[87]

The reasons for the urban bias are not hard to find. First, the law prevents peasants from numerically dominating the congresses, thus ensuring at least symbolic control for China's most "progressive" class—the proletariat. Second, cities in China have traditionally been the centers of discontent and, since 1949, occasional rioting. In the 1960s and 1970s, the Cultural Revolution (1966–1969) was fought in China's cities: workers struck and demonstrated in Hangzhou in 1975; urban discontent erupted in rioting in Tiananmen in 1976; rusticated youths demonstrated in Beijing in 1979; and returned sent-down youths rioted in Shanghai and Hangzhou in 1979. Challenges to elite authority have been largely urban-based. Third, China's cities act as the processing plant for turning agricultural surpluses into industrial wealth. The concentration of financial and technical resources in the cities makes the control of urban areas a matter of strategic importance.

In spite of their relative deprivation and powerlessness, Chinese peasant culture was characterized by values that permit group action in politics. To be sure, peasants, like other Chinese, respected authority and sought harmony, consensus, and security in social relationships.[88] One recent study concludes that achieving consensus was an important precondition for taking action in many Chinese villages.[89] Peasants, like other Chinese, deferred to and respected their leaders in exchange for protection and support. As Vivienne Shue points out for the 1950s, peasants expected their leaders to "protect the village against undesirable central demands."[90] Villagers rarely disagreed with leaders in formal public settings, such as at meetings, and seldom spoke out publicly against unpopular policies.[91] A general presumption in favor of authority existed in Chinese villages.

Under some conditions, however, peasants believed that an active and direct role in politics—passive resistance or collective violence—was legitimate. Faced with economic crisis and the failure of legitimate channels, peasants sometimes pressed their demands through strikes, corruption, riots, and demonstrations.[92]

An extensive private economy, developed over thousands of years, linked peasants to rural markets and taught them the value of rational, self-interested economic activity.[93] During times of famine, this meant looking out for the safety and security of one's family, but, during better times (in spite of their conservatism),[94] it meant trying to get ahead and even taking risks.

During the 1949–1951 land reform, party authorities tailored their policies in the countryside to meet the needs of a rational peasantry. Peasants were induced to join mutual aid teams and cooperatives by promises that they would receive higher incomes and that they and their families would enjoy higher living standards.[95] The liberal agricultural policies of the early 1960s and the post-1978 period reflected this understanding of what motivated peasants in China.

The Chinese peasant is not a free operator, however, because he is embedded in networks of moral obligation.[96] Peasants, like other Chinese citizens, are motivated in part by the belief that one ought to have concern for the welfare of others in one's network of personal relations. Historically, this network has included the household and other kin, those who live in the same village, and work and school mates.[97] Villagers expect that others within their network will help them in times of need and in other ways express human feeling toward them.

Peasants identify with those in their network and believe that to be interested in the welfare of their extended group is perfectly legitimate.[98] Rational behavior means not so much individual self-interest as concern for the welfare of one's group. Chinese peasants believe that it is legitimate to pursue the interests of the group or network, and they expect that others will do the same.

Previously, I outlined factors that tended to increase community solidarity in pre-1949 Chinese villages. Many of these factors, such as relying on irrigation and cultivating in groups also characterized the contemporary period. In addition, when authorities organized rural China into cooperatives and then into communes, they vested ownership of the land in the new organizations, and they required collective responsibility for meeting quotas and levies. These measures also undoubtedly increased feelings of group solidarity.

Among the many ties that bind the rural Chinese together, lineage has continued to play a significant role in some places, especially in South China. Although the economic basis of kinship groups was destroyed in the 1950s land reform,[99] subsequent organizational policies tended to strengthen these groups. Cooperatives and communes left intact traditional residential patterns, which in many villages were largely kin-based.[100] The implementation of household contracting since 1980 in South China has been accompanied by the strengthening of kin-based behavior in the organization of work and in collective violence.[101]

In the absence of data from North China, it is difficult to speculate on the importance of kinship as a basis of political action for the country as a whole. For the pre-1949 period, lineage groups played a significant role in many North China communities. Although recent studies of North China villages do not give a prominent place to the political role of lineages,[102] it is likely that, where they were relatively strong in the past, they continue to be influential. The same rural organizational policies were applied uniformly to both the South and the North.

Either because they view formal institutions as relatively ineffective or because they lack the resources to use them effectively, villagers prefer to work through informal channels to achieve their goals. Networks of personal relations are the preferred channel for seeking redress or change. Leaders should be open to this kind of influence, in the peasant view.

Conclusion

In general, political participation has meant, for most Chinese, mobilization into various forms of elite-determined political activity in support of party and state policies. Political participation in this view is a method of policy implementation. The dominant elite theory of leader-mass relations—the mass line—is explicitly mobilizational and sees policy making as exclusively the domain of China's leaders. The theory does not recognize the possibility of citizen-initiated attempts to influence public affairs.

At the same time, authorities recognize that China is composed of diverse interests: Both classes and strata within classes have their own interests. Further, officials acknowledge that individuals and households have interests of their own different from those of the collective or the state. In the elite view, citizens may legitimately pursue these interests in the economic realm within certain limits. But authorities do not acknowledge that any individual or group has a legitimate political interest other than the interest of the whole.

Although China's leaders have given high priority to mobilizing the peasantry into various political and economic activities, they have relatively neglected the countryside in China. Officials have provided neither the services nor the resources to permit the peasantry to initiate political activity. Nonetheless, peasants have had a keen interest in their own welfare and the welfare of relatives, friends, and neighbors. Although the conditions for building group solidarity existed, villagers highly valued personal ties to communicate their interests to authorities and to reduce insecurities. Officials provided institutions for mobilizing Chinese peasants, but only under some conditions did peasants themselves seek to use these institutions to influence public affairs.

3

The Organizational Context of
Political Participation in Rural China

Elite economic and organizational policies and the process of their implementation provided the context of political participation in the countryside. As a result of their rural economic policies, central authorities came into conflict with local vested interests. These conflicts formed the bases of rural politics in China from 1962 to 1984. In general, the period was characterized by two different policy tendencies: one was moderate and emphasized economic growth at the expense of rural class differentiation (from 1962 to 1965 and after 1978); and a second was radical and sought to reduce rural class differentiation, even at the expense of economic growth (from 1966 through 1978). These policies sparked conflict both between the state and rural society and, within rural communities, between wealthier and poorer households and production units. Political participation in the countryside was largely restricted to attempts to influence the implementation of these policies.

In 1958, to administer its program, local authorities established in the countryside 26,578 communes (*renmin gongshe*), varying in size from 20,000 to 80,000 people. These were further subdivided into brigades (*shengchan dadui*), often natural villages, and production teams (*shengchan xiaodui*) or hamlets within villages.[1] Although these organizations were designed to implement policy, their structure has provided peasants with opportunities to participate in politics. First, rural organizations were staffed by locals, who shared similar backgrounds with other villagers, making them more approachable. Second, organizational rules and regulations required the formal participation of the peasantry in some decisions. Third, the organizations centralized power in the hands of a few senior officials, which facilitated general mobilizations. Fourth, because the organizations were both residential- and production-based, they consolidated the group structure of rural society, which could be mobilized to influence public affairs under certain conditions.

Finally, the process of policy implementation itself provided opportunities for peasant political participation. The style of policy implementation and, in particular, whether authorities mobilized the masses into a campaign, determined the context of attempts to influence public affairs. In general, during campaigns, the opportunities for citizen-initiated participation were few. However, interelite conflict often emerged in the course of policy implementation, and this sometimes facilitated citizen-initiated political participation. When local leaders were divided among themselves or resisted the directives of their superiors, peasants had a greater opportunity to enlist the aid of some (especially higher-level) leaders to influence others. Thus, both the content of the rural policies and the process of implementing them have shaped the nature of political participation in the countryside.

Rural Policies

China's leaders adopted moderate, economic development–oriented policies during the early 1960s and after 1978, which relaxed restrictions on private income-earning activity and which resulted, at least after 1978, in substantial decollectivization. Between the 1960s and 1978, authorities maintained much tighter control over the private economy and enforced measures to strengthen collective agriculture. The implementation of these policies served to sharpen conflicts in China's villages, and the process of implementation provided opportunities for villagers to participate in politics.

In the wake of the Great Leap Forward, China's leaders undertook a series of reforms that greatly increased the number of communes by reducing the size of each to more manageable proportions. Authorities increased the number of communes from about 24,000 in 1959 to 74,000 in early 1962 and increased the number of brigades from about 500,000 to more than 700,000. Production teams grew from 3 to 7 million.[2] China's leaders also restructured the incentive system to reward individual households and small groups of cultivators. Local officials restored private plots and encouraged the expansion of household sideline activities and rural markets. The "free supply" distribution system was replaced by a piece-rate payment system that tied income to labor contributions.

At the same time, authorities first made the brigade[3] and then the production team[4] (usually composed of twenty to fifty households) the unit of ownership and accounting, a move that caused difficulties for less well-endowed teams and tended to increase income differentials in the countryside. It did, however, spur production by rewarding wealthier teams. These policy changes were symbolized by the slogan "three freedoms and one guarantee" (san zi yi bao). The policy encouraged the free extension of private plots, sideline production, and rural markets, and sought to guarantee or "fix" output quotas to households. Local authorities experimented with these policies in many parts of China from 1961 to 1963,[5] actions for which they were severely criticized during the Cultural Revolution.

These policies tended to strengthen the cohesiveness of teams and brigades (villages), but to reduce horizontal integration among villages. One consequence of organizing rural units of production around residential units was that lineage boundaries often came to be coterminous with team or brigade boundaries. This development was largely unanticipated by China's leaders and undermined their goals of weakening kinship ties while strengthening rural class solidarity. Educational policies encouraging self-sufficiency in rural village schooling, marketing policies restricting the number of intermediate market towns, and marriage policies encouraging marriages within villages—all worked to reduce horizontal integration, isolating villages from their surroundings,[6] but sometimes leaving intact lineage group solidarity.

The liberal policies of the 1960s saw a number of problems emerge in the countryside. Designating production teams as ownership and accounting units increased the opportunities for corruption among local cadres.

As a result, some brigade and team leaders accepted bribes, embezzled funds, set prices, and expropriated work points.[7] Along with this development was the reemergence of "feudal" and wasteful practices associated in the minds of the leadership with the pre-1949 period. The families of bridegrooms paid bride prices for marriage contracts; cadres held extravagant wedding and funeral banquets; and peasants exchanged gifts at holidays, marked bumper harvests with extravagant feasts, slaughtered pigs privately, and took over state property for private use.[8] Reports of these deviations made their way to Beijing and prompted authorities to launch the Socialist Education Campaign in 1963, in an attempt to change the thought and behavior of peasants and local officials alike.

In May 1963 Mao issued the "First Ten Points," initiating the Socialist Education Campaign.[9] This document called for "cleaning up" local cadre corruption, establishing "poor and lower-middle peasants' associations," and recording local histories. Moderate in tone, the document emphasized that errant cadres and peasants should be treated leniently and reformed through education and persuasion. It was later seen as the opening salvo of the "Four Clean-ups Campaign" (cleaning up abuses in accounting, granaries, work points, and the use of collective property), which directly attacked local cadre corruption.[10]

Deng Xiaoping, then secretary-general of the party, and Liu Shaoqi, head of state, took charge of the campaign and issued two subsequent directives: the "Second Ten Points" (September 1963), and the "Revised Second Ten Points" (1964). Mao later claimed that these undermined the campaign and obstructed the true interests of the party. These directives took a harsher line with local cadres and resulted in the dismissal of large numbers of local rural leaders.

The Beijing leadership relied on work teams to implement the Four Clean-ups Campaign, much as they had during the land reform in the 1950s. Work teams not only took temporary control of many local units, but they also set up new poor and lower-middle peasants' associations and charged them with the supervision of local cadres, newly installed in work team–managed elections.[11] At the same time, they attempted to implement the new Campaign to Study Dazhai, which featured brigade-level accounting, no private plots, and wage payments based not only on the amount of work performed, but also on political attitudes and behavior. The campaign required local leaders to convene periodic mass meetings to assess the worth of each villager, a practice that soon declined in the face of sometimes bitter disputes over work point assessments.[12] Work teams often called on the first wave of "sent-down youths," urban middle school graduates, rusticated to the countryside in 1964 to help them investigate cadre corruption and mobilize the peasantry for the campaign.[13] Work teams in many places carried out their tasks zealously, with the result that between 1 and 2 million local cadres lost their posts.[14]

The campaign took a new turn when Mao issued the "Twenty-three Points" in January 1965, identifying for the first time the source of the problem as "powerholders within the party who are taking the capitalist road." The focus of conflict now shifted to the party bureaucracy in Beijing and in the provinces, thus setting the stage for yet another attack on local leaders in the Cultural Revolution.[15]

Although the Cultural Revolution (1966–1969) was primarily an urban campaign,[16] with limited impact on the countryside,[17] still struggles between rival Red Guard factions and attacks on commune and brigade party officials spilled over into some rural and suburban areas.[18] Informants from Guangdong, for example, reported several months of anarchy (*wu zhengfu zhuyi*) in 1967 when local leaders, who had been attacked and suspended during the Four Clean-ups Campaign in 1963–1965, found themselves again under attack and refused to carry out their official duties.[19] In many areas, Cultural Revolution rivalry exacerbated old, pre-1949 kinship- and neighborhood-based conflicts.[20]

Authorities restored order in the countryside in 1969 with the Cleaning-up Class Ranks Campaign, a movement that witnessed the return of many pre–Cultural Revolution officials to their posts. The new regime dismissed or arrested many rebel Red Guard leaders and reinstated the old order in the form of "revolutionary committees."[21]

The campaigns of the mid- and late 1960s had important consequences for local rural politics. They increased the intensity of local leadership conflicts. Local leaders, battered by several rounds of investigations, dismissals, and reinstatements, sought security by strengthening ties with higher-level leaders and rebuilding ties to the peasants. The campaigns deepened communal conflicts: local leaders mobilized groups of supporters to fend off the attacks of their opponents. Thus, the campaigns probably strengthened group solidarity in some places, as lineages and "insiders" or "outsiders" sought to protect their own positions. Conflict among local leaders and group solidarity among peasants have both enhanced opportunities for peasants to participate in politics.

The Cultural Revolution was followed by a period of "ultra-leftist" excesses.[22] Middle-level leaders,[23] many of whom achieved their positions in the Cultural Revolution, demanded that production teams be amalgamated (thereby effectively expanding the size of the unit of accounting, perhaps to brigade level); that brigades and communes be permitted to take over team sideline enterprises; and that private plots and family sideline production be curtailed.[24] China's leaders charged local authorities with carrying out the "One Hit and Three Antis" Campaign (*yi da san fan*), designed to root out opponents of the new policies.[25] Press commentaries criticized "spontaneous capitalist tendencies" in the countryside and demanded the implementation of the Dazhai system. By the early 1970s authorities had reduced the number of communes to about 50,000, a figure that was to remain relatively stable for the next decade.

By late 1971, however, authorities decided that these policies were hampering production and they were scrapped.[26] Although "learning from Dazhai" continued to be a slogan until 1980, local units no longer had to do without private plots, pay time rates, or adopt brigade-level accounting. This decision was followed by a campaign that criticized "ultra-leftist" excesses in the countryside.

Dissension within the central leadership in Beijing throughout the 1970s continued to influence rural policies. Although authorities moderated the radicalism of 1968–1971, they continued to emphasize rural unit self-sufficiency and taking "grain as the key link." Thus, progress in the diversification of the rural economy, opposed by radicals in Beijing, was slow. In 1975–1976 leaders initiated a nationwide campaign to limit bourgeois rights, which had implications for the countryside. Local officials in some areas understood the campaign to mean that once again they should reduce the size of private plots, for example, and cut back family sideline production.[27]

Although the death of Mao Zedong and the arrest of the Gang of Four had a critical impact on Chinese politics, the effect was slow to reach the countryside. Indeed, during the subsequent two years, agricultural policy appeared to be in disarray.[28] A major conference on the development of agriculture, called in December 1976, for example, endorsed many of the leftist policies of the past, such as brigade-level accounting.[29] These poli-

cies were, however, tied to a commitment to modernize agriculture as part
of the new emphasis on economic development.[30]

Rural incomes throughout the 1970s stagnated,[31] and productivity
continued to be low. With the radicals out of power, Deng Xiaoping, in
coalition with moderate central and provincial party leaders, began push-
ing for major reforms aimed at increasing rural productivity and living
standards.[32]

Provincial authorities in Hunan and other areas started experimenting with policies to give greater autonomy to production teams and to
"lessen the burden on the peasants."[33] Authorities relaxed central control
in a number of areas, allowing peasants more opportunity to engage in
individual and household enterprises. Peasants began cultivating larger
private plots, expanding sideline production, and trading more actively in
rural markets. Villagers in some places started cultivating the land in small
groups, not in the larger production teams, and they began to calculate
income according to the amount of work actually performed.

In December 1978 the Third Plenum of the Eleventh Central Committee ratified these changes.[34] The "Regulations on the Work in Rural
People's Communes (Draft for Trial Use)" legitimized the above trends
and emphasized that local authorities must respect the rights of the production team, the approved unit of ownership and accounting. Under
these policies, the leadership permitted small groups of peasants to contract for the use of collective land, seeds, and tools, as long as they turned
over a fixed quota of their output to the state procurement authority.[35]
Contracting output to households, however, was expressly forbidden.[36] In
keeping with the liberal tone of the documents, authorities declared that
all but unrepentant landlords and rich peasants (and their descendants)
would henceforth be considered "commune members" and should not be
discriminated against.[37]

In early 1979 authorities in Guangdong, Sichuan, and Anhui began
experimenting with small-group farming, organized around groups of
three to five families, often kinship groups.[38] Peasants in Hunan, Jiangxi,
Guizhou, and Fujian pushed things further, however, by demanding that
local authorities permit individual farming and by trying to divide up the
land for household use.[39] Although authorities initially resisted, by April
1980 they acknowledged the usefulness of contracting output to households (*baochan dao hu*). Under the new policy,[40] production teams con-

tinued to own the land, but households could contract with teams for the use of the land for up to fifteen years.[41] Initially authorities sought to limit household contracting to poor, low-yielding areas (about one-third of production teams),[42] but the policy permitted commune members to decide which of many variations of the responsibility system to adopt.[43]

By the end of 1985, 90 percent of production teams had adopted *baogan dao hu,* or "contracting tasks to the household."[44] Under this system, households contracted with production teams for the use of fixed plots in return for payments to the team (to cover collective overhead, such as local welfare funds and cadre salaries). The team distributed land to households either on a per capita basis or to adult workers (labor powers, *laoli*).[45] Households retained for their own use or marketed the remaining products produced on the contracted land. Unlike other forms of the responsibility system, under *baogan dao hu* authorities did not use work points to distribute income to individual households. Peasants were basically self-employed and were responsible for their own food needs.[46]

This system contrasts sharply with the 1962 to 1979 practice. Then peasants worked collectively under the daily guidance of production team officials to produce a crop, most of which was sold to the state at below market prices. Peasant income from collective work was determined by calculating their labor contribution through a work point system that tended to equalize income. Although households could supplement their income by cultivating private plots or through sideline production, authorities restricted these activities for much of the period and required peasants to work for the collective to earn grain rations.[47]

Under the new policies, peasants' incomes have risen dramatically. Surveys report that the percentage of households making more than 300 yuan annual per capita income rose 20 percent from 1978 to 1981 (now 22.6 percent of households earn 300 yuan or more), while the percentage of households below 150 yuan annual per capita income fell 40 percent (to 19.7 percent of households) during the same period.[48] Substantial increases in the state purchase price of grain and other agricultural commodities[49] and relaxing market controls to permit crop surpluses to be sold in the market have contributed to this prosperity.

Peasants were quick to take advantage of the liberal policies. They shifted rapidly away from grain production and into cash crop and sideline production, which reduced the area under grain cultivation after 1978 by

100 million *mou* (one mou is one-sixth of an acre). Still total grain output rose during this period.[50] With new opportunities, the gap between rich peasant households and their poorer neighbors, many of whom opposed the new policies, widened.[51] Rural China's "specialized households" have led the economic growth in the countryside. Now forming 13 percent of the rural population, up from 10 percent in 1983,[52] many of these households have been able to earn 10,000 yuan or more annually, by specializing in grain production, livestock raising, fish farming, or other activities.[53] Still, a considerable number of China's peasant households live in poverty.[54] Although press data and field research report income differentials in China's villages,[55] this situation will not lead to class polarization in the official view. All peasants can rely on "collective arrangements and state support. . . . There is only a difference of people's livelihood."[56]

In the rush for profits, some peasants took over farmland to build houses[57] or tried to buy, sell, rent, or mortgage land owned by the team.[58] Speculation and corruption increased so rapidly that authorities implemented nationwide and local campaigns from 1977 to 1982 to deal with the problem.[59]

The reforms have produced additional problems, however.[60] In many areas cadres resisted the reduction of their authority that implementing the responsibility system entailed.[61] In some cases, local officials forced systems they favored on unwilling villagers. In Guangdong's Hainan Island, for example, county party authorities ordered a brigade to stop implementing *baogan dao hu,* although central policy permitted local units to carry out this system.[62] In other cases, local officials resigned from their posts. In Fujian's Longhai County, for example, authorities reported in 1982 that, in 20 percent of the county's 3,700 production teams, team leadership positions had either fallen vacant or were held "in name only."[63] In the areas that distributed not only land to households, but virtually all collective assets, cadres had little to do (peasants complained that the cadres were unnecessary—*baochan dao hu, bu yong ganbu*), and cadre morale suffered, producing a local leadership crisis.[64] As early as 1980, officials discovered weak or paralyzed leadership in many communes and brigades.[65]

Authorities coupled new agricultural policies with new attempts to reform rural administration. In 1982 officials stripped China's communes and brigades of their political and administrative power, and set up separate governments (townships, *xiang,* and villages, *cun*) at each level.[66] Beijing designed these reforms to encourage commune and brigade leaders to rely on economic or market forces to increase production, not political campaigns or the security apparatus.[67] By October 1983 authorities had set up 12,786 township governments in 902 of China's more than 2,000 counties. The reform was completed in June 1985, when authorities reported that they had set up 92,000 township governments and 820,000 directly elected village committees.[68] However, in 1982, when my study concludes, most peasants were still organized into approximately 54,352 communes, 719,000 brigades, and 5,977,000 production teams, which retained political and administrative functions.[69]

The process of implementing rural policies from 1962 to 1984 has been punctuated by periods of intense campaigning. As we have seen, the Four Clean-ups, the Cultural Revolution (1966–1969), and the Cleaning-up Class Ranks campaigns have had a major impact on local rural politics: They disrupted local leadership, factionalized local politics, and so dominated the local political scene that local politics, if it could not use the campaigns for its own ends, was all but smothered. Where group solidarity was strong, however, the campaigns may have provided an opportunity for groups to pursue their interests. For example, in some parts of the country, groups out of power, using the rhetoric of the campaign, could force concessions from those in power. Still, during campaigns, local officials were preoccupied with fulfilling the directives of their superiors and had little time to entertain the grievances of ordinary villagers. As campaigns subsided and village routine returned to normal, leaders were better able to grasp local problems.

The process of implementing these rural policies also exposed conflicts among local leaders. Interelite conflict provided some opportunities for citizen-initiated participation. Under these conditions, peasants could attempt to ally themselves with leaders at one level to pursue their interests vis-à-vis other leaders. In addition to providing opportunities for participation, elite policies have initiated conflicts between state and rural society, and within rural society.

Rural Organization Structure

Since 1962 authorities have organized Chinese peasants into the "three-level" system of ownership and production, centered around communes (or townships, often standard marketing areas of several natural villages), production brigades (or villages), and production teams (often neighbor-hoods within villages or small hamlets). These units, combining both gov-ernment and production functions, were supervised by party secretaries and party branch committees, which reported to county authorities, the next level up the administrative hierarchy. The organization, functions, and leadership of these units influence opportunities for local-level politics.[70]

In particular, because authorities staffed village organizations with local people, most of whom shared the same social background as ordinary peas-ants, local officials have been approachable. This facilitated the personal contacting, which characterized political participation in rural China. Sec-ond, the rules and regulations of local organizations stipulated a certain amount of mass participation: regulations required that some issues be dis-cussed democratically and that leaders be elected. Third, authorities cen-tralized power over a wide range of political, economic, and social activities in the hands of a relatively small group of leaders: party secretaries and party committees. Centralization facilitated the mobilization of the peasantry into politics. Fourth, because residential and production units largely overlapped, authorities have strengthened local group identifications. Where kinship groups were strong, for example, lineages have continued to have interests and, under certain conditions, have been able to pursue them. Finally, the formal organization structure was supplemented by an informal structure that gave informal leaders some power and that linked leaders to both their superiors and followers in networks of personal rela-tions. These linkages, maintained to enhance the security of local leaders, may have served as a channel to transmit popular grievances to higher levels.

Commune Structure

The population of China's communes grew from 1962 until the early 1970s, as the number of communes fell from 74,000 to about 54,000, but it has remained stable since that time, averaging about 15,000 people (ranging from 5,000 to 50,000). Each commune cultivated approximately 1,800 hectares of land.[71]

Political control within the commune was centralized in the hands of a party secretary, usually not a native of the commune in which he served, who, along with a party committee (*dang weiyuanhui*), supervised politi-cal, economic, and social activities in the commune.[72] The county party committee, through its organization department, appointed commune party secretaries, and nominated candidates for party committee posi-tions, who were ratified by commune party congresses (*dang daibiaohui*). These bodies, which numbered several hundred delegates, were elected by party members in the commune on the recommendation of the party com-mittee. Although there was considerable variation, party members prob-ably numbered about 1 percent of commune populations and were mostly concentrated in suburban areas. In contrast, party members were about 4 percent of the population nationwide.

Party committees varied in size from seven to thirty members (the larger committees often appointed standing committees of six or seven members). Typically, a party committee included the commune party sec-retary, two deputy secretaries, a small staff office (*bangongshi*), and com-mittee members in charge of political work, organization, propaganda, military/security matters, and youth and women's affairs.

The party structure paralleled and, for most of the period, was inter-locked with the commune administrative structure, with party committee members usually also serving on the commune management committee (*guanli weiyuanhui*).[73] The management committee (seven to thirty mem-bers, depending on the size of the commune) was to be elected every two years by a commune people's congress.[74] Delegates to the congress, num-bering several hundred, were directly elected by commune members. In practice, the commune party committee, with the approval of county au-thorities, nominated the commune management committee. The com-mune people's congress (*renmin daibiao weiyuanhui*) then ratified pre-selected lists of nominees.[75] In the early 1960s provision was made for the election of a "supervision" or "control" committee of one to three cadres to oversee the overall operation of the commune.[76]

The commune head (*shezhang*), together with the management com-mittee, supervised production in the commune. Committee members, aided by a small staff office, supervised the departments:[77] agriculture, in-dustry, commerce, education, public health, and military/security.[78] In large communes, these departments were more disaggregated. In addition to the departments, which were responsible to the commune head and the commune congress, a number of branch offices of county (*xian*) organizations were also located in the commune. These included a tax office, grain station (*liangshi zhan*), supply and marketing cooperative, and perhaps a water conservation office, a branch of The People's Bank of China, a middle school, and a public security office (*paichusuo*). Although their policies were coordinated with commune administration, these units came under the direct authority of the county.

The departments of the commune management committee were usually headed by state cadres (*guojia ganbu*). These officials, divided into two streams (administrative and specialist), were part of the nationwide civil service system. The state hired them on a 26-grade cadre pay scale and paid them a monthly salary. Personnel assignments for state cadres were made centrally, although the party organization bureau of the next higher level (here, county) probably made initial appointments.

In one Fujian commune of 30,000 people (twice the average size), two to three state cadres were distributed among the following commune departments: industry, transportation, military/security, education, and public health. The agriculture and commerce departments had more state cadres (six and thirteen, respectively), however. In all there were sixty administrative and specialist state cadres in the commune.[79] In addition to state cadres, communes recruited and paid office workers (*zhiye gongren*) and assistants (*zhuli*) to staff most departments.[80] The commune bureaucracy, then, included over 100 full-time functionaries.

Throughout the 1970s the number of commune officials grew, in part a response to new functions and in part due to overstaffing. From 1973 to 1976 in one Hunan commune, for example, commune and brigade office staff grew by 80 percent, so that by 1976 each brigade was staffed by a staggering twenty-eight cadres. Many of these officials were recruited from brigades to staff commune organizations and enterprises.[81]

The extensive number of state cadres in the commune and the existence of offices directly accountable to the county, such as the supply and marketing cooperatives, indicate that decisions on many issues lay beyond the influence of ordinary peasants. These officials were principally charged with implementing county (provincial and national) policy. They took their orders from above and depended on the evaluations of their superiors for their careers. Power in the commune was, then, centralized in the hands of party and state officials.

Although there are no comprehensive data on the characteristics of commune leaders, Michel Oksenberg's study of the backgrounds of local cadres in the early 1960s reveals that most commune-level leaders were recruited from among peasant activists who emerged during the 1950s collectivization drive and from among demobilized soldiers. Most commune cadres in Oksenberg's study (86 percent) were locals, natives of the same county, but probably born outside of the commune(s) in which they served. Although most commune cadres were party members at lower levels in the administrative hierarchy, fewer cadre positions were held by the party. Between 1962 and 1965, a gap emerged between political cadres and those with expertise in finance, trade, or education. Political officers (such as secretaries, deputy secretaries, and those in charge of political/legal or security work) tended to be older, less well-educated, and more often party members than did their more "expert" colleagues, who increasingly had middle school education. Although the average age of commune cadres in the sample was 33, political cadres were usually older. At the commune level, the turnover rate for cadres was lower than the rate for brigade and team cadres, reflecting the importance of seniority in the promotion of state cadres.[82]

According to a 1980 survey published in *Sichuan Ribao,* commune heads and their deputies in the Yongxing district of Sichuan (N = 21) averaged 38 years of age; in my own data commune cadres in an area of Fujian (N = 13) averaged 43 years.[83] If these data are representative, they indicate that by 1980 commune cadres were older than they were in the early 1960s. However, there has been considerable turnover. The impression of my informants of a gap between political and technical cadres supports Oksenberg's findings. Political cadres tended to be older, have less education, and to have been in office longer than their more technical colleagues.[84]

Communes combined political, economic, and social functions.[85] In the political realm, communes were charged with supervising brigades and teams in the implementation of party and state policy. They approved brigade and team leadership changes, initiated national and local campaigns from anticorruption to birth control, and cooperated with county authorities in a wide range of areas, including public security (maintaining public order and supervising class enemies), and military recruitment and militia training.

In the economic realm,[86] communes distributed quotas for output, sown area, and costs to brigades, and supervised lower levels in the completion of these targets; coordinated interbrigade projects, such as building roads and water conservation works; provided some agricultural inputs, such as fertilizer; initiated and managed commune-level enterprises, from which communes derived income; and coordinated tax collection, grain procurement, and the supervision of markets with county authorities. Commune enterprises grew remarkably during this period; by 1979 each commune had on the average six enterprises, which contributed about one-quarter of total commune gross output nationally.[87] By 1981, there were 1.3 million commune and brigade enterprises, employing 30 million people.[88] In the social realm, most communes managed, under the supervision of county bureaus, one middle school and a clinic or hospital.[89]

Commune authorities monitored the activities of brigades and teams through an extensive reporting system, regular inspections, the "guarantee cadre" (*baodui ganbu*) system, and special investigations carried out by investigation and work teams.

Production brigades and teams filed periodic reports with communes on their agricultural and sideline activities, including details of the area under cultivation, seed and fertilizer use, yields, costs, and production output. It was on the basis of such reports that the state fixed surplus grain (*yuliang*) and tax grain (*gongliang*) quotas. Production planning continued under the new responsibility system, and teams and brigades continued to send statistical profiles to commune offices. Commune authorities kept in touch with grassroots production activities through these reports.[90]

In addition, regular inspection visits by what were in many provinces called "guarantee cadres," ensured that commune policies were effectively implemented.[91] In one commune in Fujian, for example, each member of the commune management committee was assigned three or four brigades for which he was responsible (*guanli pian*). He visited these brigades often, presided at brigade election meetings, ensured that the brigades met their production quotas, and tried to solve disputes among the brigades under his charge. He did not necessarily speak for the brigade in commune meetings, but brigade cadres tried to cultivate good relations with him. This system was extended to the production teams.[92]

Finally, commune cadres organized periodic inspection and work teams to investigate political or economic problems in brigades that were doing

particularly badly, to investigate outstanding performance, or to implement national or local campaigns.[93] Information about local conditions
was then transmitted to commune headquarters.

As I noted above, since 1981 China's leaders have relieved communes of
their nonproductive, largely administrative functions. New township governments, responsible for economic planning, education, culture, public
health, civil affairs, public security, and family planning,[94] freed the communes to implement agricultural plans and develop commune industries.
The market plays a larger role in the allocation of inputs, such as fertilizer,
and in motivating peasants to produce more. Both township and commune
officials are supposed to be popularly elected under the new arrangements.

Brigade Structure

By 1982 rural China was organized into 719,000 production brigades,
averaging approximately 13 brigades per commune, each with an approxi-
mate population of 1,000 people. Brigades often consisted of one large
natural village or a group of smaller villages and hamlets, farming approximately 120 hectares of land.[95]

The party branch secretary was the most powerful local official in the
brigade—the basic level at which the party was organized in the countryside. Party members in the brigade, numbering twenty to thirty (or more
in larger brigades), formed the brigade party branch (*dang zhibu*), and
under the guidance of the commune party committee, elected a party
branch committee (*zhibu weiyuanhui*) of six to nine members.[96] The committee was usually composed of the party secretary, a deputy secretary, and
members in charge of political affairs, organization, propaganda, study,
and, sometimes, others in charge of women's affairs and youth. The brigade party branch committee may have included production team cadres
who were also party members.[97] A substantial minority of party members
in the brigade were probably recruited during the Cultural Revolution; in
Guizhou's Pingba County, for example, 40.9 percent of the county's 1,522
party branch members were recruited from 1966 to 1976.[98] Most rural
party members entered the party in the 1950s and early 1960s.

The brigade party branch has played an important role in the selection
of brigade leaders, because it usually nominated candidates for the brigade
congress (*daibiao dahui*)—the general assembly of representatives of con-

stituent production teams in the brigade. The brigade party committee, under the supervision of the commune party committee, also usually nominated candidates for brigade head (*daduizhang*) and the brigade management committee (*dadui guanli weiyuanhui*), elections which in theory were held every one or two years by the brigade congress.[99] Interview and press data from Guangdong and Fujian provinces support the impression that before 1978 these elections were often only ritual ratifications of party branch decisions.[100]

Although there was considerable variation, brigade management committees were usually composed of seven to nine brigade cadres, including the brigade leader, a deputy leader, an accountant, cashier, militia/public security official, women's affairs official, and, often, a secretary/clerk.[101] In practice, for much of the period, brigade party officials frequently also held positions on the management committee. Since 1981 authorities have attempted to separate party branch and brigade functions, and to that end they issued regulations on party branch work that explicitly forbade party secretaries from concurrently holding the position of brigade head. The new regulations also warned party branches not to encroach on the work of management committees.[102] Because the officials were paid by the brigade (they were not usually state cadres),[103] their income depended on local productivity. As a result, they were much more sensitive to the needs of villagers than their commune counterparts.[104] In general, brigade cadre incomes were lower than commune cadre incomes, but higher than the incomes of most other villagers.

In addition to these formal institutions at brigade level, Chinese authorities organized peasants into mass organizations under central party leadership. Work teams set up poor and lower-middle peasants' associations at brigade level in most rural areas during the Four Clean-ups Campaign from 1963 to 1965 and charged them with supervising local cadre behavior, and, in particular, with guarding against financial mismanagement and corruption.[105] Under this plan, peasant representatives from each production team were to meet periodically in the brigade under the leadership of an association head. In practice, these organizations have been largely inactive since the mid-1960s, in spite of attempts to revive them in 1974 and 1980–1981.[106]

Authorities also organized women's federations at brigade level and recruited women's affairs representatives from each production team. Offi-

Table 1.   Average Age of Rural Party Branch Cadres, 1980–1981

	Age	Number
Pingba County, Guizhou		
Secretaries	48.0	195
Party branch members	46.3	954
Yongxing District, Sichuan		
Secretaries	39.7	46
Interview Data		
Secretaries	42.0	8
Party branch members	39.0	49

SOURCES: "Zhonggong Pingba xianwei zhengdun, gaixuan dadui dang zhibu de qingkuang baogao," *Zhonggong Yanjiu* (Taibei) 195 (March 15, 1983): 140; *Sichuan Ribao*, Sept. 22, 1980; and Interview Files.

cials used these organizations to propagate a wide range of policies, from mobilizing women into the labor force to enforcing birth control targets. The youth league was also represented at brigade level and enrolled prospective party members from production teams. Like the women's federation, the youth league has chiefly served as a channel for China's leaders to mobilize the local population.

Studies of brigade cadre backgrounds indicate that from the early 1960s to the mid-1970s there has been little change in the characteristics of these cadres. Brigade cadres were overwhelmingly male, of poor and lower-middle peasant class background, had received primary education or less, and were mostly party members (from 80 to 100 percent).[107] The average age of brigade cadres, now in their mid-30s,[108] indicates a substantial turnover of brigade officials since the early 1960s.

Although party branch cadres in 1980–1981 tended to be older than other brigade cadres (table1), both groups probably had about the same levels of education. In 1982 in Guizhou's Pingba County, for example, 35.5 percent (N = 339) were illiterate, 50.8 percent (N = 485) were primary school graduates, and 13.6 percent (N = 130) were graduates of junior or senior middle schools.[109] These figures indicate that low educational levels persisted from 1962 through 1984 and that brigade officials have gotten older. Still, replacements were probably made of more senior brigade cadres (through promotions, retirements, or dismissals), while younger specialized cadres have remained in place.

Brigade administrators performed a variety of functions. In the political arena, the brigade supervised the selection of production team leaders; initiated and carried out local and national campaigns as instructed by the commune; supervised public security and militia work in the village; and supervised peasants' political education through study meetings and an extensive print and broadcast media network.[110]

In production, brigades had three principal functions: [111] First, they supervised production teams in the implementation of economic policy, including record keeping, distribution practices, and fulfilling quotas. Brigade officials were responsible for supervising the delivery of team grain to the supply and marketing cooperatives, and for enforcing regulations on the use of team land (regulations that have in the past limited the amount of land devoted to private plots and available for housebuilding). As Steven Butler observes:

> The relationship [between teams and brigades] is a complex one. Brigades do not have the resources simply to take over team management, so sometimes they let teams drift. A give-and-take relationship develops, with teams often looking to the brigade for a clean decision, in order to avoid assuming responsibility, but at times also resisting the policy set by the brigade.[112]

Second, brigades coordinated multiteam projects, such as the building of large-scale reclamation projects, waterworks, and roads, and they also provided services to teams, such as loans from the brigade credit cooperative. Finally, brigades developed and managed their own enterprises, including brickmaking works, oil presses, repair stations for agricultural machinery, orchards, tea farms, and livestock breeding stations. Although since the early 1970s this sector of the economy has grown quickly, still by 1979, each brigade on the average had only two such enterprises, employing fourteen workers, and contributing up to one-quarter of brigade and commune income.[113]

In the social arena, brigades operated public health stations, staffed by paramedics, and primary schools, and supervised local welfare programs, such as the "five guarantees." [114]

Because brigade cadres resided in the production teams, little escaped their notice. They made periodic inspections of team activities, and, like their colleagues in the commune, in many provinces they relied on guarantee cadres to ensure that teams were complying with official policy. The brigade management committee appointed guarantee cadres, who were

Table 2.   Number of Cadres Before and After Reform, Henan Province, 1980

	Prereform	Postreform
Dancheng County		
Brigade cadres	5,070	3,003
Team cadres	27,700	15,026
Liuhe Brigade		
Nonproductive cadres	146	42
Subsidized cadres	146	21

SOURCE: Xinhua, Aug. 25, 1981, in FBIS 165 (Aug. 26, 1981): K1–K3.

NOTE: Before the reform, all of Liuhe brigade's cadres were subsidized. After the reform, only one-half of them received subsidies. The other half may have been unsubsidized team cadres. When household contracting was implemented, authorities in some counties began to require brigades to subsidize team cadres.

themselves usually members of the committee, and who lived in the teams they "guaranteed." They reported regularly to the management committee on problems in their teams.[115] Brigade authorities also regularly inspected team accounts, cashiers' receipts, work point logs, and other records to ensure that policies were being carried out.

Unlike their superiors in the commune, however, brigade cadres were locals, part of the village kinship and personal networks. All brigade and team cadres were caught in a web of relations that made their job of mediating between the demands of the state and their kin, friends, and neighbors difficult. The dilemma was aptly captured by one former deputy brigade leader who tried to explain why he appeared to have changed his mind when he publicly criticized his neighbors in 1979 for trying to divide their production team into small work groups against the wishes of higher authorities. He observed: "Officials have two mouths" (*Guanzi liang-ge kou*), one for speaking to higher authorities (or publicly, in their presence), and another for speaking to the peasants, their neighbors.[116] He was caught in the crossfire because privately he supported the villagers' plan.

With the introduction of the responsibility system in 1979–1980, some brigade functions have been decollectivized to households. Under household contracting, fewer brigade-level cadres were required, and the functions of both brigade and team officials have been reduced. The number of brigade cadres in some areas has fallen as well (table 2). Authorities in Henan's Fan County, for example, cut the number of brigade cadres by as much as 60 percent.[117] In all, Liaoning, Gansu, Zhejiang, Hebei, Hunan, Anhui, Henan, Jiangxi, and Shanxi provinces reported reductions in the number of brigade cadres.[118] These changes prepared the way for the setting up of new village (*cun*) governments.

Team Structure

Brigades in 1982 were subdivided into approximately 6 million neighborhoods or hamlets, called production teams, each farming an average of 15 to 20 hectares of land, and made up of twenty to fifty families (each team averaged 139 people).[119] The size of production teams varied considerably from 1962 to 1984. Although authorities forced many teams to amalgamate from 1969 to 1971, they have permitted smaller teams since the mid-1970s. In the early 1960s and again since 1979, although the team remained the formal unit of accounting and land ownership, teams often have been further divided into work groups, sometimes with elected leaders.[120]

Overall responsibility for team affairs rested with the team leader, who, with a team management committee of five to seven members, was supposed to be elected by production team members every one or two years.[121] Brigade party officials were to supervise the elections, but their actual occurrence has varied widely during the past twenty years. The team management committee usually included the team leader, a deputy leader, a cashier/accountant, a political study leader, a storehousekeeper, a militia official, and a women's federation official.

With so many production teams and so few rural party members, party resources were thinly spread at the production team level. Although one study indicates that in 1962–1965 as many as 60 percent of production team officials were party members,[122] a mid-1970s study finds only 20 percent of team cadres to be members.[123] The latter figure may also be too high. In my data, the party was completely absent from many teams, especially those in remote areas.

In general, team cadres, who were all local people, tended overwhelmingly to be male, modestly educated, and of mostly poor and lower-middle peasant class background. Evidence from Guangdong indicates that team cashiers, accountants, and other specialists were considerably younger than team leaders (by eight years), and better educated (33 percent had seven

Table 3.　　Average Age of Production Team Cadres, 1980–1981

	Age	Number
Yongxing District, Sichuan		
Team leaders	36.7	306
Renyang Commune, Zhejiang		
Team leaders	38.0	133
Interview Data		
Team leaders	42.0	14
All team cadres	38.0	46

SOURCES: *Sichuan Ribao,* Sept. 22, 1980; *Xinhua Ribao,* Dec. 7, 1980; and Interview Files.

NOTE: After team elections in 1980, Renyang authorities announced that the average age of team leaders had dropped to 33.5 years.

years of education or more, compared to only 10 percent for team leaders and their deputies).[124]

As with brigade-level leaders, there has been considerable turnover of team-level officials. According to data from Guangdong, the average age of team officials has changed little from 1962–1965 to the mid-1970s, rising only from the mid-30s to the late 30s.[125] (See table 3.) Many peasants were unwilling to become team cadres because the duties were too onerous, the chances of alienating one's kin or friends were too great, and the compensation was too low.

Production team management committees had largely economic functions. Although they convened meetings to propagate official policy, raised and trained a militia, and carried out public security policies, most political work was directed from the brigade. Teams were responsible for some local welfare activities, but the brigades and communes usually ran the schools and hospitals.

From 1962 to 1984 in the economic arena, the team managed both the local collective and private economies.[126] Collective income came largely from the sale of required amounts of surplus crops to the state at below-market prices and from investments in small team-owned enterprises. The team organized day-to-day collective production in these areas, made work assignments, recorded labor contributions in the form of work points, and distributed income to team members. Public discussion of these processes was required in the regulations governing agricultural production.[127]

The team also monitored the scope of the private economy. For most of the period, authorities permitted peasants to cultivate up to 5 percent of the team's arable land as private plots (*ziliudi*),[128] the produce from which they could sell in rural markets. Produce from these plots contributed an estimated 30 percent of total agricultural income in 1979.[129] The size of private plots was expanded to 15 percent of arable land in 1981, before being replaced by household contracting.[130]

With these responsibilities, production teams required some autonomy, which was provided for in the regulations governing rural work. Production teams had the right to manage their own manpower and to make production-related decisions (what to plant, when to plant and harvest, and what techniques to use).[131] These matters were to be discussed by team members themselves and decided democratically. In practice, brigade, commune, and county authorities often violated the autonomy of production teams, which sometimes prompted team leaders and members to refuse to follow orders from above.[132]

With the introduction in 1979–1980 of the responsibility system in agriculture and, especially, with the emergence once again in 1981 of household contracting (*baogan dao hu*), the duties of production team cadres have changed. Team leaders no longer assigned labor and supervised its completion. Under *baogan dao hu,* the recording of the tasks completed by each team member was unnecessary (thus dispensing with the job of work point recorders). Where authorities distributed tools to villagers, storehousekeepers were no longer needed. If officials contracted out team enterprises to peasant entrepreneurs, they, and not the team, employed the cashiers and accountants.[133]

The remaining team cadres now sign contracts with households to fulfill team quotas, supervise the division of land for household use, and manage what is left of collective enterprises. Authorities, recognizing the reduced need for team cadres, have ordered the streamlining of team organizations. As we saw above, Zhejiang, Liaoning, and Guangdong provinces have reduced the numbers of team cadres in some communes by as much as 60 percent (from eight to three cadres).[134]

Informal Rural Networks

Thus far, I have focused on the formal organization of rural China. Sketching the broad contours of informal relationships, however, is essential to complete the picture. In addition to the pull of family and kin, discussed earlier, villagers are sometimes swayed by identification with other groups. In South China, which was settled by migrants from the North, for example, peasants may be divided into "insiders" (oldtime residents) and "outsiders" (recent arrivals).[135] Peasants in Hebei's Neiqiu County were loyal to either a "mountain" faction or a "plain" faction.[136] Jiangsu's Daya village was divided into an "East clique" and a "West clique".[137] These identifications can have political and economic consequences. Authorities complained, for example, that "insiders" in Fujian villages discriminated against "outsiders" in the distribution of land under the household contracting system.[138] Authorities in Anhui and Guangdong have used "personal influence" to obtain benefits, such as better jobs or urban residence permits, for their "relatives and friends."[139]

Rural leaders are, of course, not immune to the pull of these special relationships. Indeed, they use them to exercise power, according to Richard Madsen.[140] In this view, leadership in contemporary rural China is founded on competing bases of power, including both "traditional" and class-based authority. The traditional village leader ("communist gentry") uses his control over such resources as land and supplies to build patronage networks, mostly of extended kin. His power is based on patronage, which makes him politically vulnerable. For his own protection and to further the particular interests of his network, the traditional leader is loyal to his supporters and is essentially conservative and inward looking. He recognizes that the community is based on a multiplicity of interests, and he is flexible in the implementation of policy.

The power of the class-based village leader ("communist rebel") rests on his ability to mobilize the resentment of the dispossessed within the community. He embodies the rebellious hopes of the community and adopts an austere personal style. His goal is to make the village into "a single, hardworking, relatively egalitarian 'big family.'" His uncompromising dedication to the good of the community as a whole inspires selfless dedication. Both types are essentially limited in their horizon to their communities.

These competing bases of local leadership have consequences for rural political participation. We would expect traditional leaders to mobilize their clients into politics by appealing to kinship loyalties and group interests. Class-based leaders, however, use appeals for social and economic justice to mobilize their followers. If the village is divided into two or more kinship groups, some wealthier than others, these bases of power may overlap. Finally, peasants have used these relationships to influence the course of public affairs, especially where community solidarity was strong.

Further, it is likely that, in China's villages, informal leaders (called *sheyuan tou* in rural Fujian) have had an impact on rural politics. Particularly obvious in the early 1960s[141] and since 1979, these villagers may have taken the lead in putting largely economic proposals to the formal leadership. Informal leaders in my data were usually the heads of households with many skilled laborers and may themselves have been retired cadres or relatives of cadres. In Fujian they were particularly active in the economic arena but were less visible during the Cultural Revolution. Interview data suggest that they took the lead, for example, in proposing to authorities that small group and individual farming be permitted in 1978–1979, before it was official policy.[142]

Finally, village leaders are linked to commune and county authorities in relationships that became factionalized during the Cultural Revolution.[143] As a result of the attacks on local leaders that characterized the campaigns of the mid- and late 1960s, officials formed alliances with both superiors (patrons) and followers (clients) in a search for personal security.[144] Years after the event, these ties continue to be factionalized, and many officials treat their subordinates as "private property." "Instead of relying on the party and the masses," *Renmin Ribao* points out, "they rely on finding 'patrons' in the upper levels and on arranging 'confidants' in the lower."[145]

Rural leaders, recruited into factional networks, sometimes mobilized peasants to protect factional interests. The leadership struggles that emerged during the mid-1960s were often seen as the source of the conflict. As one rural leader observed, "From the Four Clean-ups Campaign, over and over again, when your group took office you oppressed us, and when our group took office we oppressed you—the line between us was very deep."[146] These conflicts emerged from a particular heritage of group conflict and tended to deepen existing cleavages.

Both formal and informal rural organization, then, has provided opportunities for peasants to participate in politics. If, however, the structures and functions of teams, brigades, and communes have remained relatively stable during the period, economic policies have changed dramatically. These policies initiated conflicts between the state and rural society and within rural communities that have formed the substance of local politics in the countryside.

Issues in Chinese Village Politics

From 1962 to 1984 political participation in rural China was largely restricted to influencing the implementation of a relatively narrow range of economic policies. Absent from these concerns was a wide range of what might be called "potential" issues, such as the provision and distribution of housing, education, social welfare, transportation, and the regulation of labor. I have found little evidence that peasants have attempted to influence policies beyond those that had an immediate impact on their livelihood, narrowly conceived in economic terms.

The content of the issues in Chinese rural politics has shifted with the policies being pursued by China's leaders. During the Cultural Revolution, the state sought to maintain or expand the collective sector and to squeeze the private sector; to aid the rural poor and prevent the reemergence of class divisions; to increase capital accumulation from agriculture, while at the same time limiting state investments in agriculture; to rely on administrative measures to make distribution and investment decisions; to control the movement of the rural population; and to ensure a local rural leadership responsive to its will.

These policies often conflicted with the perceived interests of local rural communities and, in particular, with the needs of wealthier, more productive households and units. They sought to raise local income by expanding the private sector, even if it meant increased class polarization. Local units sought to retain as many resources as possible and to increase the amount of assistance they received from outside. Finally, peasants sought relaxed migration controls and liberal birth-control policies. From their point of view, local leadership should be responsive, first, to local interests. These conflicts have formed the basis of political participation in rural politics for much of the period.

From 1962 to 1965 and after 1978, the central authorities adopted policies that removed some of the issues that alienated them from the peasantry. During these periods, the state sought to expand the private sector through decollectivization, even at the expense of renewed class polarization; to reduce the burden of accumulation on the peasantry; to increase state investment in agriculture; to rely in part on markets for distribution and investment decisions; and, though still controlling population growth, to ease restrictions on migration. However, higher-level authorities continued to value a local leadership responsive to them.

The Scope of the Collective Sector

During the Cultural Revolution, authorities attempted to maintain or expand the scope of the collective sector and to limit or restrict the private economy. They took direct control over the development of the collective economy, such as approving a growing number of team and brigade investments in sideline industries. Although team and brigade management committees were eager to expand rural sidelines,[147] they had to apply for commune approval first;[148] they also resisted the attempts of higher-level officials to take over direct control of the sidelines.[149] Officials attempted to control profits from village sideline industries through tax regulations, and teams and brigades tried to manipulate this to their advantage.[150] Communes and counties also attempted, sometimes successfully, to take over village land for their own projects.[151] These actions sometimes provoked retaliation. In one case, villagers in Hunan Province, incensed by the "illegal" enclosure of their land by a supply and marketing cooperative, tore down the wall around the property and destroyed equipment.[152]

In practice, even team autonomy over its own manpower resources was limited by commune and county demands for workers to build large construction projects.[153] Peasants sometimes resisted working when there was little benefit to themselves. In spite of the regulations prohibiting higher levels from requisitioning team labor, this practice was common.[154]

During the same period, authorities sought to restrict the private economy. They put narrow limits on the amount of land devoted to private cultivation (private plots) and to housing; the amount of time devoted to family sideline occupations and the type of occupation; and, finally, the extent of free markets and marketing activities in general.

Although private plots were abolished in 1958 during the Great Leap Forward[155] and came under attack in some places during the Cultural Revolution (1966–1969),[156] authorities from 1962 to 1984 only sought to limit the plots to 5 to 7 percent of the cultivatable area of each production team.[157] Peasants in many places, however, tried to extend them, either by opening up new land or by taking over collective land in violation of the regulations.[158]

Chinese authorities also attempted to restrict two other key components of the private economy: the scope of household sideline production and rural marketing. Officials attempted both to reduce the amount of time peasants spent working privately[159] and to control the kinds of crops they could produce. Some products were banned from private production during certain periods, prompting peasant complaints.[160] The location, frequency, and scope of rural markets were also controlled.[161] For most of the period, authorities established state monopolies on major products, such as grain and cooking oil, and restricted what could be sold in markets. By both limiting middlemen and "speculation"[162] and by operating a system of state-owned supply and marketing cooperatives, authorities controlled the growth of commercial institutions in the countryside.

During the early 1960s and after 1978, authorities reduced the scope of the rural collective sector (now effectively decollectivized) and substantially expanded the scope of the private economy. Still, with the control of land now in the hands of peasant households, the regulation of its use has become more urgent. From early 1980 on peasants and local cadres began taking over collective land for housebuilding,[163] a move that prompted the State Council to issue a circular in April 1981, prohibiting the illegal seizure of land by peasants and local cadres.[164] In spite of the regulations, peasants have continued to build houses on land suitable for cultivation.[165] Peasants in some areas began treating land distributed to them for their use as their own private property and tried to rent, sell, or mortgage it,[166] a practice specifically outlawed in a State Council circular of October 7, 1981.[167] Land use has become an important issue in rural China, and authorities have tried to control it through administrative regulations.

Class Divisions

During the Cultural Revolution, China's leaders sought to prevent the reemergence of rural class divisions. These policies restricted the ability of potentially well-to-do peasant households to improve their standard of living.

Officials sought to minimize income differentials among rural households (generally based on labor power [*laoli*]) and among neighborhoods (generally based on factors of production and proximity to cities).[168] Some policies pitted labor-rich households against their poorer neighbors. In general during this period, households with more adult laborers preferred piece-rate payment systems (*baogong*) to time rate systems, when work points were used to distribute income.[169] Piece rates encouraged them to be more productive, and left them more time for lucrative household side-lines. Because labor-rich households received more work points, they also preferred increasing the share of annual income distributed according to work point earnings and reducing the basic "fixed" distribution to each household.[170] Finally, they favored distributing private plots on a per cap-ita basis, not equal shares for each household.[171]

Households with few adult laborers favored standard payment for each labor day (time rates), which tended to equalize income within the vil-lage.[172] If, however, piece rates were the principal mode of payment, as happened in the early 1960s and increasingly since 1972, poorer house-holds favored higher basic-level distribution, with only a small percentage of income actually tied to work point earnings. They also preferred that authorities organize production collectively, so that they could rely on their stronger neighbors,[173] and that officials distribute private plots on a household, not a per capita, basis. In general, authorities sought to limit the income of potentially well-to-do peasants by popularizing time rates, by maintaining "fixed" distributions, and by distributing private plots on an equal shares basis.

Policies to protect the rural poor were reflected in debates over the ap-propriate size of production teams. Wealthier neighborhoods, in general, preferred smaller teams, so that they would not have to share their more favorable factors of production with their poorer neighbors.[174] Poorer neighborhoods favored amalgamating with their better-off neighbors in order to improve their standard of living. Although official policy for most of the period favored stable, relatively small teams,[175] officials resisted at-tempts to divide up larger teams[176] and, in some cases, even forced amal-gamations.[177] Since 1978 many larger units have been split up and reduced in size.[178]

During the early 1960s and after 1978, authorities have pursued rural policies that increased class differentiation. A "new rich peasant" class has emerged from among China's 26 million "specialized" households.[179] Denying that this will lead to increased class polarization, Chinese officials argued that the phenomenon was simply a difference in living standards.[180] Still, authorities acknowledged the existence of the rural poor in both households and production units.[181] One rural survey, for example, found that the income of about 10 percent of "five-guarantee" households (so poor that they receive welfare payments) had fallen as a result of the introduction of the responsibility system in agriculture.[182] Officials proposed tax rebates and loans to the poor to help redistribute rural incomes, and at the same time they boosted rural productivity by allowing some peasants to "become rich first."[183]

Accumulation and Investments

Cultural Revolution policies required high levels of savings, restricted consumption, and sought to determine distribution and investment decisions by administrative means, rather than relying, at least partially, on market forces. The state sought to regulate a wide range of economic behavior through production quotas and allocation plans.

In the collective sector, brigade and commune officials distributed annual production quotas to peasants in production teams, which for most of the period specified crop type, output targets, sown area, production costs, and the amount of the crop to be sold to the state. Authorities required that quotas be filled,[184] although peasants sometimes complained that they were too high or too restrictive.[185] Particularly from 1966 to 1978, when authorities limited rural diversification and emphasized grain production and self-sufficiency, teams were left with little autonomy on the issue of what they could plant. On occasion, local cadres ordered villages to destroy cash crops, if, in their view, they interfered with the policy of maximizing grain output.[186]

Authorities expanded the use of administrative measures during the Campaign to Study Dazhai, when they attempted to regulate such diverse practices as cropping patterns[187] and the reclamation of wasteland.[188] Where these measures interfered with the traditional way of doing things or appeared too risky or too time-consuming, peasants sometimes resisted implementing them.

Finally, for most of 1962 to 1984, the state distributed some supplies, such as chemical fertilizer, through a central allocation system. Although county agents, responsible for this system, devised formulas for the distribution of fertilizer (usually based on sown acreage), chemical fertilizer has been in chronic short supply,[189] and a "black market" in fertilizer emerged in the mid-1960s and the 1970s.

During the early 1960s, but especially after 1978, authorities have taken measures to reduce the scope of the administered economy. Substan-

tial decollectivization has been accompanied by a greater reliance on market forces to make key economic decisions. Since 1978 the state has made
fertilizer available outside the central allocation system, for sale at competitive prices.[190] Well-to-do peasants stand to benefit by greater reliance on the
market. This policy, then, may result in increasing rural class differentiation.

Population Control

Although Cultural Revolution leaders sought to control migration,
they did not have, for most of the period, an effective birth-control policy.
Since 1949 Chinese authorities have strictly controlled the migration of
peasants to the cities.[191] Rural laborers have occasionally been recruited for
urban industrial and construction projects, but, in general, officials have
kept peasants on the land.[192] This has been accomplished through the
household registration system and the practice of issuing food and clothing
ration tickets only at one's place of work.[193] Peasants who wished to leave
the countryside could do so only by joining the party or the army. These
policies were coupled with an ineffective birth control policy, particularly
in the countryside.

During the early 1960s and since 1978, although authorities have not
relaxed policies to keep peasants from migrating to the cities, they have
recruited peasants into noncultivator jobs. As household contracting has
been implemented, much of China's rural labor force has been freed from
cultivating the land, and some of this surplus labor has been recruited into
mining and construction.[194]

These policies have been accompanied by a serious effort to limit population growth in the countryside. The measures have taken the form of a
series of positive incentives, sometimes cash payments, for couples having
only one child.[195] Ironically, while authorities were trying to curb rural
population increases, their new agricultural policy encouraged families to
have more children. Although some provinces have successfully reduced the
number of births, nonetheless the countryside has lagged behind the cities.
More children remained the peasants' principal form of social security.[196]

The Urban/Rural Gap

In general, up until 1979, authorities gave a high priority to the development of China's cities and industrial infrastructure at the expense of the

countryside. On a societywide basis, many redistributive policies have favored urban workers at the expense of the peasantry. As Lardy has shown, although real urban and rural incomes increased only modestly during the 1960s and 1970s, consumption of cereals, vegetable oil, and cotton cloth increased more rapidly in the cities than in the countryside from the mid-1950s to the late 1970s.[197] As a development strategy, Chinese leaders kept the purchase price of agricultural produce low, passing on the savings to urban consumers. Although authorities recently raised purchase prices, for most of the period peasants complained that they were too low.[198] In addition, authorities demanded high rates of savings in the countryside.[199] Teams and brigades have had to provide their own welfare and investment funds.[200] Finally, policy makers have given urban centers a higher priority in the distribution of scarce consumer goods and building materials.[201] Severe shortages have been chronic in the countryside.

Under the new post-1978 policies, authorities have abandoned the previous high levels of accumulation.[202] They have also substantially improved the urban/rural terms of trade by increasing the prices paid for agricultural products.[203]

Conclusion

Contemporary China's rural economic and organization policies and the process of their implementation provided opportunities for peasants to participate in politics. Rural policies focused on conflict between the state and society and sharpened or dampened conflict within rural communities. These policies were the issues of village politics. Many other "potential" issues, such as housing, education, and social welfare, existed beyond the scope of peasant influence throughout the period.

China's rural organization policies, by concentrating control over resources in the hands of village-based groups, reinforced localism in the countryside. In some places this resulted in a resurgence of lineage-based politics. In addition, the formal organizations required some amount of political participation and provided the peasantry with access to their leaders, if only in the sense that village bureaucracies were locally staffed. Nonetheless, these arrangements centralized power in the hands of party secretaries, which enhanced their ability to carry out mass mobilizations in support of party/state policy.

The process of policy implementation from 1962 to 1984 has been punctuated by a series of elite-initiated campaigns, periods of intense political activity that, though mobilizing peasants into politics, also severely limited their opportunities to influence public affairs. In the course of implementing policy, however, conflicts emerged among the local and the higher-level elite. Peasants have occasionally used these divisions to make a limited impact on public affairs.

Changes in both economic and organizational policies from 1962 to 1984 influenced opportunities for participation. First, the new policies altered the substance of conflicts in the countryside. Thus, some conflicts over the scope of the private sector were removed by the implementation of household contracting, but other conflicts, particularly between the rural rich and poor, reemerged. Second, the new policies, by putting decision-making power in the hands of households, both reduced the power of local village leaders and made the exercise of power (now centralized in township governments) more remote and diffused. Third, the reform of rural administration has shifted the locus of political influence from commune and brigade leaderships to the new rural governments. Authorities hope that peasants will be able to influence the policies of these communes and brigades in the marketplace.

4

Speaking Out:
Village Assemblies and
Mass Organizations

By 1962 authorities had established a network of local assemblies in China's communes, brigades, and production teams. During the Cultural Revolution, local cadres called frequent meetings of these assemblies, which soon became highly formalized affairs. In the post-Mao era, as officials abandoned the campaign style of politics, they dramatically reduced the numbers of village and subvillage meetings. At the same time, they attempted to institutionalize the popularly elected commune and county people's congresses. Little information is available about the deliberations of these people's congresses, but participation was largely confined to party members and local activists. For most peasants, participation in meetings and formal gatherings meant attending village assemblies and branch meetings of mass organizations.

Even during the Cultural Revolution, peasants influenced public affairs in these forums under certain conditions. Peasants were more effective in meetings of production teams, where gatherings were smaller; in meetings convened during lulls between campaigns; when they had the support of higher-level elites; and when group solidarity on an issue was high. Mass organizations were chiefly effective as a further tool of elite mobilization; they have not been a particularly effective channel for peasant-initiated influencing of public affairs.

Village assemblies and mass organizations served a variety of functions, including elite-initiated communication, mobilization, and legitimization. Powerful constraints prevented peasants from using these forums to articulate their interests. First, educational levels were low in the countryside, and peasants were generally inarticulate. Second, peasants have never particularly valued open confrontations with authority in formal settings. Third, the power to control the proceedings of these institutions rested with local leaders, who sometimes retaliated against the few peasants who opposed them in these forums. Finally, authorities frequently relied on campaigns during this period, and the campaign style of policy implementation often inhibited peasants from speaking out.

Since 1962 official policy has encouraged villagers to participate in "democratic discussions" (*minzhu taolun*) on a range of local issues. The Sixty Articles (1962), for example, stipulated that "production team production plans must be fully discussed, supplemented, and revised by commune members; in particular, the opinion of experienced peasants must be solicited and the plans must be submitted to members' general meetings for adoption."[1] Within the guidelines laid down by the state, production teams were given "free will to manage production and distribute gains."[2] Teams also had the right to manage their own land and manpower[3] and to set up and develop their own sideline industries.[4]

The center reaffirmed its intention to make local decision making on production and distribution issues more democratic in policy documents issued in 1971 and 1978. In late 1971 commune members' assemblies were charged with discussing and deciding on rates of production team accumulation, the applicability of the Dazhai model, cadre compensation, and providing labor for construction projects sponsored by the commune or higher levels.[5] In 1978 the New Sixty Articles reiterated:

> On important issues including production and capital construction, operation and management, distribution, supply and marketing, credit, and the collective welfare, the administrative organs at various levels of a people's commune should extensively seek suggestions from the masses and then let the authorized organs at various levels make their decisions in a democratic way.
>
> *(Art. 9)*

Commune members have the right to raise questions, criticize and make suggestions on . . . financial affairs; also democratic conferences . . . have the right to veto unreasonable expenditures.

(Art. 39)

With the introduction of the new responsibility system in 1979–1980, central authorities attempted to push local leaders toward more flexibility by insisting that peasants in each area had the right to determine which form of the responsibility system they would adopt. From late 1980 through 1981, authorities demanded that local leaders in Guangdong, Zhejiang, Guizhou, Fujian, Shanxi, Sichuan, Anhui, Jilin, and Shandong provinces stop forcing units to adopt particular systems and permit peasants themselves to decide which system they would implement.[6] Provincial authorities in Guizhou, for example, pointed out:

Any system selected by the commune members through democratic discussion should not be changed. In some production brigades, because of better economic conditions, the system of fixed work quotas on the basis of households is not well suited, but if the system has already been put into effect and if most commune members do not want to do away with it, we should allow them to continue that system.[7]

Renmin Ribao endorsed this view a few weeks later.[8] Through democratic discussions, peasants themselves were to decide amounts of team reserves, distribution questions, revisions of contracts, and the numbers of team cadres and their subsidy levels.[9]

The authorities' insistence on democratic decision making at this level served a variety of functions. First, the process was part of the mass line theory of policy implementation, which emphasized persuasion. If peasants thoroughly discussed the policy, they would understand it and could implement it more smoothly. Second, higher-level leaders could justify removing local leaders who opposed popular policies, such as implementation of the responsibility system, by appealing to "democracy." Third, granting some autonomy to local units, provided they implemented central policies, reduced the negative consequences of rigid overcentralization. Finally, "democratic" decision making was morally appealing.

From the official account, one would expect frequent, lively meetings with suggestions, argument, and discussion from the floor. In fact, however, Chinese authorities have limited the theoretical scope of production team decision making. Even in the liberal Sixty Articles, the right to manage production and distribution was circumscribed by the requirement that teams accept state production plans and the quotas for surplus grain that went with them,[10] that natural resources be conserved,[11] that distribution be according to output,[12] and that teams reserve at least a stated minimum amount before distributing income to team members.[13] In addition to these constraints, production teams must in practice obey the regulations and orders of higher authorities on all issues, many not covered by the general regulations on rural work cited here. Higher authorities used guarantee cadres, investigation and work teams, and the reporting system to ensure compliance.

Village Assemblies

One of the most dramatic changes in rural China since 1949 has been in the organizational life of the peasants. From 1962 to 1984 peasants in production teams attended, in addition to production team mass meetings (*sheyuan dahui*), a range of specialized meetings for women, youth, party members, the militia, and informal ad hoc meetings. Peasants elected representatives to attend brigade congresses or representatives' meetings (*sheyuan daibiaohui*), and peasants who had no other official duties were sometimes elected to these as delegates. Team and brigade cadres also attended local management committee meetings, party branch meetings, and informal cadre meetings.[14]

Village assemblies or mass meetings can be analyzed in terms of a four-part typology of two variables: First, whether the outcome of the meeting was broadly political or economic; and second, whether the meeting occurred during a campaign or during a lull between campaigns. "Political" meetings included political study meetings, meetings designed to transmit political messages through the discussion of newspaper editorials or party documents, and meetings designed to select local leaders. "Economic" meetings included production planning and distribution meetings, and meetings that discussed local investment and accumulation issues.

"Campaign" meetings here indicate those meetings called to implement campaigns, such as the Four Clean-ups and the Double Hits campaigns (both designed to combat corruption); the Cultural Revolution (1966–1969); the Cleaning-up Class Ranks Campaign; and the Campaign to

Study Dazhai. They were characterized by the reading of documents, political discussion, and moral exhortation to carry out the campaign or to implement a policy. Examples include the half-hour team mass meetings called in many places every morning and afternoon during the Cultural Revolution. Leaders read quotations from Mao from pamphlets or newspapers, and a commentary followed, usually delivered by the team's political officer or political study leader.[15] Those who spoke up in these meetings to support party policy were usually party members, formal leaders, and activists. "Noncampaign" meetings were those called during lulls between rural campaigns and focused primarily on local issues. Using this typology, then, four types of local mass meetings can be distinguished: campaign political, campaign economic, noncampaign political, and noncampaign economic.

Not all meetings can be neatly fitted into the typology. Local mass meetings often discussed both political and economic issues. But some meetings, such as election meetings, were purely political. Others, such as work point distribution meetings, had clearly economic outcomes. Similarly, not all meetings held during campaigns were mobilizational meetings. Some meetings were held for reasons unrelated to campaigns, such as to discuss production plans. By using the typology, however, we can highlight important differences in outcomes and in the timing of local meetings.

Campaign political mass meetings were those called by work teams during campaigns. For example, in one case, in July 1965 a work team of fourteen people arrived in a suburban Shanghai commune to carry out the Four Clean-ups Campaign. On their arrival, they called a meeting of commune, brigade, and team cadres to explain the campaign. The work team then spread out to brigades and production teams in the commune, calling mass meetings at each level to explain the purpose of the campaign and to persuade peasants and cadres to cooperate with the work team. After an intensive investigation, they discovered that several of the production team cadres had embezzled public funds or had otherwise been corrupt. When the work team members confronted the local cadres with evidence of their wrongdoing, cadres in one production team refused to admit their mistake, even after lengthy private discussions with the work team. This problem was overcome when the work team called a team mass meeting, attended by all work team members. As the former work team investigator relates:

> I presented the case against the [production team] cadres at the meeting and asked these nine cadres to cooperate with our work team. If not, I threatened them, after the meeting each of them would be accompanied home by one of the work team members to discuss the problem until it was solved. . . . The cadres got scared when they heard this. But they didn't say anything at the meeting. Immediately after the meeting, each of us work team members took one of the nine and talked to him at length.[16]

Publicly humiliated in front of their friends and neighbors, the production team cadres admitted their mistakes. Villagers began to see the power of the work team, and, from this meeting onward, they volunteered examples of cadre corruption.

A former participant in a work team–sponsored meeting to expose cadre corruption in rural Guangdong Province during the same campaign recalls:

> During any big struggle meeting, you had to rely on militiamen to push things forward. Old people or middle-aged persons don't like to struggle against people. They're afraid to hurt the feelings of people. But young people aren't afraid to do these things. They don't know anything about these close personal relationships, and during the struggle meetings they'll struggle and attack with all their might.[17]

Campaign political meetings, then, served to mobilize villagers to accomplish the goals of the campaign. The meetings were political because they dealt with questions of leadership.

Campaign economic mass meetings included those that were held during the campaign to learn from the national model Dazhai brigade. In January 1972, for example, a work team arrived in a brigade in Guangdong to implement the Dazhai campaign. It called a meeting of all production team and brigade cadres to explain the purpose of the campaign. This meeting was followed by a series of daily "struggle" meetings called by the production teams. These team mass meetings were designed to prepare members for agricultural construction work, digging new irrigation ditches, and reclaiming wasteland, supervised by work teams. The work team targeted for special attention the peasants who refused to follow orders (*bu ting hua*), especially those with "bad class backgrounds."[18]

Although, according to my informant, the campaign was unpopular, peasants did not dare to speak out against the movement in work team–supervised meetings. When the work team left, however, the agricultural construction work, the focus of the campaign, abruptly stopped.

These two examples of local mass meetings held during campaigns may be exceptional cases because they were supervised by outsiders. Local leaders also presided over meetings during campaigns. During the Socialist Education Campaign, which preceded the Four Clean-ups, "political officers" in production teams convened mass meetings designed to instill socialist values and criticize petty capitalist tendencies in the villages.[19] In a 1972 case, brigade party secretaries were charged with convening local campaign meetings to criticize former Minister of Defense Lin Biao. These meetings, which usually consisted of local cadres reading from party newspaper editorials or from parts of official documents, served the purpose of transmitting central policy to the peasantry. In any event, meetings held during campaign conditions tended to be dominated by political activists and were characterized by an atmosphere of conformity, emotional appeals for unity with the party and the party line, and even of intimidation. They actively discouraged expressions of even minor dissent.

Noncampaign political mass meetings included routine political study meetings (from which "four bad class elements" were excluded for most of this period), meetings to transmit political directives from higher levels, and meetings to evaluate or endorse local leaders. Examples of mass meetings to elect local leaders are provided in the next chapter.

Noncampaign economic mass meetings included meetings to discuss production and distribution plans or investment and accumulation issues. At production-team level, these meetings took several forms, as the following example illustrates.

On May 7, 1981, twenty-four production team members tore down the newly constructed walls of a workers' dormitory at a commune-run medicine factory in Guangdong. The commune party secretary, after discussing the incident with his two deputies, convened a commune party committee meeting to discuss what action should be taken. The meeting resolved that the incident should be handled "politically," and not with immediate arrests.

The next day, in an effort to find out what had happened, the commune party secretary, some party committee members, local police and court officials, convened a discussion meeting (*zuotanhui*) in the team, attended by the team's cadres, the team members who had participated in the incident, and team cadres who worked in the commune. During the meeting, team members protested that the dormitory was being built on their team's land, which had been transferred to the commune factory without the team's agreement. Team members also protested that an insufficient number of jobs in commune-run rural industries had been distributed to them. During the course of the meeting, it emerged that, although the commune had distributed more jobs to the team, team cadres had reserved them for their relatives.

After discovering the team members' grievances, the commune secretary called a team mass meeting to "propagate central policies, and to oppose anarchy and individualism." The commune then allocated the team six additional jobs, paid compensation for the land, and helped the team to repair its water pond.[20]

This incident reveals the complicated interplay of actions that peasants occasionally used to influence public affairs. In this case, authorities called political crisis meetings only after peasants destroyed commune property. These were followed by meetings to discuss economic issues, at which some peasants spoke up and protested against commune policy. What started out as a series of political meetings concluded with a discussion of local economic issues.

At brigade level, leaders also sometimes called mass meetings to resolve such issues as the appropriate level of collective reserves. Brigade authorities in one case suggested an initial amount that villagers thought was too high. At team mass meetings (*sheyuan dahui*) and at the brigade congress (*sheyuan daibiaohui*), they complained to brigade party officials and insisted that the amount of the reserves, the method of accumulation, and the problem of how to use reserves be discussed carefully, item by item. The brigade party branch accepted this idea and called meetings of production team leaders (*shengchan duizhanghui*) and the brigade congress to discuss the matter. The accumulation goal set for the brigade was reduced by 45 percent over the previous year.[21]

In this case, peasants also spoke out to reduce the amount of accumulation at a series of meetings. Brigade authorities did not permit the brigade congress alone to resolve the issue, however, and they apparently sought to dilute the decision-making power of the congress by also convening a meeting of team leaders. National policy at the time encouraged local units to reduce levels of accumulation in the countryside, and this must have had an impact on brigade officials.

During noncampaign periods, mass meetings probably provided peasants with their greatest opportunity to influence local policies. These periods of reduced political activity were characterized by more relaxed supervision, which permitted villagers to devote more attention to local problems. During campaign periods, however, outside work teams were sometimes present, checking on team and brigade compliance, and the agendas of team and brigade meetings were crowded with campaign issues. In addition, my data indicate that peasants spoke out more frequently at meetings that produced largely economic outcomes. Although peasants were usually politically passive and generally inarticulate in political debate, they were keen to protect their own interests.

Variations

Meetings varied according to their outcome and according to whether they were called during campaign or noncampaign periods. They also varied according to their frequency, participants, and their democratic character.

According to regulations governing rural work, brigade authorities were obliged to call brigade congresses from two to four times a year [22] and team mass meetings monthly. [23] In practice, however, the frequency of local mass meetings varied according to whether authorities were carrying out a campaign and according to the agricultural production cycle.

During campaigns, such as the Cultural Revolution (1966–1969), authorities called brigade and team mass meetings much more frequently than during noncampaign periods. In 1966–1967, for example, Guangdong and Fujian informants report weekly brigade-level congresses. [24] At the same time, team leaders called daily team mass meetings. [25] During the 1970s, however, leaders called brigade and team mass meetings less frequently. Brigade leaders called brigade congresses only once or twice a year. [26] Fujian and Guangdong informants report that, in addition to informal nightly gatherings to record work points in their teams, political study meetings were held two or three evenings a week from 1970 to 1976. [27] If

no problem needed particular attention, meeting nights functioned as social occasions in some suburban Guangdong teams, with games and perhaps a television broadcast. Peasants received work points for attending
meetings during working hours. Since 1979, under the new responsibility
system, leaders have called even fewer mass meetings.[28]

Usually adult work point earners participated in team mass meetings.
The period was characterized by the steady participation of this group.
The participation of "bad class elements" has varied over time, however.
During the early 1960s and since 1979, when discrimination against landlords and rich peasants and their offspring was reduced, more people participated in team mass meetings. During the Cultural Revolution decade,
however, "bad class elements" were excluded from mass political meetings.
They met separately under the surveillance of local public security officers
and the brigade party branch.

Finally, the democratic character of local mass meetings varied during
the period. After 1978 authorities offered frank appraisals of the effectiveness of local assemblies in the 1960s and 1970s for democratic decision
making. In one commentary, the author points out that commune and village management lacked a democratic tradition:

> Management tended to stress only its control over the members and ignored
> their democratic rights. This was fully reflected in its paternalistic style of man-
> agement. In some communes and villages, the appointment and dismissal of
> cadres did not reflect the opinion of the people. Team mass meetings (*sheyuan
> dahui*) and brigade congresses (*sheyuan daibiao dahui*) were little more than
> rubber-stamp organs. Important issues of the collective economy were deter-
> mined by a few cadres without consultation or debate. Daily management work
> was done on the orders of a few. Leaders failed to use democratic working
> methods. . . . [29]

After 1978 some local authorities insisted that this problem was reme-
died,[30] while others point out that local leaders continued to make major
decisions, such as determining the content of production plans, "without
discussion by the masses."[31]

These generalizations obscure the fact that peasants have been able to
influence decisions under certain conditions. In general, peasant-initiated
participation in *team mass meetings* was more likely than at higher levels.
Informants from Guangdong indicate that, in the 1960s and early 1970s,
peasants in team mass meetings discussed and took part in decisions on
economic issues.

Meetings to assess work points were in some ways typical of the period. These meetings set work point values for individual workers and for specific tasks. Frequent reassessments of workers were required when the Dazhai time-rate system was introduced, particularly from 1968 to 1972, in Guangdong. The meetings were characterized by intense argument and bitter disputes as peasants tried to have their work point values raised. What started out as weekly assessment meetings became monthly and then semi-annual affairs over time. As the meetings became more troublesome, authorities called them less frequently, and team management committees began to play a more active role. Although after 1971 many places abandoned Dazhai time rates, team leaders continued to call periodic work point assessment meetings to evalute work tasks.[32] Where work points were used after 1979, authorities also called meetings to make these assessments.[33]

More recently, after prodding from higher authorities, team leaders have occasionally permitted formal team mass meetings to choose which responsibility system the team would adopt. In one 1981 case, commune authorities first provided an assessment of various systems, which was transmitted to team mass meetings, where peasants "actively participated and warmly discussed" them. According to the official report, 86 percent of the adult workers in one brigade attended these meetings. In the end, the brigade's seven teams chose four different systems, a result endorsed by the authorities.[34] Still, informants also report that in the village, "if you had some criticism (*yijian*), you would not raise it at a public meeting. You would not dare to." Fear of alienating local leaders often inhibited peasants from speaking up. Peasants preferred to contact officials informally. For these reasons, responsible village leaders collected opinion by visiting their friends and neighbors at home, where talk was less inhibited.[35]

Informants from Guangdong and Fujian contrasted the atmosphere of the smaller team mass meetings with brigade-level mass meetings, attended usually by several hundred people. Authorities called brigade meetings infrequently, and peasants rarely spoke out at them: "Peasants didn't really dare to directly disagree with brigade cadres—they were afraid it would cause trouble," one informant reports.[36]

Cadres met in team management committee meetings, which they called frequently, perhaps several times a week, and always before a team mass meeting. The cadre meetings were often informal, with the team leader canvassing opinion on an issue and perhaps discussing a problem with committee members a few at a time.

The team management committee had its own decision-making sphere. Guangdong informants reported that in the early 1970s management committees took action on loan applications,[37] team participation in brigade or higher-level projects,[38] team size,[39] and team investments,[40] without referring these issues to mass meetings. They did discuss these issues with the brigade leadership, however. On many other issues, team management committees made preliminary decisions, which were then put to mass meetings for ratification. However, rarely in my data did peasants at mass meetings overturn team cadre decisions.

Participants perceived team management committee meetings as more democratic than mass meetings. According to one former production team leader, speaking of the 1970s:

> Team [management committee] meetings were very democratic. You could express freely various points of view and no one gave you a "hat" to wear [labeled you a "bad element"]. Arguments were common. . . . In general, we could decide a policy only after getting the opinion of the brigade. [Within the team] if only a "small person" disagreed with a policy, we could still carry it out, and not have to pay any attention to his objection. But, if the team leader opposed it, it could not be done. If several people were opposed, it could not be carried out.[41]

Nonetheless, the leadership style of local cadres undoubtedly varied enormously. Some team leaders dominated their teams, made important decisions themselves, and did not consult either other team cadres or mass meetings. In one model team, for example, peasants complained that a new team leader barked out orders, worked peasants too hard, and held too few meetings to arrange work.[42] In still other teams, management committees were divided by factional or kinship disputes that undermined their effectiveness. Some local officials were petty tyrants, and others squabbled with rivals. Although the style that local officials used to conduct team management committee meetings seems to have varied widely, because teams were small, the opportunity for consultation seems to have been greatest at this level.

Cadre meetings at brigade level included party branch meetings and brigade management committee meetings.[43] Leadership style varied considerably at this level as well—from "one-man rule" (*yige ren lingdao*), perhaps the norm, to "collective leadership." In Zhejiang, for example, a brigade party secretary writes that he had permitted the party branch committee to overrule him temporarily on the issue of whether pigs should be bred collectively or privately. Although peasants preferred privatization, the party branch committee resisted. "I did not exercise my power to veto their decision," the party secretary writes, "but put the issue before the masses for discussion." "The masses" in this case were the party branch and the brigade congress, both of which supported private pig breeding. The party branch committee then changed its mind and permitted the new policy.[44]

This example is revealing for several reasons. First, the language of the story indicates that the party secretary's power to make decisions was not checked by local institutions. He "permitted himself to be overruled" by the party committee. Although he could have vetoed the committee's decision, he chose not to. Second, the secretary was attempting to implement a popular official policy over the objections of local party notables. In the end, he could not but have succeeded. Finally, the secretary did not put the measure directly to the peasants, but to production team officials meeting as the brigade congress. Had he put the issue to the peasants directly, the result might have been even more embarrassing. This anecdote may not be representative of brigade cadre decision making, but it is likely that many brigade cadres did share power with other local officials.

In other brigades, however, the leadership group was divided by factional loyalties. In one suburban Fujian brigade, for example, Cultural Revolutionary factions were institutionalized within the brigade management committee up to and beyond 1978. Disunity impaired effective cooperation within the brigade.[45] Factions also sometimes checked and balanced one another, however, which permitted some measure of power sharing and prevented the dictatorship of the party secretary.

In general, peasants were effectively able to influence public affairs through meetings only under certain conditions. First, when local cadres disagreed on a particular issue, as they did in the pig breeding example, leaders sometimes put the issue to mass meetings. By implication, had the cadres been united, the secretary would not have asked the congress for its views.

Second, peasants have occasionally been able to take advantage of cadre inertia or indecision to make changes in local policy. They were effective when the community was united on a particular issue. In 1971, for example, higher levels relaxed tight controls on private plots (*ziliudi*). Local cadres in Guangdong, some of whom had campaigned against private plots during the Cultural Revolution (1966–1969), were perplexed and unsure about what they should do. In one Taishan County brigade, cadres asked production team heads to call team mass meetings to give villagers an opportunity to express their opinions on the issue of whether plots should be redistributed to take into account recent population changes. Production team leaders called the meetings, and, according to one participant: "The team members' opinions followed their own interests. Some said to keep the present system, while others wanted changes."[46]

Brigade authorities then called team cadres to a meeting to report on the views of the villagers. In the discussions that followed, it became clear that the peasants overwhelmingly favored readjustment, a view expressed forcefully by several team cadres, many of whom themselves did not have private plots. Brigade cadres then approved of the readjustment.

These meetings were an effective forum for peasants to influence local policy because, first, community solidarity on the issue was high, and, second, because they occurred during a period when higher-level officials relaxed their opposition to private plots.

In 1971–1972 higher-level authorities also relaxed their opposition to small teams and brigades. Peasants living in a large production team in Guangdong's Zengzheng County then took the initiative to divide up their team into smaller units.[47] Although commune and brigade authorities resisted this move (higher-level authorities had only recently disapproved of smaller units), team cadres called successive team mass meetings, during which villagers resolved to divide up the team. Commune and brigade authorities finally acquiesced in the face of widespread opposition. In this case, the team was effective because it was united on the issue that the unit ought to be split up.

Third, peasant opportunity to influence local politics increased when they had the support of higher-level elites. Particularly since 1979, central authorities have attempted to mobilize villagers to participate in local politics as a strategy for curtailing and overcoming the resistance of intermediate and local cadres to the new, more liberal post-Mao agricultural policies. Several of the cases presented above can be interpreted in this light.

A number of factors have constrained peasants from speaking out in formal settings. First, because of their generally low educational level, peasants were both relatively inarticulate spokesmen for their own interests and relatively ignorant of the wider community in which they lived.

Second, peasants tended to value harmony and to respect or fear authority. They felt uncomfortable challenging their neighbors and leaders in public, although they sometimes did so, as we saw in the example of the Dazhai work point assessment meetings.

An example will serve to illustrate the passivity of Chinese peasants. In 1979 one team agreed during a mass meeting in Guangdong to grain output quotas that were unrealistically high. It soon emerged that they could not be met, according to team cadres, without uprooting an orchard to plant more grain, an unpopular proposal. Villagers then complained directly to the brigade party branch secretary who intervened. He called a meeting of team cadres, who resolved to plant grain among the trees (thus saving them) and to reclaim some previously uncultivated wasteland.[48] In this case, the villagers who attended the initial meeting probably realized that the quotas were too high, but they refused to question their team cadres or to oppose them in public.

Peasants sometimes concealed their true feelings when they ran counter to the wishes of their cadres not only because they were politically passive, but because they feared that local officials might retaliate against them. Peasants may have believed that, if they criticized their leaders, they would be discriminated against by them, or, if they criticized higher levels, brigade and commune authorities would penalize them in some way. *Renmin Ribao* in its 1980 expose of fraud and other malpractices in Xiyang County, where the former national model Dazhai brigade is located, asked incredulously (if disingenuously) why none of the relatives of the more than 140 villagers killed "unnaturally" during the "ultra-leftist" period of the Cultural Revolution lodged complaints with higher authorities: "They [the peasants] have to be urged to speak out."[49] Had they spoken out, however, local authorities could have applied a wide range of political and administrative sanctions to discipline them, including class labeling and arrest.

Informants from Guangdong and Fujian indicate that peasants sometimes considered these risks when they were tempted to complain. Speaking of the early 1960s, one former peasant says: "Peasants talked among themselves in the fields and to friends. They didn't air their opinions at meetings. If there was dissatisfaction with a policy, the dissident would have to wear a "three-flags" hat, and would not simply be struggled with, but would be arrested."[50] Local cadres sometimes demonstrated excessive zeal in their labeling of nonconformists. During the height of the Cultural Revolution (1966–1969) and during the Cleaning-up Class Ranks Campaign, local officials detained and struggled with peasants in many Guangdong villages.[51] Throughout the 1970s some cadres confiscated the property of peasants who they thought spent too much time in private enterprise and labeled them "capitalist tails."[52]

Higher-level authorities also had means of enforcing compliance, which ranged from ignoring popularly made decisions to open retaliation. In the early 1960s, when household contracting was being considered in Fujian, authorities commended production team cadres for being resolute and not giving in to pressure for *baochan dao hu,* "even though commune members raised disturbances [spoke out for it] at each meeting that was held."[53] Later, in 1979, brigades in some areas ordered peasants to uproot crops that authorities ruled to be contrary to the production plan.[54]

In 1980, during the confusion over Beijing's position on household contracting, commune authorities in Guangdong vetoed production team plans to implement *baochan dao hu,* which peasants in mass meetings had endorsed. The plans were temporarily scrapped as a result.[55] In one case, local authorities convened a commune congress to publicly criticize eleven households for carrying out the policy. And as late as 1981, Dehua County and some commune authorities in Fujian continued to ban household contracting. They withheld chemical fertilizer and credit, and increased quotas to punish the brigades that went ahead with *baochan dao hu,* although central authorities had already approved of the policy.[56] These examples indicate the power of intermediate officials to veto or negate popular central policies in China's villages.

The ability of authorities to ensure compliance with unpopular policies and their apparent willingness to overrule popular local decisions were further constraints on peasant attempts to influence government decisions. From the official point of view, majority rule was less important than that the policy outcome was "correct." Earlier I cited the example of Secretary Tian to illustrate the willingness of senior leaders to overrule apparently popular decisions that some authorities perceived as undermining collective and state interests and the long-term interests of the peasantry. Although popular endorsement of party policy was always welcome and in some sense necessary, it was less important than that the outcome conformed to party policy. Legitimacy was derived primarily from conformity to the party line, and only secondarily from the fact that it was formulated democratically. In each of the cases cited above, where higher authorities vetoed or overruled popular policies, they did so in the belief that they were carrying out "correct" policy. This concept of "correctness," then, further constrained peasant participation.

Finally, meetings held under campaign conditions were influenced by an atmosphere of conformity and demands for complete support of the party's position. These circumstances encouraged local leaders to mobilize peasants into the intense activity of the campaign. To resist was to risk social ostracism or to be targeted as an object for "struggle." Pressure from the party and local formal leaders, eager to comply, severely restricted the limited opportunities for peasant-initiated participation that China's local political institutions provided.

Mass Organizations

In addition to rural assemblies, China's leaders have organized peasants into associations designed, at least in theory, to supervise cadre behavior. Although peasants' associations played a key role during land reform,[57] with the departure of land reform work teams, they went into a steep and rapid decline.[58]

From 1962 to 1984 authorities organized new associations (called "poor and lower-middle peasants' associations") in conjunction with the Four Clean-ups Campaign. They were designed to supervise production team and brigade cadres, particularly in the areas of financial management and corruption.[59] Although draft rules prohibited local cadres from concurrently serving as association representatives, the rules explicitly put the associations under party supervision.[60]

In 1974 and then from 1980 to 1982, authorities attempted to revive the associations, first during the campaign to criticize Lin Biao[61] and then as part of an effort to establish independent, democratic local institutions. In his 1980 speech Liao Gailong urged that independent peasants' associations be established throughout the country. He pointed out that peasants, although they accounted for 80 percent of the Chinese population, had "not yet formed organizations that represent their interests." Although peasants were represented in national assemblies, Liao noted, still these congresses were "not devoted to representing the peasants; they represent the whole people, the people of various strata." Liao denied that peasants in their own association would "rise up in rebellion." Only through independent associations could peasants safeguard their own interests, he said.[62]

By 1982, however, although authorities argued that both mass organizations and people's congresses ought to supervise the government, political commentators in China saw the power of mass organizations as only advisory.[63] Unlike the 1964–1966 period, when peasants' associations in theory took a more active role in the supervision of cadres, by 1982 officials conceived of their power as substantially reduced. In response to appeals to rejuvenate or reestablish peasants' associations, authorities in Yunnan, Guangdong, Hubei, Jiangsu, and Hunan provinces held meetings of local and provincial peasants' associations.[64]

During the period of our study, local cadres in practice gave a low priority to establishing strong, independent peasants' associations. Authorities observed in 1974 that "some of the [commune] comrades of the party committee at that time [Nov. 1973] had an insufficient understanding of the role of the poor and lower-middle peasant organizations, and failed to list the poor and lower-middle peasant organizations' work on the party committee's daily agenda."[65] Poor and lower-middle peasant congresses, called at higher levels from 1964 to 1966 and again in 1973–1974, acted as devices to mobilize labor and gain peasant compliance and increasingly took on the character of meetings of model workers and "progressive elements." In fact, these meetings were called "congresses of poor and lower-middle peasants and agricultural progressives" in some places. I have no evidence of peasants making demands in these higher-level forums, and indeed press reports and radio broadcasts summarizing their tasks in 1974 and from 1980 to 1982 rarely include "supervising cadres" among them.

At village level, however, during the Four Clean-ups Campaign, press reports claim that peasants exercised considerable power over team and brigade cadres.[66] According to the press, the representatives raised such issues as production problems (for example, water management and the supply of chemical fertilizer),[67] the implementation of the incentive system,[68] the collectivization of sideline production,[69] and cadre corruption.[70] In each of these areas, representatives reportedly criticized or exposed errors of local cadres.

Data from interviews do not confirm this activist role for association representatives. Rather, interviewees suggest that poor and lower-middle peasant representatives were generally weak and ineffectual during and after this campaign. As one former peasant puts it: "The poor and lower-middle peasant representative in my team was basically of no use."[71] In this Guangdong team, the representative was an old experienced peasant "without any leadership ability," who attended team management committee meetings but did little else. If a team member had a problem, he would go to the team leader or to other cadres for help, not to the representative. "The representative couldn't solve problems," so in the informant's view, he was simply a "buddha made of mud."[72] Most informants from Guangdong and Fujian concur with this evaluation for the period.[73]

If villagers did go to association representatives for help or to make demands, it was for reasons other than their official positions; these representatives were team leaders, party members,[74] or former cadres.[75] Association representatives did occasionally disagree with team management committee members on production issues[76] and in one Guangdong case demanded the dismissal of a team leader for his "bad" work style.[77] However, the representatives had standing in the community to speak out because they were either *concurrently* local cadres (as happened in a few places, in spite of the 1964 draft rules), former cadres, currently party members, or "old experienced peasants." Only representatives with these characteristics appear to have intervened in management committee decisions.

The data from interviews can be reconciled with official reports for 1963 to 1966 if we consider that the associations "supervised cadres" while the Four Clean-ups work teams were present but did not do so after the work teams withdrew. Informants saw the measures taken by the associations against corrupt cadres as initiated by the work teams. As the work teams completed their investigations of local cadres, they set up the associations and used them to make announcements on the fate of the local officials and to legitimize their decisions. In general, since 1966, neither the press nor my interviewees have reported that the associations exercised significant power.[78] Indeed, as I note above, Liao Gailong referred to the absence of these associations in 1980.

In addition to peasants' associations, mass organizations organized at village level included the women's federation and the youth league. Although authorities have used both kinds of mass organizations to mobilize villagers into campaigns ranging from birth control to socialist education, neither served as a significant channel for peasants to influence government policy.[79]

Conclusion

In theory China's leaders implemented the mass line through both village assemblies and mass organizations, and, as a result, China's citizens should have been able to supervise local leaders in the execution of their duties through these institutions. In practice, however, they have mainly served to mobilize the peasantry to carry out party policy. Powerful constraints limited the peasants' opportunities to influence public affairs through these formal channels.

Nonetheless, peasants occasionally spoke out at meetings in an effort to influence the implementation of local economic policy. Peasants were most effective when they could ally themselves with higher-level leaders to influence the implementation of a popular central (and, therefore, "correct") policy; when group solidarity on an issue was high; when intermediate leadership groups, especially at commune or brigade level, were divided or their authority was low; and during lulls between campaigns. Authorities probably always intended mass organizations to be mobilizational, and I found only modest evidence that peasants used them to influence public affairs.

5

Voting:
Village Elections

In recent times in spite of regulations that required frequent elections of local leaders, China's officials did not mobilize the peasantry to elect their leaders and deputies to local assemblies until 1980. Although officials carried out national elections of deputies to township (commune) congresses in the 1950s and early 1960s,[1] during the intervening years most local authorities did not call elections. However, in some places, even during the Cultural Revolution, local officials called elections that gave peasants an opportunity to influence public affairs. In particular, where they could mobilize a high degree of group solidarity and where they had higher-level elite support, villagers participated in politics through elections effectively.

During the period of my study, official policy encouraged peasants to participate in local elections. By 1962 the Sixty Articles required that peasants directly elect production team cadres and delegates to brigade congresses (*sheyuan daibiaohui*).[2] In addition, state constitutions required that authorities call elections of deputies to commune people's congresses.[3] Nonetheless, my data indicate that, for most of the period, local authorities either failed to enforce these provisions or did so only nominally.

87

In December 1978 party leaders reported that the "democratic life of the country" had seriously eroded during the previous ten years. They re-emphasized the need for "democratic management" and the election of cadres in production teams, brigades, and communes,[4] a policy that subsequently appeared in the New Sixty Articles. These regulations stipulated that team members were to elect production team cadres every two years and that all village elections were to be by secret ballot.[5] The national and provincial press then demanded that local officials carry out village elections and argued that voting should be seen as evidence of the autonomy of production teams.[6]

In 1979 authorities enacted a new election law, which for the first time extended to all citizens, including peasants, the right to elect directly delegates to county-level people's congresses.[7] From 1979 to 1981 and again in 1984, officials throughout China carried out direct elections under the new law.[8] At the same time, in many parts of China, local authorities carried out elections of production team cadres.[9]

The new state constitution, enacted in 1982, required that peasants elect village (brigade) officials, including the brigade head and brigade management committee.[10] In addition, this document, like all previous state constitutions and election laws, stipulated that all citizens of the republic over 18 years of age were eligible to vote and to hold office, unless they were deprived of their political rights by law (as were unrepentant landlords and rich peasants, counterrevolutionaries, and "bad elements").[11]

In 1983, three years after authorities called the first nationwide elections under the new election law, officials in Beijing issued regulations to govern elections at county level and below. According to these rules, the standing committee of the county people's congress should appoint a township election committee to oversee elections in the township. The election committee was charged with a wide range of functions, including voter registration, examining voter qualifications, publishing a list of qualified voters, defining the boundaries of election wards, determining the number of deputies to be elected by each ward, determining and publishing official lists of candidates, setting the election date, and validating the election results.[12]

During the 1984 elections, officials issued additional guidelines for local elections,[13] which followed closely the amended 1979 election law. For example, under the regulations, political parties, organizations, and any three registered voters (now ten) could make nominations, which election committees were obliged to accept. The election committee was to publish the list of nominees twenty days before the election. This was to be followed by "democratic discussions," and, if the list was too long, the committee was to publish a revised list five days before the election. In general, the list of nominees should be no longer than two candidates for each post. During the five days before the elections, election committee members were to present the backgrounds of the candidates to the electorate. Voters were to cast secret ballots; to be elected, a candidate needed to secure at least one-half of the votes.[14]

In the 1960s and 1970s, however, authorities carried out elections without the benefit of published national regulations. As a result, I have based my discussion of the elections that occurred during that time on actual practices, as reported in press accounts, interviews with participants, and short stories.

After 1978, China's media reexamined election functions. First, elections legitimized China's leadership selection process. As one publication points out, elections "demonstrate that people are the masters of a socialist state."[15] Second, by making local cadres more responsive to local opinion, central authorities hoped to undermine opposition to their new agricultural policies. Officials linked the right of peasants to elect their own leaders with the introduction of the responsibility system in agriculture.[16]

One 1979 commentary, for example, traces the history of leadership selection in a Sichuan brigade. In 1975 local authorities removed a team leader, whom peasants had "democratically elected" in 1964 and replaced him with a peasant who, it turned out, "lacked organizational ability." Grain production fell rapidly, and the villagers were angry. In 1977 brigade authorities attempted to rectify the situation with another appointee, who "mechanically carried out instructions of the upper levels and issued blind commands," with the result that production continued to fall. Finally, in 1979, after "peasants made strong demands to brigade and commune party organs for democratic elections," the original team leader was elected, and production rose. The commentator points out:

> Democratically elected production team leaders fully reflect the will and desires of the masses, uphold their interests, and proceed from reality in carrying out instructions from upper levels . . . [while] a production team leader appointed by the upper levels can only think about the upper-level leadership, watch what

they do before taking action himself, fulfill responsibilities only to them, and neglect the cries and interests of the masses.[17]

The commentator only hints at the views of the production team leaders on the implementation of household contracting, but undoubtedly they were crucial. Brigade authorities permitted the democratic election of the original leader, who probably favored household contracting, only after higher levels legitimized experiments with the responsibility system. From 1979 to 1981 national elites supported the villagers' use of elections to replace local leaders who were obstructing party policy.

Third, authorities hoped that elections would stabilize village leadership groups.[18] In letters to the editor of *Nanfang Ribao,* for example, writers argue that elections would increase both stability and productivity.[19]

Nonetheless, some local officials doubted the effectiveness of village elections. In a letter to the editor of *Renmin Ribao,* for example, one soldier writes that, as a result of elections in his home village, team leaders were replaced annually: "I have heard that, when the villagers hold a meeting to elect a team leader, they vote for incompetents. Nothing can be done about it, except perhaps to draw lots!"[20] Reports from Zhejiang also expressed doubts. Zengguan commune reported that, as a result of elections, each year one-third of the production team heads were replaced.[21] In other areas of Zhejiang, team leaders resigned every year at the end of the agricultural busy season in anticipation of new elections, which created instability and a lack of continuity.[22]

Local officials also argued that team leaders should be appointed, rather than elected. If brigade authorities wisely chose young agricultural technicians as team leaders, production would increase,[23] especially if the team was divided by factional or kinship rivalry and incapable of electing a competent leader.[24] Although these views were perhaps minority ones, they indicated that some local officials did not share Beijing's enthusiasm for elections.

Production Team Elections

The 1979–1981 and 1984 county elections provided peasants with some experience with elections that were directly under the supervision of Beijing. Local officials set up election committees and divided communes into election districts. Authorities registered peasants to vote, lobbied them by publicly backing their favorite candidates, and supervised the casting of secret ballots for candidates to county people's congresses.[25] In Tianjin's Wuqing County, for example, thousands of villagers deprived of their political rights before 1978 were registered as electors, an estimated one million peasants listened to reports on election work, 82 percent of voters took part in nominating candidates, and 97.3 percent cast ballots.[26] During the period of my study, these elections were virtually the only time when national authorities took a direct interest in village-level balloting.[27] Although not required to by the regulations on rural work, local leaders may have attempted to implement certain features of the national election procedures in their own village elections.[28] After all, in 1979–1981 and in 1984 authorities expected peasants to participate in county-level elections.

Preparatory Meetings and Nominations

Once authorities had decided to carry out team elections, they held a series of preliminary discussions on the procedures to be followed.[29] If team elections were a high priority, as they were in some counties from 1979 to 1981, county authorities issued guidelines to local officials.

During these preliminary discussions, officials sometimes suggested that the election procedures vary according to different team situations. In one Zhejiang county, for example, commune and brigade cadres determined that production teams fell into three general groups. In the first group, team leaders had been in office a relatively short time, there were few conflicts, and the peasants were relatively satisfied with their leaders. Hence, villagers would be allowed to make nominations themselves in a team mass meeting, which would be followed by voting (by a show of hands or secret ballot). In the second group, peasants were relatively dissatisfied with their leaders, and there was some dissension. Under these circumstances, officials should first call a team mass meeting and by secret ballot elect nominees for team leadership positions. After a general discussion of these candidates, officials should hold an election for the team leader. In the third group, large teams characterized by many "opinions" (yijian) and entrenched kinship rivalry, officials should "take the household as the unit for repeated discussions, and then carry out an election using ballots." Authorities were urged to first carry out this work at "test points" (shidian) and then to implement elections in most other teams.[30]

If the team elections were a matter of routine, not requiring the attention of county or commune authorities, the brigade party branch and team management committees would meet with guarantee cadres to discuss them. These discussions were important if vacancies were being filled or if the brigade was determined to replace a particular team official.

In general, either higher levels (brigade party branches or visiting work teams) or team members (and their management committees) nominated candidates for production team cadre elections.[31] Data sources conflict on which of these two methods predominated. For the post-1978 period, interviewees overwhelmingly report that the brigade made these nominations, while most of the press reports that team members made the nominations.[32]

Prior to 1977, it is likely that brigade or work team officials made the nominations in most cases.[33] This method was justified, according to one former deputy brigade leader, because "permitting team members to make nominations would be too disorderly. If we allowed this, they would all nominate themselves." Reflecting on the role of brigade cadres in nominating team candidates, the interviewee points out:

> We were the responsible persons. The brigade can order leadership changes. . . . Usually the team members approve of our suggestions. We suggested particular names for specific posts. Team members didn't make nominations. In general we were looking for a team leader who would listen to brigade and commune orders (*tinghua*). We needed someone who could persuade commune members to carry out our orders.[34]

Guarantee cadres usually played a pivotal role in brigade nominations of team cadres. They were most familiar with the team and were trusted by their brigade colleagues.

When work teams supervised production team elections, they also often nominated team leadership candidates.[35] During the Four Clean-ups Campaign, for example, work teams sent to purge villages of corrupt cadres often supervised team and brigade elections before they left. In one case, a former work team member reports that, after conducting a detailed investigation of the production team for which he was responsible, he uncovered corruption among the current team cadres. The work team called for new elections, and each work team member made an evaluation of the production team cadres he had investigated. This culminated in a recommendation to the work team (not to brigade or team cadres) of whom to dismiss from office. The work team leader met individually with each work team member to discuss the member's recommendations, from which emerged a list of acceptable nominees for team cadre positions: "He [the work team leader] first looked at the materials I had submitted to him. Then, he listened to my explanation of the situation. . . . In every case he supported the recommendations of the work team member in the particular team concerned."[36] This list then became the candidate list for the production team. Work teams have not always completely taken over the process, however. When they participated in team elections, they usually shared supervision with brigade cadres. The Four Clean-ups Campaign was exceptional in this regard.

Nonetheless, according to press reports and interview data, in some production teams, villagers were permitted to nominate their own candidates.[37] One Guangdong informant describes the procedure in 1974:

> First, the current [team] cadres call a team management committee meeting and formulate a candidate name list. This list [in our team] always has more names on it than positions to be filled. For example, in 1974 we needed eight cadres, but the list included twelve names, mostly old cadres plus new activist elements. Afterwards the list of names was presented to the team members for their vote.[38]

In this case, the team cadres, not the brigade or an outside work team, nominated candidates for team positions. Production teams have sometimes demanded the right to make nominations, for example, in one Guangdong county in 1979. Although some party members objected, the brigade party branch eventually relented.[39] In another case, two letter writers from Hebei complain that, after peasants in their production team nominated three candidates for team leader, the commune "guarantee cadre disagreed with the practice of nominations open to everyone, and demanded that he alone be permitted to appoint the team leader." Villagers opposed this, and because the incident occurred at the beginning of the agricultural busy season, the guarantee cadre backed down and agreed that a team mass meeting could be called.[40]

Only a small minority of the press reports (three out of fifty-five) discussed the number of nominees for each post.[41] These reports indicate that more candidates were nominated than positions, and in one case authorities had to call a primary election. Of the six cases discussed in interviews for the post-1977 period, the same number of candidates were nominated as there were posts available in five cases.[42] Given the difficulty of recruiting team cadres, this undoubtedly was the dominant trend.

Campaigning and Propaganda

Nominations were usually followed by a few days of discussion among team members, during which they evaluated the candidates.[43] This was particularly true when the election was more than a ratification of the current team cadres. During this time, brigade or commune cadres sometimes attempted to influence the outcome. In one county in Guangdong, for example, just prior to countywide team elections, brigades "sent delegates to production team meetings to help ferment [*yunniang,* promote] the new candidates for leading posts."[44] In another case, a secretary in Bi County, Sichuan, discovered that peasants in a production team he had taken a special interest in were unlikely to reelect the team's leader. He instructed brigade officials to do "some work among the commune members, to ensure that the current team leader would be reelected."[45]

The press and short stories indicate that, during this stage, candidates sometimes tried to persuade villagers to vote for them during preelection team meetings.[46] Campaign speeches took the form of promises to increase rural income in some villages. In the short story "Gathering Beans," for example, several candidates are competing for election.

> "I'm willing to continue the revolution, and to serve the people," said one. Candidate Shengwei said, "O.K., if you elect me team leader, I guarantee each labor day will be worth 2 yuan." "What a joke!" exclaimed Fish King, "One yuan is more realistic." The student observed: "Yesterday two yuan, today one yuan, tomorrow half a yuan, day after tomorrow you take office, and won't it still be 0.25?" Everyone laughed.[47]

The stakes were higher during work team–supervised elections, and work team members often made the rounds of team members' houses to campaign for their nominees. If villagers resisted, as they did in one work team–supervised election in suburban Shanghai during the Four Cleanups Campaign, the work team member would make repeated visits to the villagers. A former work team member relates that he had a difficult time persuading peasants not to vote for the team's current accountant, whom the work team had determined to be corrupt.

Some [peasants] said that the accountant was good, that he had ability and knew how to do his job. His attitude was bad, but so what, that is not a big problem. And what is more, he is willing to do the job. But I said he should be changed. . . . If they disagreed, I would go to their house again and again, trying to persuade them.[48]

Few press reports or interviewees mention campaigning as a stage in real team election cases. Nominations were usually followed shortly afterward by the election meeting. Campaigning occurred only in unusual cases, where choices were offered or where higher-level authorities supported unpopular candidates.

The Election Meeting

A few days after authorities published the list of nominees, they called a meeting of all adults (often those over 16 years of age) to vote on the candidates. Brigade officials or work team members usually attended these meetings, and the guarantee cadre often presided. The presence of brigade or commune cadres was sometimes intimidating, especially if they had an interest in the outcome. According to one former peasant informant, when the brigade party secretary attended election meetings in the informant's team in Guangdong, "we watched to see what the secretary wanted." Brigade views were weighty, especially if the secretary's family lived in the team.[49] Not all brigade officials had this effect, of course, but the presence of a "local emperor" could be important.

The brigade official or work team member might open the proceedings by reminding villagers that the purpose of the meeting was to elect local leaders and, especially since 1978, by emphasizing the method that would be used. In the short story, "Gathering Beans," for example, the six conditions for electing village leaders were read out at the beginning of the meeting. These conditions were suggested by the educated youth in the team and consisted of "some rules from land reform days, some new, some old, some local and some foreign," an eclectic list that probably only imperfectly reflected national regulations.[50]

One former deputy brigade leader reports that he spoke at elections of the team cadres in teams that he "guaranteed." He said, for example:

The current team leader is older now, and has heavy responsibilities at home. He is unwilling to continue. So, we [the brigade] want to replace him in the interests of team members and of production. The brigade party committee has studied the situation, and we suggest Lao Wang as team leader, and Lao Chen and Xiao Yang as the two deputy team leaders. Their behavior (*biaoxian*) is good, they are activists in their work, they listen to the party, they are young, and of good class background. Does anyone have anything to say? Any opinions (*yijian*)? If not, all who agree raise your hand. [The result was that they were overwhelmingly elected.][51]

Introductory comments such as these might be followed by discussion, during which authorities wrote the candidates' names on a blackboard, sometimes next to a summary of the team's past economic performance, such as workday rates. Some informants report that villagers were free to add names to the list of nominees, and that this occasionally happened. The additional nominations came from the team's informal leadership, "those with relatively more prestige, and with self-confidence . . . not necessarily [political] activists . . . but those who were skilled farmers."[52]

If a work team supervised the election, the officials might resist additions to their list of nominees. Rather, the meeting would start off with a detailed look at each of the current cadres and conclude with a clear recommendation from the work team, stating who should be elected. Nominations from the floor might be interpreted as interference and generally were not welcome, particularly during campaigns such as the Four Clean-ups.[53]

Following the discussions, peasants voted, either by secret ballot or by show of hands. For the mid-1970s, Guangdong and Fujian interviewees report that both methods were used in their teams.[54] For the post-1978 period, however, of those informants who discuss the method of voting, all indicate that their teams used a show of hands.[55] Most of the press reports do not mention the balloting method (N = 46), but of those that do, in virtually every case peasants cast secret ballots.

In surburban areas, peasants may have used secret ballots, especially because authorities also required peasants to vote by secret ballot in county elections. However, in more remote areas, where literacy levels were low, more traditional methods probably prevailed. Returning to the short story "Gathering Beans," the narrator reports that the three candidates sat at the front of the room with their backs to the voters. Behind each chair was a bowl, into which voters dropped a bean if they wished to vote for that candidate. It soon became apparent that the wives of the candidates (they were all male) would be able to see who the villagers voted for, thus violating the "secret ballot." So they were ordered to sit beside their husbands, and the voting proceeded. Further complications developed when one peasant called out, "Where is Lao Xi's bowl? Yes, here it is, O.K., I'll vote for him." The wife of one of Lao Xi's competitors unleashed a string of abuse at the peasant who had not voted for her husband. Finally everyone voted, and authorities counted the beans.[56]

Review and Approval

Team cadres then sent a list of successful candidates to the brigade for review and approval. In Guangdong, in teams that elected the entire team management committee, brigade officials usually assigned team cadre positions to the newly elected (or reelected) committee members.[57] After giving their approval, brigade authorities sent the name lists to the commune, which issued a certificate of authority (*renmingshu*) to the team leader.[58]

In general, cadres or peasants nominated individuals who they thought were suitable for specific team posts. But, even in the case where the team nominated, elected, and assigned jobs to cadres, the brigade supervised the process through team party members (who participated in the early consultative stages) and through its ability to veto a candidate that the team had elected. In one 1978 case, for example, a commune guarantee cadre, after permitting an election of production team leaders in the team he was "guaranteeing," overruled the outcome when his favorite lost. He attended the election meeting and told the villagers when the result was known, that "the commune party committee cannot agree [with the election]." He then forced the brigade party branch to send a brigade official to manage the team's affairs during the busy season. The letter writer who relates the incident demanded that the situation be corrected.[59]

In a second case, commune authorities in 1979 refused to allow a candidate favored by the majority in a Guangdong production team to be a team leader because "he was too much interested in promoting the income of individual [team] members, and not so much interested in completing a commune irrigation project." Brigade officials, following commune orders, announced this decision to the team.[60] The report of the incident, which denounces it as undemocratic, aroused heated debate in the local press. One writer feels that overruling the masses was justifiable: "The masses' choices should not be supreme," because peasants did not understand the situation comprehensively, they were influenced by feudal and kinship ties, and they only wanted to protect their individual or family interests. In an election, they would just choose the "sociable" man to be a cadre, "in the belief that he would give them more of a chance to earn money."[61] Other writers criticize the commune leadership. Everyone was eligible to be elected a leader, they point out, and, if the elected team cadre proved incompetent, he could be replaced in a subsequent election.[62]

Guangdong interviewees also report cases of brigade officials appointing as team cadres candidates who had lost an election,[63] and cases of candidates with the most votes not becoming the team leader.[64] In general, then, brigade and commune cadres had considerable power to overturn disagreeable election results. How often they intervened in this way is unknown.

Variations

My discussion of the election process above has highlighted certain common features of production team elections. From 1962 to 1984, however, there were significant variations in the frequency and scope of team elections, as well as in the willingness of villagers to serve as cadres, their qualifications, and the issues in these elections.

Frequency and Scope

Neither national nor provincial authorities have published comprehensive statistics on the numbers of teams carrying out elections, the numbers of elections held, or data on which cadre positions were usually filled through elections. The only data available are scattered reports appearing in the provincial press, based on statistics compiled by authorities in some communes and counties. Nonetheless, since 1978 the retrospective accounts of local politics appearing in the press indicate wide variations in the practices of local leadership recruitment over the past several decades. Some data are available on the extent of production team elections, the timing of the elections, and which of the team cadre positions was elective.

Recently published accounts of the selection of local leaders in specific production teams and material derived from interviews indicate that, from 1966 to 1976, authorities held some kind of elections in more than one-

Table 4.   Percentage of Teams Holding Elections, 1966–1976

	Percentage	Number
Teams with elections*	65.6	21
Annual	57.1	
According to need	42.9	
Teams without elections	34.4	11

SOURCE: Derived from election data in n. 28, chap. 5.

*In five of the teams (23.8 percent), authorities described the elections as "mere formalities."

half of the production teams in the sample. In 57 percent of the production teams, these were annual elections; in the remainder, "according to need" (table 4). In 23.8 percent of the production teams, however, press reports describe the elections as "formalities." This probably understates the case, because I included in this category only elections that were explicitly identified as "formalities" in the press. There were probably many more. Certainly, the retrospective accounts of rural elections in general highlight the lack of choice that peasants often had during Cultural Revolution elections. As one writer points out in a discussion of the period: "Although in some isolated occasions officials were chosen through some democratic procedures, to a great extent these were little more than formal procedures."[65] Some informants concur with this evaluation of the period.[66]

In 34 percent of the teams (N = 11) in my data, authorities failed to call any elections from 1966 to 1976. In most cases, brigade or commune officials or visiting work teams simply appointed the cadres. A few production teams relied on pre-1949 practices. In one team management committee, for example, members sometimes drew lots for the team leadership post and sometimes rotated it among brigade management committee members. In another case, the position of team leader was rotated between the team's two party members. In approximately one-half of the production teams in the data, there were no elections, or the elections were reported as "formalities." Press reports indicate that before 1966, however, some teams elected team cadres and abandoned the practice only during the Cultural Revolution.

These data may not represent the frequency of production team elections throughout China. The number of units that held annual elections that were anything more than verbal ratifications of cadre-determined decisions is probably overstated. Authorities may have called team elections only to fill a vacancy or in response to outside pressure. If this was true, then annual elections were not the norm for most production teams.[67] The data also indicate that many different systems were adopted to recruit team leaders. Even within the same brigade, different methods were used: some teams elected their leaders, but the brigade or commune party branch appointed the leaders of other teams.[68]

Authorities called production team elections under at least four conditions. First, officials in some areas have had annual elections, probably dating from the 1950s. In these areas, local officials apparently have adopted rural work regulations requiring annual elections and have given villagers the opportunity of ratifying the existing leadership or new (probably cadre-sponsored) nominees. (But many of these elections may have been "mere formalities.")

Second, in the teams that held occasional elections, need or a vacancy may have been the determining factor. Vacancies arose because of a cadre's ill health,[69] because he was unwilling to continue (he may have wished to concentrate on family sidelines, for example),[70] or because of some perceived inadequacy in his performance. Brigade, commune, or work team officials may have felt that he was unreliable or corrupt, as happened during the Four Clean-ups and Double Hits campaigns,[71] or peasants may have become dissatisfied with his performance (he was "too selfish" or "incompetent") and have demanded a change.[72] In the latter case, however, peasant dissatisfaction itself was usually insufficient for cadres to call an election, but in each of these cases a vacancy might have occurred, which could be filled by an election.

Third, changes in brigade or commune personnel might have resulted in production team elections. If team cadres were bound to brigade or commune leaders in patronage relationships, the transfer or loss of position by a brigade or commune patron could force changes in the team leadership. In one case from the Shanghai suburbs, for example, a team election was called in 1981 to replace a leader with close ties to a just-deposed brigade cadre. A participant in the election meeting explains: "There was . . . a factional problem in the brigade. In 1980 brigade cadres were replaced. Afterwards, our team leader lost the support of the brigade."[73] In another case, a young woman, who became brigade party sec-

Table 5.   Percentage of Teams Complying with County or Commune
            Election Campaigns, 1979–1981

	Percentage	Number
Fujian Province		
Bingnan County	99.7	1,460
Jiangxi Province		
Xuanhuang County	80.0	—
Jiangsu Province		
Renyang Commune	62.7	212

SOURCES: *Fujian Ribao,* July 7, 1982; *RMRB,* Jan. 21, 1979; and *Xinhua Ribao,* Dec. 7, 1980.

retary during the Cultural Revolution and then brigade secretary, appointed her mother as a production team leader. When the young woman
was transferred to the commune to do women's federation work (seen,
by the informant, as a demotion), her mother was abruptly replaced.[74]
Factional and kinship alignments sometimes forced changes in the team
leadership group.

Finally, authorities sometimes called team elections as part of a national
or local campaign. We have seen how work teams replaced team cadres
during the Four Clean-ups Campaign. Work teams were also dispatched to
brigades and teams in some areas after the fall of the Gang of Four. One
of their purposes was to "root out hidden Gang supporters" in local
leadership groups.[75]

Local campaigns may also have mandated production team elections.
During the county-level election campaign from 1979 to 1981, for example, some counties apparently ordered countywide production team
elections. Officials in Guangdong's Lian County, Fujian's Bingnan County,
and Jiangxi's Xuanhuang County all report that elections were held in production teams throughout their counties.[76] Zhejiang authorities also report the October 1980 election of over 150 production team leaders.[77]
These reports indicate a concerted campaign to hold production team
elections, during which county authorities convened meetings of commune and brigade officials to prepare them for election work.[78] They also
indicate that provincial or county authorities placed a higher priority than
usual on team elections at that time. Nonetheless, even in areas where pres-

sure was exerted from above, not all teams complied. Table 5 indicates that not all teams held elections in these areas.

Finally, most production teams report that villagers elected the team leader and the team management committee, although there were some variations here as well. In a minority of cases, peasants either elected the team leader only or the team leader and one or two deputies. In other cases, villagers first elected the team leader, who was then permitted to nominate the committee (his "cabinet"), who were voted on by the villagers.[79] In general, however, villagers voted for the leader and the committee.[80]

Willingness to Serve

Although throughout the period authorities experienced difficulty in recruiting enough leaders to staff the nation's 6 million production teams, they experienced greater difficulties during liberal periods. During the early 1960s and after 1978, when China's leaders implemented more liberal agricultural policies, villagers often were unwilling to sacrifice time to serve as cadres, when they could promote family interests. In Fujian, during the 1961–1962 experiments with household contracting, for example, "refusal to serve as a cadre" was a serious abuse, reportable to commune authorities.[81]

After 1978 the rapid decline in the functions and powers of team cadres under the responsibility system increased the peasants' unwillingness to take on the burden of serving as a team cadre. Letters, press reports, and interview data all reveal that peasants were reluctant to be cadres, especially during these two periods.[82] Only the most unfortunate became team leaders in one poor Yunnan team, according to an informant: "No one wants to be a team cadre in this team. . . . His life was very bitter."[83]

During the Cultural Revolution, Guangdong informants also report that many peasants were unwilling to become team leaders, but for different reasons.[84] Work teams criticized and deposed local cadres during the Four Clean-ups Campaign, and in suburban areas some rural cadres lost power during the Cultural Revolution (1966–1969) to small leadership groups of urban sent-down youth and rebellious young peasants.[85] These political campaigns undoubtedly deterred many. Many teams reported instability in their leadership: "They bounced around faster than beads on an abacus." Leadership changes were reported annually, for example, in one-third of Zhejiang's Chengguan commune.[86] Every adult male in the neighborhood had served as a team cadre in a production team in Fujian.[87] Local stability, however, was restored in many areas by the early 1970s, following the Cleaning-up Class Ranks Campaign.

Becoming a team cadre meant risking the alienation of friends, relatives, and neighbors, on the one hand, and brigade and commune officials, on the other, especially if the interests of these parties could not be compromised. In addition, it meant being periodically investigated and perhaps removed from office, especially during the 1960s and early 1970s. One letter writer sums up the situation this way: "First, being a team leader is a thankless task. If you do a good job, no one notices, but if you do a bad job, you'll be cursed like hell; Second, if you become a team leader, you have no opportunity to go out to earn a little more money; Finally, some people are afraid of power." [88]

William Parish and Martin K. Whyte point to some of the benefits that team leaders enjoyed, particularly during the early and mid-1970s, when authorities restricted family income-earning activities. Team cadres were in a better position to help their family and friends. Brothers of team leaders often became cadres themselves, and sons of team cadres attained a higher educational level than the children of other peasants.[89] Further, in villages where kinship or factional politics were important, faction leaders sought to protect the interests of their groups. One former village cadre points out that, although the advantages were not great, faction leaders could distribute benefits to their members, usually kin, in the form of middle-school places, jobs outside the village, loans, and the like: "It was of no particular benefit to my family, but if I didn't pay attention to our group's interests, they would curse me!" [90] There was an expectation of favoritism in many villages.[91]

In spite of these benefits, by the early 1980s peasant unwillingness to serve as a cadre had reached worrying proportions. Leadership positions in many teams simply fell vacant.[92] Symptomatic of the problem was a 1982 *Renmin Ribao* editorial, which, after twenty years of production team organization, felt compelled to list the duties of team cadres.[93] Authorities attempted to counter what they saw as a general rural "leadership paralysis" by reducing the number of team cadres to fit their reduced functions and by demanding that teams begin to pay subsidies to team officials, based at least in part on local productivity.[94] In addition, officials in some communes extended the term of office of team leaders by one to three years.[95] Commune authorities also issued authorization papers to production team leaders, a move intended to boost their prestige. Finally, authorities organized work teams to conduct elections in teams where the post of leader was vacant.[96]

Unwillingness to serve as a cadre characterized production team politics in particular. As a result, few candidates stood for team elections, and cases of "disgruntled losers" were rare. Authorities had little difficulty recruiting brigade and commune cadres, however, who received stable incomes or state salaries. The recruitment problem was probably worse in poorer areas and poorer production teams where the advantages of leadership were few.

Qualifications for Team Leadership

Peasants valued as their leaders middle-aged males who were skilled cultivators (*nengli*) and who were able to represent the interests of the team to brigade and commune officials when necessary and when given the opportunity. The CCP accepted this view in part but added its own qualifications. Since 1980 central authorities have deemphasized class and political criteria and have pushed teams to select younger, more technically competent cadres, both male and female.

The regulations on rural work provide general guidance on the qualities of production team leaders. They emphasize attitudinal traits ("Love and care for the collective," "Firm class standpoint") as well as behavioral characteristics ("Obey the party," "Persist in scientific research," "Run the brigade democratically").[97] In the official view, for much of the period peasants should have selected "five-good" cadres and commune members, and true "revolutionary successors" as team cadres.[98] Since 1978, however, authorities have emphasized youth and technical ability, downplaying revolutionary zeal and political characteristics.

Chinese peasants preferred leaders who demonstrated ability in production, who had generally good relations with most other villagers, and who were able to defend the interests of the team. First, peasants considered whether a potential leader could manage his own production activities well. As one former sent-down youth from Guangdong observes: "[The peasants] looked at his private plot—was it managed well or not, and they would consider how he usually did agricultural work."[99] Although peasants were usually unable to dismiss leaders who neglected production, they were dissatisfied if output fell for too many years. The emphasis on agricultural ability usually limited the leadership post to physically strong males in their working prime.[100] Age was important, and peasants complained when brigade authorities appointed young, inexperienced youths as team leaders.[101] During the 1979–1981 production team elections, authorities continued to stress the need for skilled, able cultivators to assume leadership duties.[102]

Second, a prospective team leader should have good relations with most team members. He should be respected, authoritative, and able to give direction to the team. Thus, for example, an elderly team leader who could not keep his team in the fields was perceived by others as ineffectual.[103] He could be gruff at times and something of a bully ("Our team leader gave orders. If you gave your opinion . . . he'd say: "Who's in charge here?"),[104] but he had to be able to win the cooperation of most team members, and this required consideration for others. Team leaders who failed to win the cooperation of their teams risked dismissal.[105] A minority of villagers in one Shandong team, for example, forced brigade authorities to intervene when they refused the orders of a newly elected team leader that they did not like ("He made the lazy ones work"). They were later criticized in *Renmin Ribao* for their narrowmindedness.[106] In teams deeply divided by kinship or factional conflict, group leaders might select as cadres those who were mediators rather than authority figures. Thus, for example, an "outsider" with relatively little production experience was chosen in one Guangdong team precisely because she consulted the various groups in the team and shared power with them.[107]

If team leaders were expected to maintain relatively good relations with team members, they could still, within the bounds of traditional propriety, help their friends and relatives (or clients). Peasants expected some favoritism from their leaders, as long as it remained within certain limits. This, after all, was one of the attractions of team leadership. They criticized leaders, however, who were too insensitive to the public weal or who appeared to be too selfish.[108]

Finally, peasants expected team leaders to defend team interests. Press reports indicate that economic issues were a crucial concern in team elections.[109] When asked what they would do for the team, candidates almost invariably replied in terms of improving villagers' incomes. During election meetings, according to one informant, it was not necessary to ask candidates if they would protect team interests—this was understood: "In general, those who are elected very naturally protect their team's interests. Peasants don't need to study this question in particular."[110] So, for example, peasants refused to reelect a team leader who had unilaterally increased the quota of grain the team had to supply to the state.[111] And they supported as team leader a Guangdong peasant who openly criticized brigade authorities for plowing under their crops.[112] Villagers expected that team leaders would protect their interests to the extent that they could.

In addition to these qualifications for team leadership, the CCP added a few of its own. First, team leaders, like other leaders in post-1949 China, ought to be of "good" class background. In the countryside, this generally excluded landlords, rich peasants, and their offspring from leadership posts and favored the vast majority of villagers who made up the "poor and lower-middle" peasantry. During the early 1960s and after 1978 (when most landlords and rich peasants were relabeled "commune members"), class origin was not a particularly important qualification for leadership. Indeed, after 1978 peasants elected some descendants of rich peasants and landlords to team cadre positions, actions that would have been unthinkable only a few years before.[113]

The party also insisted, for part of the period, that peasants consider the candidate's political activism when selecting production team cadres. This was probably most important for those who lacked production skills or who were physically weak. Especially during political campaigns, if they could speak out articulately, they could give direction to the team. The content of political activism, however, changed with the ebb and flow of political currents in the commune (and higher levels). Today's disgruntled minority lineage (or faction) leaders became tomorrow's team leaders in the wake of campaigns, such as the Four Clean-ups Campaign's crackdown on corruption, the Cultural Revolution (1966–1969), and the dismissal of the Gang of Four. In practice, brigade and commune authorities valued the ability of team cadres to follow orders (*ting hua*), regardless of the policy they were required to implement. One's political character (*biaoxian*) often meant little more than toeing the line.

Finally, in some areas, although this was not official policy, authorities only recruited team leaders from among party members. From 1979 to 1981, for the first time in many years, authorities replaced some existing team leaders who were party members with nonmember cadres.[114] According to press reports, peasants in these areas previously believed that only party members were eligible, and local party officials probably did nothing to discourage this belief.

After 1978 authorities placed new emphasis on recruiting young rural leaders of both sexes with expertise in specialized fields of agriculture or the handling of small rural businesses. In some areas, commune authorities appointed young middle-school graduates to team leadership positions, hoping that their higher education level would help boost rural productivity.[115] As men left for jobs in the cities, suburban production teams also recruited more women to team leadership posts, to staff what in previous years had been virtually an all-male preserve.[116] Finally, some teams recognized that new expertise and managerial experience were required to manage sideline industries. Insofar as brigades and communes tried to force teams to accept younger specialists, however, they undermined the election system.

In general, if team members participated in elections, they were likely to nominate (or support) those persons as team cadres whom they felt could and would protect the team's interests—which usually meant raising the standard of living of team members, either by increasing production or by fending off unreasonable claims from the state. Brigade cadres, for their part, preferred team cadres who would follow instructions (*ting hua*) and carry out the directions of higher levels. Brigade cadres also had an interest in the prosperity of the teams and so wanted team leaders who were respected by team members and who possessed production skills (*nengli*). Brigade income was tied to team income to a great extent, and because the families of brigade cadres lived in the teams (they were all local people), their own family income was directly affected by the outcome of team activities. Team members, in turn, were aware of the needs of the brigade and would neither nominate nor select cadres totally unacceptable to the brigade leadership. They would be most likely to select or support those persons who, while most of the time appearing to carry out brigade instructions, also protected team (and now household) interests.

Issues in Team Elections

In production team elections, peasants have occasionally been able to influence the resolution of conflicts on local political issues. In general,

where villagers have been influential, they have had an impact on economic issues, such as houschold incomes for team members or on what
can be called "security" issues. Security issues revolved around kinship or
factional conflict. Electing members of one's own group to power ensured
better treatment for the group and better protection in conflicts with
outsiders.

After 1978 the press argued that, through elections, peasants chose
leaders they trusted to implement the party's new economic policies,[117]
which implies that peasant participation in team elections to dismiss local
leaders who obstructed central policy has aided the implementation of
government policy.[118] Interviewees from Fujian and Guangdong lend further weight to this interpretation, as the following examples indicate.

"Sidelines Are Capitalist Tails"

In 1977 the brigade nominated X, a party member, to be leader of a
coastal Fujian production team, and he was duly elected.[119] Over the years,
peasants became increasingly dissatisfied with his "inability to manage
production." Although neighboring brigades were gradually relaxing policies on the marketing of sideline produce, X continued to refuse permission for peasants to sell surplus seafood in the free market where it
brought substantially higher prices. When peasants confronted him, he
denounced these liberal policies as "capitalist" and continued to supervise
the seafood marketing closely.

Then, in 1980 new commune authorities suddenly replaced several brigade cadres, and X lost the support and protection he had previously enjoyed. When it came time to elect the team leader in 1981, the villagers
(not the brigade party branch this time) nominated three candidates.
These included X and two other current members of the team management committee, neither of whom were party members. During the discussion of the candidates that followed, villagers criticized X for holding
down their income and for not permitting them to market surplus seafood privately. The new brigade officials listened to the criticism, with
which they agreed. When authorities called for the vote, peasants elected
(by a show of hands) one of the other team management committee members to replace X, who became the team's deputy leader.

Peasants had been dissatisfied with X for a number of years, but, because from 1977 until 1981 authorities had not called team elections, they had been unable to replace him. Their opportunity came in 1981 when the commune intervened to reorganize the brigade leadership. It is likely that the brigade called the 1981 elections to replace the team leader, a precondition for implementing new, more liberal agricultural policies.

In this example, elections played a part in expressing popular dissatisfaction with the way local officials were implementing government economic policies. In other cases, however, elections served more diffuse purposes, as villagers attempted to place in power or maintain in official positions friends or group members who could protect the interests of the group.

"Us and Them"

Two groups (*pai*), the numerical strength of which varied over time, dominated the electoral politics of a production team (a natural village) in rural Guangdong.[120] The relationship of each cadre to his support group determined the outcome of team elections. The key factor was the waxing and waning of the numerical strength of each group. Group A, surnamed Yang, was composed of seven households of local people. Group B was a heterogenous mixture of five households, all outsiders: one Li household, two Lin households (one of the Lin household heads was the brigade party branch secretary), and two newly arrived Yang households (the team leader and his brother were the heads of these two households).

In 1969 one of the Group A households moved into the Group B camp, for reasons that were largely personal. The defecting Yang household head got along well with the Lins, but his relations with his own Yang relatives were bad. He was hot-tempered and was constantly arguing with his relatives. The precipitating incident occurred when someone from outside the team insulted his wife, and his relatives refused to come to her defense. With his defection, the division of households became six to six.

The balance continued until 1973 when the remaining six Yang households split up their common property, an exercise that proved so rancorous that three of the six Yangs went over to Group B. They were cultivated by the Lins, a process that resulted in the household split becoming three to nine.

The brigade party branch deputy secretary (Lin) helped to win over the

Table 6.   "Us and Them," 1968–1975

	Households		Cadres from	
	A	B	A	B
1968	7	5	—	—
1969–1972	6	6	3	3
1973	3	9	0	6
1974	3	10	0	6
1975	5	7	2	4

SOURCE: Interview File CN4D (Guangdong).

three defecting Yang households in a calculated way. He hated the remaining three Yang households, in part because of their strident criticism of him during the Cultural Revolution, when they charged him with corruption. Until 1971 one of the Yang household heads (Group A) had been the team's accountant. He knew about the deputy secretary's corruption and posted a big-character poster exposing him, which resulted in authorities suspending Lin from his post for two or three months. Although the Yang accountant was subsequently reelected each year to the team management committee, by 1971 Lin had sufficient power in the brigade to see that he no longer received brigade approval. Lin then set out to divide and isolate Group A, which he accomplished by 1973.

In 1974 a family moved into the team from outside for one year and promptly joined Group B, making the balance of households three to ten. In 1975 there was a further realignment when two of the Yang households that defected in 1973 returned to Group A after a furious argument with the original defector, Yang Xi. These returning Yangs accused Yang Xi's family of beating their children and their dog, and of deliberately placing a drainage ditch too close to their house. In addition, a work team arrested deputy secretary Lin for corruption and "licentious behavior" during the same year, thereby depriving Group B of its driving force. By the end of 1975, Group A had five households, and Group B, seven households.

As the size of the groups changed, so did their share of team cadre positions (table 6). From 1969 to 1972 each group had three team cadre positions. The team leader, storehousekeeper, and militia official belonged to Group B, and the deputy team leader, accountant, and women's federation official were from Group A. The two groups maintained a rough job equivalence: each group got a team leader position, an economic or accounting position, and a lesser position.

By 1973 and again in 1974, cadres from Group B dominated the team, reflecting the new strength achieved through defections. By 1975, however, the situation had changed, as Group B's fortunes waned.

In 1973–1974, the two years when Group B dominated all cadre positions, production fell drastically: "The two groups would argue every chance they got, at work, at meetings, and in the fields." Lin, the deputy secretary, accused the Yangs of "sabotaging production." When the other brigade cadres discussed the dispute, they suggested giving Group A a few of the team cadre jobs, although election results would not have warranted it. Lin vetoed this proposal, and the brigade dropped the matter.

In early 1975 a commune-level work team came to the team to sort out its problems and appointed a deputy team leader from Group A. He was subsequently elected to the team management committee at the next election, along with another member of Group A, reflecting the new alignment after Lin's fall.

In this case, elections faithfully reflected the strength of the two different groups contending for committee positions. The election outcomes were not in doubt, however, and simply formalized the balance of power struck through negotiations. During some years, the minority group held no posts, indicating that even informal agreement to share power could not be reached. Each group sought to capture as many jobs as possible to protect themselves from possible encroachment from outsiders. Stripped of its cadres in 1974, Group A obviously felt the situation was unfair and refused to cooperate with its neighbors. Thus, group solidarity played an important role in these elections.

Brigade and Commune Elections

According to the regulations on rural work, in addition to voting for team cadres, peasants had an opportunity to elect delegates to brigade and commune congresses, which in turn chose brigade and commune officials.[121] Internal party regulations also gave party members in the teams the opportunity to elect a brigade party branch committee and party branch secretary.

I have little data on the election of these congresses or their deliberations.

During the Cultural Revolution, it is likely that county and commune party officials appointed commune and brigade cadres, which people's congresses at these levels subsequently ratified. After 1978, however, authorities attempted to implement elections in some brigades and communes. In the discussion that follows, I have had to rely on the only sources available: scattered press reports and anecdotal material from interviews.

Brigades

Peasants chose brigade officials, according to one report from Guangdong, by first convening team mass meetings, which nominated candidates for the brigade management committee. The brigade congress then elected brigade cadres from among the nominees.[122] Other reports of the procedures were even less detailed. In one Jiangsu case, for example, commune authorities first assigned a cadre to work in a brigade for two years (1977–1978). Then in 1979, "according to the opinion of the masses and after an investigation of the situation, the commune requested that the relevant higher authorities approve of him becoming the brigade leader."[123] No election was mentioned; commune and county cadres played the determining role.[124]

Little evidence was available on the frequency and scope of brigade congress elections. Officials in one commune in Guangdong, however, reported that the election of brigade congresses in their thirteen brigades in 1979 was only the second election of its kind since higher-stage cooperatives were set up in 1956. Previously, either "higher-level" party committees appointed them or "although they were elected, this was a mere formality" (liuyu xingshi). In this case, the commune party committee, "reacting to the opinion of the masses" (but also undoubtedly spurred on by pressure from the county to hold elections as part of the nationwide campaign), decided to adopt democratic elections to change brigade leadership groups.[125] Most interviewees concur with this assessment: for most of the period, commune party committees usually appointed brigade officials.

During campaigns, work teams sometimes ordered brigade cadre elections, as the following example indicates.[126] In a suburban Fujian brigade, lineage politics had been important long before 1949. When the Communist party entered the village, it gave power to a weaker lineage and its allies, displacing the traditional local leaders. Since 1949 and especially

since the Four Clean-ups Campaign, these two groups had contended for
power in the village. Cultural Revolution factionalism deepened the division that already existed in the brigade. The "ins" in 1965 became the con-
servatives, and the "outs," the rebel challengers (*zaofanpai*). Factional alliances played an important role in the brigade's subsequent experience
with elections. By 1977, the brigade management committee was split
into two factions, four "Dengists" and three "Gang" members.[127]

Ostensibly as part of the 1977–1978 Double Hits Campaign (*shuangda
yundong*),[128] but also setting out to settle old scores, the district authorities
in early 1978 dispatched a work team to the brigade to rid it of corruption
and to reorganize its leadership group. Both factions in the brigade had
built networks of personal connections linking them to the commune, district, and county administrations to provide them with support and advance information on impending policy or personnel changes. Warned in
advance that the work team were Gang of Four supporters, both factions
in the brigade were on their guard.

In October 1978, after an intensive and sometimes acrimonious investigation of corruption charges, during which the work team openly played
favorites, supporting their "own" and exposing or emphasizing the corruption of the "others," the work team called for villagers to elect delegates
to a brigade congress (*sheyuan daibiao dahui*), which in turn would choose
new brigade leaders. The work team and the brigade authorities together
worked on a list of nominees, two or three from each team to be elected as
delegates to the fifty-six-member congress. To say that they worked together, however, was something of a misnomer: the work team and its faction among the brigade committee set out to nominate its supporters, and
the other faction sought to nominate its followers. In a series of meetings,
a candidate list was finally agreed on.

A period of intense campaigning followed, during which representatives of each faction canvased households for support. Work team members visited many households in key production teams and urged them to
support their candidates. The opposing faction did the same: "We also had
relatives and family ties, and we mobilized them. Team members benefited
by having their *pai* in power. They could get what they wanted more easily
from the cadres." In public, however, the leaders did not acknowledge the
conflict: "We didn't say vote for our *pai* at team meetings, because the
work team was always present. We just said it informally." After several

mass meetings in the production teams, attended by representatives of both factions, peasants chose the delegates.

The overall factional composition of the newly elected brigade congress was unclear, because some delegates refused to be dragged into the factional fighting. In this air of uncertainty, the work team and brigade authorities met to nominate the new brigade management committee. Through discussion with the delegates in their homes and other informal locations, it emerged that the work team's faction would be able to command more votes in the congress. During the nomination meetings, the work team insisted that they nominate only a sufficient number of candidates to fill the seven vacancies. The minority faction argued for more (nine) but lost. In the end, the authorities nominated four candidates supported by the work team and three candidates supported by the minority faction.

Undaunted, the minority faction then began lobbying congress delegates to write in the names of four others of their faction (to make seven): "All three groups [both factions and the independents] had meetings in various peasants' homes. We asked the delegates to come. It was very informal. We sounded out the delegates." In November 1978 the congress met and elected the candidates as nominated. Of the seven management committee members, the brigade head, a deputy head, and a secretary (*wentou*) belonged to the minority faction, while a second deputy secretary, the cashier, a water conservancy station head, and the women's federation representative belonged to the dominant faction. These results were then approved by the commune party committee.

Power changed hands as a result of the election. It is unlikely that this radically altered any brigade policy, but it may have reassured the new majority faction members that they would get a fair hearing if they had a grievance that village officials could solve.[129] Although the motives of peasant voters were unknown, it is likely that many of them voted for delegates who would protect their group's interest. Some favoritism was expected of village cadres and to have representatives of one's group in power could only be advantageous.

In this case, authorities had not called such an election since before the Cultural Revolution. During that time, the PLA appointed a brigade revolutionary (management) committee, half from each faction. The 1978 election was a chance for the two competing groups to test their strength. In the end they proved about equally matched.

Brigade Party Committees and Secretaries

Because party and government personnel overlapped for much of the period from 1962 to 1984 and because power in China's villages was centered in the party secretary, it is appropriate to raise the issue of the selection of village party committees and their secretaries. It is likely that the commune party secretary appointed brigade party officials and the brigade party committee and thus had considerable power.

During the 1979–1981 elections, party members aired complaints about the lack of democracy in their party branches. For example, in a letter to the editor of *Nanfang Ribao* in 1979, a party member complains that the commune deputy secretary, presiding at a meeting of the brigade party branch, personally selected the nominees to join the party committee and refused demands to remove an unpopular candidate. The secretary replied: "The commune party committee chose all five of these candidates, so they must be nominated. Our democracy is guided democracy, not anarchism." "Is this right?" the reader queried.[130]

Since 1981 central authorities have adopted new rural party branch regulations, which require annual elections of branch committees and the direct election of branch secretaries (although no term of office is specified for secretaries).[131]

Press reports indicate that authorities used party elections to rid local party branches of personal opponents and those who obstructed central policies. For example, officials in one Guangdong commune authorized party branch elections "without advance nominations," although the commune did send officials to production teams to "help out." The result was that two of nine party branch secretaries lost their posts.[132] Apparently, commune authorities used the elections to oust the two village secretaries.

Brigade party branch elections were sometimes part of local party rectification campaigns. In 1982 Guizhou's Pingba County, for example, dispatched work teams to carry out party rectification and the reelection of party branch committees throughout the county.[133] The process typically took several days, with sessions of document reading, criticism, and self-

Table 7.   Results of the Party Branch Elections, Pingba County, 1982

	Percentage	Number
Committee members reelected	62.2	593
Committee members losing	25.7	246
Incorrect party style	42.3	
Opposed birth control policy	8.5	
Low education and/or lacked ability	32.5	
Other reasons	16.7	
New committee members	12.1	115

SOURCE: "Zhonggong Pingba xianwei zhengdun, gaixuan dadui dang zhibu de qingkuang baogao," *Zhonggong Yanjiu* (Taibei) 195 (March 15, 1983): 144.

NOTE: The number of new committee members is probably less than the number who lost, because authorities reduced the total number of serving cadres.

criticism preceding the elections. The work team led local party members and "representatives of the masses" in the assessment of nominees. They sought experienced leaders, who were characterized by a correct work style, fairness, initiative, and activism on behalf of the people. Authorities excluded the "good old boys" (*lao hao ren*) who were influenced by kinship ties and factionalism. Through a process of "going up and down several times," the work team produced a list of nominees that had more names on it than there were positions available, a characteristic of the new-style democratic elections. The work team called an election meeting of the party branch, and voting was by secret ballot.

The newly elected party branch committees in Pingba County were both more highly educated and younger than their predecessors. Not everyone was satisfied with the results, however, because 25.7 percent of the incumbent committee members lost their seats (table 7). The losses indicate that county authorities used the elections to dismiss from the committees 21 local cadres who refused to endorse the party's new birth control policies, 104 cadres deemed to have an incorrect party style, 80 cadres lacking sufficient education or ability, and 41 cadres for other reasons. County authorities probably took the opportunity of the rectification to rid local branches of factional opponents. The same report characterized as "seriously divided" the situation in 29 percent (N = 57) of the county's party branches prior to rectification. Even after the work team–sponsored rectification, authorities reported satisfactory results in only 49 of these branches. Winning in this situation was usually temporary because one's opponents were one's neighbors, and they did not leave. Authorities may have understated the case when they reported only a handful of divided party branches.

Communes

If higher-level authorities (usually the commune) dominated brigade cadre selection during this period, this was even more the case in the selection of cadres for commune posts.

In 1979–1981 some provinces (Jiangsu, Shandong, Heilongjiang, Gansu, Hunan, and Sichuan) carried out elections for delegates to commune congresses in conjunction with county people's congress elections. According to one report, the "trial point" election of delegates to Shengli commune in Sichuan's Emei County closely resembled the election of county congress delegates.[134] In mid-September 1979 commune authorities began propaganda on the election law and citizen duties in the election. They then set up an electoral committee and organized the commune into districts, each under the supervision of an election small group. These groups rallied peasants to participate in the elections and registered peasants to vote.

The electoral committee accepted nominations from the people, who put forward 294 candidates, 200 percent more than the places available. The committee then reduced the list to 184 percent more candidates than positions. Voters received literature identifying the candidates and their records. In the end, 97 percent of those eligible voted in the election. This rather mechanical report indicates that the election followed closely the county-level procedures. The activity went through virtually the same stages and probably was conducted as part of a county election.

According to another source, in a Fujian commune in 1980, brigade party committee officials nominated one cadre (usually the team leader) from each team in the brigade, plus two or three brigade officials, as delegates to the commune congress. Peasants then endorsed these delegates in team mass meetings. In all, the congress had more than 500 delegates, including representatives of schools, banks, and other units.[135]

A few other reports indicate that commune cadres sometimes interfered in the elections in much the same way that other officials tried to subvert the county-level elections. For example, commune leaders in Xixiang County, Shaanxi, advised villagers how to mark their ballots, forged ballots, and added the names of cadres who were not elected to the list of deputies.[136] The press also reported isolated cases of cadre interference in Sichuan.[137]

It is difficult to know what to make of all this. Guangdong and Fujian interviewees report that from 1962 to 1980 authorities failed to conduct regular elections of delegates to commune congresses.[138] It is likely that county and commune officials dominated the nomination and election stages of these congresses. They probably recruited delegates from among party branch members and trusted brigade and commune cadres and controlled the elections if there were any. There is little evidence that peasants could use these congresses to influence public affairs.

Conclusion

Village elections performed certain functions in Chinese society. Like elections in other one-party systems, they mobilized the populace into the political process, educated and socialized them into the norms of Chinese society, integrated them into the larger community, legitimized the selection of village leaders, and occasionally influenced public policy.[139]

Peasants influenced the course of public affairs through elections under limited circumstances. In some areas village politics was characterized by annual elections and fixed terms of office. Although these may have provided no more than an opportunity for peasants to endorse the existing village leadership, they may have offered opportunities for peasants to register disapproval of current policies or to dismiss unpopular leaders. This was particularly the case where group solidarity, sometimes based on lineage identifications, was strong, and where peasants could ally themselves with higher-level leaders. Community groups sometimes provided the solidarity necessary to challenge brigade authority. In some cases, this happened when villagers felt that brigade officials had overstepped their authority and violated the historically accepted way of doing things (such as by appointing a minority lineage representative as leader). High levels of community solidarity made real elections feasible under these circumstances, but they also presented a threat to brigade (party) authority.

When national elites supported village elections, as they did from 1979 to 1981, to ensure the selection of local leaders who were sympathetic to policies favored in Beijing, peasants were more effective. During this period, so confident were national leaders that peasants favored their policies, they turned to the peasants to throw out village officials who were obstructing them. The strategy appears to have worked in a great many areas but also to have contributed to the unattractiveness of team leadership positions.

In general, however, from 1962 to 1984 village-level elections were neither a reliable nor an effective method for peasants to influence government policy. They were unreliable because they were not institutionalized, and they were ineffective because the elite dominated them. This state of affairs was symptomatic of elite ambivalence toward elections as a leadership recruitment device and symptomatic of peasant political values.

Authorities called team-level elections infrequently and irregularly in many places. This stemmed from chronic underregulation of the village-level election process. Not until 1982 did authorities recognize village-level elections in the constitution, and not until 1983 did they publish supplementary regulations for elections at county level and below. For most of the period, the only public guidance offered to local officials charged with implementing village-level elections was contained in the Sixty Articles, which were extremely general and provided no means for their enforcement. They remained "draft" documents, "for trial use."

According to Zhang Qingfu and Pi Chunxie, to institutionalize democracy, authorities must carry out elections, and moreover they must follow certain procedures, including secret ballots, relatively open nominations, and more candidates than posts, within a framework of rules specifying responsibilities and penalties.[140] The Sixty Articles were woefully inadequate in this regard. Although they specified that village leaders must be chosen every one or two years by mass meetings of team members voting by secret ballot, they said nothing about nomination procedures or the appropriate number of candidates. Moreover, there were no penalties for cadres who flouted the regulations.

The authoritative status of the regulations on rural work is in doubt. Contrary to the regulations, county, commune, and brigade authorities, for example, extended terms of office for production team leaders from three to five years, presumably with the approval of higher authorities. In some areas, officials did not acknowledge "terms of office," and cadres continued to wield power as long as they retained the support of their superi-ors. In these areas, elections, if they were held, were little more than en-dorsement rituals. Also, many villages chose not to implement voting by secret ballot. And the regulations were vague on mass participation in the affairs of brigade and commune congresses. Why were communes in Sichuan, twenty years after the Sixty Articles first appeared, still carrying out "trial point" elections for commune congress delegates? Apparently, local officials treated the regulations as advisory.

There were good reasons for underregulation, however. Peasants were, in general, unwilling to become team cadres. Their unwillingness in-creased in recent years under the new agricultural policies. Authorities were hard-pressed to require every local unit to nominate more candidates than positions. Also, because literacy rates were low in the countryside, authorities had to rely on alternatives to the secret ballot.

Second, village-level elections were ineffective because, in general, they remained tightly under the control of local elites. Where authorities car-ried out elections, brigade and commune leaders sometimes nominated their own candidates, refused to permit popular additions to the list of nominees, campaigned for their favorites, forged ballots, and overruled or vetoed results they considered unacceptable, all in the name of "guided democracy." In 1979 and 1980 the press reported cases of cadre inter-ference or sabotage without indicating whether higher authorities took any disciplinary action. Letter writers debated the appropriateness of some cadre intervention. There were few regulations at this level, and those that did exist appeared to be advisory.

In addition, powerful outside work teams, dispatched by higher authori-ties during campaigns, such as the Four Clean-ups and the Double Hits, intervened directly in the leadership selection process. They chose their own nominees, campaigned for them, and supervised the balloting and ap-proval stages of the election.

This state of affairs was symptomatic of a basic elite ambivalence to the value of choosing village-level leaders through elections. First, in addition to propagating democratic selection procedures, national officials have also pursued other goals. They recruited younger team cadres with higher edu-cational qualifications, perhaps with specialties in agricultural science. Vil-lagers, however, had their own notions of who was best qualified to lead their teams. If left to their own devices, they might not have chosen the younger specialists. Thus, in many pre-1978 discussions of local leadership recruitment, authorities propagated the qualities they desired in local leaders, adding as an afterthought: "And by the way, they ought to be elected to their posts."[141] National leaders also wished to encourage stability in local leadership groups. There is some evidence that elections led to instability, and officials may have been loath to intervene in a process that was largely governed by past practice.

Local leaders, further, were ambivalent about local elections because they complicated their means of retaining power. During the 1979 to 1981 elections, some leaders expressed the fear that, if elections were implemented in their area, they might lose their positions.[142] This fear was not baseless, because one of the objectives of the central leadership during this time was to replace local cadres who opposed or obstructed their new agricultural policies, and they were successful in many cases.

Finally, elite ideology in China has not valued power sharing or popular participation in the recruitment of leaders. Historically, leadership was paternalistic and autocratic. The mass line further emphasized the distance between leaders and the masses, conceiving of the people as objects to be solicited, a process that in theory the elite ought to control. If elites have not placed a particularly high value on village elections, then, in all likelihood, neither have the peasants. Villagers valued harmony and respect for authority. Raucous election meetings, campaigning, and standing for office were not a part of their world.

6

Contacting:
Insiders and Outsiders

Authorities in contemporary China encouraged peasants to contact them, primarily to expose instances of maladministration, corruption, and local cadres who obstructed central policies. In the early 1960s and after 1978, officials attempted to institutionalize contacting by encouraging peasants, for example, to visit government offices. During these more relaxed periods, local leaders were probably more receptive to informal contacting.

During the Cultural Revolution, however, authorities sent waves of outsiders, organized into work teams, into the villages to replace "corrupt" local leaders and to force the implementation of new policies. In general, the campaigns of the 1960s and 1970s were not conducive to peasant-initiated political activity. Nonetheless, even during these years peasants occasionally used visiting outsiders to influence public affairs.

High levels of group solidarity, linking peasants with local leaders (insiders), improved the effectiveness of peasant political participation. Peasants expected village leaders to protect local interests and to respond to group members' views. When local leaders pursued unpopular policies, peasants could effectively protest only if they could ally themselves with visiting higher-level leaders (outsiders).

The Insider Networks

In rural China, peasants have been linked to their neighbors and to local leaders in networks of "five kinds of personal relations [*guanxi*]" (same surname, kinship, village, school, and workplace).[1] Because post-1949 authorities organized primary schools and production units geographically,[2] peasants sometimes found that they were bound to their neighbors not just by kinship, but through school ties and as coworkers, that is, by all five kinds of personal relations.

The peasantry's dependence on local leaders during the 1960s and 1970s for the distribution of grain rations, work points, private plots, outside employment, and other benefits encouraged the development of a rural clientelism.[3] Some peasants cultivated connections with local patrons to ensure favorable treatment and to obtain individual benefits. Local leaders, often under attack during this period, also sought supporters or clients from among the villagers. In addition, local officials sometimes looked to patrons in brigade and commune organizations for protection against the unfavorable consequences of campaigns launched from higher levels.[4]

The new agricultural policies reduced the functions of local leaders, lessening somewhat the hold they had on community resources. Nonetheless, peasants still depended on them to approve outside employment and loans and for access to certain agricultural inputs,[5] thus perpetuating the economic basis of clientelist politics. In addition, in some South China communities, implementation of the new agricultural policies has strengthened one kind of personal relationship—kinship solidarity. As production teams decollectivized, villagers found that they had to rely on the help and support of kin, organized into production small groups.[6] Thus, for example, in one Guangdong area after 1978: "The patrilineal kinship group has now replaced the team as the unit for recruiting labor in agriculture," a development that led to the strengthening of kinship ties in some rural areas.[7]

During the 1960s and 1970s, peasants sometimes used insider connections to influence the implementation of public policy. During the grain-short years of the early 1960s, for example, peasants in Sichuan brought to the government's attention the extent of food shortages among them through personal ties to the People's Liberation Army (PLA). Through letters and the visits of relatives, peasant-soldiers learned of serious food shortages in their native districts. The soldiers turned letters from their relatives over to the army and themselves "became restive." In the end, the PLA responded by dispatching groups to help those families in difficulties.[8]

Peasants also used personal ties to influence the distribution of goods and services or to waive inconvenient rules and regulations. Guangdong informants report that, during the early and mid-1970s, for example, villagers "with good connections" approached leaders privately to get loans from credit cooperatives,[9] to get permission to work outside the team,[10] and to get scarce goods, such as chemical fertilizer and building materials.[11]

Typical of politically significant contacting were the efforts of relatives of a Fujian brigade cadre to persuade him to allow group contracting in the late 1970s, before commune authorities permitted it. In 1979 he "guaranteed" several production teams, which, after discussions among themselves, tried to divide the teams into smaller production groups. Each group had twenty or so households, most composed of close relatives. On hearing of the action, commune authorities sent a work team to stop it:

> We brigade "guarantee cadres" were in a difficult spot. We couldn't advocate it [group contracting], nor could we prevent it. If we said "Go ahead," we'd be criticized [by the commune]. But our relatives put pressure on us to do it. When the commune cadres came and asked "How could you let them do this?" I just said, "I didn't encourage it." I had told the team members, "Do whatever the central documents say." This is what I told the team cadres in the team I was guaranteeing. All the brigade cadres secretly supported group contracting, but we couldn't say so publicly. We'd be accused of being tails of the masses.[12]

In this case, commune authorities dispatched a work team to bring the brigade back into line with central policies (as the commune perceived them) at the time. Outsiders were used to curb the tendency of local cadres to give in to their friends, relatives, and neighbors.

Because peasants usually contacted officials privately, most cases are difficult to document. Nonetheless, there is some evidence that peasants attempted to circumvent state distribution policies by using personal ties. Where regulations were inconvenient, villagers sometimes attempted to bend them by asking for special consideration from their cadre friends and relatives.

Relations with Outsiders

As part of their method for problem sovling in policy implementation at local levels, Chinese leaders regularly dispatched work and investigation teams, individual cadres, and reporters to local units to investigate difficulties, feed back information to government departments, and to help local officials solve problems. These officials sometimes solicited the views of peasants on particular issues and relayed them back to their superiors, and peasants occasionally used these visiting outsiders to influence policy implementation.

Both theoretical and practical considerations justified the leaders' reliance on work and investigation teams. Mao Zedong's theory of leadership required that leaders conduct investigations before they made policy: "No investigation, no right to speak." [13] To prevent bureaucratism, cadres were charged with making the investigations personally. [14] Work and investigation teams also filled a practical need in rural China where the leaders of local work units were usually local people. Higher levels sent outside teams and cadres to try to prevent local leaders from catering to the needs and wishes of their constituents, neighbors, and relatives at the expense of party and state policy. [15]

There were, however, significant differences among these "outsiders." For example, work teams tended to be larger and more powerful than investigation teams and had a greater impact on village life. [16] When work teams accepted the views of peasants, rather than trying to change them (as occurred especially during campaigns), they could be strong allies of the peasants in influencing the course of local policy implementation.

Investigation Teams

Authorities usually dispatched investigation teams on a regular or an ad hoc basis to report back on the progress of policy implementation, although teams were also sent out to assess damage in cases of natural disasters. [17]

The teams sometimes conducted surveys of peasant attitudes on government policy, which were relayed to policy makers at higher levels. For example, an investigation team sent to assess the spread of household contracting in the early 1960s in one Fujian area reports:

Of the fourteen team households, only four households of affluent middle peasants were actually resolutely advocating household contract production; there
were six households whose ideology was confused and who were at times irre-
solute; and there were four households of poor peasants who resolutely opposed private contracting.[18]

Although the survey may have been inaccurate (the survey method was not
reported), the report highlights the complexity of views among the villagers at the time.

After 1978 national authorities placed renewed emphasis on the activities of investigation teams.[19] For example, officials urged delegates to national and provincial assemblies to inspect local conditions before they
convened the assemblies.[20] As a result, from February to September 1981,
authorities in Henan, Jiangsu, Zhejiang, Gansu, Shanxi, Jilin, Jiangxi,
Shandong, and Anhui provinces sent out inspection teams.[21] In the course
of checking on the implementation of rural economic policies, the officials
were also charged with soliciting "the views of the masses."

Sent-down Cadres

Authorities also sometimes dispatched individual cadres to survey local
conditions and to help local officials overcome problems in the course
of policy implementation (called "squatting at a point," *dundian*). During
and after the Cultural Revolution, officials sent their colleagues to the
countryside in large numbers.[22] Press reports indicate that sent-down
cadres, especially if they came from powerful units, sometimes intervened
to support peasant demands. When Liu Jie, first secretary of Henan Province, visited Xinye County in June 1980, he saw that local cadres had
erected housing for themselves on collectively owned farmland.

He got out of his car and asked about this. Peasant masses working in the fields
there gathered around. . . . The peasants angrily said: "These houses were put
up by a few people who consider themselves lords over everyone. . . . " The
masses objected to this on many occasions . . . but the county party committee
had not been able to solve the problem.[23]

Based on this experience, the secretary demanded that local officials enforce the policy of prohibiting cadres from building on collectively owned
land.

Interview data indicate that peasants occasionally appealed to sent-down cadres to intervene on their behalf on politically significant issues. In one Guangdong brigade in 1968, for example, the brigade leadership decided to remove a production team leader after a disastrous harvest. Team members, however, objected, pointing out that insects were responsible for the decline in production, not the team leader's mismanagement. Commune officials decided to investigate the problem and dispatched a cadre to the brigade. After initially agreeing with the brigade's decision, the commune official called a meeting to announce the result. At the meeting, villagers objected to the team leader's dismissal. (What could he have done about the insects, they asked?) The commune cadre saw that support for the team leader was substantial and gave in. The commune then ordered the brigade to permit the team leader to continue in office.[24]

Reporters

Both national and local newspapers dispatched reporters to the countryside to investigate conditions there and to report on the implementation of government policy. Although generally these reports highlight model experiences ("*haoren, haoshi,*" good people, good things), they also sought to teach by negative example.[25] Especially after 1978, editors have reemphasized the importance of investigative reporting, which has exposed problems in the implementation of policy.[26]

Peasants occasionally contacted reporters who visited their village to try to influence the course of local public affairs. In one 1979 case, a *Nanfang Ribao* reporter discovered that a brigade in Guangdong, in clear violation of government policy, decided "after discussion" to ban all sales from the free market of produce grown on private plots. This appeared to brigade officials to be the only way to stop villagers from pilfering collective vegetables for sale in the market. The reporter concludes his story by pointing out that the new regulation was "unfair" to the holders of private plots who intended to sell their produce on the market and ran counter to the party's policy on private plots.[27] In response to his story, the brigade withdrew its regulation.[28]

In another case, members of a fishing brigade in Guangdong, upset with the corruption and oppressive leadership style of the brigade's deputy secretary, complained to the Guangzhou offices of *Nanfang Ribao*. The newspaper investigated the villagers' complaints, and on January 12, 1979, published the results in an article entitled, "We must solemnly deal with the offenders." The paper demanded that the deputy secretary be arrested and that other cadres who supported him be educated on the importance of "democracy and the legal system."[29]

The recently exercised power of visiting journalists is illustrated by the report of a *Hebei Ribao* reporter in 1979, which criticized a commune for violating the party's policy of permitting villagers to farm private plots. The reporter visited a commune and discovered that peasants were farming all the private plots collectively. Commune cadres reported that the villagers had "agreed" to this arrangement, although central policy at the time encouraged peasants to cultivate plots individually. The reporter's own investigation showed that the peasants were dissatisfied with the commune's policy.

> In the daytime, this reporter casually chatted with the commune members in the autumn fields, and on the vegetable farms and threshing grounds. Then in the evening I called on them from door to door meticulously getting to the bottom of things. My first-hand investigation turned out to be just the opposite from the situation stated by the commune and the cadres.[30]

The reporter discovered that over 90 percent of the villagers preferred to farm their own private plots. When asked why they had agreed to collective cultivation, one peasant replied: "It was a trap set by the cadres; I was just compelled to take what's given in silence like a dumb person tasting bitter herbs."

Soon after local authorities received the new policy documents on agriculture in early 1979, they discovered that peasants wanted to decollectivize the private plots, which the cadres felt was unacceptable. The officials then formulated new regulations, requiring villagers who chose to farm their own private plots to buy pumping equipment for wells, chemical fertilizer, and agricultural machinery at their own expense. Faced with massive additional expenditures, most peasants agreed to the old arrangements. They then were required to sign documents of agreement, kept on file in brigade headquarters, to protect local cadres against charges that they were violating party policy (to leave them "room for maneuver," in the words of the reporter). The reporter's article was reprinted for national circulation in *Renmin Ribao*.

Interviewees also occasionally reported that peasants approached members of rural reporting groups, staffed during the early and mid-1970s by rusticated urban youths. Organized at commune and brigade level to feed local stories to commune- and brigade-run broadcasting stations,[31] members of these groups had some discretion about what they reported, although mostly they served as an additional investigation unit for their cadre supervisors.

These examples indicate that peasants sometimes approached investigation teams, sent-down cadres, and reporters in an effort to influence the implementation of local policy. They were most successful when they used these outsiders to force local cadres to implement national policies or when they brought obvious inequities to the attention of senior leaders. When policy lines were changing, reporters were most active in rooting out local opposition. The media then published these cases of opposition as negative examples to pressure other local leaders to accept the new line.[32]

Work Teams

Work teams (*gongzuo dui*) were groups of two or more cadres organized at one level of the government or party to go down to lower levels in order to investigate and report on conditions there, to supervise the implementation of policy, and to solve problems as they arose. In the past they exercised much more power than investigation teams or sent-down cadres.

Although the party has relied extensively on work teams to implement official policy,[33] on three occasions since 1962 officials debated their function and effectiveness.[34] The "human wave" tactics that sent thousands of work team members incognito to some local areas, under the direction of Wang Guangmei during the Four Clean-ups Campaign, prompted Mao to see them as obstructionist.[35] Radicals in Beijing denounced work teams a second time when party bureaucrats sent them out to shore up conservative party committees in schools and factories during the early stages of the Cultural Revolution.[36]

The most revealing criticism of work teams appeared in the press in early 1979, however, authored by county and district authorities. First, critics pointed out that rural work teams were often composed of incompetents. In many units everyone, except "the old and the weak," took a turn on work team duty, and novices ended up helping experts (*waihang bang neihang*), because the teachers, accountants, skilled workers, and other experts drafted into the work teams knew little about farming.[37]

Second, work teams, because they were temporary organizations, whose membership was usually rotated, tended to value short-term outcomes. In their drive for quick fixes and rapid increases in output of the units they were investigating (to demonstrate the work team's success), they "enthusiastically went searching for chemical fertilizer and tractors" for their units, ignoring the costs. Work team members thus became "purchasing agents" for the production teams.[38] When the work team left, production often collapsed.

Third, because of dual lines of authority, the areas of responsibility and power between work teams and commune and brigade party branches were unclear. This led to conflict between the work team and local party organizations, which undermined the unity of local organizations. Work teams either ended up in conflict with these organizations or became a constituent department of them, both of which rendered the work team ineffective.[39]

Fourth, during the Cultural Revolution, work teams tended to take over completely the work of the units they were investigating.[40] This undermined the authority of local leaders and made it difficult for them when the work team left. It also created instability, increased opportunities for factional infighting, and sometimes resulted in falling production.[41] Every time work teams came to communes and brigades in one Jiangsu county, for example, they carried out "struggle, criticism, and changing the leadership" (*yi dou er pi san huanban*). In one brigade, work teams visited eight times and made nine changes in the brigade leadership group.[42] In a Shandong case, county authorities blamed work teams for replacing a brigade secretary six times in as many years, and a team leader ten times during the same period: "When the cadre situation is unstable, commune members resort to factionalism, and production falls."[43]

If these cases accurately reflected the performance of work teams, it was not surprising that some team members reported that peasants were indifferent or hostile to them.[44] Indeed, one member of a work team in Fujian reports that his 1981 team was only "the second since land reform to be welcomed by the peasants."[45] The tendency of work teams to take over local units was especially unsuitable for the new, post-1980 agricultural policies, which required decentralization and local production unit autonomy. This, then, was seen as a serious defect.

Finally, staffing work teams undermined the effectiveness of the units dispatching them, because large numbers of officials left the office for long periods of time, and, because work teams were often overstaffed, they wasted manpower. In one recent case, the press derisively reported that 150 officials, one-third of whom were section or bureau chiefs, were sent to a commune in Shandong, "enough to form a commune party committee" among themselves.[46] Local units had to subsidize the living expenses of these visitors, which drained local resources.[47]

These commentaries also reveal that authorities sometimes staffed work teams with officials who had lost their jobs during "organizational simplification" campaigns. Dispatching work teams did not really solve the problem of overstaffing, one commentator notes, because organizations then tended to fill the temporary vacancies by promotions.[48] During times of instability, factional politics also played a role in the recruitment of work teams. The victors at higher levels dumped the losers, unsure of whether their jobs would still be available when they returned, into work teams.[49]

Although the critics proposed either abolishing or reforming work teams (for example, by transforming work teams into less powerful and smaller "investigation teams"),[50] other officials were quick to come to their defense. They pointed out that the apparent disadvantages of work teams were really disadvantages of the leftist policies of the Gang of Four period. Political campaigning, frequent policy changes, and factionalism did not nullify work teams as an organizational tool. They too, however, cautioned work teams and commune guarantee cadres not to take over the work of local production units. Work teams must give advice only, respect local party leadership and commune, brigade, and team autonomy. They should be smaller than before and be sent less frequently, but they were still seen as effective.[51] In mid-1979 authorities reaffirmed the usefulness of work teams and senior officials continued to dispatch them throughout the rest of the period.[52]

In general, work teams can be analyzed in terms of their setting (were they implementing a campaign or not?) and their goal (either political or economic change). Some work teams implemented either national or local campaigns. They tended to be larger and more authoritative than noncampaign work teams. Noncampaign work teams, sent out by county and commune authorities, concentrated on isolated problems, such as leadership failures or production problems. Both campaign and noncampaign work teams were dispatched throughout 1962 to 1984.

Although the distinction between what is "political" and "economic" is often in practice arbitrary, my analysis differentiates work teams that focused on political change from work teams that focused on economic change.

Work teams whose goals were *political changes* replaced or disciplined leaders, supervised or controlled class enemies, and stabilized public order. They worked in campaign settings, such as Socialist Education, Four Clean-ups, Cultural Revolution, Criticize Lin Biao and Confucius, Rectify and Rebuild the CCP, Criticize the Gang of Four, and Double Hits. In noncampaign settings, they worked to maintain or reestablish CCP leadership and control.

Work teams whose goals were *economic changes* attempted to further develop collective and individual production, introduced changes to production techniques, and reformed the incentive system. They operated in, for example, the Campaign to Study Dazhai. In noncampaign settings, they investigated problems and implemented policies in rural commerce, sideline production, and the responsibility system.

Campaign Political Work Teams

Although work teams in political campaigns solicited the opinions of villagers, their focus was narrow, and the results were largely predetermined by the demands of the campaign. The following example,[53] taken from a Four Clean-ups work team operation near Shanghai in 1965–1966, illustrates campaign work team methods.[54]

When the work team, composed of fourteen urbanites, mostly recent college graduates under the command of an experienced party leader, arrived in the commune, its leader called a meeting to explain the anticorruption campaign to local officials. Authorities assigned a work team member to each production team, who in turn convened meetings of village leaders and peasants to explain the campaign. Peasants listened passively.[55]

During the early information-gathering stage of the work teams' activities, the work team member visited households in the team, often several times, to complete the detailed information required. In the course of these investigations, members asked villagers about the production team cadres. How much money did the cadres spend? Did cadres have any unofficial income? Were there any complaints about their style of work? Were they fair? The work team, thus, prepared the ground for their attack on local cadre corruption. At this early stage, peasants were in general reluctant, even unwilling, to make accusations against their leaders.

After the work team member collected general background information on the cadres, he investigated the financial affairs of the team and discovered that the accountant had embezzled public funds. When the work team member confronted the accountant and other team officials with his findings, however, they were hotly denied. The campaign at this stage was still a matter between the work team and the cadres.

Confronted with the resistance of local cadres, the work team called a mass meeting of all production team members during which it exposed the local cadres and invited the villagers to denounce them. Each cadre would be placed under house arrest if he did not cooperate, the work team threatened. This frightened the local cadres, and although they did not confess to wrongdoing, it fundamentally changed their attitude toward cooperating with the work team. A few continued to resist, however.

As a result of the meeting, the peasants saw that the work team, because it could detain and depose local cadres, had real power. Villagers began to speak out and reported instances of local cadres abusing their power. Still, the work team took the initiative and solicited the opinions of villagers, going to their houses, and asking them about specific cadres: "The peasants were angry! Because of the high level of their hostility [the former work team member reports] we did not put [additional] pressure on the cadres. But the peasants put pressure on them." The new material generated from interviews with villagers made up the bulk of the charges now investigated by the work team.

After the investigation and intense grilling from work team members over several weeks, most local cadres admitted that they had made mistakes. The attack on the cadres affected their morale, however, and some refused to exercise leadership responsibilities. The work team had undermined their prestige in the eyes of the villagers and reduced their authority. The work team decided that some of the leaders needed to be replaced and then, in work team–supervised elections, installed a new leadership group.

In this case, the work team mobilized peasants to reevaluate the criteria for local leadership and to replace corrupt village leaders. Peasants initially hesitated to make charges against local leaders, either out of fear of cadre retaliation after the work team departed,[56] a desire to protect friends and relatives who were also patrons, or because peasants felt that some cadre corruption was acceptable, and that it was a local concern, which should not be dealt with by outsiders. The work team had first to gain the confidence and respect of villagers, which it did in the above case at a mass meeting during which it denounced and threatened the local cadres. Peasants came forward with their own complaints against the cadres after this episode.

Campaign Economic Work Teams

Work teams also implemented campaigns designed to change the rural economy. During the period of my study, the most prominent economic campaign work teams were those sent to implement the Campaign to Study Dazhai, a national model brigade in North China, known for its emphasis on normative incentives, self-reliance, and massive efforts to transform a barren, mountainous area into cultivatable land. During successive campaigns, some starting in the mid-1960s, authorities dispatched work teams to local areas throughout China to popularize the experience of this model. One such work team spent a month and a half in a Guangdong brigade in January and February 1972.[57]

Composed of three commune-level cadres, all party members, the work team first called a series of meetings of local officials to explain the significance of the campaign. The work team then convened a series of daily "struggle" meetings to mobilize the peasants to participate in the campaign. They took as their targets the poor and middle peasants who they judged to be lacking in discipline and the villagers who failed to follow orders (*bu ting hua de*). Held up to public criticism and ridicule, the example of these peasants persuaded others to comply with the work team's requests.

The work team used struggle meetings to mobilize the peasants for agricultural construction work, which was the focus of the campaign. The work team directed villagers to prepare barren land for cultivation, level existing fields, and repair and extend the irrigation and drainage system. The work was unpopular, and peasants grumbled that leveling the land only caused other problems (water then had to be pumped into the fields by hand because the work team did not supply pumps). Scraping the topsoil off some of the fields and dumping it on other less fertile fields left the original fields covered with patches of hard, infertile clay. "Leveling the land is useless," peasants complained, "it just looks better." In addition, each villager had to work longer hours, cutting into time for private sideline production. Incomes from that sector subsequently fell: "Peasants were unhappy. They could not disobey orders and go on strike, however. Some, though, secretly did not go out to work, but went about their own family business. Others officially 'at work' just sat around and told stories."[58]

Peasants did not dare to verbalize their dissatisfaction with the campaign. They worked the longer hours, but without enthusiasm. Production team leaders, aware of the ill feeling about the campaign, did little except to warn the villagers to comply while the work team was present. When the work team left, however, villagers abruptly stopped the agricultural construction work.

Recent retrospective accounts of work team methods in campaigns, such as the Campaign to Study Dazhai, confirm that work teams relied on struggle meetings and public criticism to gain peasant compliance, which sometimes resulted in tense relations between the work teams and local villagers.[59]

Noncampaign Political Work Teams

County and commune officials also dispatched work teams on an ad hoc basis to investigate specific leadership problems or on a more routine basis to enforce rules and regulations on such issues as corruption and social order.

In the wake of county-level elections from 1979 to 1981, some production teams carried out local elections under the supervision of work teams, dispatched in particular to production teams where the position of team leader was vacant (*mei ren dang duizhang*).[60] Retrospective press accounts indicate that work teams, along with brigade and commune party committees, often played active roles in the selection of pre-1978 team cadres.[61]

Peasants sometimes used visiting work teams to dislodge unpopular leaders. In one 1974 Guangdong case, for example, commune authorities dispatched a work team to a seriously divided brigade in which an ambitious party secretary took over, on behalf of the brigade, profitable side-line industries that previously had been owned by the production teams.[62] The work team visited the villagers and found them eager to denounce the party secretary for violating the rights of production teams. Although peasants refused to take the initiative and seek out work team members, they did not require a conclusive demonstration of work team power before they spoke out. This may have been because work team members, although not from the village, were known to the villagers as commune officials. Also, many brigade cadres disapproved of their secretary's actions and undoubtedly made their feelings known to the villagers.

Unlike the campaign experiences reported above, the work team avoided struggle meetings to humiliate the secretary. Nonetheless, "he was frightened and had no power. The work team had the power to manage production. The work team also chaired brigade meetings, not the secretary. . . . If a production team had a problem, it went to the work team."[63] In the end, commune authorities, acting on the results of the work team investigation, transferred the unpopular secretary out of the brigade and returned the sidelines to the teams. In this case, peasants allied themselves to the work team to get rid of an unpopular leader. In other cases, villagers sided with brigade authorities to prevent work teams from installing unpopular candidates.

Noncampaign interventions by work teams in local leadership selection were almost always trouble-shooting exercises. Commune and county authorities were alerted to leadership problems in the villages, through the reports of dissatisfied local leaders themselves, through routine visits, or through falling production figures. The evidence suggests that, in some cases, villagers used these work team visits to influence local public affairs.

Noncampaign Economic Work Teams

Officials sometimes dispatched work teams to implement economic policies or to check up on production plans during noncampaign periods. Press and interview data indicate that work teams acted on some peasant complaints and modified unpopular local policies. In one Guangdong case from 1963, for example, county authorities dispatched a work team to a brigade that had failed to meet its surplus grain quota for the year. The work team discovered that the commune had arbitrarily raised the brigade's quota, although it had little additional land suitable for rice cultivation. The work team lowered the quota, and "the commune party committee corrected the original unrealistic demand."[64] The press has reported other cases of work teams lowering quotas to ease peasant dissatisfaction.[65]

More recently, county and commune authorities dispatched work teams to help local officials implement the agricultural responsibility system. In areas where local cadres resisted these initiatives, authorities dispatched work teams to replace the cadres or to persuade them to implement the policies. In one 1980 case, authorities in Fujian[66] dispatched a work team to a brigade to propagate the new agricultural policies: "The cadres and peasants [of the brigade] were very conservative. They remembered all the criticism of the *san zi yi bao* period,[67] during the early 1960s, and were reluctant to implement the new policy." At these meetings peasants asked why the new policy was being implemented now, especially because, during the Cultural Revolution, the same officials had severely criticized it: "It was declared to be a mistake then, so why do you ask us to change? Why do you cadres change your mind? We [work team members] said, 'This is the policy from above. We also don't know why [it is being implemented now].'"[68]

When some villages attempted to implement small group or household farming in 1978–1979, before the central authorities approved, county and commune officials sent out work teams to discipline them.[69] This happened in the Fujian brigade discussed above, which made the work of the 1980 work team, sent out a year later to support household contracting, all the more difficult.

Authorities sent work teams, then, to implement the policy of the day, and whether or not the policy was popular had a lot to do with whether peasants could use the work team to influence government decisions. If local officials obstructed the implementation of a popular policy, peasants sometimes allied themselves with the visiting outsiders to force a change of policy on local cadres.

Conclusion

The rural poor have few political resources, and, as a result, they have tended to rely on individual contacts to participate in politics. In China, where personal relationships are highly valued, some peasants cultivated relations with local leaders to influence the distribution of public goods. From time to time, they also attempted to use visiting outsiders for their own ends. These became politically significant acts when they resulted in leadership changes or influenced the implementation of public policies.

Contacting was usually an individual activity, but, when peasants acted together, they were more effective in persuading both local leaders and outsiders to help them. High levels of group solidarity enhanced their chances of success. Peasants also sometimes approached visiting officials, journalists, and work and investigation teams to expose instances of cadre abuse of power or obstruction of the implementation of policies. When these visitors were investigating the implementation of popular policies, villagers could more easily use their visit to ensure that local leaders complied with central directives.

The institution of outside visits was, from the peasants' point of view, however, neither a reliable nor an effective method for them to influence public affairs. Some work teams, for example, opposed popular official policies, such as household contracting.[70] In addition, higher-level cadres decided by themselves when to dispatch outsiders to local levels. Especially during national campaigns, work teams put new issues on local agendas, which left relatively little opportunity for peasants to raise other issues, and the style adopted by many campaign work teams, which relied on struggling with and criticizing local leaders and peasants, made contacting work team members on any issue other than implementing the campaign of the day less attractive.

7

Writing:
Letters, Petitions, and Posters

For the same reasons that authorities urged citizens to contact them, they also encouraged the people to write to them to expose instances of local cadre corruption, maladministration, and obstruction of higher-level policies.[1] During the early 1960s and after 1978, newspaper editors published thousands of communications on these themes. In the interim, however, occasional letters appeared, often praising the authorities and their policies.

The authenticity of published communications to authorities in China, such as letters to the editor, is difficult to establish. Although officials may have manufactured letters to suit their purposes, it is likely that, during the period of my study, many letters were authentic. During the Cultural Revolution, authorities themselves may have authored some forms of written communication to a greater extent than during other periods.

The Cultural Revolution witnessed an explosion of big-character posters, particularly in China's cities. To a lesser extent, rural residents also used posters to attack faction leaders and to expose instances of cadre abuse. In the post-Mao period, authorities withdrew the constitutional right of

China's citizens to use big-character posters.[2] Mindful of the slanderous and uncontrolled poster attacks that characterized the Cultural Revolution, since 1980 officials have curbed the use of this channel.

Peasant-initiated letter and poster writing was most effective during the early 1960s and since 1978, when it drew the attention of higher-level authorities to instances of local cadre abuse or insubordination. Although peasants preferred other methods of communicating their demands, they occasionally used written modes, even during the 1960s and 1970s, to influence the course of public affairs.

Letters from the Masses

In the early 1960s and after 1978, Chinese authorities emphasized the importance of "letters and visits" work as a means of facilitating the implementation of policy.[3] The party newspaper, *Renmin Ribao,* took the lead in 1978 and urged authorities to take seriously "letters from the masses."[4] In response, people (including, undoubtedly, some peasants among them) flooded the party with tens of thousands of letters, and by the end of 1978 the paper had "handled" over 800,000 letters in that year alone. Although the number of letters declined in 1979, the volume continued to remain high.[5]

In 1979 authorities at *Renmin Ribao* reported that local cadres, to whom they routinely circulated the bulk of the letters, had failed to investigate many complaints aired in them or had ignored the letters altogether.[6] The newspaper remarked that, as a result, anonymous letters from readers would continue to be favorably received. At the same time, authorities publicized model cases of local cadres handling complaints raised in letters to *Renmin Ribao*. In Kaifeng district, for example, on the first and fifteenth of each month a district party secretary spent time at the "letters and visits" office of the district government to receive visits from citizens, and, "together with office staff, to solve difficult problems raised in letters."[7]

Provincial authorities reported that from 1978 to the end of 1979, the number of letters and visits they received had gone up 400 percent, while personnel to deal with this flood had only increased by 40 percent. Delays and confusion resulted.[8]

Senior officials in the provinces attempted to demonstrate the efficacy of letters from citizens by responding to them. In 1979 letters from "cadres and masses" reportedly prompted Vice-Premier Wan Li to investigate problems in Jinzhai and Yuexi counties.[9] Officials pointed out that by strengthening the work of handling letters and visits they would improve the democratic life of the country:[10] "The masses, being the masters of the country, should publicly criticize an erring cadre, a public servant, in the press. Such a practice can enhance the democratic rights of the people, as well as enliven the atmosphere in both the party and the state organs."[11]

Although some county governments appointed senior cadres to supervise the handling of letters (in one county this cadre made the rounds of communes in the county, investigating complaints),[12] many local cadres ignored the letters. These problems prompted Shanghai's *Jiefang Ribao* to comment that, in their "letters work" they had encountered three types of problems. First, after receiving a letter of complaint, the newspaper had great difficulty in "gathering material and checking the facts" due to the obstruction of the office or cadre about whom the complaint was made. Second, having ascertained the facts and decided to publish the letter, the newspaper often could not get the necessary approval from higher-level authorities to print it: "Submission for approval often turns out to be submission for execution." Finally, if the letter was printed, there was no guarantee that any action would be taken. The offending office or cadre would simply stall, ignore the letter, or appeal to a higher-level patron for protection, which, often enough, was granted.[13]

Finally, in 1980 provincial party authorities in some areas issued notices to local cadres, criticizing them for "not paying sufficient attention" to the letters. Provincial officials demanded that personnel at all levels be assigned to deal with the letters, that results of their investigations be reported to their superiors, and that the newspaper that originally received the letter be informed of the outcome.[14] Thus, aware that some cases of serious maladministration could be uncovered through complaints from citizens, some authorities in China have attempted since 1978 to encourage complaints of certain kinds and have attempted to respond to them.

In their study of letters to the editor which appeared in *Renmin Ribao* in 1966–1967 and 1976–1978, Godwin Chu and Leonard Chu found that, of all the letters published, peasants had authored only 10.2 percent during the Cultural Revolution; by the post–Gang of Four period, peasants' letters had fallen to 4.8 percent (18 of 376 letters).[15] These figures indicate either that writing to this official daily was a strategy not often employed by villagers or that, although peasants wrote in greater numbers, their letters were rarely published. The former is more plausible, for reasons that are discussed below.

In the Chus' post–Gang of Four sample, most letters to *Renmin Ribao* were signed, while less than one-half of the Cultural Revolution letters identified the writer. In my data of letters to the editors of provincial newspapers, written by peasants or rural residents from 1979 to 1981, 99 percent (N = 21) were signed by individuals or collective units.[16] It was impossible to determine the status of the authors of these letters, however. Many letter writers signed their names and indicated only which county, commune, or brigade they came from. In only 8 of 59 cases did the newspaper explicitly identify the letter writer as a cadre.

The letters published in the provincial press from 1979 to 1981 discuss either conflict over leadership issues (69.5 percent, N = 41) or conflict over the allocation of human or material resources (30.5 percent, N = 18). Rural residents more often raise leadership issues, complaining either that cadres had been improperly selected or that they had abused their power. Rural letter writers from Guangdong, for example, ask whether team leaders had to be party members [17] (implying that this qualification ought to be unnecessary), complain that brigade authorities had overturned the election of a popular villager as a production team leader,[18] and point out that appointed team leaders lacked popular support and were "always at odds with the masses."[19] Other letters question the value of cadres under the responsibility system.[20]

Village dwellers also wrote to provincial papers to expose cadre misbehavior. Cadres abused their power in Hunan by taking over collectively owned farmland to build private housing for themselves,[21] and they sometimes engaged in authoritarian behavior, such as beating and arbitrarily arresting peasants.[22]

In their letters to the provincial press, rural residents also raise issues over the allocation of resources. Some letters complain that local cadres did not follow regulations in the implementation of agricultural policy. One writer to *Gansu Ribao* complains that brigade cadres dug up trees planted privately in 1979, in violation of the new, more liberal agricultural policy.[23] A peasant in Heilongjiang points out that in 1981 team authorities in his village took over private plots and "commune members are extremely dissatisfied" (again, an action explicitly prohibited in the New Sixty Articles).[24]

Letters from the countryside also discuss redistributive issues in the provincial press. Writers in both Shaanxi Province and Inner Mongolia point out that, by amalgamating production teams, local authorities had caused productivity to drop. Richer teams saw their assets shared out to their poorer neighbors, and they lost interest in the new larger collectives.[25] Finally, some writers complain about the distribution of consumer goods and agricultural implements in the countryside.[26]

Of the letters written by those explicitly identified as rural cadres, 75 percent (N = 6) concentrate on resources issues (only 2 letters raised leadership issues), while in letters written by the remainder, 76.5 percent (N = 39) raise leadership issues. For rural residents who wrote to newspapers, then, leadership issues appear to have been more important from 1979 to 1981 than they were for those who signed themselves as rural cadres.

Cadres complain about being mistreated by other cadres and demand that the working conditions of local officials be improved. In one case, the women's federation representative of a production team wrote to complain that she had been beaten up by the leader of her production team when an earlier letter of hers, complaining about the leader's authoritarian work style, was published in a provincial paper.[27] In another case, an official of a brigade in Zhejiang wrote to explain why villagers were reluctant to become team leaders.[28] In most of their letters, however, cadres complain that the resources available in the countryside were inadequate. They urge, for example, improved transportation facilities[29] and greater protection of the country's natural resources, such as forests.[30]

Chu and Chu found in their study of letters to *Renmin Ribao* that during the post–Gang of Four period, peasants raised conflicts with cadres more often than with any other group. In their study, conflicts over leadership issues and resource allocation issues were present in letters published during both the Cultural Revolution and post–Gang of Four periods. Conflicts over ideological issues, important in 1966 and 1967, declined in the post-Gang letters.[31] There were none in my provincial press survey.

Finally, authorities took action to redress villagers' complaints on 64.4 percent (N = 38) of the letters published in the provincial data. In some cases, several letters were required before any action was taken. Of the letters authored by rural cadres, in none of the cases in my data was there any indication that action was taken to correct the situation.

Examples of conflict resolution in the provincial press data included a reply by the Guangzhou Municipal Agricultural Committee to a writer's complaint that production team cadres refused to permit villagers to breed their own cattle. The committee advised the cadres to change their decision.[32] In the case of a villager beaten to death by two party members, a letter writer's complaint prompted the provincial newspaper to conduct its own investigation. When the investigation team, sent from the paper, raised the matter with the commune party secretary, he was incredulous that anyone would care: "He's dead. So what?" The paper persisted, and eventually county authorities intervened, expelled the accused from the party, and arrested them.[33]

In another case, a writer's complaint that local officials had uprooted privately planted trees (violating party policy at the time) brought newspaper pressure on county authorities to investigate, and an investigation confirmed the writer's allegations.[34] Whether the peasants were compensated, however, was not stated. In other cases, authorities did not report any action to correct abuses that were publicized in the press. When a writer demanded that commune officials in Guangdong not be permitted to overrule team-level election outcomes, the newspaper printed the letter but did not indicate that any action had been taken.[35] (Perhaps printing the letter itself was considered sufficient censure.)

Chu and Chu found that more than one-half of their Cultural Revolution sample of letters mentioned the resolution of conflict. This declined to 25.1 percent in the post-Gang sample.[36] These data would indicate that letters to provincial papers, especially from non-cadres, were more often accompanied by an indication that the conflict had been resolved than were the letters published for virtually the same period in *Renmin Ribao*, the CCP daily. Provincial authorities may have felt more pressure to report the resolution of conflict, and, because they were were closer to the source of the letters, may have been in a better position to resolve the issues. *Renmin Ribao* depended on these provincial and local governments to solve cases raised in the letters.

Although my analysis concentrates on the recent periods, newspapers also published letters to the editor from rural residents during the early and mid-1960s. In general, these letters mirrored elite concerns. Thus, for example, during the Four Clean-ups Campaign, letters complaining about local cadres abusing their position and engaging in corruption were common in the press.[37] During the more liberal early 1960s, rural letter writers demanded that brigade and commune cadres respect the rights of production teams to manage their own land.[38] These examples indicate that central and provincial authorities used the "Letters to the Editor" column in the newspapers to mobilize support for their policies and to expose the shortcomings of local cadres who failed to implement them.

Villagers also sent letters to party and government offices and to radio stations. Throughout the period of my study, officials have in theory encouraged peasants to write and visit party and government offices, to "expose incidents of violation of the law and discipline, and to criticize unhealthy trends."[39] Like the published letters to the editor, published letters to party and government offices and to radio stations also mirrored government policy at the time. Rural residents sent letters criticizing officials for corruption during the mid-1960s drive against cadre abuses.[40] In one extraordinary case, two old peasants in Shengshi brigade in Guangdong wrote to both the Guangdong Provincial Party Committee and to the Central Committee General Office in Beijing to denounce their brigade party secretary for corruption. They were beaten up by the secretary for their trouble, but in the end, Wang Guangmei, the wife of the powerful head of state, Liu Shaoqi, came to the brigade to investigate the case.[41] Since 1978 authorities have become more concerned with local cadre behavior and have once again published villagers' letters denouncing local cadres for corruption and other abuses.[42]

Recent letters to local radio stations exposed officials who falsely reported grain output in Hebei, asked that the state buy more pigs at free market prices, and demanded that usurers be punished.[43] All of these demands and complaints confined themselves to improved implementation of existing policies. In no case, however, did the published letters demand that party policies be changed; rather, they criticized local officials for failing to implement them.

Insofar as these letters were written by peasants, they were an effective means of influencing public affairs only when they raised contemporary issues, as defined by the leaders of the day. If they exposed local cadre abuses or obstruction of higher-level policies, the letters could force investigations or public comments, which had an impact on local politics.

Nonetheless, the elite have seriously limited letter writing as a channel for participating in politics. First, of the citizen-initiated letters, authorities probably have published only a fraction. Although papers such as *Ren-*

min Ribao published "representative" letters on some topics, officials have not revealed the contents of other letters. Second, in general, citizen-initiated letters that were published probably fell within the broad guidelines of what the writers perceived to be acceptable at the time. For example, to criticize local cadre corruption in the mid-1960s and since 1978 was legitimate, and this was reflected in the letters from those periods. Letters demanding that more liberal agricultural policies be implemented also appeared during this time. Through political socialization, Chinese citizens learned to be sensitive to the limits of permissible criticism, and these limits are reflected in the published letters.

Although I have been unable to determine the status of many of the letter writers, I suspect that most of those identified here as rural residents were team or brigade officials, schoolteachers, demobilized soldiers, secondary school graduates, or urbanites rusticated to the countryside. That is, it is likely that very few "ordinary peasants" wrote letters to the authorities.

There were several reasons for this. First, especially in more remote areas, rural literacy was low. The 1982 census counted over 210 million "illiterate and semi-literate" persons in the countryside,[44] one-quarter of all rural inhabitants. This helps to explain why, although peasants made up 80 percent of the population at the time, only 4.8 percent of the letters published by *Renmin Ribao* were written by them. As one former Shanghai youth, sent down to Yunnan, said of the 1970s when asked about peasant letter writing: "There was a lot of illiteracy there. No letters were written to the media. . . . We sent-down youth wrote letters to Beijing and Shanghai about our plight. But it was of no use."[45] None of my peasant interviewees had ever written a letter to a newspaper or to any other authority (apart from applying for an exit permit to come to Hong Kong), nor did they know personally of anyone who had.

In addition, local cadres, often the target of letters from villagers, sometimes retaliated against letter writers, making this means of expression unattractive. Newspapers turned over their letters to local authorities for solutions, but these same authorities were often the targets of the complaints. Local officials had every reason to ignore the letters; to do otherwise would have been to admit that they had made a mistake, which could affect a cadre's standing in the eyes of his peers and superiors. By sending letters of complaint to the offenders themselves for action, the authorities demonstrated the weakness of this channel for redressing grievances. Peasants undoubtedly felt that private channels were more effective.

Signing Petitions

According to official policy, Chinese citizens may make written complaints to government authorities.[46] During 1979 thousands of petitioners, fresh from the countryside, exercised this right in Beijing. They demanded that authorities change class and administrative labels wrongly given to them in previous campaigns, that suitable jobs be found for them, and, in many cases, that they be allowed to return to their homes in the cities.[47]

During the period of my study, peasants rarely petitioned government authorities as a means of influencing policy, but authorities have reported a few cases. For example, in 1980 eight villagers (two of whom were cadres) petitioned prefectural and county authorities to require the commune to return land, nurseries, and forests it had occupied since 1976. Villagers saw the petition as the only course open to them after the commune ignored repeated requests to return the assets and then jailed brigade cadres for permitting villagers to dig up saplings planted on the disputed land. Prefectural and county authorities, informed of an investigation team's findings, ruled that the commune had to return the land or compensate the villagers.[48]

Interviewees indicated that peasants in Guangdong occasionally petitioned local authorities to redress their grievances. In one 1963 case, for example, villagers petitioned county authorities to allow them to sell flowers in Guangzhou markets, a practice that local officials had recently banned. Although the author of the petition was arrested, when commune officials intervened on behalf of the village, county authorities eventually relented.[49] In another case, villagers petitioned a brigade party branch in 1973 to permit them to split up their large, unwieldy team. After several years of agitation in the team to divide it up into two units, local leaders drafted a petition. The brigade passed the petition to the commune, which dispatched an investigation team to visit the village. In the end, the petition was granted.[50]

In these cases, as in the cases of letters to authorities, peasants petitioned senior officials to complain that local cadres had not implemented official policy. During the early 1960s and after 1978, peasants complained that some local cadres violated official policy when they refused to permit peasants to expand their sideline undertakings or to permit brigades and teams to manage their own land and manpower. Other peasants complained that, although smaller teams had been legitimate since late

1971,[51] local officials stood in the way of dividing up a large team that could not work together.

Petitioning was not well developed or widely used by the peasants. Unlike letter writing, however, petitions were almost exclusively citizen-initiated. There is, thus, little doubt about the authenticity of the few examples of petitions reported above.

Big-Character Posters

Although authorities used them extensively in mass campaigns to mobilize the people and to denounce factional rivals, not until 1959 did Zhou Enlai announce that big-character posters (*dazibao*) (and the other three "greats": mass meetings, debates, and discussions) would become a part of China's regular political life.[52] Posters appeared in great numbers in urban China during the Cultural Revolution and were legitimized as weapons of factional attack in Mao Zedong's "Sixteen Points."[53]

Rival Red Guard groups wrote and put up big-character posters in suburban communes and villages as part of the Cultural Revolution, but during these years the posters were mostly authored by urban youth sent down to the countryside.[54] In one Guangdong village, for example, after the first posters appeared attacking commune officials and the local work team, ordinary peasants were reported to be "almost as nervous as the commune cadres and the work team."[55] Urban youth continued to fight their battles during the campaign through posters, while the peasants remained largely indifferent.[56]

Although by 1969 citizens were airing fewer grievances in big-character posters, authorities continued to permit ordinary people to post them. The first major poster critical of the post–Cultural Revolution regime, authored by Li Yizhe, appeared in Guangzhou in 1974 and demanded a return to socialist democracy and legality.[57] Authorities responded with their own poster and arrested the Li Yizhe group.[58] Nonetheless, the new 1975 state constitution explicitly endorsed the use of posters in mass movements to consolidate party control of the state.[59] Three years later, the 1978 state constitution reaffirmed the right of Chinese citizens to use posters.[60]

In 1978 and 1979, however, activists in Beijing and other Chinese cities used posters to spread their ideas critical of the regime and to support their struggle for democracy, human rights, and the rule of law.[61] Although Deng Xiaoping initially endorsed some of the critical views that appeared in the posters, by 1980 he no longer saw big-character posters as a "positive force."[62] Indeed, by 1979 the official press began to criticize citizens who aired their grievances in posters. In May 1979, for example, just before authorities convened the National People's Congress, officials criticized "persons who use big-character posters to slander people."[63] At about the same time, in Liaoning's Jin County authorities adopted regulations that forbade citizens from posting *dazibao* that contained false accusations, slander, or personal atacks on cadres.[64]

During the campaign against posters in 1979, Liaoning authorities revealed that villagers had attacked a team leader in Zhuanghe County, accusing him of embezzling money and grain. Investigations revealed, however, that the charges were false.[65] In another case, poster writers, signing themselves "some among the masses" (*bufen qunzhong*), attacked a brigade party branch secretary in Liaoning's Jin County as "the despotic ruler of the south." The poster, put up outside a county "hero's rally," accused the secretary of twenty crimes. County authorities tore down the poster and launched an investigation, which revealed that the author was a disgruntled accountant who had been fired for graft and corruption. The investigators also discovered, however, that the accusations were at least partially accurate (although they "exaggerated his [the secretary's] mistakes").[66] Still, the authorities attacked the poster because, they said, it undermined stability and unity. Rather than reporting the matter to the appropriate legal authorities, the poster writer(s) had taken the matter into their own hands.

During 1979 authorities used previously radical Liaoning Province as a test case. If Beijing could convince local authorities, who had been seriously influenced by the Gang of Four, to criticize the use of posters, other provinces would fall in line. As a result, officials in Liaoning led the attack on the posters.

During the June 1979 National People's Congress, a peasant deputy from Liaoning proposed that the right to use the posters should be withdrawn. He pointed out that posters were a tool of Cultural Revolution factionalism; that they were particularly suited to slander; and that "big-character posters cost a lot in ink and paper, and result in great waste." There were many other means for rural leaders to learn what was bothering the masses: monthly mass meetings, leaders soliciting peasants' views, suggestion boxes, party branch activities, and cadre meetings at all levels.[67] Deng Xiaoping obviously endorsed these sentiments, because in September 1980 authorities amended the 1978 state constitution to delete the right of citizens to use big-character posters.[68] Only the few remaining "democracy movement" activists protested the change.[69]

Peasants, like other Chinese citizens, occasionally used posters to influence public affairs. In 1974, for example, villagers authored a poster in Shanxi that criticized the insensitivity of the party secretary to the plight of a fellow villager who had become ill. Many peasants demanded that the secretary resign. Although commune authorities intervened to protect the secretary, they decided to demote him to deputy secretary. Feeling remorseful, the secretary resigned and agreed to a demotion (he became a team leader).[70] In this case, apparently, the poster played a positive role in the eyes of authorities by drawing public attention to a leadership problem.

In another case, from Fujian, a small group of rural youth put up a poster in 1979 attacking their team leader, who had been appointed to his post before the Cultural Revolution. Although criticism of the leader first surfaced in 1977, team members had been unable to replace him. In the poster they claimed that the leader was incompetent, could not raise team income, and had little leadership ability. Brigade authorities intervened, dismissed the team leader, and called for elections. The new team leader instituted new policies, which raised the value of a workday from 0.3 yuan to 0.8 yuan, satisfying many in the team.[71]

Many interviewees, however, reported that they had seen no posters during the 1970s.[72] None of my interviewees had themselves written a poster nor had most of them known anyone who had. As one informant reports: "There were no posters in my brigade or in the county that I knew about. There were lots of them during the Cultural Revolution. But they mostly had to do with factional problems."[73]

The nature of village society helps to explain why peasants used big-character posters so infrequently. There were no anonymous *dazibao* in the countryside, where everyone knew everyone else's business, and villagers who wrote posters were immediately recognized by their neighbors and local cadres.

Officials sometimes criticized, ostracized, or took revenge against rural residents who were sufficiently bold or foolish to write posters. Interviewees from Guangdong and Fujian provinces report occasionally seeing posters in their communes during the Cultural Revolution, but they often provoked angry reactions and retaliation from local cadres. In one Guangdong case, for example, a peasant who put up a poster that attacked a commune cadre was immediately identified by the cadre and scolded.[74] In another case, a team cashier who criticized a brigade cadre in a poster was dismissed from his post.[75] More recently, in 1978, rural primary teachers put up a poster in one Fujian commune that criticized the commune party secretary for treating them badly during the Cultural Revolution. Commune authorities quickly tore down the poster, and the teachers put up no others.[76]

Other characteristics of the Chinese peasantry, such as their illiteracy and their tendency to respect legitimate authority, also inhibited them from choosing this mode of participation.

Conclusion

When peasants, through written channels, raised issues that mirrored elite concerns, they could use these channels more effectively to participate in local politics. Thus, when higher-level leaders campaigned against corrupt local officials, they welcomed letters and posters written by peasants that denounced local cadre abuses. In addition, written communication, like other modes of participation, helped to identify problems in policy implementation.

Still, probably few peasants chose to participate in politics by writing to authorities. This method was viewed as less effective than contacting an influential patron, relative, or friend. Only if contacting or speaking out in a meeting failed would villagers consider writing as an alternative. Rural schoolteachers, cadres, middle school graduates, and sent-down urbanites probably used this channel most frequently. It is likely that few "ordinary" peasants wrote to authorities or used posters to attempt to influence public affairs.

Unlike the other modes of participation discussed, the potential for elites to mobilize peasants through written modes was not very great. Citizen-initiated letters brought troubles and difficulties and were usually ignored. Only officials interested in the relatively long-term concerns of increasing the efficiency of their organization or preventing the abuse of regulations, neither of which were high priorities for many officials during the late 1960s and 1970s, would have responded without the pressure of a campaign. With indifferent elite support or even outright opposition, then, these activities remained weak and ineffective as channels for citizen-initiated political participation.

8

Withholding, Bribing, and Demonstrating

Historically, when Chinese peasants were unable to use legitimate channels effectively to express deeply felt grievances, they sometimes resorted to illegitimate activities. In recent years, these ranged from defensive strategies, such as withholding goods and services from authorities, to aggressive strategies, such as bribery, violence, or spontaneous demonstrations. Even during the 1970s, when authorities tightly controlled the political arena, peasants sometimes used these methods to participate in local politics.

Many of these activities, such as bribery, were individual initiatives designed to win particular benefits from the authorities. Violence and demonstrations, however, were more likely to be effective if peasants first mobilized group solidarity. Local leaders played a crucial role as organizers of these collective acts. During the 1970s villagers of generally "good" class background tended to use defensive or protective strategies, but during the more relaxed early 1960s and after 1978 they relied on more aggressive strategies.

Official Policy

Of these activities, China's leaders recognized as legitimate only the rights to strike (withhold labor) and to demonstrate during part of the period. Although both the 1975 and 1978 state constitutions legitimized the right to strike, it was omitted from the 1982 constitution, which, however, did not make strikes illegal.[1] The state constitutions also acknowledged the right of the people to demonstrate.[2] Chinese citizens could only legitimately engage in these activities, however, if the party led them, and they upheld the "four principles" (Marxism–Leninism–Mao Zedong Thought, the rule of the Communist party, the dictatorship of the proletariat, and socialism).

Throughout the period of my study, officials outlawed such activities as bribery, withholding of goods and services, violence, and sabotage. The "Regulations Regarding the Punishment of Corruption," promulgated in 1952, for example, proscribed specific forms of corruption, including bribery.[3] Courts sentenced cadres guilty of serious corruption to death, and authorities executed Chinese citizens, mostly cadres, in extreme cases.[4] In addition, administrative rules and regulations governing cadre behavior forbade officials from accepting bribes.[5] In the mid-1960s authorities attempted to curb rural cadre corruption in the Four Clean-ups Campaign.[6] Then, from 1977 to 1978, officials in Guangdong, Fujian, and Zhejiang provinces dispatched work teams to implement the anticorruption and antispeculation goals of the Double Hits Campaign in the countryside.[7] Further, in the 1979 criminal code, authorities reinforced earlier laws proscribing corruption.[8] In 1981 and 1982 they then launched a concerted drive against the corrupt activities of local (mostly urban and county-level) officials. The State Council "Decision on the Severe Punishment of Serious and Harmful Economic Crimes," adopted in 1982, and stiffer penalties for corruption added to the criminal code indicate that senior authorities intended to deal severely with corrupt local officials.[9]

Since 1954, under the unified purchase and sale regulations, China's leaders have required peasants to turn over surplus agricultural produce to the state and prohibited peasants from withholding these goods.[10] Even under the new, liberal agricultural policies, peasants continued to fulfill state-determined quotas. Deliberate withholding of goods from the state or its agents was illegitimate.

China's leaders also outlawed the use of political sabotage and violence. Both the 1953 and 1979 election laws, for example, prohibited individuals or groups from sabotaging elections, either by deliberately refusing to participate in the electoral process or by using illegal means to influence election outcomes.[11] Finally, although the draft and official criminal codes outlawed violence in the 1960s and again since 1979,[12] the turbulent years of the Cultural Revolution may have legitimized the use of violence to a certain extent. During those years, officials mobilized supporters for often violent confrontations with rival factions, especially in urban China. Since 1979, however, China's leaders have again explicitly forbidden the use of violence.

Withholding and Sabotage

Peasants occasionally attempted to influence the course of public affairs by withholding cooperation from authorities, such as by refusing to participate in a mobilized political activity. By the late 1960s and 1970s, many local leaders in Guangdong and Fujian discovered that they had to pay the villagers to attend team mass meetings.[13] One interviewee reports that, if household heads did not attend important discussions, such as those in 1980 to discuss the implementation of the responsibility system, village leaders would go to their houses to round them up.[14]

Although these cases were mostly nondeliberate, and, therefore, politically insignificant, in other cases villagers intentionally refused to cooperate. In some villages, where the leadership was divided (usually along kinship or factional lines), local cadres deliberately refused to cooperate with their colleagues in an effort to force policy changes. In a Shanxi village, for example, a disgruntled former brigade leader, recently demoted to deputy leader, refused to cooperate with other village officials to solve local problems.[15] In another case, a former brigade cadre in suburban Shanghai, demoted to take charge of a brigade enterprise, refused to attend meetings or to have anything to do with the other leaders. As a result, the work of the village was seriously affected.[16] Finally, earlier we saw that when a peasant from a minority lineage in a Guangdong village was appointed team leader contrary to the expectations of the members of the majority lineage, villagers refused their cooperation, and production fell rapidly.[17] In this case, the active noncooperation of the villagers forced the brigade party branch to rescind its earlier unpopular decisions. These instances of "nonparticipation" were significant, because, by withdrawing their cooperation, the peasants undermined the performance of others in the village and forced changes on public issues.

In the late 1960s through the mid-1970s, observers report that exhausted peasants slept through late night meetings called during political campaigns.[18] Although the peasants who stayed away from these meetings probably did so because they were too tired or bored to do otherwise, some of them may have refused to attend the meetings to express their dissatisfaction with local policies. Local cadres sometimes did not attend for the same reason.

In addition to withdrawing from meetings or cadre deliberations, some peasants withheld their cooperation by refusing to be a cadre or by sabotaging elections. As early as 1961 peasant unwillingness to take on the tasks of team cadre in Fujian Province was so widespread that some local party branches included "refusal to be a cadre" on forms reporting local problems to their superiors.[19] This sort of withdrawal was a problem throughout the period and has intensified under the new agricultural responsibility system.

During the 1979 to 1981 elections of production team cadres, some peasants deliberately refused to participate in local elections as a protest strategy. Use of nonparticipation strategies also characterized formal and informal leaders in some villages. In one March 1980 case, for example, peasants demanded that authorities call an election to replace a team accountant accused of embezzling 456 yuan of team funds. Because the accountant "knew he would lose, he deliberately caused chaos to the orderly arrangements." He refused to attend a meeting to discuss the election and returned the entreaties of brigade officials with curses. When he physically attacked the brigade deputy secretary, however, other brigade officials intervened and jailed him for three years.[20]

In another case, in 1978, a former Fujian brigade cadre organized his kinsmen to sabotage a production team election. As a production team accountant and also the informal leader of ten or so households of close relatives in his production team, he had repeatedly run into trouble for his outspokenness and honesty. He had criticized the Study Dazhai work team for failing to recognize that village youth were basically lazy and needed close supervision, and he had attacked the birth control campaign for depriving villagers of security in their old age. In each case visiting work teams struggled with him and sent him to study classes. He reacted by refusing to attend meetings in the brigade: "You don't let me speak my mind, so what's the use [of attending]?"

After a series of clashes with the leader of his production team (they were each the informal leader of different kinship groups), the team leader demanded the accountant's ouster, and brigade officials concurred. In the subsequent election, the accountant

> organized his kinsmen not to participate. They didn't attend the team election meeting. . . . [He] talked to his kinsmen informally. "They won't let me say what is on my mind," he said. They met in peoples' houses after work or at dinner. [He] said that to elect the team leader without [the participation of his group] was illegal, and [he] demanded that the team be divided.[21]

The accountant raised the issue of splitting up the team informally with the local guarantee cadre and then drafted a letter to a county-level work team with the same request. The accountant's kinsmen refused to work with the team leader's supporters and forced a de facto split. In the end, implementation of the responsibility system solved the problem, because it permitted the new situation to continue.

In addition to withdrawing from politics in an attempt to influence local political outcomes, peasants sometimes withheld both their labor and agricultural products to protest against government policies.[22] Villagers refused to send laborers to help build collective construction projects, either to prevent the projects from being carried out or because they were not sufficiently compensated for the work. Peasants also slowed down or went on strike to protest the implementation of incentive schemes, such as the Dazhai work point system, which tended to equalize income from collective labor.

Villagers sometimes refused to send the required number of laborers to water conservation work sites,[23] to roadbuilding projects,[24] or to construct schools or meeting halls.[25] In one case, during winter 1978, county authorities mobilized peasants from a number of villages on the outskirts of Shanghai to build a canal. The villagers complained bitterly that digging the canal in the frozen ground was too difficult and of no use to them, and they went on strike (*daigong*), stopped working, and returned to their homes. In the end, authorities abandoned the project.[26]

To these collective acts of withholding, peasants sometimes added deliberate slowdowns to protest low pay. When authorities attempted to implement the more egalitarian time rate remuneration system (Dazhai work points), skilled villagers in many areas began slowing down and producing less.[27] In one late 1960s case from Guangdong, for example, strong workers moved only two or three *dan* (1 dan = 110.23 lbs.) of night soil in four hours when the Dazhai system was introduced. When piece rates were restored, during the same time period they each moved five times as much.[28] Peasants slowed down to express their dissatisfaction with the system that paid everyone about the same, regardless of their labor contribution.

Peasants also occasionally withheld grain and other agricultural produce through elaborate false reporting schemes. Villages sometimes underreported grain output so that they could distribute more among themselves.[29] Although marginal false reporting by itself was not usually an activity peasants adopted to influence government decisions, authorities perceived the act as being politically motivated when villagers withheld substantial amounts of grain or other resources. For example, Vice-Premier Wan Li reported in November 1982 to a rural work conference that villagers in Anhui Province's Funan County withheld grain from authorities: "The masses *intended* to arouse the attention of the county CCP committee to solve the problem. Therefore, they stored the grain in their houses and were unwilling to hand it out."[30] In this case, central authorities interpreted the withholding as a deliberate protest by villagers against the overaccumulation policies of local cadres. According to the report, "the problem was solved, and in only one day the state purchase quotas were overfulfilled."

Bribing Officials

Although central authorities have twice during the period deemed corruption among rural cadres to be serious enough to warrant national campaigns,[31] politically significant corruption is more difficult to document. Bribery, a form of corruption, became political participation when peasants used it to influence the implementation of public policy. Villagers have attempted to bribe local officials not so much to change policies, but to waive "inconvenient" requirements, such as those forbidding housebuilding on land suitable for cultivation or to jump long lines of their neighbors queueing for scarce commodities, such as building materials or travel permits.

Peasants sometimes bribed cadres in exchange for special favors. For example, villagers plied local officials with cigarettes, good meals, bottles of liquor, peanuts, and sometimes money to speed up the processing of requests for scarce goods and services.[32]

Emigrés report that peasants bribed local cadres to get scarce chemical fertilizer, allocations of land for housing, building materials, job opportunities in cities or in brigade industries, to join the PLA (before 1980), to overlook transgressions of the law, or to evade the birth control policy.[33] "If you did not bribe local cadres," one informant from rural Fujian relates, "you got what was left over. To get what you wanted, you had to *yanjiu, yanjiu*." This pun plays on the double meaning of *yanjiu*—to research or cigarettes and wine.[34]

From 1978 to 1982, press attention in China focused on urban and higher-level cadre corruption.[35] Nonetheless, reports in the provincial media commending brigade authorities for resisting attempts to bribe them indicate the scope of the problem. For example, a brigade cadre charged with distributing permits to build new houses was presented two geese by one applicant and 70 yuan by another. He resisted both bribes.[36] In another case, authorities commended a youth league member, charged with distributing building material (then in short supply), for refusing bribes.[37]

Neither the national nor the provincial press has reported comprehensive data on the scope of corruption in rural China. Even if authorities published such data, however, it would indicate only a portion of the activity, because, to be successful, peasants carried out the bribery in secret.

In general, the goods and services provided to cadres in exchange for favors have been so modest that one might conclude that villagers were simply being friendly and hospitable, not engaging in bribery. Peasants explained to visiting journalists from Xi'an, for example, that local custom required that they invite their neighbors for meals. Why, then, asked Radio Xi'an, were the "people" invited by the peasants always cadres and not other villagers. This was "far from being a small matter," the report concludes.[38]

Violence and Demonstrations

In January 1979 dissident Fu Yuehua led hundreds of peasants to demonstrate in front of Zhongnanhai, the seat of party and state power in Beijing. Raggedly dressed and obviously poor, they squatted in front of party headquarters for several days and demanded that authorities punish local officials who had abused their power, that officials provide them with jobs, and that appropriate arrangements be made for their livelihood.[39] This was the first "spontaneous" demonstration of peasants in the nation's capital since the founding of the People's Republic in 1949. These activities coincided with reports of scattered riots of sent-down youth in a number of other cities.[40]

Beating gongs and waving banners, party and youth league members mobilized peasants into countless demonstrations through large villages and county towns to support campaigns from the Socialist Education Movement in the mid-1960s to the ouster of the Gang of Four. In addition to participating in these mobilized demonstrations, however, villagers occasionally organized their own, outside of party leadership.

Since 1979 incidents of collective violence have apparently become more common. Authorities report, for example, clan fights over graveyards and other communal property in Guangdong and Hunan and attacks by angry commune members on state farms in Yunnan.[41] Of the many instances of violence or demonstrations, however, in only some of them were peasants politically motivated. Where they were, in my data, peasants resorted to violence to protest against local cadre abuse of power or their failure to implement popular central policies; food shortages; or insufficient compensation for village resources taken by the state.

In a report that reveals that cadres made up 76 percent of those apprehended for violations of the law in Guangdong in 1980, authorities condemn local officials who took the law into their own hands.[42] In one case, 1,000 peasants from a brigade in Hebei's Xingtai County demonstrated against and held captive authorities of the county people's court, whom the villagers accused of beating, manhandling, and kicking litigants; illegally confiscating their property; and illegally arresting bystanders who attempted to come to their rescue. The villagers surrounded the judge and other officers of the court and only freed them after the intervention of commune party authorities. A county investigation later criticized the high-handed manner of the court officials.[43]

If peasants occasionally protested against cadre abuse of power, they also sometimes demonstrated to demand that local cadres implement popular central policies. On Guangdong's Hainan Island, for example, county party officials in 1983 ordered a brigade to stop implementing *dabaogan,* well after central policies permitted local units to carry it out. The new brigade officials complied (the county authority had dispatched a work team to the unit in March 1983 to replace the brigade leaders), but incomes fell as a result. In May brigade authorities convened a meeting of 600 villagers to demand that the county lift its restrictions. When county authorities ignored their plea, peasants visited county government offices. County public security authorities, on instructions from the party secretary, arrested some villagers to intimidate them. When the peasants returned home, county officials published the "crimes" of those they had arrested and demanded that some villagers attend group study meetings. That night over 100 villagers assembled outside the quarters of a delegation of visiting county party officials and demanded the release of those who had been arrested. Still, the officials held their ground. Finally, "higher authorities" heard of the incident, intervened, and ordered the county to change its policy.[44]

In this case, peasants, under the leadership of village officials, used a variety of collective means to protest against government action, culminating in meetings and a demonstration. Clearly the villagers had a keen sense of their own interests and sought to pursue them vis-à-vis county authorities. Nonetheless, the peasants were only successful after the intervention of higher authorities.

In the only case in my data for the mid-1970s, peasants demonstrated to protest against food shortages and the imposition of arbitrary restrictions on household income-earning activities. Short of food and desperate, villagers cut grass to sell in the market. A visiting commune-level work team criticized them for "spontaneously developing capitalism" and called individual villagers to struggle meetings. Furious, a group of twenty to thirty peasants marched on commune headquarters and demanded help. Although several of the protesters were arrested, the commune then intervened to solve the food shortages.[45]

Peasants also sometimes resorted to violence or demonstrations in an effort to win higher compensation for village property taken over by the state. In one Hunan case, 500 commune members destroyed and carted away the property of a local colliery, "committing acts of violence" to pro-

test against "a reservoir problem which had been solved after negotia-
tion."[46] The problem had obviously not been solved to the villagers'
satisfaction.

In another case, sixty peasants tore down a wall that a supply and marketing cooperative had erected to enclose land belonging to the village.[47]
And in Shandong peasants forcibly retrieved saplings that they had planted
on land confiscated from them by commune authorities.[48]

Most interviewees report that not since the violence of the Cultural
Revolution had peasants organized themselves in demonstrations. Although there are few instances of violence in their reports, nonetheless
some informants relate stories of fights between villages, between kin
groups, and between villages and nearby factories.[49] Although much of
this violence was probably not aimed at political participation, it sometimes appears to have a political purpose, especially when the target of the
rioting was rural political authority.

In one 1979 case from Guangdong's Hainan Island, for example, 300
villagers, "under the pretext of applying for an audience with the higher
authorities to appeal for help," occupied the county broadcasting station
and used it for "agitating propaganda" broadcasts; trashed the county
party committee's general office, security office, and conference room; occupied the county cadre guesthouse; searched and confiscated property
from the house of the county party first secretary; and stole state and private property, including "official seals, documents, papers and files."[50] This
violent attack on state and party authority had clear political implications.
Authorities failed to report the causes of the violence, however. We can
speculate that during a period of clan violence on the island county officials prompted the attack by favoring one village or kinship group over
another. In any event, villagers deliberately attacked local political authorities in this case. These and other examples of rural violence indicated the
decline in the authority of local formal leaders after 1978.

The legitimacy of violence and demonstrations was ambiguous in rural
China. On the one hand, since 1978, authorities have encouraged citizens
to adhere to the laws of the land, which clearly forbade violent acts and
required the people to respect party authority (the "four principles"). On
the other hand, China's leaders in the recent past have openly condoned
violent solutions to political conflict and approved of the largest spon-

taneous demonstration in recent memory, held in April 1976 in Beijing's Tiananmen.

In general, violence and demonstrations organized by forces outside the party and directed at political authority were illegitimate. Authorities reserved for themselves, however, the power of defining the legitimacy of these acts as warranted by the situation as they saw it at the time.

Conclusion

Peasants adopted reactive strategies, such as withholding goods or services, during the tightly controlled periods of the early and mid-1970s, but they adopted more aggressive strategies, such as bribery and violence, when central authorities relaxed controls during the early 1960s and after 1978. Decollectivization placed more resources in the hands of individual households. Not since the 1950s have peasant families had control of so wide an array of resources and in quantities surplus to their needs. Since 1979 many villagers, especially the "new rich peasantry" have, for example, been in a better position to offer advantages to authorities in exchange for special favors.

The same liberalization witnessed a decline in the authority and prestige of formal leaders in the countryside. They have become less able than before to impose their views on the villagers. Peasants sometimes violently expressed their dissatisfaction with cadres who abused their power and with some local officials who failed to implement popular official policies. In addition, the authorities, in their pursuit of economic development under the "four modernizations," sparked an unparalleled expansion of state institutions in the countryside and in the suburbs. State offices and organizations have expanded and have physically moved into and displaced villagers, but at the same time they have provided relatively low levels of compensation. Peasants sometimes protested against this situation by using violence or demonstrating.

Second, the class composition of the peasants who have adopted illegitimate strategies to influence politics has changed during the past thirty-five years. During the 1950s landlords, rich peasants, and well-off middle peasants evaded taxes, hid surplus grain from the authorities, and instigated or even organized some acts of open resistance.[51] By 1962, however, public security measures and the party's penetration of institutions in the countryside were sufficient to control these activities. The state continued to be unable to meet demands for scarce goods and services, however. As a result, the "poor and lower-middle" peasantry turned to informal channels to meet their needs. Since 1962 peasants of "good" class background came increasingly to be associated with withholding strategies, bribery, and even violence.

Third, some strategies were almost exclusively individual attempts to reach accommodation with inconvenient policies, while others were employed by groups. Bribery, for example, was an individual affair, carried out in secret. Its goals were specific, usually the waiver of inconvenient, lengthy, or costly regulations or the provision of commodities in short supply. The collective impact of this corruption changed patterns of allocation, however, as goods and services went to those with "good connections" or other resources.

Groups adopted other strategies. Although important data on the collective use of informal strategies are lacking, in many cases peasants relied on group solidarity to pursue their interests. Peasants mobilized a community support network to resist encroachments of the state and neighboring units and to advance local group interests. Because collective groups adopted such strategies as withholding, violence, and demonstrations, authorities saw them as more threatening than individual acts.

Finally, both formal and informal local leaders played an important role in organizing the peasantry to carry out illegitimate strategies. Without the resources of these leaders, ordinary peasants would have been ineffective. On an individual level, local cadres accepted bribes and waived requirements or provided resources outside of the plan. On a collective level, formal and informal local leaders provided organizational talent and direction to peasant efforts to protest unreasonable accumulation goals or low compensation. Press data link local officials to acts of violence and withholding of grain and other resources, and informal leaders actively supported these protests and probably encouraged the few local demonstrations reported here as well.

Depending on their choice of allies, peasants used different arenas to participate in politics. When allied to higher-level authorities to oppose unpopular local leaders, peasants relied largely on legitimate channels (meetings, elections, contacting outsiders, and the media). However, when allied to local leaders to oppose higher-level officials and their policies, peasants often resorted to largely illegitimate channels. In this situation, they viewed legitimate channels as ineffective to oppose policies that higher-level authorities had already determined to be "correct."

That Chinese peasants sometimes engaged in politically significant illegitimate activities is a clear indication of the existence of peasant-initiated attempts to influence the course of local politics. But even here, because of the crucial role played by the local elite, the autonomy of the peasants' action is in question. Local officials organized and led peasants in many of the protests and undoubtedly pursued, at least in part, their own objectives. Even in these the most "autonomous" of actions, there was, then, an element of mobilization directed either at influencing other local officials or at influencing higher-level elites.

9

Conclusion:
Modernization, Participation,
and Chinese Peasants

Peasants in contemporary China engaged the state and its agents in various arenas in an effort to influence the course of public affairs. Their activities have also served China's political system. Elections, for example, not only legitimized the regime, but socialized the citizenry into elite norms and furthered the implementation of public policy. Speaking out at meetings or contacting work team members facilitated leader-mass communication and helped to knit local communities together with intermediate government and party units.

The significance of political participation can be evaluated from a comparative developmental perspective.[1] Students of one-party states argue that postrevolutionary regimes typically go through stages of development that lead to a dramatic expansion of "spontaneous" forms of participation.[2] Having consolidated their power and transformed the economy, the leaders then embark on an ambitious development program. In the course of socioeconomic change, strategically important groups emerge from among specialists, technicians, and other skilled people, on whom the party must depend to implement its policies. The party grants these groups some

166

autonomy, especially within their own fields of expertise, and the party agrees to share power with them to a limited extent. In its attempts to foster modernization and industrialization, the party ultimately faces challenges from a variety of sources, including "demands by local and popular groups for participation in and influence over the political system."[3] These groups gradually develop a group consciousness and begin to demand more political participation.

Both party leaders and citizens come to value this increased participation, and it eventually spreads to less strategic groups in society. Thus, "at the level of the workplace, the quantity and quality of worker and peasant participation plays an increasingly crucial role in the regime's efforts to promote modernization and development."[4] At this stage, the party assumes a new role—that of mediator among groups pursuing their own interests in the development process.

The mechanisms that lead to these changes include

> increases in the average socio-economic level of the population and of particular groups within it, increased organizational involvement, heightened group consciousness (and, often heightened intergroup conflict), expanded government activities impinging on more and more of the population, and the gradual acceptance among elites and nonelites of the idea of citizen responsibility and participation as a concomitant of the modern state.[5]

Two features of established one-party states are especially noteworthy: first, they are characterized by the emergence of "interest groups" or "specialized interest groups," which, though not reducing the need for the party's overall guidance, restrict the party's role;[6] and, second, the character of political participation is dramatically altered because the modernization process itself encourages "higher levels of participation, more diverse forms of participation, more complex bases of participation (with socioeconomic class of rising importance), and a higher ratio of autonomous to mobilized participation."[7] Thus, Samuel P. Huntington argues that, "as societies become economically well off and socially complex . . . [their] political systems also have to become more open, participant and responsive."[8]

If the process of modernization, other things being equal, leads to increased participation, as Huntington and Joan Nelson point out, "other things are rarely equal."[9] The process is neither steady nor uniform and can be influenced by a complex array of factors, including the policies and attitudes of the political elite, group cohesion, and other contingencies, such as the opportunity for migration.[10] Elite attitudes to political participation, Huntington and Nelson argue, are "the single most decisive factor" in influencing the nature of participation in any particular society.[11] Group cohesion is also important, because, where "family, ethnic, religious, or territorial groupings and associations" are strong, political participation from these groups is likely to increase. Development will reinforce these identifications and enhance the ability and motivation of individuals to organize for political action on the basis of these ties.[12]

Modernizing communist systems, so the argument goes, including among them presumably postrevolutionary China, have gone through or are going through these changes. The peasants in China, however, have not formed an "interest group," nor have they joined autonomous organizations that have had an impact on politics. The nature of political participation in China has been determined by a particular historical context, in which authorities created a strong, relatively centralized party/state authority and reestablished a relationship of dependence between themselves and the peasantry. Elite conflict has had a decisive impact on the development of political participation in China. Nonetheless, during the period of my study, the modernization/participation paradigm is not adequate to explain the development of peasant political participation.

Peasants as a Group in Chinese Politics

In his discussion of groups in Soviet politics, H. Gordon Skilling defines a political interest group as "an aggregate of persons who possess certain common characteristics, and share certain attitudes on public issues, and who adopt distinct positions on these issues, and make definite claims on those in authority."[13] He excludes from this category "broad social groups," such as workers or peasants, which he labels "categoric groups" and instead seeks to focus attention on "occupational" groups, such as writers, economists, and party officials and "opinion" groups, such as leftist writers, centrist economists, and conservative military officials.[14] His study of interest groups in the Soviet Union is confined to these categories.

Although Skilling admits that "categoric" groups are politically relevant for the study of Soviet politics ("their needs and wants are in some degree taken into account and articulated by political leaders"),[15] broad categories of workers and peasants lack "a high degree of mutual awareness and interaction and have at present much less effective means to express their interests explicitly and to press them upon those responsible for policy-making."[16] Skilling points out that peasants in the Soviet Union, for example, had no formal association for pressing their interests. Although he admits that elites established mass organizations of peasants, he argues that these associations were unable "autonomously" to express or defend the interests of peasants. They functioned, rather, to transmit party decisions to villagers for their implementation. Still Skilling admits that these broad social categories had the potential for being represented by "latent" or "potential" interest groups in the future.[17]

Other scholars have applied the group approach to the study of Chinese politics.[18] Recent studies of occupation groups, however, conclude that interest groups have yet to emerge in post-1949 China.[19] Agreeing with Skilling, I see the peasantry as a broad social or "categoric" group. It perceives itself not so much as "the peasantry," but as members of other significant groups, based on an identification with social class, production unit, and family. It is not surprising that such a large category as "the peasantry" is divided into numerous subcategories or groups.

For much of the period of our study, the class labels that authorities distributed to all peasants in the course of land reform have had a significant impact on peasants' lives. Officials placed under surveillance landlords and rich peasants (and their offspring), and denied them political rights, admission to the party, army, or higher education, and, in some cases, saw to it that their incomes were lower than the incomes of other householders. The party rewarded poor peasants, the victors in the revolution, with higher incomes, improved access to the benefits of education, and political leadership. Because one's class label had such an important impact on one's life chances, peasants came to think of each other in class terms. One indication of this phenomenon appeared in marriage patterns. Offspring of "good" class families were loath to marry sons or daughters with "bad" class backgrounds.[20] Although by 1957 the economic conditions that produced this class differentiation had disappeared, the categories continued to influence the way peasants thought about and dealt with each other.

In 1979 officials relaxed the policy of discriminating against "bad" class elements, and they introduced household contracting, which encouraged some peasants to "get rich first." In spite of official denials, this policy is likely to lead to increased class polarization in the countryside, as larger families farming poorer land are left behind.[21] With the emergence of new rich peasants, I expect that conflicts of interest between well-to-do "specialized" households and their poor neighbors will intensify.

In addition to class identifications, peasants usually saw themselves as members of particular local communities (coterminous with production units in the countryside). These communities/production units had their own interests, which rivaled those of other, usually neighboring, units or higher authorities. Disputes over land, water rights, and other resources were common during the period. Rivalry in the marketplace to sell cash crops or to gain approval for industrial undertakings also influenced the way peasants viewed outsiders. Although the implementation of household contracting since 1979–1980 has reduced peasant identification with weakened local production units, it has increased competition among peasant households in local markets.

Peasants in some parts of China strongly identified with family and extended kinship interests. Although the strength of these bonds varied, they were nonetheless significant. In spite of the party's attempt to undercut the power of kinship organizations, authorities have probably not succeeded in replacing these ties. During the 1950s the feeling that extended family interests ought to be protected provided the basis for much of the early cooperative agriculture in many parts of China. Particularly in South China, new rural production units, introduced in 1958, institutionalized kinship cooperation. Authorities gave these new units, often lineage-based, title to the land. In the post-1979 decollectivization, peasants have continued to rely on kin-based cooperation in many areas.

In addition to these groups, peasants belonged to a variety of others: peasants' associations, women's federations, the party, the army, and so forth. As a result, the peasantry saw itself less as a mass of 800 million cultivators and more as members of particular subgroups.

Not only did peasants belong to a multitude of groups, but interaction among the peasantry was relatively weak. First, although peasants interacted locally in markets and other settings, they lived most of their lives in their native communities and married spouses from nearby villages. Peasants joined the army, went off to school, or became state officials, but only in relatively small numbers. Indeed, state policy for most of the period tied peasants to the land. Authorities effectively prevented rural to urban migration through the household registration and rationing systems. China's leaders isolated the peasantry from itself (but not from the party) and reduced opportunities for peasant interaction unsupervised by the party.

Second, although authorities established a nationwide network of peasants' associations (the poor and lower-middle peasants' associations), with branches organized at brigade level, these organizations (when they were active) were effectively controlled by the party. Peasants' associations functioned chiefly as a method of transmitting party policy to the countryside. The mass organizations lacked their own identity—a problem recognized by Liao Gailong in 1980, when he recommended setting up additional "independent" peasants' associations.[22]

Peasants have not formed a cohesive group that could act in Chinese politics. The 1979–1980 economic reforms may have altered this situation to a certain extent, because the new policies have produced a new class of rich peasants, composed mostly of China's 24.8 million "specialized households."[23] Recent studies of the distribution of rural income report that 3 to 6 percent of households in some places have already become "rich through labor" and have earned incomes of from three to six times the national average.[24] If these households organize, they could become a political force. Authorities are likely to prohibit this development, however. They have already taken steps to recruit (and, thus, to coopt) the "new rich peasants" into the party.[25]

The modernization/participation paradigm does not posit autonomous group activity for the peasantry as a whole, but it does suggest that "the quantity and quality of . . . peasant participation plays an increasingly crucial role" in the development process,[26] and that, throughout the system (including, therefore, the peasantry), higher levels, more diverse forms, more complex bases, and more autonomous participation are obtained in the development process.[27] Does the paradigm adequately describe the experience of China's peasantry? How has the nature of peasant political participation changed in contemporary China?

The Nature of Peasant Participation in China

The political participation of China's peasantry evolved after 1949 within a particular historical context. This context was characterized by (1) the

emergence of a strong central party/state authority as a result of collectivization of the economy; (2) the exchange of peasant dependence on a
local economic elite for dependence on a new political elite, represented by
local party leaders; and (3) the dominant role played by elite conflicts in
the development of political institutions.

As a consequence of the revolution and collectivization of the economy, political leaders transformed China from a weak state system, loosely
controlled by a factionalized elite, into a strong state system, dominated
by the organized and relatively disciplined Communist party. China's political elite, through the party, played the decisive role in the development
of political participation and in the country's modernization. First, elites
have, on the whole, induced and controlled the modernization process.
Initiatives from political leaders, such as the program that emerged from
the Third Plenum of the Eleventh Central Committee in December 1978,
largely established the direction of China's economic development.
Throughout the period, though sometimes reacting to local pressures,
central party leaders determined the nature of the policies, when and how
they were introduced, amended, or abandoned, and how they should be
implemented.

Second, the party determined the nature of legitimate political participation in China. Party officials limited the right to participate in politics to
"the people" and reserved for themselves the authority to define the members of this category. Central authorities identified the legitimate modes
and institutions of participation and assumed control over the operation of
these channels. In the electoral system, for example, party influence predominated in the nomination stage, and local officials "reviewed and approved" election outcomes. As for local assemblies, party committees for
most of the period set agendas, determined the issues, decided when the
assemblies would be called, and ruled on whether state authorities should
act on recommendations or complaints aired in the assembly meetings. Political leaders decided whether existing institutions should be replaced, reformed, or ignored. In the Cultural Revolution, for example, party leaders
attacked existing institutions of participation and eventually replaced them
altogether.

Third, political elites set narrow limits on the activities of various occupational groups in Chinese society, preventing them from organizing
outside of party control to pursue their own interests. Although the lati-

tude permitted to these groups varied somewhat, elites maintained control both through networks of party-sponsored organizations, such as the All-China Federation of Trade Unions, and through periodic rectification campaigns, such as the Hundred Flowers in 1957.

Fourth, political elites, through the party's control over the media and communications, decisively influenced the content of political information. Attempts by workers in China's major cities to print and distribute unofficial political journals during the 1978–1981 democracy movement, for example, were met by strong official action to bring the distribution of political information back under party control. Finally, the party propagated an official idea system, which legitimized its commanding role in Chinese politics and which reserved for it the right to make policy and see to it that it was implemented. In each of these spheres, then, the exercise of central authority touched the lives of the Chinese people and influenced their relationship to the leadership.

During the past several decades, the impact of central authority has varied considerably, however. First, the ability of elites to determine political outcomes in China has been a function of their unity. During periods of intense conflict among national political leaders, such as during the Cultural Revolution, their grip on local political behavior and processes was considerably reduced. Second, China's vast size and relatively poor communications system reduced the influence of central authority on more physically remote areas. Local leaders may have implemented policy changes more slowly in more remote parts of the country. Third, the people have continued to develop their own informal means of participating in politics, which supplemented the formal, elite-inspired institutions and channels. Based on patterns of social interaction and group solidarity, ordinary citizens engaged in a wide range of informal political behavior, both individual and collective.

At local levels in the countryside, the revolution replaced peasant dependence on local economic elites, including landlords, merchants, and moneylenders, with dependence on local political elites, in the form of party members. After land reform, most peasants withdrew from formal politics "to become rich." Party cadres created a local bureaucracy and reestablished a relationship of dependence between themselves and the peasantry. Officials gradually took control of production, land, and movement from the countryside to the cities. By 1957, with the setting up of "higher-stage" cooperatives, the relationship was complete. The party/state, administered by local peasant-bureaucrats, commanded most resources.

During the subsequent period, village leaders, most of whom were (and continue to be) party members, controlled access to crucial resources that had a direct bearing on the peasants' lives. Team and brigade leaders, for example, controlled the distribution of agricultural inputs; distributed jobs, work points, loans, and private plots; controlled the use of land; approved opportunities for higher education, health care, and other social services; granted travel permits; administered internal security; and decided who would be admitted to the party. On a systemwide basis, the powers of local leaders were minimal, but they had an enormous impact on the lives of China's villagers. This dependence, coupled with peasant values that respected authority, accounted in large part for the reluctance of villagers to challenge their leaders in formal settings. The post-1979 agricultural policies have reduced peasant dependence, however, because they curtailed the powers of local leaders and increased the resources available to individual peasant households.

Finally, elite conflict had a decisive impact on the course of political participation throughout the period. Leaders attempted throughout the 1950s to create popular institutions of participation, such as local assemblies. In the Cultural Revolution, radical leaders attacked these institutions, however. During the late 1960s and early 1970s, the institutions atrophied and were subsequently replaced by the mass campaign and new party and state institutions. During these years, elite conflict restricted the number of people who could legitimately participate in politics and undermined the ability of the new institutions to provide remedies or to solve problems.

After 1978 China's leaders abolished many Cultural Revolution political institutions and reestablished formal, legal, and regular channels of political participation. In the new policies, authorities expanded the scope of participation by restoring political rights to "rightists" and other victims of the Cultural Revolution, and by permitting debate on a wider range of issues than was possible during the Cultural Revolution. Still, elites continued to mobilize the masses into politics in this new setting.

Elite conflict influenced the nature of political participation in the villages in the following ways: First (and probably least significantly), elite conflict redirected the institutions and modes of participation to meet the mainly short-term needs of China's leaders. Local officials replaced management committees, ostensibly responsible to local assemblies, with revolutionary committees, and more recently, with local governments, again ostensibly responsible to local assemblies. Authorities encouraged, used, and then banned "big-character posters" as required by the politics of their staying in power.

Second, elite conflict involved peasants in periodic mass campaigns, which required investments of time and energy, squeezed many local concerns off formal agendas, and forced local conflicts into a new political rhetoric. Mass campaigns often forced a reallocation of resources away from production and into the resolution, at local levels, of conflicts imported from outside. Campaigns also tended to keep the discussion and resolution of local issues outside of formal local institutions, as party leaders used these institutions to transmit messages from above. Because local conflicts over the distribution of resources and the implementation of policies persisted, however, village participants adopted the language of the elites (such as "radical" or "revisionist") to legitimize their local struggles.

Third, elite conflict provided opportunities for the "outs" to attack the "ins" and, thus, to settle old scores. During the mid-1960s, for example, the Four Clean-ups Campaign's search for corruption legitimized local attacks on leaders in office. Similarly, the Cultural Revolution made local leaders vulnerable to attack in their communities. During periods of elite dissension, the disorder gave disgruntled elements in the villages new "handles" to use to attack their enemies. Kinship rivalry, disputes over resources, and other forms of local politics took on new forms, imported from outside.

Finally, elite conflict in China sent wave after wave of high-level officials to live in the villages, with varying consequences. These influential outsiders sometimes meddled in local disputes, taking sides, and installing new leaders or policies. They also helped villages by using their connections to higher-level units to distribute scarce resources to the village. These visiting officials kept open communications between higher-level authorities and the grassroots. In a variety of ways, then, elite conflict influenced the nature of local participation.

During the past several decades, peasant political participation has developed in China within a particular context, but how precisely has it developed? Has the quantity of political participation increased in the countryside? Has participation shifted from a more "traditional" (patron-client) to a more "modern" (class) base? Have peasants begun participating to further their group interests? Have the numbers of peasants who participate increased? Have the modes of participation diversified? Has autonomous participation increased? Have the constraints on peasant participation been reduced? To these questions, the modernization/participation paradigm would answer in the affirmative. But is this an adequate answer for contemporary rural China?

Quantity

In contrast to the pre-1949 Nationalist government, which lacked the ability to organize mass participation, the Communist party mobilized the people into politics at a rapid rate. Virtually all eligible peasants participated in elite-sponsored organizations in the countryside. Hundreds of millions of "poor and lower-middle" class peasants, for example, joined local peasants' associations,[28] and, when they were active, meetings of the associations resembled mass meetings. Virtually all rural women were eligible to join the women's federation as well.[29] Other indicators of political activity reflect the same trend. In the 1979–1980 elections, for example, 96.56 percent of all registered voters cast ballots,[30] up from 85.88 percent during the 1953–1954 elections.[31] Even at the village level, interviewees report that, during the 1960s and 1970s, most household heads attended meetings.

Authorities achieved these high rates of participation through persuasion and organization and through control of institutional processes. First, local leaders exhorted villagers to attend meetings and to take part in political activities. In the countryside, they mobilized friends and neighbors to persuade reluctant participants. One former Fujian deputy brigade leader, for example, points out that, under his administration, important meetings were delayed while leaders personally asked tardy household heads to attend. In elections, officials made their preferences known and visited peasant households to explain their views if the need arose.

Second, party branches played a key role in the operation of local political institutions. Party members met prior to brigade mass meetings to set agendas and to determine issues. In the election process, leaders usually exercised control over the crucial "nominations" and "review and approval" processes that preceded and followed the actual vote. Authorities also dominated other channels. Through their control of the media, for example, officials determined which letters to the editor to print and the nature of the official response to them.

Nonetheless, the quantity of mobilized participation has varied with the ebb and flow of mass campaigns. During the Four Clean-ups, the Cultural Revolution (1966–1969), and the Cleaning-up Class Ranks campaigns, authorities maintained political activity at a feverish pitch. Since 1979, however, officials have relied less on campaigns to achieve development goals. Still, the leaders have continued to mobilize the people into political activities, such as meetings and elections, at relatively high rates.

Given the lack of data, estimates of the quantity of more autonomous political participation in the countryside must be highly speculative. Before 1949 citizen-initiated participation was mostly confined to those with the resources to participate (landlords, rich peasants, merchants, and the like). The rate of participation for these groups was probably high; for poor peasants, it was undoubtedly much lower. After 1949 the authorities stripped the rich of their political base and gave poor peasants the ability to initiate some political action during the land reform. Authorities then reduced the scope for poor peasant intervention, however, by collectivizing the economy and by using the party to further organize and penetrate society, especially in mass campaigns. During the 1960s and 1970s, the long-term declining usefulness to peasants of formal, largely ritualized institutions prompted them to rely to a great extent on contacting and other informal activities to participate in politics. Nonetheless, measured against mobilized participation, in quantitative terms, the amount of autonomous participation during these years was relatively insignificant.

Since 1979–1980 authorities have revitalized local institutions of participation at the same time that they have relaxed political controls, abandoned mass campaigns, and placed more resources in the hands of peasant households to initiate their own political activities. It is likely that these moves have increased the amount of autonomous participation in the countryside as peasants pursue their interests both inside and outside formal institutions.

Bases

The basis of peasant-initiated, collective political action in the countryside continues to be self-interest. Peasants make individual cost-benefit

calculations, weighing "the risk of trading the status quo for a lottery between successful action and failure."[32] As Samuel L. Popkin points out,
although most peasants avoid risks when they appear to be great, some are
willing to gamble to improve their lot. The gamble, in this case, is risking
the wrath of local leaders in exchange for winning economic concessions.
In general, peasants participate to maximize their own economic advantage: They attempt to distribute benefits to themselves or to minimize
their own losses by redistributing the cost of public goods to others. In
politics individual peasants also seek to increase their own status and
power or to avoid the costs of nonconformity, such as social ostracism
(which failing to participate in mobilized activities entails in contemporary China).

Before 1949 poor peasants depended on cultivating good relations with
their rich peasant, landlord, and merchant neighbors, who mediated between them and the state. These relations were often built on shared circumstances, such as kinship, community, or village ties. In South China, in
particular, the leaders of powerful lineage groups were not only the source
of patronage, but acted to relay peasants' political interests to the larger
community. Still, the basis of these relationships was undoubtedly self-
interest: peasants accepted the protection of patrons because it was in their
interests to do so.[33]

According to the modernization/participation paradigm, as one-party
states develop economically, traditional, patron/client-based politics give
way to modern, class-based politics. In the 1949 Chinese revolution, the
Communist party used political and military means to destroy the power
of the old elite and attempted to substitute for it a new class-based politics.
They succeeded in dividing communities along class lines long enough to
identify, ostracize, or eliminate relatively small numbers of landlords and
rich peasants. The party organized poor peasants to take power away from
these traditional leaders. Having taken power, however, poor peasant leaders set up a new rural bureaucracy, centralized power in the hands of local
party committees and leadership groups, and reestablished a relationship
of dependence between themselves and ordinary peasants. Thus, although
the party attempted to establish a new basis for participating in politics, it
largely failed. Patronage continued to play an important part in village affairs.[34] In the Four Clean-ups Campaign and the Cultural Revolution,
China's leaders attempted once again to replace traditional leader-mass

relations with class-based politics.[35] In the long term these campaigns became highly ritualized. They also laid factional loyalties, linking local leaders with higher-level authorities, on top of already existing local conflicts.

Politically imposed, class-based politics had an impact on the Chinese countryside, however. As Anita Chan, Richard Madsen, and Jonathan Unger make clear, leaders who demanded social and economic justice struck a responsive cord with Chen village's poor households.[36] During the 1960s and 1970s, peasants referred to themselves in terms of elite-sponsored class labels. Local authorities also distributed benefits to villagers based on class designations.

Nonetheless, for the period of my study, the basis of political participation, in spite of elite attempts to replace it, remained largely traditional. Peasants participated most effectively when they could mobilize group (kinship, community, or village) solidarity. My study indicates that the strength of group solidarity rested on several factors: (1) The group had a relatively rich resource base (fertile land, nearby markets, or cash crops), which meant that it had more to gain or to lose by collective action; (2) it existed in a geographically coterminous area, which facilitated communication and other forms of interaction; (3) it valued its collective identity, which facilitated continuing to organize; (4) it had a pre-1949 history of collective action, that is, prior experience of making demands of political authorities; (5) it had an effective leader, who defended its interests; and (6) it was confronted by a challenge to its interests, in an environment when action to defend them was possible.

Since 1980 authorities have used economic means (decollectivization) to undermine the patronage position of local leaders and to provide the basis for class-based politics. The new policies have created substantial rural income differentials, which could become the basis of new class divisions. Already authorities have reported that some poor peasants, out of envy, have confiscated the property of their newly rich neighbors, actions that may underscore the growing appeal of class-based politics.[37] China may be moving, then, toward a modern basis of political participation.

Participants

Participants in pre-1949 rural China were arranged in a bifurcated hierarchy. Nationalist party members dominated county governments, while

an entrenched local elite, mostly outside of party control, ruled in the villages. From 1927 on, the party in the cities recruited predominantly from
among intellectuals, industrialists, and merchants; in the countryside party
activists came from among landlords, rich peasants, teachers, and small
merchants.[38] Although some elements within the Guomindang attempted
to broaden the party's base in the countryside (especially in Jiangsu and
Zhejiang provinces) during these years, officials recruited relatively few
ordinary peasants into the party.

As a result of the 1949 revolution, the Communist party shifted political power in the countryside from the hands of the rural informal elite to a
new formal leadership, composed largely of party members. In contrast to
the pre-1949 situation, the party recruited the new leaders from among
the less well-to-do and the poor. Still, the qualities that peasants valued in
their village leaders remained largely unchanged.

During the past thirty years, Communist party members of peasant origin formed a substantial, although declining, proportion of all party members. In 1956, for example, 69.1 percent of party members were of peasant
origin, a figure that declined slightly in 1957, to 66.8 percent.[39] In subsequent years, especially during the early 1960s and since 1979, the party
has recruited heavily from urban areas, appealing to China's intellectuals.
Thus, since 1979, although the party has admitted 800,000 new members, it recruited only 10 percent of them from among the peasantry.[40]

Peasants have held an insignificant number of posts at higher levels
within the party, although they have done better in people's congresses.
John Lewis estimates that in 1961, for example, "very few" leaders in the
Central Committee came from worker-peasant classes.[41] Although figures
indicating the peasant composition of the Central Committee are not available, the only Politburo member whose principal occupation has been in
the countryside in recent times was Chen Yonggui.[42] In the National
People's Congress, however, peasants did better, forming 20.6 percent of
delegates in 1978[43] and, together with workers, 26.6 percent in 1983.[44]
Peasants probably made up larger percentages of delegates to provincial
and lower-level assemblies.

Peasant representation varied with the party's perception of its needs.
Authorities probably recruited most heavily from among the peasantry
during the late 1940s and early 1950s, again in 1958, and during the Cul-

tural Revolution. During more moderate periods, in the mid-1950s, early 1960s, and since 1979, when leaders pursued ambitious economic development programs, peasants have entered the party in reduced numbers. Since 1984, however, authorities have mounted another recruitment campaign among the "new rich" peasantry—the principal beneficiaries of household contracting.

Less powerful than these officially recognized participants are party-recruited activists, individuals who spoke out both in support of party policy and in defense of (their) local interests. During land reform and subsequent campaigns, authorities recruited groups of supporters to help them implement party policy.[45] Visiting work teams also cultivated local activists to support their activities. These peasants took the lead in speaking out in defense of party policies and exhorting fellow villagers to carry out the measures, often irrespective of their impact on village interests.[46]

In addition to the activists who supported party policy, influential, informal village leaders acted as opinion leaders to defend village, community, kinship, or household interests. Especially during liberal periods, these informal activists sometimes attempted to influence the implementation of policies, such as by demanding adjustments to the distribution of private plots, the extension of household contracting, or the liberalization of marketing policies. The party recruited from both sorts of activists during various periods.

Some ordinary peasants participated more frequently than others. In general, males, with "good" class origins and some education, who were strong, skilled (*you nengli*), and in their working prime, participated at higher rates. Lower rates of participation occurred among women, those of "bad" class origins and with little education, and those who were unskilled, physically weak, and either too old or too young to be in their working prime. In general, during both the Republican and contemporary periods, peasants preferred middle-aged males with agricultural skills to be their leaders. Nonetheless, during the 1970s, especially as authorities industrialized the countryside, they increasingly recruited younger, more technically competent villagers for leadership posts.[47]

Peasants in rural China had substantial choices about the extent of their participation. Individuals voluntarily decided to seek party membership or to become activists. In addition, participation in the countryside, like the cities, was differentiated into "elite" and "mass" levels. The small percentage of the population who were party members participated at the highest rates. Ordinary peasants outside of the party participated at much lower rates. Further, after years of restricting participation to those of "good" class origin, since 1979 authorities have lowered the barriers and granted the rights of political participation to more and more people.

Forms

The past sixty years were characterized by significant continuities in the channels for peasants to participate in politics. Before 1949 and in recent times, villagers relied chiefly on informal means, such as contacting, to air their grievances. Peasants left leadership selection to local officials and only rarely intervened. Indeed, Martin Yang's description of a pre-1949 election in Taitou, quoted in my introduction, is remarkably similar to recent accounts provided by interviewees. Finally, when conditions deteriorated to unacceptable levels, peasants continued to resort to passive resistance or violence.

The Communist party established several new channels of participation, however, which have greatly increased its capacity to mobilize the people. The party set up a network of mass assemblies and mass organizations linking peasants to higher levels. Elite-sponsored work teams bypassed middle-level bureaucrats to facilitate policy implementation, and the officially controlled media have penetrated the country with a new thoroughness.

Both Communist and Nationalist party leaders struggled, in fits and starts, with the problem of how to expand and to institutionalize mobilized participation. The diversity of modes of participation in the countryside varied according to the needs of the leaders. As a result, there has not been a steady and uniform diversification of channels of participation.

During the early period of my study, from 1962 to 1965, China's leaders provided institutions of participation in the countryside through local assemblies, mass meetings, elections, and offices to handle letters and visits. From 1966 on, however, these channels atrophied, and peasant participation in them became increasingly ritualized. During the Cultural Revolution, the radical attack on central party and state organizations spread to local institutions in the countryside. The radical leaders in Beijing were suspicious of existing channels because they were unreliable and sometimes unresponsive to their interests. In their place, Cultural Revolution leaders set up revolutionary committees and reemphasized less institutional forms, such as writing "big-character posters" and "speaking out freely, airing views fully, and holding great debates." The Cultural Revolution, then, saw the contraction of the modes of participation dominated in 1965 by the party and state bureaucracy, and the expansion of other, "reliable" modes, such as "big-character posters." These changes had little impact on peasant political behavior, however, both because participation in them also became increasingly ritualized and because peasants throughout the period relied on more informal channels to press their interests.

More informal channels expanded or contracted according to the peasants' perception of their usefulness. During periods of intense campaign activity, peasants relied on these channels less than during more relaxed periods, when local officials could afford to be more accommodating. During the period of my study, there has not been a steady and uniform expansion of more diverse forms of informal or illegal modes of participation. Peasants have continued to rely to a greater or lesser extent on the same channels that existed before 1949, especially personal contacts, but also petty corruption, violence, and demonstrations. As the formally established channels atrophied and became increasingly ineffective, informal and illegal channels played a more significant role for peasant interest articulation.

Since 1979 authorities have revitalized and expanded the scope of formal institutions, such as local assemblies, elections, and letters and visits. At the same time, they have abolished or restricted Cultural Revolution forms, such as revolutionary committees and "big-character posters." The new agricultural policies provided households with more resources to engage in informal participation. Although authorities undoubtedly hope that peasants will resort to the revitalized formal institutions of participation, peasants are likely to continue to rely at least in part on informal channels.

The modernization/participation paradigm, then, inadequately describes the developments in rural China during the past several decades. Authorities have both expanded and contracted channels of participation during the period to suit the requirements of their remaining in power and to pursue party policies. Peasants meanwhile relied on more informal channels when they perceived them to be effective.

Constraints on Participation

In both Nationalist and Communist party-controlled China, elite and mass values, a lack of resources, and party domination have constrained the development of citizen-initiated political participation in the countryside. In pre-1949 China, although elites acknowledged the sovereign rights of the people, they decided that the people needed an extended period of "tutelage" before they could exercise self-government. In the Communist party's view, although elites should consult the people, the mass line charges leaders with initiating the process, determining its course, and producing policy outcomes, based on their world view. Further, although CCP authorities recognized that different interests exist in Chinese society, they forbade citizens from organizing to press these interests vis-à-vis party/state authority. The paternalistic attitudes of Chinese statecraft, inherited from the past, buttressed these views and fostered a respect for legitimately constituted authority.

In general, peasant values reinforced the conservative tendencies among pre- and post-1949 officials, many of whom were of peasant origin. Respect for authority and a desire to avoid conflict made open challenges to officialdom in the countryside unlikely. Peasants did not particularly value public, formal institutions of political participation. They were, however, keenly aware of their own economic interests and believed that local leaders should protect them, failing which, they could legitimately take informal, even illegal, action.

These views have not supported formal, public adversarial politics. Nor have they legitimized the formation of interest groups to make demands of party/state authority. Rather, they suggest that peasants perceived leader-initiated forms of political activity as the most legitimate. Ordinary peasants need only pursue their interests when leadership has failed, and then the activity ought to be largely informal, through individual contacts for private benefits. In this view, only as a last resort should peasants rely on more aggressive strategies.

Peasants as a group have also commanded few resources to allow them to have a significant impact on public affairs. Poverty and their low social status have deprived China's peasantry of opportunities to participate in politics. In collectivization, central authorities took control of the land—the key economic resource in the countryside. Then, through household registration and rationing policies, they took control of peasant labor. These measures have contributed to preventing peasants from accumulating sufficient economic resources to become a political force.

Although literacy rates have undoubtedly increased in rural China over the decades, 31.9 percent of the adult population in 1982 remained "illiterate or semi-literate," and most of them lived in the countryside.[48] In addition, the peasantry was scattered throughout the countryside and was geographically isolated from the centers of power. The vastness of the peasant population indicates the extent to which its interests were divided along family, production unit, community, and other lines.

The Nationalist party was much less able than the communists to organize and to control popular participation. As a result, in pre-1949 China, much political activity occurred outside of Guomindang control. This situation changed abruptly in the 1949 revolution, however, as the CCP penetrated and gained control over most rival political organizations or eliminated them.

In the countryside, although the Communist party recruited peasants with leadership skills into the party, these peasant party members have been unable to articulate the specific needs of China's peasantry. The party monopolized most forms of legitimate collective political action and prohibited citizens from organizing political groups beyond party control. The party set up mass organizations with an exclusively peasant membership, such as the poor and lower-middle peasants' associations, to mobilize the peasantry. These organizations have not served peasant interests independently of the party, however. Finally, through its control of the media, the party controlled to a large extent the dissemination of political information, which precluded peasants from using this channel for making autonomous demands. In general, then, peasants have had neither the inclination nor the resources to become active articulators of their own interests.

If political efficacy means the perceived effectiveness of an individual or group in formal political institutions, then during the past several decades ordinary Chinese peasants have been largely ineffective.[49] In the late 1960s and 1970s, as participation became increasingly ritualized, peasant apathy was at least partly a consequence of the ineffectiveness of formal institutions. The belief that formal participation had little meaning only reinforced the tendency of peasants to seek informal solutions.

Trends and Prospects

Since 1949 Chinese authorities have created a strong and centralized party/state, collectivized the economy, and propagated norms that, though they require mass activism in policy implementation, value "correctness" more than participation in the formulation of policy. In spite of their weak position, peasants have sometimes challenged political authority and occasionally have won limited victories. Although leaders during the Cultural Revolution trumpeted conformity and viewed with disdain individual or small group claims on the party/state, peasants continued to be sensitive to, and to defend, their own and their community's interests.

Peasants engaged the state on largely economic issues. They resisted attempts by authorities to expand the scope of the collective economy and to restrict distribution through markets. They protested high levels of accumulation and relatively low levels of state investment in agriculture. They evaded birth control policies when they were introduced, and, in violation of state policies designed to keep peasants in the villages, they sometimes sought job opportunities in the towns and cities. Wealthier and more skilled rural households protested against policies designed to prevent a polarization of incomes. Generally, the peasants responded to elite initiatives.

Through the party's rural organization policies, authorities provided peasants with the means to react. By organizing China's villagers into units that were both residential and production-based, officials consolidated group or community interests. From time to time, peasants drew on these resources to challenge political authority. For the most part, communes, brigades, and teams were staffed by locals, who were already embedded in networks of personal relations within the community. This facilitated relatively easy and informal contacting. Power was centralized in the hands of a party secretary, which facilitated mobilization. Finally, and least significantly, the regulations governing the operation of local units required mass participation in decision making. Local leaders who wished to consult other villagers as they made decisions could look to the regulations for support.

Institutions, such as local assemblies, mass organizations, elections, and letters to the editor, have all had a heavily mobilizational character. Elites used these channels to inform or to educate and to encourage peasants to implement party/state policy. Even in these forums, however, peasants have occasionally taken the initiative to influence the course of public affairs. Local leaders sometimes solicited the opinions of peasants when they disagreed among themselves on a policy or on how it ought to be implemented. Still, it is likely that peasants preferred more informal institutions of participation and, in particular, relied more often on individual contacts to secure particular benefits.

Peasants addressed authorities about deeply felt grievances through visits to their offices or by means of petitions or posters. When these means failed, they sometimes resorted to quasi-legal or illegal strategies, such as bribery, demonstrations, or violence.

Peasants have been effective when they could mobilize group solidarity, whether based on kinship, community, or village loyalties, to confront unpopular policies. They were also more effective where they could exploit divisions among local leaders; where they could ally themselves with local leaders to protest against the policies of higher-level authorities; or where they could ally themselves with higher-level leaders to demand local changes. In different circumstances, peasants have used each of these strategies.

Local leaders played a pivotal role in this process. The party/state charged them with the implementation of its policies and the protection of its (wider) interests. Villagers expected them to guard against the encroachment of outsiders (including the party/state and surrounding communities) and to uphold local interests. When the demands of higher-level political authorities became too great, local leaders often sided with their friends, relatives, and neighbors. They played a crucial role in the organization of peasant-initiated participation, and without them it would have been impossible.

Citizen-initiated action to influence the implementation of policy is significant, especially when policy making is incremental and when the outcome of political struggles depends largely on the success or failure of policy. During the Maoist era, authorities made major decisions, such as

collectivizing agriculture and setting up communes, that departed radically from past practice. They justified them and implemented them, in
part, by relying more on the leader's personality cult and less on results.

In the post-Mao era, however, authorities took incremental decisions to
decollectivize agriculture. They relied increasingly on results to stay in
power. In this environment, peasant-initiated political participation has
had a significant, if indirect, impact on the policy process. By cooperating
with authorities or enthusiastically implementing policy (as with household contracting), peasants provided reformers in Beijing with the am-
munition to maintain and extend the reformist course. In addition, the
peasants' lack of enthusiasm for Cultural Revolution policies undoubtedly
contributed to the reevaluation of those measures in the late 1970s.

An indication of the relative weakness of peasants vis-à-vis the party/
state was their inability to prevent collectivization or, when it occurred, to
decollectivize agriculture sooner. The weaknesses of the peasantry as a
force in Chinese politics stem from many sources: its conservatism; its limited resources and economic dependence on local leaders; its relative deprivation; and its lack of cohesion, except on a small group or community
basis.

Paradoxically, authorities have both strengthened and weakened the latent power of the peasantry in contemporary China. Post-Mao reforms,
which put more resources in the hands of peasant households and reduced
their dependence on village leaders, have strengthened the political position of the peasantry. Rural incomes have grown substantially, which has
reduced the rural/urban gap. Still, the size of the peasantry as a group is
declining. By the hundreds of thousands, villagers have responded to post-
Mao reforms and moved into the towns and cities to take up urban occupations. Thus, the latent political power of the peasantry is weakening,
while the strength and political significance of China's urban centers are
increasing.

APPENDIX

In the preparation of this manuscript, I have used official sources to make a preliminary identification of the issues and participation strategies. For the period considered here, however, a rich provincial press has only been available outside of China from 1962 to 1965 and again since 1979. In addition to the national and regional press, I have canvassed as many of these provincial presses as possible. Although there is considerable regional variation within China, I have found greater similarities than differences in the reportage of issues and strategies. Where the sources differ, however, I have brought them to the reader's attention.

To supplement the press reports, I have relied on interviews with former residents of rural China, most of them from South China's Guangdong and Fujian provinces. These interviews were designed to check the reliability of the press data and, especially, to determine the extent of variation in the implementation of policies articulated in the national press. In the first set of interviews, conducted from May 1975 to October 1976 at the Universities Service Center in Hong Kong, I questioned twenty-five informants, all but three of whom were from Guangdong (the others, one each, were from suburban Shanghai, Xinjiang, and Shanxi). Half of the group were urban middle-school graduates, rusticated from Guangzhou to the Guangdong countryside in 1964 or 1968, during two successive *xiafang* campaigns. Another ten were former peasants, born in Guangdong villages, and the remaining three were village cadres. All of these informants arrived in Hong Kong before 1974, mostly as illegal immigrants or as "refugees."

From June to September 1982, I conducted a second set of interviews in Hong Kong to update the study. The group was composed of eleven former residents of rural China, most of them from Fujian (and one each from Guangdong, Yunnan, suburban Shanghai, and Xinjiang). Most of the second group had some experience as schoolteachers or village officials. There were only two rusticated youths and one peasant among them. Unlike the first group, all of the second group arrived in Hong Kong legally from 1978 to 1981. That is, none of the second group were "refugees," an important difference.

I recruited candidates for interviews for the 1975–1976 study through personal contacts in the "refugee" community in Hong Kong. I contacted the 1982 group through advertisements placed in local newspapers. I paid informants by the hour for each three-hour session, which in some cases extended over fifteen sessions. I did all of the interviewing myself, although a Cantonese-Mandarin translator was present for interviews with exclusively Cantonese-speaking informants. Detailed transcripts were kept of each interview, and it is from these transcripts that data for this study are drawn. Copies of the transcripts may be obtained from me directly. I have also deposited the transcripts in Columbia University's East Asian Library.

I asked each informant to complete a personal background data sheet before I began a series of open-ended questions designed to elicit information on local leadership, campaigns, meeting styles and content, local issues, and other topics. The questions were designed to produce factual information about events and procedures. Although I did not probe the attitudes or feelings of interviewees, it became obvious that many of the first group of "refugees" had negative feelings about their experiences in China, from which they had fled. These attitudes were in stark contrast to the much more positive attitudes held by the 1982 group, all legal immigrants to Hong Kong, who regularly traveled back and forth between Hong Kong and the Chinese interior.

I tried to eliminate the effects of biasing by asking only factual questions about which there was no obvious "correct" answer (Was there such and such a campaign in your area? When did it take place? How did it start?). Each interviewee's information was checked for internal consistency and with the other sources of data, such as the press. It was occasionally possible to verify information by checking it with other informants from the same area. More rigorous verification was usually not possible, but the fabrication of information over an extended series of interviews would have been extremely difficult without obvious contradictions. After several years of experience of interviewing in Hong Kong, I am confident of the reliability of the data presented here. In general, the different data sources used in this study are consistent, complementing and reinforcing each other. Where contradictions among the data sources occur, however, I have drawn them to the reader's attention in the text.

An additional source of data might have been interviews with peasants and cadres carried out in China, but interviewing in China has its own problems. Participant-observers become part of the village situation, and answers to questions are given accordingly. Insofar as powerful outsiders accompany researchers to village sites, and observers befriend members of different factions or lineages within the village, peasant and local cadre co-operation is modified to suit their ongoing relationships and obligations within and without the village. Interviewing in Hong Kong has the advantage of catching interviewees after they have left this network of relationships. It has other problems, however, which I have acknowledged here.

I have adopted the following notation to identify the interviewees: "NM" is "peasant"; "CN" is "sent-down youth" interviewed in 1975–1976; "NCN" is "sent-down youth" interviewed in 1982; "KB" is "cadre" interviewed in 1975–1976; "NKP" is "cadre" interviewed in 1982; "T" is "teacher" interviewed in 1975–1976; and "NT" is "teacher" interviewed in 1982. After the prefix, I gave each individual interviewee belonging to the category a number. For the 1975–1976 interviews, a further letter, ranging in alphabetical order, identifies the date of the interview session. This is followed by the page number of the transcript. For the 1982 interviews, I have used the date of the interview, rather than a code. In each case, I have identified the province where the interviewee lived in the countryside.

LIST OF ABBREVIATIONS

CQ	*The China Quarterly*
FBIS	Foreign Broadcast Information Service. *Daily Report: People's Republic of China* or *Daily Report: Communist China*. Washington, D.C.: U.S. Department of Commerce.
JAS	*Journal of Asian Studies*
JPRS	Joint Publications Research Service. *China Report: Political, Sociological, and Military Affairs, Translations on Communist China,* and *Red Flag*. Washington, D.C.: U.S. Department of Commerce.
Lianjiang Documents	C.S. Chen and Charles Price Ridley, *Rural People's Communes in Lien-chiang*. Stanford, Calif.: Hoover Institution for the Study of War and Peace, 1969.
NCNA	New China News Agency
NFRB	*Nanfang Ribao* [Southern Daily]. Guangzhou.
NPCRS	*News from Provincial Chinese Radio Stations*. Hong Kong: British Information Service.
RMRB	*Renmin Ribao* [People's Daily]. Beijing.
SCMM	*Selections from China Mainland Magazines*. Hong Kong: U.S. Consulate General.
SCMP	*Survey of China Mainland Press*. Hong Kong: U.S. Consulate General.
SWB	*Summary of World Broadcasts, Far East*. London: British Broadcasting Corporation.

NOTES

Chapter 1

1. See D. Richard Little, "Mass Political Participation in the U.S. and the U.S.S.R.," *Comparative Political Studies* 8, no. 4 (Jan. 1976): 449–51; Theodore H. Friedgut, *Political Participation in the USSR* (Princeton: Princeton University Press, 1979), p. 16. See also Merilee S. Grindle, ed., *Politics and Policy Implementation in the Third World* (Princeton: Princeton University Press, 1980), p. 15, for the importance of policy implementation and its significance for political participation in Third World countries. The "process of implementing public policies is a focus of political participation" in Third World countries because of "characteristics of the political systems themselves, such as the remoteness and inaccessibility of the policymaking process to most individuals and the extensive competition engendered by widespread need and very scarce resources" (Grindle, p. 15). The importance of the implementation process is increasingly realized by students of Chinese politics, e.g., David M. Lampton, ed., *Policy Implementation in Post-Mao China* (Berkeley and Los Angeles: University of California Press, 1987).

2. Recent studies of rural Chinese politics and society include William Parish and Martin King Whyte, *Village and Family in Contemporary China* (Chicago: University of Chicago Press, 1978); Anita Chan, Richard Madsen, and Jonathan Unger, *Chen Village* (Berkeley and Los Angeles: University of California Press, 1984); and Richard Madsen, *Morality and Power in a Chinese Village* (Berkeley and Los Angeles: University of California Press, 1984).

3. See James R. Townsend, *Political Participation in Communist China* (Berkeley and Los Angeles: University of California Press, 1969), chaps. 5 and 6, which identifies people's congresses, elections, legal organs, democratic parties, mass organizations, and local residential and production units. Marc Blecher, "Leader-Mass Relations in Rural Chinese Communities" (Ph.D. dissertation, University of Chicago, 1978), identifies meetings, informal discussions, local grapevines, contacting, big-character posters, mass organizations, local elections, interviews with visiting officials, and work and investigation teams. Tony Saich, "Workers in the Workers' State," in David S. G. Goodman, ed., *Groups and Politics in the People's Republic of China* (Armonk: M. E. Sharpe, 1984), pp. 159–69, identifies workers'

congresses, trade unions, elections, and the party. Victor C. Falkenheim, "Political Participation in China," *Problems of Communism* 27 (May–June 1978): 22–25, includes quasi-legal modes, with written forms, meetings, elections, and lobbying.

4. Studies devoted wholly or in part to political participation in contemporary China include James R. Townsend, *Political Participation in Communist China* (Berkeley and Los Angeles: University of California Press, 1969); Andrew J. Nathan, *Chinese Democracy* (New York: Alfred Knopf, 1985); John Gardner, "Political Participation and Chinese Communism," in Geraint Parry, ed., *Participation in Politics* (Manchester: University of Manchester Press, 1972), pp. 218–45; Lucian Pye, "Mass Participation in Communist China," in John Lindbeck, ed., *China: Management of a Revolutionary Society* (Seattle: University of Washington Press, 1971), pp. 3–33; Victor C. Falkenheim, "Political Participation in China," *Problems of Communism* 27 (May–June 1978): 18–32; Falkenheim, ed., *Citizens and Groups in Chinese Politics* (Ann Arbor: University of Michigan China Monograph Series, 1987); Charles Hoffmann, "Worker Participation in Chinese Factories," *Modern China* 3 (July 1977): 291–320; Stephen Andors, *China's Industrial Revolution* (New York: Pantheon Books, 1977); Martin Lockett and Craig R. Littler, "Trends in Enterprise Management, 1978–82" (paper prepared for the Conference on China in Transition, Queen Elizabeth House, Oxford, Sept. 7–10, 1982); Andrew Watson, "Industrial Management—Experiments in Mass Participation," in Bill Brugger, ed., *China* (London: Croom-Helm, 1978), pp. 171–202; Andrew Walder, "Participative Management and Worker Control in China," *Sociology of Work and Occupations* 8, no. 2 (May 1981): 224–52; Walder, "Some Ironies of the Maoist Legacy in Industry," in Mark Selden and Victor Lippitt, eds., *The Transition to Socialism in China* (Armonk, N.Y.: M. E. Sharpe, 1982), pp. 215–37; William Brugger, *Democracy and Organization in the Chinese Industrial Enterprise, 1948–53* (Cambridge: Cambridge University Press, 1976); Tony Saich, "Workers in the Workers' State," in Goodman, ed., *Groups and Politics,* pp. 152–75; James Cotton, "Intellectuals as a Group in the Chinese Political Process," in Goodman, ed., *Groups and Politics,* pp. 176–96; David G. Strand, "Reform of Political Participation" (paper prepared for the Conference on Reform of the Chinese Political Order, Harwichport, Mass., June 18–23, 1984); Marc Blecher, "Consensual Politics in Rural Chinese Communities," *Modern China* 5, no. 1 (Jan. 1979): 105–26; Blecher, "Leader-Mass Relations in Rural Chinese Communities" (Ph.D. dissertation, University of Chicago, 1978); Brantly Womack, "The 1980 County-Level Elections in China," *Asian Survey* 22, no. 3 (March 1982): 261–77; Barrett L. McCormick, "Election Campaign in Nanjing" (paper prepared for the 33rd Annual Meeting of the Association of Asian Studies, San Francisco, March 1983); McCormick, "Reforming the People's Congress System," in David M. Lampton, ed., *Policy Implementation in Post-Mao China* (Berkeley and Los Angeles: University of California Press, 1987); John P. Burns, "Chinese Peasant Interest Articulation," in Goodman, ed., *Groups and Politics,* pp. 126–51; and Burns, "The Election of Production Team Leaders in Rural China, 1958–74," *CQ* 74 (June 1978): 273–96.

5. For a definition of "modernization," see Samuel P. Huntington, *Political Order in Changing Societies* (New Haven: Yale University Press, 1971), pp. 33−34. For the view that the political participation of workers and intellectuals will increase as one-party socialist states evolve, see Huntington, "Social and Institutional Dynamics of One-Party Systems," in Huntington and Clement H. Moore, eds., *Authoritarian Politics in Modern Society* (New York: Basic Books, 1970), pp. 3−47; Huntington and Joan Nelson, *No Easy Choice* (Cambridge, Mass.: Harvard University Press, 1976), chap. 3; Myron Weiner, "Political Participation," in Leonard Binder et al., eds., *Crises and Sequences in Political Development* (Princeton: Princeton University Press, 1971), pp. 159−204; Donald E. Schulz, "On the Nature and Function of Participation in Communist Systems," in Schulz and Jan S. Adams, eds., *Political Participation in Communist Systems* (New York: Pergamon Press, 1981), pp. 26−78. See Lucian Pye, "Mass Participation in Communist China," in John M. H. Lindbeck, ed., *China: Management of a Revolutionary Society* (Seattle: University of Washington Press, 1971), pp. 3−33, for a discussion of the impact of participation on modernization. See also Friedgut, *Political Participation in the USSR*, p. 290−97, for a discussion of the link between modernization and participation in the Soviet Union.

6. Hsiao Kung-chuan, *Rural China* (Seattle: University of Washington Press, 1972), p. 264.

7. For general accounts of elite-level politics during the Nationalist era, see Lloyd E. Eastman, *The Abortive Revolution* (Cambridge, Mass.: Harvard University Press, 1974), and Eastman, *Seeds of Destruction* (Stanford: Stanford University Press, 1984).

8. Bradley K. Geisert, "Power and Society" (Ph.D. dissertation, University of Virginia, 1979), p. 167.

9. Philip A. Kuhn, "Local Self-Government Under the Republic," in Frederic Wakeman, Jr., and Carolyn Grant, eds., *Conflict and Control in Late Imperial China* (Berkeley and Los Angeles: University of California Press, 1975), pp. 282−87.

10. See Ch'ien Tuan-sheng, *The Government and Politics of China, 1912−1949* (Stanford: Stanford University Press, 1970), pp. 133−36; Robert E. Bedeski, *State-Building in Modern China* (Berkeley: University of California China Research Monograph, 1981), pp. 153−71. On local self-government, see H. G. W. Woodhead, ed., *The China Yearbook, 1929−1930* (Tianjin: Tianjin Press, 1930), p. 1215.

11. Geisert, "Power and Society," p. 180.

12. Kuhn, "Local Self-Goverment," p. 286.

13. For definitions of "local elite," see Geisert, "Power and Society," p. 9; Kuhn, "Local Self-Government," pp. 287−93; and Lenore Barkan, "Nationalists, Communists, and Rural Leaders" (Ph.D. dissertation, University of Washington, 1983), pp. 369−71.

14. See also Guy S. Alitto, "Rural Elites in Transition," in Susan Mann Jones, ed., *Select Papers from the Center for Far Eastern Studies, 1978−1979*, no. 3 (Chi-

cago: University of Chicago, 1979). Alitto has characterized those who "virtually monopolized" local self-government during this period as a "symbiotic coalition of bandits, militarists, officials, functionaries, landlords and local bullies and evil gentry" (p. 225).

15. Geisert, "Power and Society," p. 181.

16. Ibid., p. 183.

17. Philip Huang, *The Peasant Economy and Social Change in North China* (Stanford: Stanford University Press, 1985), p. 238.

18. See Sidney D. Gamble, *North China Villages* (Berkeley and Los Angeles: University of California Press, 1963), pp. 41–42. See the list of qualifications for village leadership established by the Guomindang (p. 52): candidates must be at least 25 years of age and have performed at least one of the following: "Passed civil examinations; served the Kuomintang [Guomindang]; served the Nationalist government as an officer of the fourth rank; taught in a primary school or graduated from a middle school; taken training in self-government; and had a record of service in the local hsien [*xian*] government," (ibid., p. 52).

19. Geisert indicates that elections for these positions were held in Jiangsu ("Power and Society," pp. 183–84).

20. Gamble, *North China Villages,* p. 42. In North China, various methods were used to choose official village leaders: rotation, drawing lots, nomination, or self-appointment. Where the post was rotated (common, e.g., in Shanxi), power was shared among the village elite. In most cases, leaders served for indefinite terms (ibid., pp. 4, 33, 55, 57, 60, 187, 199, 268).

21. Martin C. Yang, *A Chinese Village* (New York: Columbia University Press, 1965), pp. 175–76.

22. Ibid., p. 179.

23. Huang, *The Peasant Economy,* p. 240.

24. Geisert, "Power and Society," pp. 181–85. See M. C. Yang's statement: "In spite of these changes [the implementation of village elections], the official leaders in Taitou are still essentially of the old category and function in the old manner" (*A Chinese Village,* p. 174).

25. Ch'u T'ung-tsu, *Local Government in China Under the Ch'ing* (Stanford: Stanford University Press, 1969), pp. 176, 182, 184–85.

26. Huang, *The Peasant Economy,* p. 237.

27. Hsiao, *Rural China,* pp. 72 and 264.

28. Evelyn S. Rawski, *Education and Popular Literacy in Ch'ing China* (Ann Arbor: University of Michigan Press, 1979), pp. 5, 14, 18, 23. See also Gamble, *North China Villages,* p. 108.

29. Rawski, *Education and Popular Literacy,* p. 3.

30. See Hsiao, *Rural China,* pp. 154–65, who argues that during the late nineteenth century the gentry and not "ordinary peasants" petitioned the authorities. See Barkan, "Nationalists, Communists and Rural Leaders," p. 309, for an example of petitioning in 1930.

31. See, e.g., Gamble, *North China Villages,* pp. 246–47; William Hinton, *Fanshen* (New York: Vintage Press, 1966), p. 52, writes of the situation in Long Bow: "So ruinous were court cases that most families avoided them like the plague." Still, in other places, a "tradition" of litigation existed. See, e.g., Barkan, "Nationalists, Communists, and Rural Leaders," p. 220.

32. Gamble, *North China Villages,* pp. 199–200.

33. Elizabeth J. Perry, *Rebels and Revolutionaries in North China, 1845–1945* (Stanford: Stanford University Press, 1980), p. 80.

34. Geisert, "Power and Society," pp. 225–26.

35. Lucien Bianco, "Peasant Movements," in John K. Fairbank and Albert Feuerwerker, eds., *The Cambridge History of China,* vol. 13, part 2 (Cambridge: Cambridge University Press, 1986), pp. 280–81.

36. For CCP organizing prior to 1927, see Roy Hofheinz, *The Broken Wave* (Cambridge, Mass.: Harvard University Press, 1977), pp. 67–138. For the organization structure of the post-1927 associations, see Hsiao Tso-liang, *The Land Revolution in China, 1930–1934* (Seattle: University of Washington Press, 1969), pp. 170–86.

37. Chen Yung-fa, "Rural Elections in Wartime Central China," *Modern China* 6, no. 3 (July 1980): 267–310; Mark Selden, *The Yenan Way in Revolutionary China* (Cambridge, Mass.: Harvard University Press, 1971); Brantly Womack, *The Foundations of Mao Zedong's Political Thought, 1917–1935* (Honolulu: University of Hawaii Press, 1982); Chen Yung-fa, *Making Revolution* (Berkeley and Los Angeles: University of California Press, 1986).

38. Huang, *The Peasant Economy,* pp. 220, 234.

39. Ibid., pp. 258–74.

40. The evidence is reviewed in Jack Potter, "Land and Lineage in Traditional China," in Maurice Freedman, ed., *Family and Kinship in Chinese Society* (Stanford: Stanford University Press, 1970), p. 130. See also Maurice Freedman, *Chinese Lineage and Society* (London: Athlone Press, 1971).

41. Rawski, *Education and Popular Literacy,* p. 87.

42. Huang, *The Peasant Economy,* p. 233; Gamble, *North China Villages,* p. 315.

43. Potter, "Land and Lineage," pp. 127, 129, 130.

44. Ibid., pp. 132–36.

45. Ibid., p. 131. See Rawski, *Education and Popular Literacy,* p. 85.

46. Huang, *The Peasant Economy,* pp. 238, 260; and M. C. Yang, *A Chinese Village,* p. 241.

47. See, e.g., Gamble, *North China Villages,* p. 55.

48. M. C. Yang, *A Chinese Village,* p. 176.

49. Isabel and David Crook, *Ten Mile Inn* (New York: Pantheon, 1979), p. 76.

50. Andrew J. Nathan, *Chinese Democracy* (New York: Alfred Knopf, 1985), pp. 107–12.

51. For definitions of political participation, see Sidney Verba and Norman H. Nie, *Participation in America* (New York: Harper and Row, 1977), pp. 2–3; Her-

bert McClosky, "Political Participation," in *International Encyclopedia of the Social Sciences,* vol. 11 (New York: Macmillan, 1968), p. 252. (See the select bibliography for additional references.) See also Myron Weiner, "Political Participation," in Leonard Binder, et al., eds., *Crises and Sequences in Political Development* (Princeton: Princeton University Press, 1971), p. 165; Robert H. Salisbury, "Research on Political Participation," *American Journal of Political Science* 19, no. 2 (1975): 323–41; Huntington and Nelson, *No Easy Choice,* pp. 4–10. For general studies of the problem of conceptualizing political participation in communist systems, see Robert S. Sharlet, "Concept Formation in Political Science and Communist Studies," in Frederic J. Fleron, ed., *Communist Studies and the Social Sciences* (Chicago: Rand McNally, 1969), pp. 244–53; and Donald E. Schulz, "Political Participation in Communist Systems," in Schulz and Jan S. Adams, eds., *Political Participation in Communist Systems* (New York: Pergamon Press, 1981), pp. 1–25.

52. See Marc Blecher, "Leader-Mass Relations," e.g., which omits any discussion of passive resistance or other illegitimate strategies. Hoffmann, Andors, and Saich (see n. 4) restrict their comments to legal and legitimate (or "sanctioned") channels of participation. Although more general accounts by Townsend, Pye, and Gardner (see n. 4) do not explicitly exclude these activities, they omit any discussion of them.

53. Townsend, *Political Participation,* pp. 4–5. See also John A. Booth, "Political Participation in Latin America," *Latin American Research Review* 14, no. 3 (1979): 31–32, who argues that political participation is "behavior influencing or attempting to influence the distribution of public goods." "Public goods" consist of "special kinds of collective goods supplied by governments or by communities through their collective expenditure." Thus, Booth argues, communities also supply public goods, even though they lack formal governments.

54. See Townsend, *Political Participation,* p. 173. According to Townsend, this behavior is related more to the affairs of "small economic and social units that are not part of the formal government structure." Apparently agreeing, Hoffmann, Walder, Andors, Saich, and Lockett and Littler (see n. 4), also discuss the activities of workers' congresses as cases of "worker participation" or "mass participation," not as "political participation."

55. See Huntington and Nelson, *No Easy Choice,* pp. 132–34; and Verba and Nie, *Participation in America,* p. 52.

56. See Salisbury, "Research on Political Participation," p. 325.

57. See the excessively inclusive formulation adopted by Friedgut. Political participation is "the involvement of citizens in any activities relating to public affairs" (*Political Participation in the USSR,* p. 19).

58. Alex Pravda, "Elections in Communist Party States," in Guy Hermet et al., eds., *Elections Without Choice* (London: Macmillan, 1978), pp. 169–95.

59. See, e.g., McClosky, "Political Participation," p. 252; Weiner, "Political Participation," p. 164; Friedgut, *Political Participation in the USSR,* p. 20; and Townsend, *Political Participation,* pp. 4–5.

60. Thomas P. Bernstein, "Leadership and Mobilization in the Collectivization

of Agriculture in China and Russia" (Ph.D. dissertation, Columbia University, 1970), pp. 11–12.

61. Samuel L. Popkin, *The Rational Peasant* (Berkeley and Los Angeles: University of California Press, 1979). Popkin points out: "By rationality I mean that individuals evaluate the possible outcomes associated with their choices in accordance with their preferences and values. In doing this, they discount the evaluation of each outcome in accordance with their subjective estimate of the likelihood of the outcome. Finally, they make the choice which they believe will maximize their expected utility" (p. 31). See also Joel Migdal, *Peasants, Politics, and Revolution* (Princeton: Princeton University Press, 1974), pp. 210–21.

62. Popkin, *The Rational Peasant,* p. 31.

63. See Madsen, *Morality and Power in a Chinese Village.*

64. Vivienne Shue, *Peasant China in Transition* (Berkeley and Los Angeles: University of California Press, 1980), p. 190. Those peasants who did less well in land reform, however, soon began to evidence what Shue calls "the old, radical, egalitarian, expropriationist syndrome."

65. Shue, *Peasant China in Transition,* pp. 176–77.

66. See Bernstein, "Leadership and Mobilization."

67. Xinhua, Feb. 22, 1983, in FBIS, *Daily Report: People's Republic of China* (Washington, D.C.: U.S. Department of Commerce) 37 (Feb. 23, 1983): K33. In 1984 authorities reported that 73.72 percent of China's labor force was employed in "agriculture, animal husbandry, forestry, and fishing." See also *Beijing Review* 20 (May 1984): 25.

68. The national media include newspapers, such as *Renmin Ribao* (*RMRB*), and periodicals, such as *Hongqi* and *Jingji Guanli.* Since 1979 some provincial papers from South China have been available, e.g., *Nanfang Ribao* (*NFRB*), *Sichuan Ribao, Fujian Ribao,* and *Xinhua Ribao.* Other provincial sources are included in the *Nongye Jingji* volume of the Zhongguo renmin daxue shubao cailiao she collection (Chinese People's University Book and Newspaper Materials Society). The English translation serials include Foreign Broadcast Information Service (FBIS), *Daily Report: People's Republic of China* or *Daily Report: Communist China* (Washington, D.C.: U.S. Department of Commerce); *Survey of China Mainland Press* (*SCMP*) (Hong Kong: U.S. Consulate General); Joint Publications Research Service (JPRS), *China Report: Political, Sociological, and Military Affairs, Translations on Communist China,* and *Red Flag* (Washington, D.C.: U.S. Department of Commerce); *Summary of World Broadcasts, Far East* (*SWB*) (London: British Broadcasting Corporation); and *News from Provincial Chinese Radio Stations* (*NPCRS*) (Hong Kong: British Information Service).

69. C. S. Chen and Charles Price Ridley, *Rural People's Communes in Lien-chiang* (Lianjiang Documents) (Stanford: Hoover Institution, 1969); *Baoan Bulletin,* trans. in Union Research Service, vol. 27, nos. 7, 8, 9 (April 24, April 27, and May 1, 1962) (Hong Kong: Union Research Institute).

70. Jack Potter, "The Economic and Social Consequences of Changes in China's Rural Economic Policies, 1978–1981"; Greg O'Leary and Andrew Watson, "The

Production Responsibility System and the Future of Collective Farming," *Australian Journal of Chinese Affairs* 8 (1982): 1–34; David Zweig, "Opposition to Change in Rural China," *Asian Survey* 23, no. 7 (July 1983): 879–900; Zweig, "Peasants and the New Incentive System," in William Parish, ed., *Chinese Rural Development* (Armonk: M. E. Sharpe, 1985), pp. 141–63; Helen Siu, "The Nature of Encapsulation" (paper prepared for the Workshop on Recent Reforms in China, Cambridge, Mass.: Harvard University, April 30, 1983); Graham E. Johnson, "The Production Responsibility System in Chinese Agriculture," *Pacific Affairs* 55 (1983): 430–51.

Chapter 2

1. The two characters *minzhu* first appeared in the classical *Shujing* (Book of history), where they meant both "the ruler of the people" and "the people as masters." See Yan Jiaji, "Minzhu shi yi zhong guojia xingshi" [Democracy is a state form] in *Minzhu Wenti Jianghua* [Talks on the question of democracy] (Beijing: Qunzhong chubanshe, 1980), p. 14. The modern usage of *minzhu*, which equates it with the Western concept of "democracy," reentered Chinese from Japanese. See Li Yuning, *The Introduction of Socialism Into China* (New York: Columbia University Press, 1971), p. 81. I am grateful to Andrew Nathan for drawing this to my attention.

2. Wu Jialin, "Some Questions Concerning Socialist Democracy," *Beijing Review* 24 (June 15, 1979): 9–13, in Brantly Womack, ed., "Electoral Reform in China," *Chinese Law and Government* 15, nos. 3–4 (Fall-Winter 1982–1983): 96.

3. These "four principles," are explicitly mentioned in each of China's post-1949 state constitutions.

4. See Wu Jialin, "Some Questions," pp. 96–97.

5. *Hongqi* 9 (May 1, 1982), in JPRS 81379, July 28, 1982, p. 33.

6. Mao Zedong, "Talk at an Enlarged Working Conference Convened by the Central Committee of the Communist Party of China, January 30, 1962," in Qi Xin et al., *China's New Democracy* (Hong Kong: Cosmos Books, 1979), p. 253.

7. Special Commentator, "Uphold the Correct Orientation of Socialist Democracy," *RMRB*, Jan. 18, 1980, in Womack, "Electoral Reform," p. 100.

8. See Mao Zedong, "On the Correct Handling of Contradictions Among the People," *Selected Readings from the Works of Mao Tse-tung* (Beijing: Foreign Languages Press, 1967), p. 353.

9. Ibid., p. 353. The state is defined as a "people's democratic dictatorship" in the 1954 and 1982 state constitutions. The 1975 and 1978 state constitutions refer to the state as a "dictatorship of the proletariat." These are now seen as the same in the official view.

10. See the 1953 election law in Theodore H. E. Chen, ed., *The Chinese Communist Regime* (New York: Praeger, 1967), pp. 65–75.

11. See "Decision of the Central Committee of the Chinese Communist Party

Concerning the Great Proletarian Cultural Revolution," Aug. 8, 1966, in *Peking Review* 33 (Aug. 12, 1966): 6.

12. The ultra-leftist perspective is drawn from Hunan Provincial Proletarian Revolutionary Great Alliance Committee (Sheng wu lian), "Whither China?" reprinted in *The Revolution is Dead, Long Live the Revolution* (Hong Kong: The Seventies, n.d.), pp. 180–200.

13. Ibid., pp. 183, 188.

14. This view was also held by the more moderate Li Yizhe poster writers, in "Concerning Socialist Democracy and Legal System," reprinted in *The Revolution is Dead, Long Live the Revolution*, pp. 249–83.

15. Hunan Provincial Alliance, "Whither China?" p. 198.

16. During this period, Mao openly denigrated such procedures as elections as meaningless. See John Bryan Starr, *Continuing the Revolution* (Princeton: Princeton University Press, 1979), p. 212.

17. Hunan Provincial Alliance, "Whither China?" p. 199.

18. For a discussion of the Li Yizhe poster, see Susan L. Shirk, "Going Against the Tide," *Survey* 24, no. 1 (Winter 1979): 82–97; and Stanley Rosen, "Guangzhou's Democracy Movement in Cultural Revolution Perspective," *CQ* 101 (March 1985): 1–31.

19. *April 5 Forum*, April 1, 1979, in JPRS 73987 (Aug. 9, 1979): 21. See *Peking Spring*, Jan. 27, 1979, in JPRS 73421 (May 10, 1979): 15. Wang Xizhe held the same view in *Mao Zedong and the Cultural Revolution* (Hong Kong: Plough Publications, 1981), p. 29.

20. *April 5 Forum*, April 1, 1979, in JPRS 73987: 21; *Exploration*, March 11, 1979, in JPRS 73421: 33; and Li Yizhe, "Concerning Socialist Democracy and Legal System," p. 255.

21. *April 5 Forum*, Dec. 10, 1978, in JPRS 73787 (June 29, 1979): 17.

22. *Peking Spring*, Jan. 9, 1979, in JPRS 73421: 1.

23. See Li Yizhe, "Concerning Socialist Democracy," p. 255, and Liu Qing, "Prison Notes," trans. in *Spearhead* 14/15 (Summer/Autumn 1982): 39–40.

24. April 1, 1979, in JPRS 73987: 5. Similar views were expressed by *Exploration*, Dec. 1978, in JPRS 73756: 22; *Enlightenment*, Jan. 1, 1979, in JPRS 73215 (April 12, 1979): 45; and the Li Yizhe poster writers, in Rosen, "Guangzhou's Democracy Movement," pp. 3–12.

25. *April 5 Forum*, Nov. 1978, reprinted in *Dalu Dixia Kanwu Huibian* (Collection of underground publications from the Chinese mainland), vol. 1 (Taibei: Institute for the Study of Chinese Communist Problems, 1980), p. 43.

26. Li Yizhe, "Concerning Socialist Democracy," p. 228.

27. *April 5 Forum*, March 11, 1979, in JPRS 73922 (July 27, 1979): 24.

28. *Exploration*, Jan. 29, 1979, in JPRS 73787: 32.

29. Ibid., Dec. 1978, in JPRS 73756: 17.

30. Ibid., Jan. 29, 1979, in JPRS 73787: 41.

31. Ibid., March 11, 1979, in JPRS 73421: 31.

32. Ibid.

33. See Nathan, *Chinese Democracy,* pp. 3–44; Chen Ruoxi, *Democracy Wall and the Unofficial Journals* (Berkeley: Center for Chinese Studies, Studies in Chinese Terminology no. 20, 1982), pp. 1–39; James Seymour, ed., *The Fifth Modernization* (Stanfordville, N.Y.: Human Rights Publishing Group, 1980), pp. 1–40; Kjeld Erick Brodsgaard, "The Democracy Movement in China, 1978–1979," *Asian Survey* 21, no. 7 (July 1981): 742–74; and Fu Po-shek, "The 'Unacknowledged Phase' of the Chinese Democractic Movement, 1980–1981" (unpublished paper, 1982).

34. Deng Xiaoping, "Speech to the Enlarged Meeting of the Politburo," Aug. 18, 1980, in FBIS 77 (April 22, 1981): W1–W14.

35. Liao Gailong, "The 1980 Reform Program of China" (part 4), in FBIS 50 (March 16, 1981): U13.

36. Liao, "1980 Reform," p. U13.

37. Sun Qimeng, "Carry Out Two Kinds of Supervision of Different Natures," *RMRB,* July 1, 1982, in FBIS 131 (July 8, 1982): K1–K4. Elections ought to be "legal, disciplined, orderly, and regular."

38. Xiao Weiyun, "The Socialist Democractic Principles of our Country's Election Law," in Womack, "Electoral Reform," p. 63. See also Zhang Qingfu and Pi Chunxie, "Revise the Electoral Laws to Institutionalize Democracy," *RMRB,* May 22, 1979, in FBIS 103 (May 25, 1979): L5–L8, which links implementing certain procedures (secret ballot, more nominations than positions, and universal suffrage) to institutionalizing democracy.

39. NCNA, Sept. 13, 1953, in *SCMP, Supplement* 651 (Sept. 16, 1953): 12.

40. *RMRB,* May 25, 1953.

41. Hu Jian, "Wealth of the People and Wealth of the Nation," *RMRB,* Feb. 1, 1983, in FBIS 25 (Feb. 4, 1983): K3.

42. Radio Jiangxi, Nov. 20, 1964, in *NPCRS* 84 (Nov. 26, 1964): 16.

43. Interview File NM1.

44. Lianjiang Documents, p. 114.

45. *RMRB,* Feb. 1, 1983, in FBIS 25 (Feb. 4, 1983): K3.

46. FBIS 77 (April 22, 1981): W11. See also *Hongqi* 2 (Jan. 16, 1982), in JPRS 80431 (March 30, 1982): 62. For an earlier statement, see also Liu Shaoqi, "Report on the Draft Constitution of the People's Republic of China (1955)," in Townsend, ed., *Political Participation,* p. 68.

47. See, e.g., *Xinhua Ribao,* June 30, 1953, in *SCMP, Supplement* 677 (July 1953): xx; *RMRB,* Nov. 15, 1953, in *SCMP* 689 (Nov. 17, 1953): 21; *RMRB,* Jan. 26, 1970, in *SCMP* 4597 (Feb. 16, 1970): 7; *Guizhou Ribao,* June 29, 1982, in FBIS 134 (July 13, 1982): Q2; and *Liaoning Ribao,* Feb. 12, 1982, in FBIS 38 (Feb. 25, 1982): S2.

48. Radio Henan, Oct. 22, 1963, in *NPCRS* 29 (Oct. 24, 1963): 4; and Radio Henan, Sept. 12, 1963, in *NPCRS* 24 (Sept. 19, 1963): 28.

49. Mao Zedong, "On the Correct Handling of Contradictions Among the People," *Selected Readings,* pp. 350–88.

50. Mao Zedong, "Analysis of the Classes in Chinese Society," *Selected Readings,* pp. 11–20. In 1978 authorities removed the class labels of "landlord" and "rich peasant" from among most villagers who had been so labeled during the 1949–1952 land reform campaign and designated them "commune members." Discrimination against them was supposed to stop. See "Regulations on the Work in Rural People's Communes (Draft for Trial Use)," Dec. 22, 1978, arts. 50, 52, in *Issues and Studies* 15, no. 9 (Sept. 1979): 111. In November 1984 authorities announced that they had concluded the program of rehabilitating landlords, rich peasants, counterrevolutionaries and "bad elements," a group that numbered 20 million from 1949 to 1984. From July 1983 to late 1984, authorities removed the "bad" labels from 28,227 landlords and 14,343 rich peasants (Xinhua, Nov. 1, 1984, in FBIS 214 [Nov. 2, 1984]: K14).

51. *RMRB,* Dec. 28, 1955, in *SCMP* 1206 (Jan. 12, 1956): 16.

52. Commentator, *RMRB,* May 20, 1982, in FBIS 101 (May 25, 1982): K101.

53. During the early 1960s, authorities acknowledged a "serious polarization" between households based on labor power, when peasants in Fujian Province experimented with household contracting (Lianjiang Documents, p. 101). See also Mark Selden, "Income Inequality and the State," in William L. Parish, ed., *Chinese Rural Development* (Armonk: M. E. Sharpe, 1985), pp. 194–203.

54. For discussions of the mass line, see Townsend, *Political Participation,* pp. 72–73; Starr, *Continuing the Revolution,* pp. 190–93; John Lewis, *Leadership in Communist China* (Ithaca: Cornell University Press, 1963), pp. 70–100; Harry Harding, "Maoist Theories of Policy-Making and Organization," in Thomas W. Robinson, ed., *The Cultural Revolution in China* (Berkeley and Los Angeles: University of California Press, 1971), pp. 117–42; Brantly Womack, *The Foundations of Mao Zedong's Political Thought, 1917–1935* (Honolulu: University of Hawaii Press, 1982), p. 61; Mark Selden, *The Yenan Way in Revolutionary China* (Cambridge, Mass.: Harvard University Press, 1971). For a recent reaffirmation of the mass line, see "Resolution on Certain Questions in the History of Our Party Since the Founding of the People's Republic of China," *Beijing Review* 27 (July 6, 1981): 10–39.

55. Mao Zedong, "Some Questions Concerning Methods of Leadership," *Selected Readings,* p. 236.

56. Zhu Tong, "Commenting on a Viewpoint of Democracy," *Beijing Ribao,* April 23, 1982, in FBIS 86 (May 4, 1982): K14. Zhu points out that democracy defined exclusively as majority rule is impossible in socialist (proletarian) China, because the working class is not in a majority in China. To adopt exclusive majority rule would give political power to the peasants, and "the authority of the workers and their political party over state leadership would come to naught."

57. Radio Wuhan, July 16, 1965, in *NPCRS* 116 (July 22, 1965): 13.

58. Mao Zedong, "Talk at an Enlarged Working Conference," p. 253.

59. Womack, *Foundations of Mao Zedong's Political Thought*, pp. 111–12; Starr, *Continuing the Revolution*, pp. 152–53.

60. Editorial, "All Power Belongs to the People," *RMRB*, Jan. 6, 1983, in FBIS 5 (Jan. 7, 1983): K2.

61. Periodic campaigns against corrupt party members, however, demonstrate that the party recognizes that *individual* party members may have their own interests.

62. See Harding, "Maoist Theories of Policy Making," p. 121.

63. See Gordon White, *The Politics of Class and Class Origin* (Canberra: Australian National University, 1976); and Richard Kraus, *Class Conflict in Chinese Socialism* (New York: Columbia University Press, 1981).

64. Mao Zedong, "Talk at an Enlarged Working Conference," p. 259.

65. See art. 86 of the 1954 state constitution; art. 14 of the 1975 state constitution, which is the most explicit; art. 18 of the 1978 state constitution; and art. 28 of the 1982 state constitution. The 1953 and 1979 election laws exclude the same categories of the population from participation.

66. The New Sixty Articles (1978), art. 50, p. 111.

67. See art. 56 of the 1954 state constitution; arts. 3 and 21 of the 1975 state constitution; art. 35 of the 1978 state constitution; and art. 97 of the 1982 state constitution.

68. See arts. 58 and 59 of the 1954 state constitution; arts. 3 and 22 of the 1975 state constitution; art. 35 of the 1978 state constitution; and arts. 99 and 101 of the 1982 state constitution.

69. See section 6 of the 1954 state constitution; section 5 of both the 1975 and 1978 state constitutions; and section 2 of the 1982 state constitution.

70. See arts. 87 and 97 of the 1954 state constitution; and arts. 34 and 40 of the 1982 state constitution. The 1975 and 1978 state constitutions added to these freedoms the freedom to "speak out freely, air views freely, hold great debates, and to write big-character posters (*dazibao*)," and the freedom of correspondence and the right to strike (arts. 13, 27, and 28 of the 1975 constitution, and art. 45 of the 1978 constitution). The 1982 constitution departed from previous constitutions by putting the section on "citizens' rights" near the front of the document, not, as traditionally, at the end.

71. Feng Shen, "Lun minzhu zhiduhua," [On democratic institutionalization]," *Sixiang Jiefang* [Thought liberation], Jan. 15, 1980, in Womack, "Electoral Reform," p. 124.

72. Sun Qimeng, "Carry Out Two Kinds of Supervision of Different Natures," *RMRB*, July 1, 1982, in FBIS 131 (July 8, 1982): K2.

73. The four great freedoms were "the right to speak out freely, air views freely, hold great debates, and write big-character posters." The 1978 state constitution was amended to delete these rights, and they do not appear in the 1982 state constitution.

74. The role of Mao Zedong during the period was ambivalent. In 1932 he felt so strongly that elections to choose leaders were necessary that, when they failed, he demanded that they be carried out again (Womack, *Foundations of Mao Zedong's Political Thought,* p. 158). He supervised the inclusion of the various freedoms and institutions in China's constitutions as well, but in 1967 he said: "I don't believe in elections. . . . I was elected by Beijing but aren't there quite a few people who have never seen me? If they haven't even seen me how can they elect me? It's nothing more than their having heard of my name" ("Conversation with Albanian Delegation, February 3, 1967," quoted in Starr, *Continuing the Revolution,* p. 212).

75. See the 1954, 1975, 1978, and 1982 state constitutions, art. 1.

76. See Sulamith H. Potter, "The Position of Peasants in Modern China's Social Order," *Modern China* 9, no. 4, (Oct. 1983): 465–99.

77. See Nicholas R. Lardy, *Agriculture in China's Modern Economic Development* (Cambridge: Cambridge University Press, 1983), chap. 4; and William L. Parish, "Egalitarianism in Chinese Society," *Problems of Communism* 30 (Jan.–Feb. 1981): 41; Randolph Barker and Radha Sinha, "Chinese Agriculture," in Barker and Sinha, eds., *The Chinese Agricultural Economy* (Boulder: Westview, 1982), p. 8. Parish and Whyte, *Village and Family,* p. 53, estimate the differential to be 2 to 1. In 1982 average per capita rural incomes were estimated to be 300 yuan, compared to 1,000 yuan for China's cities. See Xinhua, June 2, 1982, in FBIS 107 (June 3, 1982).

78. See "Rural Schools Lack Funds," *China Daily,* Sept. 27, 1983; Jonathan Unger, *Education Under Mao* (New York: Columbia University Press, 1982), pp. 49–59; Suzanne Pepper, "Chinese Education After Mao," *CQ* 81 (March 1980): 1–65; and Hubert O. Brown, "Recent Policy Towards Rural Education in the People's Republic of China," *Hong Kong Journal of Public Administration* 3, no. 2 (Dec. 1981): 168–88.

79. See John Dixon, *The Chinese Welfare System, 1949–1979* (New York: Praeger, 1981). In 1982 some wealthy villages in 11 of China's 29 provinces and regions were reported to be paying old-age pensions of from 10 to 15 yuan per month to a million peasants. This is a relatively recent development, however. See *NCNA,* Aug. 5, 1982, in *SWB* FE/7098/BII/15, Aug. 7, 1982.

80. See A. Doak Barnett, *Cadres, Bureaucracy, and Political Power* (New York: Columbia University Press, 1967), pp. 389–94; Lynn T. White, *Careers in Shanghai* (Berkeley and Los Angeles: University of California Press, 1978), pp. 154–75.

81. *China Daily,* July 2, 1984.

82. See Thomas Bernstein, *Up to the Mountains and Down to the Villages* (New Haven: Yale University Press, 1977); Interview Files CN1 and CN2. For an account that stresses the ability of youth to adapt, see Anita Chan, Richard Madsen, and Jonathan Unger, *Chen Village* ((Berkeley and Los Angeles: University of California Press, 1984).

83. See Madsen, *Morality and Power in a Chinese Village,* pp. 111, 121.

84. These survey data can be found in *Xinli Kexue Tongxun* 4 (1981): 26–31,

trans. in David S. K. Chu, ed., *Sociology and Society in Contemporary China: 1979–1983* (Armonk: M. E. Sharpe, 1984), pp. 159–69.

85. *Jiaoyu Yanjiu* 11 (1981): 6–12, trans. in Stanley Rosen, "Education and Political Socialization of Chinese Youths," in John N. Hawkins, ed., *Education and Social Change in the People's Republic of China* (New York: Praeger, 1983), p. 119.

86. See art. 14 of the 1979 Election Law. Article 10 of the same law requires that rural deputies to local people's congresses represent four times as many people as urban deputies.

87. Xiao Weiyun, "The Socialist Democratic Principles of Our Country's Election Law," *Beijing Daxue Xuebao* [Research Journal of Beijing University], May 1979, in Womack, "Electoral Reform," pp. 67–68.

88. See Richard Solomon, *Mao's Revolution and the Chinese Political Culture* (Berkeley and Los Angeles: University of California Press, 1971); and Lucian Pye, *The Dynamics of Chinese Politics* (Cambridge: Oelgeschlager, Gunn and Hain, 1981).

89. Marc Blecher, "Consensual Politics in Rural Chinese Communities," *Modern China* 5, no. 1 (Jan. 1979): 118–19.

90. Shue, *Peasant China in Transition,* p. 330.

91. A former brigade cadre observed, "If you feed them [the peasants], they will do whatever you want," (Interview File NKP2).

92. See Elizabeth J. Perry, "Rural Violence in Socialist China," *CQ* 103 (Sept. 1985): 414–40.

93. G. William Skinner, "Marketing and Social Structure in Rural China," *JAS* 24 (1964): 3–43, and 24 (1965): 195–228; Skinner, "Chinese Peasants and the Closed Community," *Comparative Studies in Society and History* 13 (1971): 270–381.

94. Vivienne Shue, "Peasant Culture and Socialist Culture in China," in Godwin Chu and Francis L. K. Hsu, eds., *Moving a Mountain* (Honolulu: University of Hawaii Press, 1979), pp. 325–26.

95. Vivienne Shue, *Peasant China in Transition,* pp. 100, 187–90, 278, passim.

96. See Richard Madsen, *Morality and Power in a Chinese Village,* esp. pp. 1–8.

97. See Ezra Vogel, "Land Reform in Kwangtung: 1951–1953," *CQ* 38 (April–June 1969): 46; and Maurice Freedman, *Chinese Lineage and Society* (London: Athlone Press, 1971).

98. On the networks that link peasants to their leaders, see Jean Oi, "Communism and Clientelism," *World Politics* 37, no. 2 (Jan. 1985): 238–66.

99. Potter, "Land and Lineage," p. 130.

100. See esp. William Parish, "China—Team, Brigade, or Commune?" *Problems of Communism* 25, no. 2 (March–April 1976): 51–65. For discussions of the significance of lineages in contemporary Guangdong, see Parish and Whyte, *Village and Family,* pp. 28, 113–14; Chan, Madsen, and Unger, *Chen Village,* pp. 32–33, 277; and Madsen, *Morality and Power in a Chinese Village,* pp. 50–51.

101. See Jack Potter, "The Economic and Social Consequences of Changes in China's Rural Economic Policies, 1978–1981" (unpublished paper). On rural violence and its link to lineages, see Perry, "Rural Violence in Socialist China," pp. 430–38.

102. See, e.g., William Hinton, *Shenfan* (New York: Random House, 1983); and Norma Diamond, "Taitou Revisited," in William Parish, ed., *Chinese Rural Development* (Armonk: M. E. Sharpe, 1985), pp. 246–70.

Chapter 3

1. Jurgen Domes, *The Internal Politics of China, 1949–1972* (New York: Praeger, 1973), pp. 97–101. For secondary accounts of the development of rural policy prior to 1958, see Vivienne Shue, *Peasant China in Transition* (Berkeley and Los Angeles: University of California Press, 1980); Peter Schran, *The Development of Chinese Agriculture, 1950–1959* (Urbana, Ill.: University of Illinois Press, 1969); Kenneth R. Walker, *Planning in Chinese Agriculture* (Chicago: Aldine Press, 1965); and Thomas Bernstein, "Leadership and Mobilization in the Collectivization of Agriculture in China and Russia." For accounts of land reform, see William Hinton, *Fanshen* (New York: Vintage Books, 1966), and Isabel and David Crook, *Ten Mile Inn* (New York: Random House, 1979).

2. *Da Gong Bao* [Impartial Daily], Sept. 17, 24, 1964, in Jurgen Domes, *The Internal Politics of China, 1949–1972*, p. 118.

3. "Urgent Directive Concerning Present Policy Problems in the Rural People's Communes," in Mark Selden, ed., *The People's Republic of China* (New York: Monthly Review Press, 1979), p. 516.

4. "Regulations on the Work of the Rural People's Communes" (Revised Draft), Sept. 1962 (hereafter the Sixty Articles), in Union Research Institute, *Documents of the Chinese Communist Party Central Committee, September 1956–April 1969*, vol. 1 (Hong Kong: Union Research Institute, 1971), pp. 695–725.

5. For a retrospective look at this policy, see Du Runsheng, "Nongcun gongzuo de lishixing zhuanbian" [Critical turning point in the history of rural work], *RMRB*, Sept. 16, 1982, p. 4; Dai Qingqi and Yu Zhan, "Study Comrade Deng Zihui's Viewpoint on the Agricultural Production Responsibility System," *RMRB*, Feb. 23, 1982, in FBIS 44 (March 5, 1982): K16–K20; and *Jingjixue Dongtai* 1 (1982) in Zhongguo renmin daxue shubao cailiaoshe, *Nongye Jingji* F2 (1982) 2: 70–74. For an account of the experience of one Guangdong commune with contracting production to the household during 1961 to 1963, see Gordon Bennett, *Huadong* (Boulder: Westview Press, 1978), pp. 32–39.

6. William Parish, "China—Team, Brigade or Commune?" *Problems of Communism* 25 (March–April 1976): 51–56.

7. See, e.g., Lianjiang Documents, p. 196.

8. Ibid., p. 197.

9. For the text of this document and others associated with the Four Clean-ups

Campaign, see Richard Baum and Frederick Teiwes, *Ssu-ch'ing* (Berkeley: Center for Chinese Studies Monograph Series, University of California, 1968).

10. For general accounts of the Four Clean-ups Campaign, see Richard Baum, *Prelude to Revolution* (New York: Columbia University Press, 1975); Byung-joon Ahn, *Chinese Politics and the Cultural Revolution* (Seattle: University of Washington Press, 1976). For an account of the campaign in a South China village, see Chan, Madsen, and Unger, *Chen Village,* chap. 2.

11. See John P. Burns, "Peasant Interest Articulation and Work Teams in Rural China: 1962–1974," in Godwin C. Chu and Francis L. K. Hsu, eds., *China's New Social Fabric* (London: Kegan, Paul International, 1984), pp. 147–55.

12. For a discussion of the Dazhai work point system (time rates), see Parish and Whyte, *Village and Family,* pp. 63–71.

13. See Chan, Madsen, and Unger, *Chen Village,* chaps. 2, 3. For a discussion of the policy of rusticating youths, see Thomas Bernstein, *Up to the Mountains and Down to the Villages* (New Haven: Yale University Press, 1977). In all, from 1968 to 1978, more than 17 million urban youths were transferred to the countryside. Since 1978, the policy has been discontinued.

14. According to one estimate, as many as 70 to 80 percent of team leaders may have been removed from office in some provinces (Michel Oksenberg, "Local Leaders in Rural China, 1962–1965," in A. Doak Barnett, ed., *Chinese Communist Politics in Action,* p. 184).

15. See Lowell Dittmer, "'Line Struggle' in Theory and Practice," *CQ* 72 (Dec. 1977): 675–712, for a discussion of the differences among national-level elite on the implementation of the campaign during this period.

16. For general accounts of the Cultural Revolution, see Hong Yung Lee, *The Politics of the Chinese Cultural Revolution* (Berkeley and Los Angeles: University of California Press, 1978); Lowell Dittmer, *Liu Shao-ch'i and the Chinese Cultural Revolution* (Berkeley and Los Angeles: University of California Press, 1974); and Ahn, *Chinese Politics and the Cultural Revolution.*

17. On the limited impact of the Cultural Revolution in rural areas, see Richard Baum, "The Cultural Revolution in the Countryside," in Thomas W. Robinson, ed., *The Cultural Revolution in China* (Berkeley and Los Angeles: University of California Press, 1971), pp. 367–477.

18. See Ken Ling, *The Revenge of Heaven* (New York: G. P. Putnam and Sons, 1972), for an account of occasional fighting in suburban Fuzhou.

19. Interview File CN2; also Chan, Madsen, and Unger, *Chen Village,* chap. 4.

20. Interview File NKP2. For the situation in a rural North China community during the Cultural Revolution, see William Hinton, *Shenfan* (New York: Random House, 1983), pp. 489–652.

21. For an account of this process in Guangdong, see Chan, Madsen, and Unger, *Chen Village,* chap. 5.

22. *RMRB,* Aug. 4, 1972, in FBIS 165 (Aug. 23, 1972): B5; *RMRB,* Aug. 7, 1972, in FBIS 166 (Aug. 24, 1972): B8; and Radio Hefei, Aug. 9, 1972, in FBIS

157 (Aug. 11, 1972). See also David Zweig, "Agrarian Radicalism in China, 1968–1978" (Ph.D. dissertation, University of Michigan, 1983), for an account of radical policies during this ten-year period. He focuses on leftist attempts to make brigades the unit of accounting, to restrict private plots, and to equalize assets through interunit transfers.

23. State and party organs never officially endorsed the policy of making brigades the unit of accounting, but the policy was pushed by some national leaders and their middle-level supporters (David Zweig, "Limits to Agrarian Radicalism in China" [paper presented to the Canadian Political Science Association, Ottawa, Ontario, June 1982], p. 11).

24. Evidence that these policies were carried out in some places can be found in Radio Zhejiang, July 26, 1972, in FBIS 150 (Aug. 2, 1972): C5; Interview Files NM4E-3 (Guangdong, 1972); NM11C-9 (Guangdong, 1971); and CCP Ssumao District Committee, "Ssumao District Party Committee's Opinion About the Implementation of the CCP Central Committee Directive Concerning the Question of Distribution in the Rural People's Commune," *Sidongfa* (1972) 22, in *Issues and Studies* 9, no. 6 (March 1973): 91–97. This and other evidence is reviewed in Dennis Woodward, "'Two Line Struggle' in Agriculture," in Bill Brugger, ed., *China* (London: Croom-Helm, 1978), pp. 153–70.

25. The slogan stood for striking counterrevolutionaries, and opposing corruption, speculation, extravagance, and waste. See Chan, Madsen, and Unger, *Chen Village*, pp. 207–10; and Woodward, "Two Line Struggle," pp. 161–62.

26. See "CCP Central Committee Directive Concerning the Question of Distribution in Rural People's Communes," *Zhongfa* (1971) 82, in *Issues and Studies* 9, no. 2 (Nov. 1972): 92–95.

27. John P. Burns, "The Radicals and the Campaign to Limit Bourgeois Rights in the Countryside," *Contemporary China* 1, no. 4 (Jan. 1977): 25–27.

28. For a discussion of the problems of the transition period, see the editorial, "Consciously Carry out the Party's Rural Policies," in *RMRB*, Jan. 26, 1979, in FBIS 22 (Jan. 31, 1979): E19–20.

29. See Zweig, "Limits to Agrarian Radicalism," pp. 13–17, who reports that by 1978, 66,700 brigades (nearly 9 percent of total brigades) had established brigade-level accounting.

30. See the discussion of the Second Dazhai Conference in Tang Tsou, Marc Blecher, and Mitch Meisner, "National Agricultural Policy," in Mark Selden and Victor Lippitt, eds., *The Transition to Socialism in China* (Armonk, N.Y.: M. E. Sharpe, 1982), p. 276.

31. See *RMRB*, July 30, 1980, in FBIS 161 (Aug. 18, 1980): L14.

32. See Nicholas R. Lardy, *Agriculture in China's Modern Economic Development* (Cambridge: Cambridge University Press, 1983), pp. 146–90; and Victor Lippitt, "The People's Communes and China's New Development Strategy," *Bulletin of Concerned Asian Scholars* 13, no. 3 (July–Sept. 1981), pp. 19–30.

33. See "Relieving the Peasants of Unreasonable Burdens," *RMRB*, July 5,

1978, which reports the results of the "Xiangxiang Experience," brought to the attention of party cadres in Central Committee Document 37 (June 1978) in Lin Chen, "The Commune System," *Issues and Studies* 18, no. 2 (Feb. 1982): 26.

34. The two documents are "Decisions on Some Questions Concerning the Acceleration of Agricultural Development (Draft)" published in *Zhonggong Yanjiu* (Taibei) 13, no. 5 (May 15, 1979): 150–62; and "Regulations on the Work in Rural People's Communes (Draft for Trial Use)" (hereafter New Sixty Articles) published in *Zhonggong Yanjiu* (Taibei) 13, no. 6 (June 15, 1979): 139–52 (in English in *Issues and Studies* 15, no. 8 [Aug. 1979]: 100–12 and 15, no. 9 [Sept. 1979]: 104–15).

35. New Sixty Articles (1978), art. 36.

36. Ibid., art. 35.

37. Ibid., art. 50.

38. Radio Guangzhou, Jan. 21, 1979, in FBIS 17 (Jan. 24, 1979): H1; *NCNA*, Jan. 21, 1979, in FBIS 17 (Jan. 24, 1979): E18; *RMRB*, Jan. 29, 1979, in FBIS 33 (Feb. 15, 1979): J4–J7; and Jurgen Domes, "New Policies in the Communes," *JAS* 41, no. 2 (Feb. 1982): 256–57.

39. Interview Files NKP2; and Domes, "New Policies," p. 257.

40. "Concerning Further Strengthening and Perfecting the System of Job Responsibility for Agricultural Production," *Zhongfa* (1980) no. 75, in *Zhonggong Yanjiu* (Taibei) 171 (March 15, 1981): 110–18.

41. See "Zhonggong zhongyang guanyu yi-jiu-ba-si nian nongcun gongzuo de tongzhi" [Party Central notice on 1984 agricultural work], *RMRB*, June 12, 1984. In poor areas authorities subsequently extended this to 30 to 50 years. See "Circular of the CCP Central Committee and the State Council on Helping to Change the Face of Poor Areas as Soon as Possible" (Sept. 29, 1984), in Xinhua, Sept. 29, 1984, in FBIS 198 (Oct. 11, 1984): K22–26.

42. See *Jingji Guanli*, Sept. 1981, p. 13.

43. See *NFRB*, June 17, 1979, p. 3. For general discussions of the different forms of responsibility systems, see Liu Xumao, "Woguo nongcun xianxing de ji zhong zhuyao shengchan zerenzhi jianjie" [Introduction to several important production responsibility systems implemented in China's countryside], *Jingji Guanli*, Sept. 1981, pp. 12–14; Ma Biao, "Anhui nongcun baochan daohu qingkuang kaocha" [Examination of the situation of contracting output to households in rural Anhui] *Jingji Guanli*, Feb. 1981, pp. 19–22. For secondary accounts, see Greg O'Leary and Andrew Watson, "The Production Responsibility System and the Future of Collective Farming," *Australian Journal of Chinese Affairs* 8 (1982): 1–34; Tang Tsou, Marc Blecher, and Mitch Meisner, "The Responsibility System in Agriculture," *Modern China* 8, no. 1 (Jan. 1982): 41–103; Zhao Baoxu, "China's Agricultural Policies, Past and Present" (paper presented at the Center for Chinese Studies, University of California, Berkeley, Dec. 1982); David Zweig, "Peasants and the New Incentive System," in William Parish, ed., *Chinese Rural Development* (Armonk: M. E. Sharpe, 1985), pp. 141–63; Zweig, "Opposition to Change in Rural China," *Asian Survey* 23, no. 7 (July 1983): 879–900; Helen Siu, "The Na-

ture of Encapsulation" (paper prepared for the Workshop on Recent Reforms in China, Harvard University, April 30, 1983); Graham Johnson, "The Production Responsibility System in Chinese Agriculture," *Pacific Affairs* 55 (1983): 430–51; and Kathleen Hartford, "Socialist Agriculture Is Dead; Long Live Socialist Agriculture!" in Elizabeth J. Perry and Christine Wong, eds., *The Political Economy of Reform in Post-Mao China* (Cambridge, Mass.: Harvard University Press, 1985), pp. 31–62. The process of implementing the policy is discussed in David Zweig, "Context and Content in Policy Implementation," in David M. Lampton, ed., *Policy Implementation in Post-Mao China* (Berkeley and Los Angeles: University of California Press, 1987).

44. Frederick W. Crook, "The *Baogan Daohu* Incentive System," *CQ* 102 (June 1985): 291.

45. *Sichuan Ribao,* July 23, 1981, p. 3; Interview Files NKP2 (Fujian) (3.9.82); NT1 (Fujian) (29.6.82); and O'Leary and Watson, "The Production Responsibility System," p. 15.

46. Kathleen Hartford, "Socialist Agriculture is Dead; Long Live Socialist Agriculture!" in Perry and Wong, eds., *Political Economy of Reform,* p. 37.

47. See Parish and Whyte, *Village and Family,* pp. 63–71, for a description of the work point system.

48. Xinhua (Beijing), June 2, 1982, in FBIS 107 (June 3, 1982), figures released by the State Statistical Bureau, based on a sample survey of 18,529 peasant households. For provincial statistics, see Xinhua (Nanjing), Oct. 12, 1981, in FBIS 203 (Oct. 21, 1981): O2; and Zhou Cheng, "On Contracting Output to Households," pp. 87–88. See also S. Lee Travers, "Getting Rich Through Diligence," in Perry and Wong, eds., *The Political Economy of Reform,* pp. 111–30.

49. See Xinhua, June 2, 1982, in FBIS 107 (June 3, 1982): K9, where it is reported that the index of the purchase price for agricultural products rose by 38.5 percent in 1981 over 1978.

50. Radio Beijing, Jan. 9, 1983, in FBIS 9 (Jan. 13, 1983): K16; Radio Changsha, May 6, 1980, in FBIS 92 (May 9, 1980): P3; Radio Shijiazhuang, July 11, 1980, in FBIS 147 (July 29, 1980): R2–R3; Radio Harbin, Dec. 12, 1980, in FBIS 244 (Dec. 17, 1980): S1–S2; Radio Guangzhou, Feb. 14, 1982, in FBIS 32 (Feb. 17, 1982): P2; and Radio Shijiazhuang, June 15, 1982, in FBIS 121 (June 23, 1982): R1.

51. Commentator, "Protect Peasants Who Get Rich Through Hard Work," *RMRB,* May 20, 1981, in FBIS 101 (May 25, 1981): K16–K18; Huo Shilian, "Much Can Be Accomplished by Peasant Households Which Have Become Rich Through Labor," *RMRB,* June 15, 1982, in FBIS 119 (June 21, 1982): K13–K18; Letter to the Editor, *Fujian Ribao,* Oct. 25, 1982; Interview File NKP2 (Fujian) (3.9.82); Jack Potter, "The Social and Economic Consequences of Changes in China's Rural Economic Policies, 1978–1981." For evidence of opposition to the responsibility system, see David Zweig, "Opposition to Change in Rural China," *Asian Survey* 23, no. 7 (July 1983): 879–900. See also John P. Burns, "Local Cadre Accommodation to the 'Responsibility System' in Rural China," *Pa-*

cific Affairs 58, no. 4 (Winter 1985–86): 607–25; and Richard J. Latham, "The Implications of Rural Reforms for Grass-Roots Cadres," in Perry and Wong, eds., *Political Economy of Reform,* pp. 157–74.

52. *Beijing Review* 8 (Feb. 20, 1984).

53. Authorities in Shanxi estimated that from 3 to 6 percent of peasants there have achieved this status already. See *RMRB,* June 15, 1982, in FBIS 119 (June 21, 1982): K14. See also Zhongguo nongcun fazhan yanjiu zhongxin cailiaoshe, *Nongcun Zhuanyehu Qin Lao Zhi Fu Yibai Li* [One hundred examples of rural specialized households becoming rich through labor] (Beijing: Renmin chubanshe, 1983).

54. See *RMRB,* Nov. 15, 1983, and *NFRB,* May 12, 1983. In 1985 authorities reported that 100 million peasants lived below the poverty line (*China Daily* [Beijing], Dec. 18, 1985).

55. *RMRB,* June 15, 1982, in FBIS 119 (June 21, 1982): K14, and *Beijing Review* 39 (Sept. 26, 1983): 27.

56. *Sichuan Ribao,* Sept. 10, 1981, in FBIS 191 (Oct. 2, 1981): Q21.

57. Radio Fuzhou, April 10, 1981, in FBIS 72 (April 15, 1981): O2–O3; Radio Guangzhou, June 19, 1981, in FBIS 132 (July 10, 1981): P3; Radio Beijing (commenting on Ningxia Hui Autonomous Region's problem), Oct. 12, 1981, in FBIS 203 (Oct. 21, 1981): T1; Xinhua (Feb. 27, 1982) in FBIS 48 (March 11, 1982): R1; and State Council Report on the Use of Farmland for Housing Construction (Oct. 29, 1982), Xinhua (Nov. 5, 1982), in FBIS 216 (Nov. 8, 1982): K16.

58. State Economic Commission, "Report on Doing a Better Job in Engaging in Agricultural Sideline Production by Industrial and Mining Enterprises," transmitted by the State Council, Oct. 7, 1981, Xinhua, Oct. 15, 1981, in FBIS 201 (Oct. 19, 1981): K3; Radio Changsha, Oct. 17, 1981, in FBIS 205 (Oct. 23, 1981): P4.

59. In Fujian during 1978, work teams implemented the Double Hits (*shuangda*) Campaign, which attempted to eliminate corruption and speculation (Interview Files NKP2). See *RMRB,* Nov. 5, 1978, for a discussion of the Double Hits Campaign in Zhejiang. A national campaign against corruption reached its height in 1981–1982.

60. For a general discussion of the problems of implementing the responsibility system, see Ma Renping, "Nongcun shixing shengchan zerenzhi hou chuxian de xin wenti" [New problems that have emerged after the implementation of the rural production responsibility system], *Jingji Guanli,* Aug. 1981, pp. 3–8.

61. See reports of cadre resistance in Radio Hangzhou, May 14, 1980, in FBIS 95 (May 14, 1980): O4–O5; *NFRB,* Dec. 18, 1980, p. 2; *NFRB,* Dec. 29, 1980, p. 2; and *Sichuan Ribao,* Nov. 7, 1981, in FBIS 224 (Nov. 20, 1981): Q2; "Hui mai mou shijian shuoming le shenme?" [What is the explanation for destroying the wheat field?], in Zhongguo renmin daxue shubao cailiao she, *Nongye Jingji* F2 10 (1981), pp. 87–89.

62. *NFRB*, July 22, 1983.

63. *Fujian Ribao*, April 12, 1982. See also *Fujian Ribao*, March 26, 1982, and April 8, 1982.

64. See Radio Guizhou, April 24, 1981, in FBIS 80 (April 27, 1981): Q1; Editorial, *RMRB*, Feb. 19, 1982, in FBIS 41 (March 2, 1982): K8–K11; *Fujian Ribao*, Feb. 28, 1982; Radio Zhengzhou, May 27, 1982, in FBIS 100 (June 8, 1982): K3; and Xinhua, June 2, 1982, in FBIS 111 (June 9, 1982): Q1–Q2; "Zhengzhi zhidaoyuan hai you gongzuo kezuoma?" [Do political thought cadres still have work to do?], *RMRB*, April 27, 1979.

65. *Sichuan Ribao*, Aug. 9, 1982, in *SWB* FE/7118/BII/12 (Aug. 31, 1982).

66. See Zhang Chunsheng and Song Dahan, "Separation of Government Administration from Commune Administration Required by the Development of the Rural Economy and the Building of State Power," *RMRB*, July 30, 1982, in *SWB* FE/7098/BII/10 (Aug. 7, 1982).

67. Wu Min, "From Integration to Separation of Government Administration and Commune Management," *Shanxi Ribao*, June 7, 1982, in FBIS 121 (June 23, 1982): R6.

68. Xinhua, Oct. 26, 1983, in FBIS 209 (Oct. 27, 1983): K18; and *NCNA*, June 5, 1985. Replacing communes with cooperatives was proposed by Lin Tian in "Guanyu renmin gongshe tizhi wenti de shentao" [Discussion of the problem of the people's commune system], *Jingji Guanli*, Jan. 1981, pp. 10–13. Sichuan and Anhui provinces have experimented with abolishing communes and replacing them with specialized companies (Liu Cheng and Chen Wuyuan, "Nongcun guanli tizhi gaige de chubu shi" [Preliminary experiment in the reform of the rural management system], *Jingji Guanli*, April 1981, pp. 37–41). See also *Liaowang* 5 (Aug. 20, 1981), in FBIS 207 (Oct. 27, 1981): K17, for Xindu County's experience; Kyodo News Service, Jan. 3, 1982, in FBIS 1 (Jan. 4, 1982): K3, for a discussion of proposed changes in Anhui; *Zhongshan Daxue Yanjiusheng Xuekan* 4 (1981), in Zhongguo renmin daxue shubao cailiao she, *Nongye Jingji* F2 (1982) 1:47–50; Radio Taiyuan, Feb. 7, 1983, in FBIS 32 (Feb. 15, 1983): R2; Xinhua, Jan. 12, 1983, in FBIS 27 (Feb. 8, 1983): O4; *Xinhua Ribao*, March 12, 1983, in FBIS 57 (March 23, 1983): O1; *Shanxi Ribao*, Feb. 8, 1983, in FBIS 44 (March 4, 1983): R4–R5; and Radio Chengdu, Feb. 22, 1983, in FBIS 39 (Feb. 25, 1983): Q1–Q2. See also Vivienne Shue, "The Fate of the Commune," *Modern China* 10, no. 3 (July 1984): 259–83.

69. *Zhongguo Baike Nianjian* (Beijing: Zhongguo da baike quanshu chubanshe, 1983), p. 393.

70. For secondary accounts of commune organization, see John Pelzel, "Economic Management of a Production Brigade in Post-Leap China," in W. E. Willmott, ed., *Economic Organization in Chinese Society* (Stanford: Stanford University Press, 1972), pp. 387–414; A. Doak Barnett, *Cadres, Bureaucracy, and Political Power in Communist China* (New York: Columbia University Press, 1967), pp. 339–424; Benedict Stavis, *People's Communes and Rural Development in China*

(Ithaca, N.Y.: Rural Development Committee, Cornell University, 1974); Frederick Crook, "The Commune System in the People's Republic of China, 1963–1974," Joint Economic Committee, 94th Congress, *China* (Washington, D.C.: U.S. Government Printing Office, 1975), pp. 366–408; Steven Butler, *Agricultural Mechanization in China* (New York: East Asian Institute, Columbia University, 1978); Gordon Bennett, *Huadong* (Boulder: Westview Press, 1978); William Parish and Martin King Whyte, *Village and Family in Contemporary China* (Chicago: University of Chicago Press, 1978), pp. 96–114; and Vivienne Shue, "The Fate of the Commune," *Modern China* 10, no. 3 (July 1984): 259–83.

71. *Zhongguo Baike Nianjian* (Beijing, 1983), p. 393; and World Bank, *China* (Annex C, Agricultural Development), Report No. 3391-CHA, June 1, 1981, p. 31.

72. This account is based heavily on Barnett, *Cadres, Bureaucracy, and Political Power;* Bennett, *Huadong;* and Interview Files NKP2 (Fujian) (10.8.82) and NT1 (Fujian) (15.7.82).

73. This was called the commune revolutionary committee from 1969 to 1981. See the New Sixty Articles (1978), art. 9.

74. Provided for in the Sixty Articles (1962), art. 8, and the New Sixty Articles (1978), art. 9. The Organic Law for the Local People's Congresses and Local People's Governments of the People's Republic of China (hereafter Organic Law), Dec. 10, 1982, art. 5, extends terms of office for township (*xiang;* formerly commune) officials to three years (trans. in FBIS 244 [Dec. 20, 1982]: K43–K54).

75. For recent examples of elections of commune people's congress delegates, see Radio Chengdu, Nov. 25, 1979, in FBIS 229 (Nov. 27, 1979): Q3; *NFRB,* June 2, 1980, p. 3; *Jiefang Ribao,* Oct. 10, 1980, in FBIS 212 (Oct. 30, 1980): O2–O3; Radio Xian, Nov. 1, 1980, in FBIS 220 (Nov. 12, 1980): T2; and *Sichuan Ribao,* Nov. 19, 1980.

76. Barnett mentions "supervision committees" in *Cadres, Bureaucracy, and Political Power,* p. 350. See also Stavis, *People's Communes,* pp. 107–8. They were provided for in the Sixty Articles (1962), art. 8, but were not mentioned in the New Sixty Articles (1978) or by my interviewees.

77. Barnett called these "departments" (*bu*), but when management committees became "revolutionary committees," authorities changed their names to "groups" (*zu*).

78. Some commune administrations also included transportation, water conservation, finance and trade, women's affairs, youth affairs, and political/legal groups.

79. Interview File NT1 (Fujian) (15.7.82). The World Bank reports that in 1979 there were on average 20 state cadres per commune (1.06 million) in China's 53,000 communes (out of a total of 20 million state cadres at all levels throughout China) (*China,* p. 31).

80. Interview File NT1 (Fujian) (15.7.82).

81. *RMRB,* July 5, 1978.

82. Michel Oksenberg, "Local Leaders in Rural China," pp. 155–215.

83. *Sichuan Ribao,* July 5, 1980; and data derived from interviews.

84. Interview File NKP2 (15.8.82).

85. See Barnett, *Cadres, Bureaucracy, and Political Power,* pp. 352–62.

86. See Stavis, *People's Communes,* pp. 81–90; Butler, *Agricultural Mechanization,* pp. 27–34; and Sixty Articles (1962), art. 10.

87. Enterprises included tractor service pools, chemical and cement plants, machine shops, canneries, paper manufacturing plants, small-scale hydroelectric plants, and consumer goods industries (The World Bank, *China,* p. 32).

88. *RMRB,* May 10, 1982, in FBIS 94 (May 14, 1982): K3.

89. Stavis, *People's Communes,* pp. 86–87.

90. Interview File KP1 (Guangdong).

91. See *Xinhua Ribao,* June 5, 1980; *Xinhua Ribao,* April 24, 1980; Jilin sheng nongye weiyuanhui, ed., "Jilin sheng nongcun renmin gongshe nongye shengchan zerenzhi shixing banfa" [Trial methods for implementing the rural production responsibility system in Jilin Province's rural people's communes], *Jilin Ribao,* Dec. 19, 1981, in Zhongguo renmin daxue shubao cailiao she, *Nongye Jingji* F2 1 (1982), p. 69; Wang Shuheng and Chen Quanyi, "Guanyu wanshan nongye shengchan zerenzhi de jige wenti" [Several questions on the perfection of the rural production responsibility system], *Jiangxi Shehui Kexue* 5–6 (1981), in Zhongguo renmin daxue shubao cailiao she, *Nongye Jingji* 1 (1982): 75–82; Letter to the Editor from Hubei, entitled "Baodui ganbu bu yinggai baoban xuanju" [Guarantee cadres should not fix elections], *RMRB,* Dec. 1, 1978; and *RMRB,* Jan. 14, 1978, which discusses the situation in Shandong. See also *RMRB,* April 21, 1978; *RMRB,* May 9, 1979; *Fujian Ribao,* Feb. 18, 1982; *Fujian Ribao,* Oct. 25, 1982; and *Fujian Ribao,* March 21, 1981. These articles indicate that guarantee cadres can be found in Jiangsu, Jilin, Jiangxi, Hubei, and Shandong, in addition to Fujian (Interview Files NCN3 [29.7.82]; NKP1 [30.6.82]; NT1 [6.7.82]; and NKP2 [10.8.82]). These informants indicate that the practice predated the Cultural Revolution. Although Guangdong Province does not use the system of *baodui ganbu,* informants from Guangdong have reported that commune and brigade authorities sometimes stationed (*zhu*) cadres in troublesome units. These cadres would serve much the same function.

92. Interview File NKP2 (10.8.82). The interviewee speculated that, under the responsibility system, guarantee cadres may no longer be needed.

93. See Burns, "Peasants and Work Teams."

94. *Zhongguo Xinwenshe,* May 14, 1982, in FBIS 95 (May 17, 1982): K8–K9.

95. *Zhongguo Baike Nianjian* (Beijing, 1983), p. 393; and World Bank, *China,* p. 30.

96. Barnett, *Cadres, Bureaucracy, and Political Power,* p. 367–70; and Bennett, *Huadong,* p. 182. Authorities reported 19 party members per branch in Guizhou's Pingba County. See "Zhonggong Pingba xianwei zhengdun, gaixuan dadui dang zhibu de qingkuang baogao" [Report on the rectification and reelection of the

party branch of the Chinese Communist party committee of Pingba County],
Zhonggong Yanjiu (Taibei) 195 (March 15, 1983): 140. Interview data from Fujian indicate that party committee size varied from 5 to 9 members.

97. Interview Files NT2 (Fujian) (25.6.82); NT1 (Fujian) (22.6.82).

98. "Zhonggong Pingba xianwei zhengdun, gaige dadui dang zhibu de qingkuang," *Zhonggong Yanjiu,* p. 141.

99. Sixty Articles (1962), art. 18, annually; New Sixty Articles (1978), art. 9, every two years.

100. *NFRB,* Feb. 24, 1980, states that the elections for brigade cadres in Huilong commune, Gaoyao County, held in Oct. 1979 were only the second time that these leaders had been democratically elected. Previously brigade cadres were all appointed by upper levels. Although sometimes "elections" were held, they were little more than formalities. For the same argument for Fujian, see Interview Files NCN1 (2.7.82); NCN3 (15.7.82); NT1 (22.6.82); and NKP2 (8.8.82).

101. Barnett, *Cadres, Bureaucracy, and Political Power,* pp. 363–67; Bennett, *Huadong,* p. 182; Interview Files NKP2 (Fujian) (29.7.82); NCN1 (Fujian) (2.7.82); NT1 (Fujian) (22.6.82); NM1 (Fujian) (3.9.82).

102. "Zhongguo gongchandang nongcun dang zhibu gongzuo tiaoli (shixing caoan)" [Chinese Communist party rural party branch regulations (draft for trial use)] (Beijing: Zhonggong zuzhibu, Dec. 1981), in *Zhonggong Yanjiu* (Taibei) 16, no. 9 (Sept. 15, 1982): 149.

103. In Fujian, if commune authorities could not find a suitable brigade secretary locally, they sometimes appointed a state cadre to the post. This occasionally happened in larger market towns. See Interview File NT1.

104. According to one Guangdong informant, the brigade secretary's basic (presubsidy) income was determined by averaging the highest household incomes of the 3 teams with the highest, middle, and lowest incomes in the brigade (NT4 [Guangdong]). According to NKP2, the brigade secretary in his brigade earned 24 yuan per month plus 5 yuan per month subsidies in 1981. In the richest brigade in NKP2's commune, the brigade secretary received 40 yuan per month, while the lowest brigade cadre salary in the poorest brigade in the commune was 10 yuan per month. Obviously, poorly paid cadres had to spend most of their time earning money to supplement their cadre income. See Interview File NKP2 (Fujian) (29.8.82). See the Fujian provincial government regulations, which restrict the number of subsidized brigade cadres. A village with 20 households or less may subsidize 3 brigade officials; a village of 200 to 500 people may subsidize 4; villages of 500 or more people may subsidize 5 cadres (*Fujian Ribao,* Feb. 20, 1982).

105. See Baum and Teiwes, *Ssu-ch'ing.*

106. See, e.g., Radio Guangzhou, Nov. 29, 1974, in FBIS 232 (Dec. 2, 1974): H2; Radio Nanning, Dec. 15, 1974, in FBIS 242 (Dec. 16, 1974): H3. More recently, see Liao Gailong, "The 1980 Reform Program of China," reprinted in *Qishi niandai* 134 (March 1, 1981), in FBIS 50 (March 16, 1981): U11, subtitled "Establish an Independent Peasants' Association."

107. Oksenberg, "Local Leaders," pp. 155–215; Parish and Whyte, *Village and Family,* pp. 102–3.

108. Ibid.; and Interview Files for 1976–1980.

109. "Zhonggong Pingba xianwei zhengdun, gaixuan dadui dang zhibu de qingkuang baogao," p. 140. After the rectification, the average age for branch members (N = 899) dropped to 42.6, and for secretaries (N = 195), dropped to 45.2 years; 206 branch members were middle-school graduates, and only 199 branch members were illiterate.

110. See Barnett, *Cadres, Bureaucracy, and Political Power,* pp. 379–86. Informants in Guangdong and Fujian report that since 1978 authorities have cut back political education and reduced the frequency of meetings.

111. See Butler, *Agricultural Mechanization,* pp. 16–27; also Barnett, *Cadres, Bureaucracy, and Political Power,* pp. 372–79. The Sixty Articles (1962), art. 19, lists the duties of brigade management committees. The New Sixty Articles (1978) does not disaggregate brigade and team responsibilities.

112. Butler, *Agricultural Mechanization,* p. 17.

113. World Bank, *China,* p. 26; Butler, *Agricultural Mechanization,* p. 22.

114. Official policy guarantees every citizen food, clothing, medical care, housing, and burial expenses (Parish and Whyte, *Village and Family,* p. 74). In Feb. 1983 the Ministry of Civil Affairs reported that there were approximately 3 million "five guarantees households" (households that had to be provided with the above necessities). See NCNA, Feb. 8, 1983, in *Ming Bao* (Hong Kong), Feb. 11, 1983. Recently, Xinhua reported that 2.73 million poor peasant households had been helped by authorities (Dec. 18, 1982, in FBIS 248 [Dec. 27, 1982]: K6).

115. See this chapter, n. 91.

116. Interview File NKP2 (Fujian) (3.9.82).

117. "Jingjian she dui fei shengchan renyuan jianjing nongmin fudan" [Simplify (the numbers of) commune and brigade nonproductive personnel; reduce the peasants' burden], *Jingji Guanli,* Jan. 1982, p. 59.

118. *RMRB,* Sept. 5, 1981; *Nongcun Jingji Wenti* 5 (1981), in Zhongguo renmin daxue shubao cailiao she, *Nongye Jinjyi* F2 11 (1981), pp. 109–15; *Zhejiang Ribao,* Oct. 28, 1981; Radio Shijiazhuang, Sept. 9, 1981, in FBIS 183 (Sept. 22, 1981): R2–R3; *RMRB,* Sept. 17, 1981, in FBIS 188 (Sept. 29, 1981): K13–K15; Radio Hefei, Sept. 25, 1981, in FBIS 188 (Sept. 29, 1981): O1–O2; Xinhua, Aug. 25, 1981, in FBIS 165 (Aug. 26, 1981): K1–K3; Xinhua, Sept. 4, 1981, in FBIS 174 (Sept. 9, 1981): O2–O3; Radio Taiyuan, Dec. 19, 1980, in FBIS 249 (Dec. 24, 1980): R6; and Radio Zhengzhou, May 10, 1981, in FBIS 90 (May 11, 1981): P4; Radio Zhengzhou, May 10, 1981, in FBIS 80 (May 11, 1981): P4; and *Nongye Jingji Wenti* 12 (1982), in Zhongguo renmin daxue shubao cailiao she, *Nongye Jingji* F2 (1982) 1: 105.

119. *Zhongguo Jingji Nianjian* (Hong Kong, 1982), p. VIII-9; and World Bank, *China,* p. 26; Team size ranged from 110 to 700 people in my sample (N = 10) for Fujian in 1978 to 1980.

120. For accounts of small groups and their elected leaderships in Gansu and Sichuan, see *RMRB,* March 2, 1982; *Sichuan Ribao,* Aug. 23, 1981; and *Sichuan Ribao,* June 17, 1981.

121. See Sixty Articles (1962), art. 38 (one year), and New Sixty Articles (1978), art. 9 (two years).

122. Oksenberg, "Local Leaders," p. 180.

123. Parish and Whyte, *Village and Family,* p. 103. But 89 percent of Jianwa County's 2,000 production team leaders were party members in 1982 (*Fujian Ribao,* May 20, 1982).

124. Parish and Whyte, *Village and Family,* pp. 102–3.

125. Oksenberg, "Local Leaders," p. 181; Parish and Whyte, *Village and Family,* p. 102, and Interview File data.

126. Butler, *Agricultural Mechanization,* pp. 8–15.

127. See the Sixty Articles (1962), art. 38, which provides that "all important things such as the team's production and income distribution must be decided through discussion at a general meeting of commune members, and not by the cadres. Before any decision is reached, opinions of the commune members should be solicited, and several different plans submitted to them, with details of each plan clearly explained to them before any decision is reached after full deliberation at a general meeting of commune members [at team level]." See the New Sixty Articles (1978), art. 9, which says: "On important issues including production and capital construction, operation and management, distribution, supply and marketing, credit, and the collective welfare, the administrative organs at various levels of the people's commune should extensively seek suggestions from the masses, and then let the authorized organs at various levels make their decisions in a democratic way."

128. See the Sixty Articles (1962), art. 40, and the New Sixty Articles (1978), art. 49. In the latter document, teams could adjust the size of private plots to take into account demographic changes only after receiving county approval.

129. World Bank, *China,* p. 29.

130. See "Notice on the Report of Actively Developing Diversified Economy in Rural Areas," *Banyuetan* 8 (April 25, 1981), in Ch'en Ting-chung, "The Prospects of the People's Commune: The 'Three Freedoms and One Contract,'" *Issues and Studies* 18, no. 5 (May 1982): 39.

131. The Sixty Articles (1962), art. 21, and the New Sixty Articles (1978), art. 7.

132. See John P. Burns, "Rural Guangdong's 'Second Economy,' 1962–1974," *CQ* 88 (Dec. 1981): 637–38.

133. See Potter, "Economic and Social Consequences," who reports activities of this sort in rural Guangdong. Press reports indicate that collective property was divided up among villagers. See Radio Changsha, July 6, 1981, in FBIS 158 (Aug. 17, 1981): P4; *Ningxia Ribao,* April 8, 1982, in FBIS 84 (April 30, 1982): T1 (which complains that peasants advocated "the more completely and thoroughly

the collective property is shared out the better"); and Editorial, *RMRB*, April 3, 1982, in FBIS 73 (April 15, 1982): K1–K3.

134. *RMRB*, Sept. 5, 1981; *Zhejiang Ribao*, Oct. 28, 1981; *Zhejiang Ribao*, Dec. 7, 1981.

135. Parish and Whyte, *Village and Family*, p. 23–26.

136. *RMRB*, Nov. 8, 1983, in FBIS 219 (Nov. 10, 1983): R2.

137. *Xinhua Ribao*, March 1, 1980, p. 2.

138. "Tuanjie 'wailaihu'" [Unite with "outsider households"], *Fujian Ribao*, April 4, 1982.

139. Xinhua, Jan. 30, 1982, in FBIS 22 (Feb. 2, 1982): O1; Lin Zeng, "Rural Workers Must Not Be Hired Indiscriminately," *Yangcheng Wanbao*, Aug. 3, 1982, in *SWB* FE/7098/BII/18 (Aug. 7, 1982); and *NFRB*, Dec. 28, 1982.

140. Madsen, *Morality and Power*, chap. 9. Madsen's typology includes two other types of leaders: the "pragmatic technocrat," usually younger, educated, agricultural specialists who can "get the job done"; and the "moralistic revolutionary," a transient category of sent-down youth.

141. See Oksenberg's speculation about the role of retired cadres ("Local Leaders," p. 169).

142. Interview File NKP2 (Fujian) (3.9.82).

143. Commentator, "Eliminate Factionalist Interference and Uphold the Principle of Party Spirit," *Shanxi Ribao*, Sept. 8, 1981, in FBIS 193 (Oct. 6, 1981): R8; *Zhongguo Xinwenshe*, Nov. 22, 1981, in FBIS 225 (Nov. 23, 1981): O1–O2; *Hebei Ribao*, Dec. 11, 1981, in FBIS 249 (Dec. 29, 1981): R1–R6; Radio Shijiazhuang, June 9, 1981, in FBIS 123 (June 25, 1982): R1; Radio Nanning, May 20, 1983, in FBIS 102 (May 25, 1983): P6.

144. Pye, *The Dynamics of Chinese Politics*. See also J. Bruce Jacobs, *Local Politics in a Rural Chinese Cultural Setting* (Canberra: Australian National University, 1981); Morton Fried, *Fabric of Chinese Society* (New York: Octagon Books, 1969); and Jean C. Oi, "Communism and Clientelism," *World Politics* 37, no. 2 (Jan. 1985): 238–66.

145. Li Qiming, "Uproot Factionalism, Guarantee Reform," *RMRB*, March 21, 1983, in FBIS 56 (March 22, 1983): K2.

146. *RMRB*, May 5, 1979, p. 2.

147. Interview File CN5C-11 (Guangdong); CN6C-12, 13 (Guangdong); NKP1 (Fujian) (5.7.82); see also Radio Nanjing, Aug. 26, 1964, in *NPCRS* 72 (Sept. 3, 1964): 18; Radio Taiyuan, Sept. 3, 1964, in *NPCRS* 73 (Sept. 10, 1964): 30; and Radio Hefei, Sept. 24, 1964, in *NPCRS* 76 (Oct. 1, 1964): 1.

148. Interview File CN5L-17 (Guangdong).

149. *RMRB*, Aug. 9, 1972, in *SCMP* 5199 (Aug. 20, 1972); Interview Files CN11A, B, C (Guangdong).

150. See Leo Goodstadt, "Taxation and Economic Modernization in Contemporary China," *Development and Change* 10 (1979): 403–21. In Feb. 1979 au-

thorities in China reduced the tax burden for newly established rural enterprises. See Radio Beijing, Feb. 4, 1979, in FBIS 26 (Feb. 6, 1979): E6; and Xinhua, Feb. 9, 1979, in FBIS 30 (Feb. 12, 1979): E12. To reduce taxes, many previously established rural enterprises "reestablished" themselves after this date.

151. See Radio Jinan, Nov. 11, 1980, in FBIS 223 (Nov. 17, 1980): O6–O8; and Sept. 18, 1980, in FBIS 187 (Sept. 24, 1980): O4–O5; Radio Xi'an, Jan. 12, 1979, in FBIS 10 (Jan. 15, 1979): M4.

152. Radio Changsha, Aug. 1, 1982, in *SWB* FE/7098/BII/19 (Aug. 7, 1982).

153. Radio Guangxi, Dec. 21, 1963, in *NPCRS* 38 (Dec. 26, 1963): 45.

154. Both the Sixty Articles (1962), art. 21, and the New Sixty Articles (1978), art. 38, give production teams control over their own manpower. For examples of peasant resistance, see Lianjiang Documents, pp. 173, 179, 181, 184, 187–92; Radio Nanchang, Jan. 1, 1967, in *NPCRS* 193 (Feb. 2, 1967), and Jan. 25, 1964, in *NPCRS* 43 (Jan. 30, 1964); Radio Beijing, Aug. 24, 1972, in FBIS 168 (Aug. 28, 1972): B5; *Guangming Ribao,* Aug. 22, 1971, in *SCMP* 4969 (Sept. 7, 1971): 1; and Interview File NM4D-8 (Guangdong).

155. *NFRB,* Dec. 23, 1960, in *SCMP* 2418 (Jan. 17, 1961): 5.

156. Ray Wylie, "The Great Debate," *Far Eastern Economic Review* (Hong Kong), Sept. 14, 1967, p. 11; "Ten Major Crimes of Private Plots," in *China News Service* (Hong Kong) 146 (Nov. 17, 1966): 2.

157. Sixty Articles (1962), art. 40, and New Sixty Articles (1978), art. 49.

158. Lianjiang Documents, pp. 145–46, 170–71, 191, 211, 231; Radio Guiyang, June 23, 1967, in *NPCRS* 214 (July 6, 1967): N10; *NFRB,* May 26, 1963, p. 2. As late as 1981, peasants continued to complain that some local officials had confiscated private plots or had refused to permit their expansion. See Commentator, *RMRB,* June 17, 1981, in FBIS 122 (June 25, 1981): K21–K22; and Letter from Heilongjiang to the Editor, *Zhongguo Nongmin Bao* [China Peasant News], March 19, 1981, in Zhongguo renmin daxue shubao cailiao she, *Nongye Jingji* F2 7 (1981): 64.

159. Radio Nanning, March 10, 1965, in *NPCRS* 98 (March 18, 1965): 21; and Radio Nanchang, May 7, 1963, in *NPCRS* 5 (May 9, 1963): 5.

160. Interview File NM1C (Guangdong); Radio Xi'an, Sept. 11, 1964, in *NPCRS* 74 (Sept. 17, 1964): 30; Radio Xi'an, Dec. 30, 1964, in *NPCRS* 89 (Jan. 7, 1965): 32; Radio Xi'an, Oct. 5, 1964, in *NPCRS* 77 (Oct. 8, 1964): 21; and Radio Changsha, Sept. 9, 1964, in *NPCRS* 74 (Sept. 17, 1964): 9.

161. See G. William Skinner, "Marketing and Social Structure in Rural China, Part 3," *JAS* 24, no. 3 (May 1965): 384–99; Radio Kunming, Dec. 21, 1969, in FBIS 247 (Dec. 23, 1969): E4.

162. See Sixty Articles (1962), art. 41, and New Sixty Articles (1978), art. 32; Lianjiang Documents, p. 226, and the definition of "speculation" in *China News Agency,* Feb. 6, 1982, in *SWB* FE/6951/BII/9–10 (Feb. 11, 1982), which includes: "the resale of industrial and agricultural means of production; violating the

state's procurement plans by forcing up prices, large-scale purchase and resale of commodities procured under the state plan; resale of planned supply tickets and negotiable securities issued by banks; and seeking profits by reselling gold and silver, foreign currency, jewelry, cultural relics, imported goods and precious medicinal materials."

163. *RMRB,* Jan. 7, 1980, in FBIS 14 (Jan. 21, 1980): L10–L11; Radio Nanning, March 23, 1980, in FBIS 60 (March 26, 1980): P1; Radio Zhengzhou, June 20, 1980, in FBIS 126 (June 27, 1980): P4–P5; Radio Fuzhou, April 10, 1981, in FBIS 72 (April 10, 1981): O2–O3.

164. Xinhua, April 20, 1981, in FBIS 77 (April 22, 1981): K24.

165. *NFRB,* June 6, 1981, p. 2; Radio Guangzhou, June 19, 1981, in FBIS 132 (July 10, 1981): P3; Radio Changsha, Sept. 26, 1981, in FBIS 188 (Sept. 29, 1981): P7; Radio Beijing, Oct. 12, 1981, in FBIS 203 (Oct. 21, 1981): T1; Radio Chengdu, Dec. 3, 1981, in FBIS 234 (Dec. 7, 1981): Q2; Xinhua, Feb. 27, 1982, in FBIS 48 (March 11, 1982): R1; *Fujian Ribao,* March 6, 1982, in FBIS 54 (March 19, 1982): O1; *RMRB,* March 19, 1982; Radio Xi'an, March 20, 1982, in FBIS 56 (March 23, 1982): T3; Radio Guiyang, April 11, 1982, in FBIS 72 (April 14, 1982): Q1; *RMRB,* April 19, 1982; Radio Wuhan, April 28, 1982, in FBIS 88 (May 6, 1982): P1; Radio Wuhan, June 20, 1982, in FBIS 131 (July 8, 1982): P3; and Xinhua, Nov. 5, 1982, in FBIS 216 (Nov. 8, 1982): K16.

166. In Guizhou, villagers in Chaoli commune "insisted that they be assigned land which had belonged to them before they joined the cooperatives," *RMRB,* April 21, 1981, in FBIS 81 (April 28, 1981): K15–K17; Radio Hangzhou, Sept. 16, 1981, in FBIS 182 (Sept. 21, 1981): O1 (reports that commune officials were jailed for selling land); and Radio Changchun, Oct. 12, 1981, in FBIS 202 (Oct. 20, 1981): S3.

167. Xinhua, Oct. 15, 1981, in FBIS 201 (Oct. 19, 1981): K3; Radio Changsha, Oct. 17, 1981, in FBIS 205 (Oct. 23, 1981): P4; *RMRB,* Oct. 30, 1981, in FBIS 215 (Nov. 6, 1981): K1; Xinhua, Nov. 4, 1981, in FBIS 214 (Nov. 5, 1981): K1; Radio Guiyang, Nov. 20, 1981, in FBIS 227 (Nov. 25, 1981): Q1; Radio Kunming, April 21, 1982, in FBIS 87 (May 5, 1982): Q3; and Radio Zhengzhou, May 28, 1982, in FBIS 107 (June 3, 1982): P4.

168. Parish and Whyte, *Village and Family,* pp. 54–71; Martin Whyte, "Inequality and Stratification in China," *CQ* 64 (Dec. 1975): 684–711; Marc Blecher, "Income Distribution in Small Rural Chinese Communities," *CQ* 68 (Dec. 1976): 797–816.

169. For a description of these work point systems, see Parish and Whyte, *Village and Family,* pp. 63–71. For evidence of the preference, see Interview Files NM11K-4 (Guangdong); NM6H-10 (Guangdong); CN5K-16 (Guangdong); *Baoan Bulletin,* p. 128; and Lianjiang Documents, p. 101.

170. See Sixty Articles (1962), art. 34, and New Sixty Articles (1978), art. 44. See also *Baoan Bulletin,* pp. 156–57.

171. Interview File NM11K-9, 10 (Guangdong).

172. See Parish and Whyte, *Village and Family,* pp. 63–71.

173. Richard Madsen Interview File WW 18/12; Interview File CN5 (Guangdong); For evidence of poor households opposing household contracting since 1980, see Jack Potter, "Economic and Social Consequences" (estimates that 20 to 30 percent of the village he investigated opposed household contracting); David Zweig, "Opposition to Change in Rural China"; and Interview Files NKP2 (Fujian) (3.9.82); NT1 (Fujian) (29.6.82).

174. Interview Files NM9B-5,6 (Guangdong); NM11C-9 (Guangdong).

175. Sixty Articles (1962), art. 5; New Sixty Articles (1978), art. 6.

176. Lianjiang Documents, pp. 102–3; Radio Guangzhou, March 3, 1967, in *NPCRS* 199 (March 23, 1967): M21; and Radio Hangzhou, July 26, 1972, in FBIS 150 (Aug. 2, 1972): C5.

177. Interview File NM9B-5,6 (Guangdong); NKP2 (Fujian) (15.8.82). See also David Zweig, "Limits to Agrarian Radicalism."

178. Interview File NKP2 (Fujian) (15.8.82); Radio Xi'an, Jan. 10, 1979, in FBIS 12 (Jan. 17, 1979): M4; Xinhua, Jan. 10, 1979, in FBIS 10 (Jan. 15, 1979): M3–M4; Radio Wuhan, Jan. 14, 1979, in FBIS 11 (Jan. 16, 1979): H2; and Gordon Bennett, "Huadong People's Commune, 1980," *Asian Survey* 22, no. 8 (Aug. 1982): 745–56.

179. See *RMRB,* June 15, 1982, in FBIS 119 (June 21, 1982): K14, which reports that some households have been able to earn 1,000 to 2,000 yuan per capita annual income under the responsibility system.

180. *Sichuan Ribao,* Sept. 10, 1981, in FBIS 191 (Oct. 2, 1981): Q2. See also Cao Ruitian, "A Talk About Poverty and Wealth," *RMRB,* May 18, 1982, in FBIS 99 (May 21, 1982): K2–K3; Radio Zhengzhou, Aug. 14, 1982, in *SWB* FE/7106/BII/2 (Aug. 17, 1982); Yu Guoyao, "A Brief Discussion of Rural Specialized Households," *RMRB,* June 14, 1982, in FBIS 121 (June 23, 1982): K8–K10; Commentator, "Protect Peasants Who Get Rich Through Hard Work," *RMRB,* May 20, 1982, in FBIS 101 (May 25, 1982): K16–K18; Huo Shilian, "Much Can be Accomplished by Peasant Households Which Have Become Rich Through Labor," *RMRB,* June 15, 1982, in FBIS 119 (June 21, 1982): K13.

181. Commentator, "Enthusiastically Assist Poverty-Stricken Communes, and Production Brigades and Teams," *RMRB,* May 18, 1982, in FBIS 98 (May 20, 1982): K1. See also "Nongcun diaocha baogao" [Rural investigation report], *Guangxi Daxue Xuebao* 2 (1981) in Zhongguo renmin daxue shubao cailiao she, *Nongye Jingji* F2 (1982)2:55–59. This investigation found that the gap between rich and poor households widened from 1978 to 1980, but that most previously deficit households were now solvent. For a discussion of the nature and causes of rural poverty in contemporary China, see Lardy, *Agriculture in China's Modern Economic Development,* pp. 169–75.

182. *RMRB,* Sept. 1, 1981, in FBIS 174 (Sept. 9, 1981): K7–K15. There are now about 3 million "five guarantees" households.

183. Xinhua, Sept. 5, 1980, in FBIS 176 (Sept. 9, 1980): L33–L34; and *Liaoning Ribao,* March 1, 1982, in FBIS 52 (March 17, 1982).

184. Interview File CN5I-5 (Guangdong). Authorities can reduce quotas, of course, in the event of a natural disaster, such as a flood or drought.

185. For early complaints, see Radio Hefei, Sept. 7, 1963, in *NPCRS* 23 (Sept. 12, 1963): 23; and Radio Hangzhou, Sept. 3, 1963, in *NPCRS* 22 (Sept. 5, 1963): 19. More recently, see Radio Beijing, Sept. 22, 1979, in FBIS 187 (Sept. 25, 1979): L8–L10.

186. Xinhua, Jan. 20, 1979, in FBIS 15 (Jan. 22, 1979): E14; Xinhua, July 21, 1979, in FBIS 142 (July 23, 1979): O1; Xinhua, July 26, 1979, in FBIS 127 (July 30, 1979): L12–L15; Radio Wuhan, Aug. 25, 1979, in FBIS 169 (Aug. 29, 1979): P5; *RMRB,* Aug. 30, 1979, in FBIS 179 (Sept. 13, 1979): P8–P9; and *NFRB,* Oct. 26, 1979, p. 1, in FBIS 216 (Nov. 6, 1979): P2–P4. These cases were from Anhui, Fujian, Hebei, Hubei, and Guangdong.

187. *Hongqi* 3 (March 3, 1973), in *SCMM* 750 (April 2, 1973): 69; *RMRB,* Jan. 1, 1972, in *SCMP* 5054 (Jan. 14, 1972): 201.

188. Radio Wuhan, July 16, 1965, in *NPCRS* 116 (July 22, 1965): 13; Radio Changsha, Dec. 27, 1964, in *NPCRS* 88 (Dec. 30, 1964): 17.

189. Radio Hangzhou, June 11, 1963, in *NPCRS* 10 (June 13, 1963): 10; Radio Xi'an, Dec. 11, 1964, in *NPCRS* 87 (Dec. 17, 1964): 30; Radio Guangzhou, Aug. 26, 1964, in *NPCRS* 72 (Sept. 3, 1964): 24; and Radio Xi'an, Sept. 2, 1964, in *NPCRS* 73 (Sept. 10, 1964): 33.

190. Radio Changsha, May 11, 1980, in FBIS 95 (May 14, 1980): P6; Xinhua, Feb. 23, 1982, in FBIS 38 (Feb. 25, 1982): K4; *RMRB,* June 3, 1982; and Interview Files NKP1, NT1, NKP2.

191. See Barnett, *Cadres, Bureaucracy, and Political Power,* pp. 394–99.

192. Since 1980 authorities in Henan, Guangdong, Liaoning, Sichuan, and Anhui have demanded that rural laborers working in the cities return to the countryside. See Xinhua, Oct. 30, 1980, in FBIS 213 (Oct. 31, 1980): P1; Radio Guangzhou, Sept. 12, 1981, in FBIS 180 (Sept. 17, 1981): P1; Radio Shenyang, Nov. 10, 1981, in FBIS 218 (Nov. 12, 1981): S1; Radio Chengdu, Dec. 6, 1981, in FBIS 235 (Dec. 8, 1981): Q1; Radio Hefei, March 21, 1982, in FBIS 55 (March 22, 1982): O1; Radio Zhengzhou, July 11, 1982, in FBIS 139 (July 20, 1982): P4; and *Yangcheng Wanbao,* Aug. 3, 1982, in *SWB* FE/7098/BII/18 (Aug. 17, 1982). For earlier periods, see Editor, "Sources of Labor Discontent in China," *Current Scene* 5 (March 15, 1968); and John Lewis, "Commerce, Education, and Political Development in Tangshan: 1956–69," in Lewis, ed., *The City in Communist China* (Stanford: Stanford University Press, 1971), pp. 153–79.

193. "Regulations Governing Household Registration" (Beijing: Standing Committee, National People's Congress, Jan. 9, 1958), trans. in H. Yuan Tien, *China's Population Struggle* (Columbus: Ohio State University Press, 1973). For the operation of the system in Shanghai, see Lynn T. White, *Careers in Shanghai* (Berkeley and Los Angeles: University of California Press, 1978).

194. See "Peasants Go Down Coal Mines Under Contract System," *China Daily* (Beijing), April 11, 1984.

195. See John S. Aird, "Population Studies and Population Policy in China,"

Population and Development Review 8, no. 2 (June 1982): 267–97; Judith Banister, *China's Changing Population* (Stanford: Stanford University Press, 1985); H. Yuan Tien, *China's Population Struggle* (Columbus: Ohio State University Press, 1973); Steven W. Mosher, *Broken Earth* (New York: Free Press, 1983), chap. 8; and Wong Siu-lun, "Consequences of China's New Population Policy," *CQ* 98 (June 1984): 220–40. Interview File NKP1 (Fujian) (30.6.82).

196. See Joyce Kallgren, "Politics, Welfare, and Change," in Perry and Wong, eds., *The Political Economy of Reform,* pp. 144–45, 151.

197. Lardy, *Agriculture in China's Modern Economic Development,* p. 157.

198. Interview File NM4D-5 (Guangdong). See the comments of delegates to the 1980 National People's Congress, in Xinhua, Sept. 5, 1980, in FBIS 176 (Sept. 9, 1980): L13.

199. Sixty Articles (1962), arts. 34, 35, 36; New Sixty Articles (1978), art. 42.

200. Recent statements of this policy can be found in *RMRB,* June 25, 1979, in FBIS 133 (July 10, 1979): L17–L18; Radio Nanchang, Feb. 16, 1980, in FBIS 36 (Feb. 21, 1980): O4–O6; and Radio Changchun, Jan. 4, 1982, in FBIS 7 (Jan. 12, 1982): S1.

201. Radio Changchun, Oct. 19, 1979, in FBIS 205 (Oct. 22, 1979): S1–S2; Xinhua, Feb. 27, 1981, in FBIS 39 (Feb. 27, 1981): L11.

202. In 1980–81, peasants sometimes protested against the previous high rates of accumulation by "dividing up everything in an uproar." See, e.g., Radio Jinan, Dec. 29, 1981, in FBIS 251 (Dec. 31, 1981): O3; *RMRB,* April 3, 1982, in FBIS 73 (April 15, 1982): K2; see also Radio Chengdu, Feb. 28, 1983, in FBIS 41 (March 1, 1983): Q1, which reports that "fees and charges" paid by peasants were 15 yuan per capita per year in one Sichuan county (too high, according to authorities).

203. Under the new agricultural policies, grain prices in free markets have risen. Peasants sometimes took advantage of this and sold all of their grain in free markets. They, thus, ignored their contracted state quota responsibilities. See, e.g., Radio Chengdu, Nov. 17, 1980, in FBIS 229 (Nov. 25, 1980): Q1; and Radio Jinan, Jan. 23, 1981, in FBIS 17 (Jan. 27, 1981): O1–O2.

Chapter 4

1. Sixty Articles (1962), art. 23.
2. Ibid., art. 22.
3. Ibid., art. 21.
4. Ibid., art. 25.
5. "CCP Central Committee Directive Concerning the Question of Distribution in Rural People's Communes," Dec. 26, 1971 (*Zhongfa*) 82, in *Issues and Studies* 9, no. 2 (Nov. 1972): 92–95.
6. *NFRB,* Nov. 2, 1980; *Zhejiang Ribao,* Nov. 17, 1980; *RMRB,* March 23, 1981; Radio Taiyuan, March 17, 1981, in FBIS 52 (March 18, 1981): R3–R4;

Sichuan Ribao, April 20, 1981; *Anhui Ribao,* April 26, 1981, in Zhongguo renmin daxue shubao cailiao she, *Nongye Jingji* F2 (1981) 9:57; Radio Changchun, May 17, 1981, in FBIS 96 (May 19, 1981): S2; *Shanxi Ribao,* June 4, 1981, in Zhongguo renmin daxue shubao cailiao she, *Nongye Jingji* F2 (1981) 11:47; *Sichuan Ribao,* Sept. 10, 1981; *RMRB,* Nov. 18, 1981; and Long Chun, "Guanyu nongye shengchan zerenzhi de jige wenti" [Several problems regarding the agricultural production responsibility system], *Jingji Wenti Tansuo* [Exploration of Economic Problems] 1 (1982), in Zhongguo renmin daxue shubao cailiao she, *Nongye Jingji* F2 (1982) 4:65–68.

7. Xinhua, Feb. 19, 1981, in FBIS 34 (Feb. 20, 1981): Q1–Q2.

8. Xinhua, March 2, 1981, in FBIS 41 (March 3, 1981): L23–L27.

9. Long Chun, "Several Problems Regarding the Agricultural Production Responsibility System," p. 68.

10. Sixty Articles (1962), art. 22; New Sixty Articles (1978), art. 36.

11. Sixty Articles (1962), art. 24.

12. Ibid., art. 32; New Sixty Articles (1978), art. 36.

13. Sixty Articles (1962), art. 35; New Sixty Articles (1978), art. 42.

14. For the range of meetings held in one Fujian brigade in 1961, see the Lianjiang Documents, pp. 174–75. See also Interview Files NKP2 (Fujian) (3.9.82), (7.9.82), (29.8.82), (29.7.82); NKP1 (Fujian) (5.7.82); NT1 (Fujian) (6.7.82); NCN3 (Fujian) (29.7.82).

15. Interview File NM11J-2 (Guangdong).

16. Interview File CN3A-2 (Shanghai).

17. Chan, Madsen, and Unger, *Chen Village,* p. 58.

18. Interview File CN5K-10 (Guangdong).

19. See Chan, Madsen, and Unger, *Chen Village,* pp. 74–102.

20. *NFRB,* Oct. 24, 1981. Examples of other team noncampaign economic meetings can be found in *Sichuan Ribao,* Sept. 13, 1981; *Fujian Ribao,* March 26, 1982; and *NFRB,* Jan. 7, 1979.

21. *Zhejiang Ribao,* Oct. 26, 1981. See also ibid., Dec. 18, 1980.

22. Sixty Articles (1962), art. 18, stipulates 2 times a year; New Sixty Articles (1978), art. 9, stipulates 4 times a year.

23. Sixty Articles (1962), art. 38; New Sixty Articles (1978), art. 9.

24. See Interview Files NM9B-32 (Guangdong); NT1 (Fujian) (6.7.82).

25. Interview File NKP2 (Fujian) (3.9.82).

26. Interview File NT1 (Fujian) (6.7.82).

27. Interview Files NKP2 (Fujian) (3.9.82); NM3A-5 (Guangdong). For the same period in Guangdong, Blecher reports that 78 percent of his informants responding to the question of the frequency of team mass meetings said that their teams held meetings at least 2 or 3 times per month, while 33 percent reported that their teams met several times per week. In some teams, meetings were held at specified intervals, and in others only when team cadres deemed them necessary (Blecher, "Leader-Mass Relations," p. 97).

28. Interview Files NKP2 (Fujian) (3.9.82); NCN3 (Fujian) (29.7.82); NT1 (Fujian) (6.7.82).

29. Pan Naiyue, "Nongcun shedui jingying guanli de huigu he gaige weiyi" [Management of rural communes and brigades in retrospect with suggestions for reform], *Nongye Jingji Wenti* 4 (1981), in Zhongguo renmin daxue shubao cailiao she, *Nongye Jingji* F2 (1981) 9 : 100–2. Pan suggests the following reforms: that team mass meetings and brigade congresses be guaranteed full use of their management power; that everyone be equal before the law; and that paternalistic leadership be "rooted out" with leaders "going to the people and listening to their opinions."

30. Xinhua, Jan. 20, 1979, in FBIS 15 (Jan. 22, 1979): E14–E15.

31. Radio Guiyang, Oct. 17, 1979, in FBIS 205 (Oct. 22, 1979): Q1–Q2.

32. Interview Files NM3A-6 (Guangdong); NM11J-3 (Guangdong); NM9C-1, 2 (Guangdong). See also Jonathan Unger, "Incentives, Ideology, and Peasant Interests in a Chinese Village, 1960–1980," in William L. Parish, ed., *Chinese Rural Development* (Armonk: M. E. Sharpe, 1985), pp. 117–40.

33. Production teams that adopted *baochan dao hu* continue to use a piece-rate work point system, while the teams that adopted *baogan dao hu* have dispensed with it.

34. "Jianli zerenzhi yao ying dui zhiyi" [Establish responsibility systems suitable to the brigade], *Sichuan Ribao*, Sept. 13, 1981.

35. Interview File NKP2 (Fujian) (29.7.82).

36. Interview File CN5L-3 (Guangdong).

37. Interview File CN5J-3 (Guangdong).

38. Interview File NM4D-8 (Guangdong).

39. Interview File NM9D-7 (Guangdong).

40. Interview File CN6C-12, 13 (Guangdong).

41. Interview File NM4D-2 (Guangdong).

42. Chu Li and Tian Jieyuan, *Inside a People's Commune* (Beijing: Foreign Languages Press, 1974).

43. During the 1970s, they were often composed of the same people. For a discussion of types of brigade cadre meetings in one Fujian brigade in 1961, see Lianjiang Documents, p. 222. See also Interview Files CN5H-6 (Guangdong); CN5L-4 (Guangdong); NM9B-7 (Guangdong).

44. "Yiyuanhua lingdao bu shi yi ge ren lingdao" [United leadership is not one-man leadership], *Zhejiang Ribao*, Dec. 18, 1980; See also Chan, Madsen, and Unger, *Chen Village*, pp. 26–37 and passim, for a discussion of the leadership styles of Chen village leaders.

45. Interview File NKP2 (Fujian) (29.7.82) and (29.8.82).

46. Interview File CN5L-1-9 (Guangdong).

47. Interview File NM4E-2, 3 (Guangdong).

48. "Yao jiena sheyuan de zhengque yijian" [(We) must accept commune members' correct opinions], *NFRB*, Feb. 19, 1979, p. 2.

49. Xinhua, Aug. 13, 1980, in FBIS 164 (Aug. 21, 1980): L3–L5.

50. Interview File NM9B-8. Wearing a "three-flags" hat meant being labeled a "rightist," "counterrevolutionary," or a "bad element" (criminal). See also NKP2 (Fujian) (29.7.82) for the same sentiment.

51. For a graphic description of the labeling process, see Chan, Madsen, and Unger, *Chen Village*, pp. 141–68.

52. See Xinhua, Jan. 17, 1979, in FBIS (Jan. 19, 1979): E20–E22, which relates the cases of Deng Shaocheng in Sichuan and Huang Shaojun in Guizhou. They and their families were labeled "capitalist upstarts" during the 1970s and "newly emerging rich peasants" after 1976, both "bad" labels. As a consequence, their property was confiscated. In 1979 it was returned, and the labels removed, however.

53. Lianjiang Documents, p. 103.

54. *RMRB*, April 24 and Jan. 6, 1979.

55. *NFRB*, Dec. 18 and 29, 1980.

56. *Fujian Ribao*, May 14, 1981.

57. See Hinton, *Fanshen*, pp. 332–40; and Townsend, *Political Participation*, p. 166, who concludes that "the peasants sometimes had a significant control over the election and removal of peasant leaders, and peasant meetings were generally quite open to expressions of popular opinons."

58. For evidence of the decline, see *Changjiang Ribao*, Aug. 28, 1951, in *SCMP* 179 (Sept. 21–22, 1951): 31–32, and *Changjiang Ribao*, Nov. 20, 1952, in *SCMP* 471 (Dec. 12, 1952): 11–12, which notes that many village peasant associations existed "in name only and do not have any members."

59. See the "Organizational Rules of Poor and Lower-Middle Peasant Associations (Draft)," June 1964, in Baum and Teiwes, *Ssu-ch'ing*, pp. 95–101.

60. Ibid., arts. 1, 2, 8.

61. See, e.g., Radio Guangzhou, Nov. 29, 1974, in FBIS 232 (Dec. 2, 1974): H2; Radio Nanning, Dec. 15, 1974, in FBIS 242 (Dec. 16, 1974): H3; Radio Guangzhou, Feb. 17, 1974, in FBIS 36 (Feb. 21, 1974): D1; Radio Wuhan, Dec. 26, 1975, in FBIS 6 (Jan. 9, 1974): D5; and Radio Hefei, Nov. 20, 1973, in FBIS 234 (Dec. 5, 1973): C3.

62. Liao Gailong, "The 1980 Reform Program of China—Part Four," in FBIS 50 (March 16, 1981): U11. For an earlier, but less eloquent, call for independent peasants' associations, see Xinhua, Jan. 16, 1980, in FBIS 13 (Jan. 18, 1980): L12–L15.

63. Sun Qimeng explicitly identified supervision by mass organizations in "Carry Out Two Kinds of Supervision of Different Natures," *RMRB*, July 1, 1982, in FBIS 131 (July 8, 1982): K1–K4.

64. See Radio Kunming, Feb. 18, 1982, in FBIS 37 (Feb. 24, 1982); Radio Wuhan, Dec. 23, 1980, in FBIS 2 (Jan. 5, 1981): P2; Radio Guangzhou, April 2, 1982, in FBIS 68 (April 8, 1982): P2; Radio Nanjing, June 24, 1979, in FBIS 139 (July 18, 1979): O5; and Radio Changsha, Feb. 22, 1980, in FBIS 38 (Feb. 25, 1980): P3.

65. Radio Guangzhou, Nov. 24, 1974, in FBIS 229 (Nov. 26, 1974): H4.

66. See general accounts in Radio Guangzhou, Sept. 3, 1964, in *NPCRS* 73 (Sept. 10, 1964): 21–22; Radio Changsha, Oct. 5, 1964, in *NPCRS* 77 (Oct. 8, 1964): 6; Radio Guangzhou, Oct. 13, 1964, in *NPCRS* 78 (Oct. 15, 1964): 25–26.

67. *NFRB*, Aug. 1, 1965; Radio Kunming, Sept. 18, 1965, in *NPCRS* 125 (Sept. 23, 1965): 50.

68. Radio Wuhan, Dec. 25, 1964, in *NPCRS* 88 (Dec. 30, 1964): 22.

69. Radio Guangzhou, Sept. 4 and Oct. 8, 1964, in *NPCRS* 73 and 78 (Sept. 10 and Oct. 15, 1964, respectively).

70. See Radio Zhengzhou, Aug. 28, 1964, in *NPCRS* 72 (Sept. 3, 1964): 8; Radio Changsha, Oct. 5, 1964, in *NPCRS* 77 (Oct. 8, 1964): 6; Radio Guangzhou, Sept. 4, 1964, in *NPCRS* 73 (Sept. 10, 1964): 24; Radio Nanjing, Nov. 8, 1964, in *NPCRS* 82 (Nov. 12, 1964): 19; Radio Taiyuan, Aug. 31, 1964, in *NPCRS* 72 (Sept. 3, 1964): 32; Radio Nanchang, Oct. 27, 1964, in *NPCRS* 80 (Oct. 29, 1964): 18; Radio Nanjing, Dec. 21, 1964, in *NPCRS* 88 (Dec. 30, 1964): 31–32; Radio Changsha, Dec. 17, 1963, in *NPCRS* 38 (Dec. 26, 1963): 6; and Radio Nanchang, Nov. 17, 1964, in *NPCRS* 83 (Nov. 17, 1964): 15.

71. Interview File NM9B-22 (Guangdong).

72. See also Interview File NM4D-1 (Guangdong).

73. Interview Files CN5H-5 (Guangdong); NM4D-1 (Guangdong); NKP1 (Fujian) (5.7.82); NT1 (Fujian) (12.7.82); NT3 (Fujian) (2.8.82); and NCN1 (Yunnan) (15.7.82).

74. Interview File NM8C-1 (Guangdong).

75. Interview Files CN5C-9 (Guangdong) and CN5B-19 (Guangdong).

76. Interview File NM5B-6 (Guangdong).

77. Interview File NM4D-1 (Guangdong).

78. For an exception, see the report of a brigade peasant association in Hubei that investigated the misappropriation of 26,000 yuan by five brigade-level enterprises in 1982 (Radio Wuhan, Aug. 30, 1982, in FBIS 171 [Sept. 2, 1982]: P2).

79. Exceptions to this general observation were the few cases in my data of women's federation members who demanded that the government's policy of equal pay for equal work be enforced. Usually, however, members had standing (such as cadre status or party membership) to speak out, other than their role in the federation. See Kay Ann Johnson, Trip Notes, May–June 1978 (unpublished).

Chapter 5

1. Townsend, *Political Participation*, pp. 115–18. Nationwide elections of delegates to commune (township) congresses were held in 1953–1954, 1956, 1958, 1961, 1963, and 1966. These elections were held under the authority of the 1953 Election Law, art. 3, trans. in Theodore Chen, ed., *The Chinese Communist Regime* (New York: Praeger, 1967), pp. 65–75. The 1954 state constitution also provided for the direct election of township congress delegates (art. 56). Since 1962 the Sixty Articles have also required the direct election of delegates to commune and brigade congresses.

2. Sixty Articles (1962), arts. 18 and 38. Article 38 required that peasants elect the production team head, accountant, a control committee member, a supervisor, and management committee members for one-year terms.

3. See the 1975 state constitution, art. 21 (which, however, omits the "direct" election of commune congress delegates); and the 1978 state constitution, art. 35.

4. "Communique of the Third Plenary Session of the Eleventh Central Committee of the Communist Party of China," Dec. 22, 1978, in FBIS 248 (Dec. 26, 1978): E8.

5. New Sixty Articles (1978), art. 9. This document called for the direct election of commune and brigade congresses, and production team leader, deputy leader, and members of the team management committee.

6. Editorial, *RMRB,* Jan. 24, 1979; Editorial, *RMRB,* Jan. 26, 1979, in FBIS 22 (Jan. 31, 1979): E18–E19; *NFRB,* Feb. 1, 1979; Editorial, *RMRB,* April 28, 1979; and *RMRB,* Feb. 27, 1979.

7. See "The Electoral Law of the National Peoples' Congress and Local Peoples' Congresses of the People's Republic of China," July 1, 1979, amended on Dec. 10, 1982. The amended version appears in FBIS 243 (Dec. 17, 1982): K14–K21. Direct election of county and commune (township) congress delegates was also affirmed in the "Organic Law for the Local People's Congresses and Local People's Governments of the People's Republic of China," July 1, 1979, amended Dec. 10, 1982. The amended version appears in FBIS 244 (Dec. 20, 1982): K43–K54.

8. See Cheng Zihua, "Summing Up Report on the National Direct Election at the County Level," Sept. 3, 1981, in FBIS 177 (Sept. 14, 1981): K2-K10. Cheng reported that by Sept. 1981, 2,368 out of 2,756 counties held direct elections for county people's congresses. In Sept. 1983, authorities announced that elections scheduled for that year would be postponed for one year because of "the structural reform, and the separation of government and commune administration" (Xinhua, Sept. 2, 1983, in FBIS 173 [Sept. 6, 1983]: K11). By Dec. 1984, officials reported that "all but ten of the country's 2,805 county-level units requiring elections by law" had conducted direct elections for delegates to county-level people's congresses (Xinhua, Jan. 30, 1985, in FBIS 21 [Jan. 31, 1985]: K13). These elections were held concurrently with elections of deputies to local congresses at *xiang* (township) and *cun* (village) levels. Because the elections were for positions in the new local governments, they fall beyond the scope of my study. For secondary accounts of the 1980 elections, see Andrew J. Nathan, *Chinese Democracy* (New York: Alfred A. Knopf, 1985), chap. 10; Brantly Womack, "The 1980 County-Level Elections in China," *Asian Survey* 22, no. 3 (March 1982): 261–77; Barrett L. McCormick, "Election Campaign in Nanjing," (paper prepared for the annual meeting of the Association of Asian Studies, San Francisco, March 1983); McCormick, "Reforming the People's Congress System," in David M. Lampton, ed., *Policy Implementation in Post-Mao China* (Berkeley and Los Angeles: University of California, 1987).

9. More than 2,350 production team elections were reported in 1979–1980 in Guangdong and Zhejiang alone. See *RMRB,* March 7, 1979; *NFRB,* Sept. 10, 1979; *Zhejiang Ribao,* Nov. 7, 1980; *Zhejiang Ribao,* Nov. 14, 1980. From 1980

to 1981, the Shanghai suburbs and Shandong, Heilongjiang, Gansu, Hunan, and Jiangsu provinces reported holding elections to elect commune people's congresses in conjunction with county-level direct elections. See *Jiefang Ribao,* Oct. 10, 1980, in FBIS 212 (Oct. 30, 1980): O2–O3; Radio Jinan, June 4, 1980, in FBIS 111 (June 6, 1980): O2–O3; Radio Harbin, June 3, 1980, in FBIS 111 (June 6, 1980): S1; Radio Gansu, July 17, 1980, in FBIS 140 (July 18, 1980): T1; Radio Changsha, Jan. 23, 1980, in FBIS 20 (Jan. 29, 1980): P1; and Radio Nanjing, May 19, 1981, in FBIS 97 (May 20, 1981).

10. See 1982 state constitution, art. 111.

11. See 1982 state constitution, art. 34; 1978 state constitution, art. 44; 1975 state constitution, art. 27; 1954 state constitution, art. 86; 1953 Election Law, arts. 4, 5; 1979 Election Law (amended in 1982), art. 3; and Xu Chongde and Pi Chunxie, *Xuanju Zhidu Wenda* [Questions and answers on the election system] (Beijing: Qunzhong chubanshe, 1980), p. 167.

12. "Certain Regulations by the National People's Congress Standing Committee Concerning the Direct Election of Deputies to People's Congresses at the County Level and Below," Xinhua, March 7, 1983, in FBIS 46 (March 8, 1983): K1–K3.

13. For Guangdong, see, e.g., Guangdong sheng xuanju gongzuo bangongshi, "Zhijie xuanju xuanchuan tigang" [Direct election propaganda outline], Dec. 29, 1983; and Guangzhou shi jiaoqu xuanju weiyuanhui bangongshi, "Guangzhou shi jiaoqu, zhen, xiang dibajie renda daibiao xuanju xuanchuan cailiao" [Guangzhou city, suburb, town, and township propaganda materials for the election of delegates to the Eighth People's Congress], Jan. 9, 1984. These regulations follow closely the amended 1979 Election Law. See also regulations for Shanxi and Beijing in "Shanxi sheng geji renmin daibiao dahui xuanju shishi xize" [Bylaws for the implementation of elections of various levels of people's congress in Shanxi Province] in Shanxi sheng renmin dachanghui bangongshi, ed., *Difang Renda Gongzuo Shouce* [Handbook for local people's congresses' work], vol. 1 (1984), pp. 147–48; and "Beijing shiqu, xian, xiang, zhen renmin daibiao dahui daibiao xuanju shishi xize" [Bylaws for the implementation of elections for district, county, township, and town people's congress deputies] in *Beijing Shi Difangxing Fagui Huibian: 1980–1985* [Selection of Beijing municipal local laws: 1980–1985] (Beijing: Zhongguo zhengfa daxue chubanshe, 1986), pp. 126–38. Other regulations governing election work in Beijing can be found in *Beijing Shi Difangxing Fagui Huibian.*

14. See Nathan, *Chinese Democracy,* pp. 197–203, for a discussion of the provisions of the 1979 Election Law as they were carried out in the 1980 elections.

15. Zhang Huanguang, "What is Meant by Direct Elections at the County Level?" *RMRB,* Aug. 20, 1980, in JPRS 76547 (Oct. 3, 1980): 30–31.

16. See *Fujian Ribao,* Feb. 21, 1981, and Liu Jianzheng, "Nongye shengchan zerenzhi cujin le nongcun de minzhu jianshe" [Carrying out the agricultural responsibility system results in building village democracy], *Guangming Ribao,* Dec. 27, 1982; Li Zaizao and Chen Jinluo, "A Talk on the Fundamental Spirit of

Election Laws and the Significance of Direct Election of People's Congresses at the County Level," *Faxue Yanjiu* 2 (April 23, 1980), in JPRS 76527 (Oct. 2, 1980): 6–13. See Zhang, "What is Meant by Direct Elections at the County Level?" p. 30; "Qunzhong xuanju ziji xinren de ganbu haochu duo" [There are many advantages of the masses electing their own trusted cadres], *NFRB*, Jan. 20, 1980, p. 1; *Fujian Ribao*, May 15, 1980; *RMRB*, March 30, 1982; *Zhejiang Ribao*, Dec. 20, 1980; *NFRB*, March 28, 1979; *Xinhua Ribao*, Dec. 9, 1980; *Xinhua Ribao*, Dec. 7, 1980; *Xinhua Ribao*, Oct. 22, 1980; *NFRB*, Sept. 10, 1980; and *NFRB*, Nov. 11, 1982.

17. Radio Chengdu, Dec. 29, 1979, in FBIS 1 (Jan. 2, 1979): J2.

18. "Xuanju neng lingdao qun zengchan de ren dang duizhang" [Elect those who can lead the masses to raise production to be team leaders], *RMRB*, Feb. 20, 1979; and *NFRB*, Sept. 10, 1979, which reported that, before elections were instituted in 1979, the team changed its leader every year.

19. "Shengchandui ganbu bixu minzhu xuanju" [Production team cadres should be democratically elected], *NFRB*, Jan. 10, 1979; *NFRB*, July 8, 1980, p. 2. See also *NFRB*, March 15, 1979, and *RMRB*, Feb. 26, 1979, for the same argument.

20. *RMRB*, April 3, 1979.

21. *Zhejiang Ribao*, Nov. 14, 1980.

22. "Wei xuan shengchan duizhang shuo ji ju hua" [A few words on the election of production team leaders], *Zhejiang Ribao*, Nov. 6, 1981; "Kuaiji duiwu xiangdui wending hao" [Relative stability of team accountants is good], *Zhejiang Ribao*, July 25, 1980.

23. "Caiqu duo zhong banfa xuanba peiyang zhong-qingnian ganbu" [Use many methods for selecting and cultivating young and middle-aged cadres], *Sichuan Ribao*, Sept. 22, 1980; *Xinhua Ribao*, April 11, 1980.

24. "Lingdao banzi bian yi nian da bianhua" [Leadership group change, in one year a big change], *Xinhua Ribao*, May 14, 1980.

25. This can be inferred from Cheng Zihua, "Summing Up Report on the National Direct Election at the County Level," Sept. 3, 1981, in FBIS 177 (Sept. 14, 1981): K2–K10.

26. *Tianjin Ribao*, March 17, 1980, in JPRS 75825 (June 4, 1980): 66–70.

27. From 1962 to 1977, *RMRB* published only one editorial dealing with election work (April 16, 1963).

28. This and subsequent sections are based on reports of production team elections found in the following sources. Fifty-five cases have been reported in the press since 1978: *NFRB*, July 8, 1980; *NFRB*, Jan. 10, 1979; *RMRB*, April 3, 1979; *Fujian Ribao*, March 21, 1982; *RMRB*, Nov. 9, 1979; *NFRB*, March 15, 1979; *NFRB*, Feb. 14, 1979; *RMRB*, Dec. 12, 1978; *Sichuan Ribao*, July 10, 1980; *Xinhua Ribao*, July 7, 1980; *NFRB*, Jan. 20, 1980; *Zhejiang Ribao*, Dec. 20, 1980; *RMRB*, March 7, 1979; *NFRB*, Feb. 13, 1979; *Xinhua Ribao*, Oct. 22, 1980; *Zhejiang Ribao*, Dec. 20, 1980; *RMRB*, June 30, 1980; *RMRB*, Feb. 20, 1979; *RMRB*, Jan. 21, 1980; *Xinhua Ribao*, Dec. 7, 1980; *Zhejiang Ribao*, Nov. 14,

1980; *NFRB*, Sept. 10, 1979; Radio Chengdu, Dec. 29, 1978, in FBIS 1 (Jan. 2, 1979): J2; *Xinhua Ribao*, May 15, 1980; *RMRB*, March 20, 1982; *NFRB*, March 28, 1979; *Xinhua Ribao*, Dec. 9, 1980; *NFRB*, Sept. 10, 1980; *NFRB*, Nov. 11, 1982; *Zhejiang Ribao*, Dec. 7, 1981; *Zhejiang Ribao*, Dec. 11, 1980; *NFRB*, March 7, 1979; *NFRB*, Sept. 12, 1979; *Fujian Ribao*, July 7, 1982; *Xinhua Ribao*, March 22, 1980; *RMRB*, May 20, 1979; *RMRB*, May 15, 1979; *RMRB*, Feb. 26, 1979; *RMRB*, April 27, 1979; *RMRB*, March 3, 1980; *Xinhua Ribao*, March 22, 1982; *Zhejiang Ribao*, Nov. 7, 1980; Radio Shijiazhuang, Nov. 15, 1979, in FBIS 229 (Nov. 27, 1979): R1–R2; *RMRB*, Dec. 15, 1980; *Sichuan Ribao*, Aug. 5, 1980.

Twenty cases were generated from interviews, mainly from Fujian and Guangdong: Interview Files NT3 (Shanghai) (15.7.82); NCN3 (Fujian) (15.7.82 and 29.7.82); NKP4 (Fujian) (26.6.82 and 22.9.82); NCN1 (Yunnan) (2.7.82); NT1 (Fujian) (22.6.82); NKP1 (Fujian) (21.6.82); NKP2 (Fujian) (29.7.82); NM5A-3, 4 (Guangdong); NM3A-4, 6 (Guangdong); NM11I-10 (Guangdong); NM9A-23 and 9B-12 (Guangdong); NM4C-7 (Guangdong); NM6A-2, 3 (Guangdong); CN4C-2 and 4D (Guangdong); CN11A, B, C (Guangdong); CN3A, B, C (Shanghai); NM10B, C (Guangdong).

29. Many provinces issued local election regulations based on the national election law. Sichuan issued "Bylaws Governing the Election of County- and Commune-level People's Congresses in Sichuan Province," which was based on the 1979 Election Law (*Sichuan Ribao*, July 31, 1980, in JPRS, *China Report* No. 140 [Nov. 21, 1980]: 14–15). See also n. 13 above. Election handbooks, such as Xu Chongde and Pi Chunxie, *Xuanju Zhidu Wenda*, were intended for distribution to commune level. See *RMRB*, Aug. 20, 1980, in JPRS 76547 (Oct. 3, 1980): 32–33.

30. "Renyang gongshe yu lingdao de minzhu xuanju shengchan duizhang" [Renyang commune leads the democratic election of production team leaders], *Xinhua Ribao*, Dec. 1, 1980.

31. In most production teams in Xuanhuang County, Jiangxi, elections were held without prior nominations (presumably reelections of the incumbent cadres). See, "Taopi gongshe minzhu xuanju shengchan duizhang" [Taopi commune democratically elects team leaders], *RMRB*, Jan. 21, 1979.

32. Of 6 cases generated through interviewing, 4 reported that the brigade made these nominations. Of the 55 press cases, only 9 addressed this issue, of which 8 reported that team members made the nominations. See Interview Files NT3 (Shanghai) (15.7.82); NCN2 (Fujian) (29.7.82); NKP1 (Fujian) (21.6.82); NKP2 (29.7.82); *RMRB*, Nov. 9, 1979; Interview File NT1 (Fujian) (22.6.82); *NFRB*, Feb. 13, 1979; *NFRB*, Jan. 20, 1980; *RMRB*, June 30, 1980; *NFRB*, March 15, 1979; *RMRB*, March 7, 1979; *Zhejiang Ribao*, Dec. 20, 1980; *Xinhua Ribao*, Oct. 22, 1980.

33. See Interview Files, NM5A-3 (Guangdong); NM6A-2, 3 (Guangdong); NM9A-12, 17 (Guangdong); and CN5G-1 (Guangdong); NT2 (Fujian) (25.6.82); NCN1 (Yunnan) (2.7.82); NKP4 (Fujian) (26.6.82).

34. Interview File NKP2 (Fujian) (29.7.82).

35. *RMRB*, March 7, 1979; *Fujian Ribao*, April 23, 1982; *RMRB*, Nov. 9, 1979; *NFRB*, Feb. 13, 1979. During some campaigns, such as the Four Clean-ups Campaign, work teams took over the supervision of production team elections from brigades in many places (Interview Files CN3A, B, C [Shanghai]; NM10B, C [Guangdong]). Informants in Fujian also reported work teams managing local elections in the wake of the fall of the Gang of Four (Interview File NKP2 [8.8.82]). Finally, if difficult leadership problems emerged that could not be handled by brigade authorities, counties or communes sometimes sent work teams to carry out local investigations and supervise appropriate team leadership changes.

36. Interview File CN3A, B, C (Shanghai).

37. Interview Files NCN3 (Fujian) (15.7.82); NT1 (Fujian) (22.6.82); *NFRB*, March 15, 1979; *NFRB*, Jan. 20, 1980; *Zhejiang Ribao*, Dec. 20, 1980; *RMRB*, March 7, 1979; *NFRB*, Feb. 13, 1979; *Xinhua Ribao*, Oct. 22, 1980.

38. Interview File NM11I-10 (Guangdong). See also NM3A-4 (Guangdong). Some informants report that, although the team management committee formally nominated candidates, they first informally sought the approval of the brigade party branch (Interview File CN5H-6 [Guangdong]).

39. "Xuan hao dangjiaren" [Elect the masters well], *NFRB*, March 15, 1979.

40. "Baodui ganbu bu ying baoban xuanju" [Guarantee cadres should not guarantee elections], *RMRB*, Dec. 1, 1978.

41. *RMRB*, June 30, 1980; *Zhejiang Ribao*, Dec. 20, 1980; *RMRB*, Dec. 9, 1979. That such a small number of the press reports indicate that the number of nominees exceeded the number of posts at a time when this was one of the much-publicized advantages of the new election law leads me to conclude that most brigades only nominated enough candidates to fill the available posts.

42. Interview Files NT3 (Fujian) (19.7.82); NCN3 (Guangdong) (29.7.82); NT1 (Fujian) (22.6.82); NKP1 (21.6.82); NKP2 (29.7.82); and NCN3 (29.7.82). In the early and mid-1970s, a number of informants report that more candidates than posts were sometimes nominated. See Interview Files NKP4 (Fujian) (22.9.82); NCN1 (Yunnan) (2.7.82); NM9A-15 (Guangdong); NM11I-10 (Guangdong).

43. E.g., "Taopi gongshe minzhu xuanju shengchan duizhang" *RMRB*, Jan. 21, 1979; and *RMRB*, June 30, 1980.

44. *NFRB*, March 15, 1979.

45. "Shei shi zhenzheng de Baili?" [Who is the real Baili?], *Sichuan Ribao*, July 10, 1980.

46. One correspondent to *Zhejiang Ribao* indicates that, in his area at the end of the busy season, most team leaders resigned and waited for the following year's election. He interprets this action as an election strategy: "In submitting their resignations, [many team] leaders were aiming at catching the attention of commune and brigade authorities, to solicit help to solve their problems. Some . . . resigned because they wanted to be reelected. To them, reelection with popular support meant that team members had faith in them." The writer deplores this conduct,

because it resulted in instability in team leadership groups ("Wei xuan shangchan duizhang shuo ji ju hua," *Zhejiang Ribao,* Nov. 6, 1981).

47. Ding Zhengquan, "Jiandou" [Gathering beans], *Yuhua* [Rain and Flowers] (Beijing) 1980, no. 3: 4–12. See also *RMRB,* June 30, 1980.

48. Interview File CN3B-1 (Shanghai).

49. Interview File CN5G-24 (Guangdong).

50. Ding, "Jiandou," pp. 4–12.

51. Interview File NKP2 (Fujian) (29.7.82).

52. Interview File CN5G-19 (Guangdong). See also Interview Files NM5A-3 (Guangdong) and NM6A-3 (Guangdong) for cases of peasants making additional nominations during team election meetings.

53. Interview File CN3B-1, 2 (Shanghai).

54. Interview Files NM11I-10 (Guangdong); NM5A-3 (Guangdong); CN4C-2 (Guangdong); and NM9A-17 (Guangdong); NKP4 (Fujian) (22.9.82); NT2 (Fujian) (25.6.82).

55. Interview Files NT3 (Shanghai) (15.7.82); NCN3 (Fujian) (15.7.82); NKP2 (Fujian) (29.7.82).

56. Ding, "Jiandou," pp. 4–12.

57. Interview Files NM8D-14 (Guangdong). Sometimes team management committees did this themselves (CN4C-2 [Guangdong] and NM4C-7 [Guangdong]). See also NM11I-10 (Guangdong); NM9A-13 (Guangdong); NM8D-14 (Guangdong); NKP4 (Fujian) (22.9.82); and NT2 (Fujian) (25.6.82).

58. In Chengguan commune [Zhejiang], commune authorities issued the *renmingshu* to the team leader, while brigade authorities gave it to the team management committee. Communes may have recently started issuing these documents to team leaders to increase their authority. See *Zhejiang Ribao,* Nov. 14, 1980.

59. *RMRB,* Dec. 1, 1978; for a similar case, see Interview File NM9A-13, 14 (Guangdong).

60. "Shangmian quanding duizhang jiu shi bu minzhu" [Upper levels choosing team leaders is not democratic], *NFRB,* Feb. 14, 1979.

61. "Zhezhong quanding shi biyao de" [This sort of choosing is necessary], *NFRB,* Feb. 21, 1979.

62. "Quanding dake bubi" [Fixing is not necessary], *NFRB,* March 14, 1979; "Cong xuanju bu xuan xiao tanqi" [Talking about elections being overruled], *NFRB,* March 15, 1979. *NFRB* reported no official reaction to this case.

63. Interview File NM1F-1 (Guangdong).

64. Interview Files CN4C-2 (Guangdong); CN11B (Guangdong).

65. "Renmin zui zhongyao de quanli shi xuanju quanli" [The people's most important power is the right of election], *NFRB,* Jan. 16, 1979. See also "Cong xuanju daibiao tanqi" [Talking about electing representatives], *RMRB,* Oct. 9, 1978; and "Wei shenme chuxian fendui xianxiang?" [Why has the phenomenon of splitting up the team emerged?], *RMRB,* May 5, 1979.

66. Interview Files NCN3 (29.7.82); NCN1 (2.7.82); NKP2 (29.7.82).

67. Writing in 1977, I concluded that, since 1970, local cadres had called an-

nual production team elections. New information indicates that this generalization was accurate for only a few teams. See John P. Burns, "The Election of Production Team Cadres: 1962–1974," *CQ* 74 (June 1978): 276.

68. For cases of this, see *NFRB*, July 8, 1980, and *NFRB*, March 15, 1979.

69. Interview File NT2 (Fujian) (25.6.82).

70. Interview File NKP2 (29.7.82); see also the section below on cadre unwillingness.

71. Interview Files CN3A, B, C (Shanghai).

72. Interview File NKP4 (Fujian) (26.6.82); see also press stories of peasants demanding the ouster of unpopular cadres. In a 1974 case, peasants put up a big-character poster protesting that their team leader "prospered by other people's misfortune" (*RMRB*, May 20, 1979). Peasants "for a long time" demanded the removal of a party member who was their team leader because of his "selfishness" (*NFRB*, March 28, 1979), and peasants demanded the removal of incompetent brigade appointees in a Sichuan brigade (Radio Chengdu, Dec. 29, 1978, in FBIS 1 [Jan. 2, 1979]).

73. Interview File NM3 (Shanghai) (15.7.82). For press reports linking team leadership recruitment problems to factionalism, see *Sichuan Ribao*, Oct. 9, 1980; *RMRB*, May 5, 1979 (which dates the problem to the Four Clean-ups Campaign); *Xinhua Ribao*, May 14 and Dec. 7, 1980.

74. Interview File NM3 (Shanghai) (15.7.82).

75. See, e.g., *Tianjin Ribao*, March 17, 1980, which points out that elections in Wuqing County were preceded by "purging the Gang of Four faction throughout the entire county [so that] . . . the power of leadership in the county, communes, and production brigades is firmly in the hands of reliable persons," in JPRS 75825 (June 4, 1980): 67.

76. *NFRB*, March 15, 1979; *Fujian Ribao*, July 7, 1982; and *RMRB*, Jan. 21, 1979.

77. *Zhejiang Ribao*, Nov. 7, 1980, and Nov. 14, 1980.

78. *Xinhua Ribao*, Dec. 7, 1980.

79. This method was used in Guangxi, Guangdong, and Zhejiang. See *RMRB*, May 15, 1979; *NFRB*, Feb. 13, 1979; *NFRB*, Jan. 20, 1980; *Zhejiang Ribao*, Dec. 20, 1980; and *Zhejiang Ribao*, Nov. 7, 1980.

80. In all of the 2,052 production teams in Lian County, Guangdong, cited above, voters elected the leader and the committee.

81. Lianjiang Documents, p. 192, also pp. 217, 235–36, 288.

82. See Letter to the Editor, *Zhejiang Ribao*, Nov. 7, 1980; *Xinhua Ribao*, June 14, 1980; *NFRB*, Oct. 10, 1982; *Fujian Ribao*, July 7, 1982; *Zhejiang Ribao*, Dec. 20, 1980; and *Xinhua Ribao*, Dec. 7, 1980. See Interview Files NT3 (Shanghai) (15.7.82); NKP1 (Fujian) (21.6.82); NKP2 (Fujian) (29.7.82); NCN1 (Yunnan) (2.7.82).

83. Interview File NCN1 (Yunnan) (2.7.82). The team leader came from a poor family, married into a wealthier one, and was supporting four daughters, a sign, in the informant's eyes, of his impoverished condition.

84. Interview Files NM9B-18 and NM9A-17 (Guangdong); CN5A-18 (Guangdong). See also Parish and Whyte, *Village and Family,* chap. 8.

85. For a description of this process in one Guangdong village, see Chan, Madsen, and Unger, *Chen Village,* chaps. 3, 4.

86. *Zhejiang Ribao,* Nov. 14, 1980.

87. *Fujian Ribao,* Feb. 5, 1981. See also *NFRB,* July 8, 1980; *Fujian Ribao,* March 21, 1982; *Xinhua Ribao,* April 19, 1980; *Fujian Ribao,* April 14, 1981.

88. Letter to the Editor, *Zhejiang Ribao,* Nov. 7, 1980.

89. Parish and Whyte, *Village and Family,* pp. 110–12.

90. Interview File NKP2 (Fujian) (3.9.82).

91. On traditional village ethics, see Richard Madsen, *Morality and Power in a Chinese Village.*

92. *Fujian Ribao,* July 7, 1982; *Xinhua Ribao,* April 19, 1980. See also Burns, "Local Cadre Accommodation to the 'Responsibility System,'" pp. 614–19, for a discussion of local cadres "exiting" in response to household contracting.

93. In FBIS 41 (March 2, 1982): K8–K11.

94. *NFRB,* Oct. 10, 1982; *Zhejiang Ribao,* Nov. 14, 1980; *Fujian Ribao,* Aug. 9, 1981; *Fujian Ribao,* April 16, 1982; *NFRB,* Jan. 29, 1981; *Zhejiang Ribao,* Nov. 7, 1980; and *Xinhua Ribao,* March 22, 1982.

95. On Dec. 1, 1980, Renyang commune, Changshu County, issued a regulation extending the term of office of team leaders to 3 years (*Fujian Ribao,* Dec. 7, 1980, which noted that the Sixty Articles limited the term to 2 years); Hetian brigade in Lian County extended the term to 5 years (*NFRB,* Jan. 29, 1981); Chengxi commune extended the term to 3 years (*Zhejiang Ribao,* Dec. 7, 1981); and Jiangdong County extended the term to 4 years (*Fujian Ribao,* April 16, 1982). This action is evidence of the difficulties that commune and county officials faced as they sought to recruit team leaders.

96. *Fujian Ribao,* July 7, 1982.

97. Sixty Articles (1962), arts. 47–51; New Sixty Articles (1978), arts. 53–55. These regulations required cadres to follow the "three main rules of discipline" and the "eight points for attention."

98. "Five-good" commune members were good in observing the laws and decrees of the government; good in protecting the collective; good in labor attendance; good in protecting public property; and good in uniting with and helping other people. "Five-good" basic-level cadres were good in holding fast to the socialist road; good in executing party policies; good in labor participation and production leadership; good in observing the PLA's three-eight work style in diligence, thrift, honesty, and concern for the masses; and good in political and ideological study. (See Baum, *Prelude to Revolution,* p. 185n.) The "five conditions for revolutionary successors" were: They must be genuine Marxist-Leninists; they must be revolutionaries who wholeheartedly serve the overwhelming majority of the people of China and the whole world; they must be proletarian political leaders capable of rallying and working with the overwhelming majority; they must set an

example in applying the party's democratic centralism, must master the method of leadership based on the principle of "from the masses, to the masses," and must cultivate a democratic style of work and be good at listening to the masses; and they must be modest and prudent, guard against arrogance and impetuosity, must be imbued with the spirit of self-criticism, and have the courage to correct mistakes and shortcomings in their work. (See *RMRB*, Aug. 3, 1964.)

99. Interview File CN5G-20 (Guangdong). In "Gathering Beans," a candidate's wife, unenthusiastic about her husband running for team leader, publicly ridicules his ability to manage their private plot (Ding, "Jiandou").

100. See Parish and Whyte, *Village and Family,* pp. 101–2.

101. See a letter to the editor, complaining about a team leader appointed by the brigade who was "too young" (*NFRB*, Jan. 10, 1979).

102. See *RMRB*, Jan. 21, 1979; *Xinhua Ribao*, Dec. 7, 1980; *RMRB*, March 7, 1979; and *Xinhua Ribao*, Dec. 9, 1980.

103. Interview File CN5G-20 (Guangdong).

104. Interview File CN5H-18 (Guangdong).

105. Interview File CN5G-21 (Guangdong).

106. "Minzhu xuanju yihou" [After the election], *RMRB*, April 27, 1979.

107. Interview File CN5H-16 (Guangdong).

108. See Interview File NKP4 (Fujian) (22.9.82) for the importance of "public mindedness." See also Madsen, *Morality and Power in a Chinese Village.*

109. "Xinshou nuoyan de hao duizhang" [The good team leader who kept his promise], *RMRB*, June 30, 1980. See also Ding, "Jiandou."

110. Interview File CN5G-23 (Guangdong).

111. Interview File CN5C-2 (Guangdong).

112. Interview File NM9A-13 (Guangdong).

113. See *NFRB*, Sept. 12, 1979; *RMRB*, May 15, 1979; and *RMRB*, Feb. 26, 1979; Interview Files NKP1 (Fujian) (21.6.82) and NT2 (Fujian) (25.6.82). Some interviewees, however, report that class origin continued to be a consideration after 1979, indicating that some past practices were difficult to change (Interview File NKP2 [Fujian] [29.7.82]). One of the major consequences of the registration of voters during the 1979 to 1981 county elections was the removal of "class hats," which gave thousands of peasants voting rights they had not had before. In Wuqing County, authorities reported that, in 1978, 5,160 people had been denied voting rights as landlords, rich peasants, counterrevolutionaries, or "bad elements." After the registration campaign was completed, 5,118 of these individuals were registered. See *Tianjin Ribao,* March 17, 1980, in JPRS 75825 (June 4, 1980): 67–68.

114. *RMRB* (about Zhejiang), Dec. 15, 1980; *NFRB*, March 7, 1979, and March 28, 1979.

115. *Xinhua Ribao,* May 14, 1980; *Xinhua Ribao,* April 11, 1980; *Sichuan Ribao,* Sept. 22, 1980.

116. Interview File NT3 (Shanghai). For reports of resistance to women serv-

ing as team cadres, see *Xinhua Ribao,* May 3, 1980, and Interview File CN3C (Guangdong).

117. *RMRB,* March 30, 1982; *Zhejiang Ribao,* Dec. 20, 1980; *NFRB,* Sept. 10, 1980; *Xinhua Ribao,* Dec. 9, 1980; *Xinhua Ribao,* Dec. 7, 1980; *Xinhua Ribao,* May 15, 1980; *NFRB,* March 28, 1979; and *Xinhua Ribao,* Oct. 22, 1980.

118. Some writers challenged this view, arguing that elections led to instability and falling incomes. To give some indication of the extent of the gains attributed to elections, see the output of Liangchu commune's [Jiangsu] team No. 5, which increased grain output after the election by 15,000 *jin* (1 *jin* = 1.1 lbs.) (*Xinhua Ribao,* Oct. 22, 1980). In another case, also from Jiangsu, the per capita distributed income from collective sources in a team that elected its leader increased in one year from 54 to 124 yuan (*Xinhua Ribao,* Dec. 9, 1980).

119. Interview File NCN3 (Fujian) (19.7.82).

120. Interview File CN4D (Guangdong).

121. Sixty Articles (1962), arts. 7 and 18, which specified that authorities should call brigade and commune congresses at least twice a year. Officials should hold elections for brigade congress delegates annually, while they should hold elections for delegates to commune congresses once every two years. The New Sixty Articles (1978), art. 9, specified that brigade congresses should meet quarterly, while commune congresses should meet twice a year. Elections for delegates to these congresses should be held every two years.

122. "Minzhu xuanchu chengxin dangjiaren" [Democratically select appropriate masters], *NFRB,* Feb. 24, 1980. See also "Dalemu cun minzhu xuanju cunzhang de diaocha" [Investigation of the democratic election of the village head of Dalemu village], *Nongye Jingji Wenti* 8 (1982): 38–39.

123. *Xinhua Ribao,* March 18, 1980. See also *NFRB,* Jan. 14, 1979, which indicates that brigade cadres, purged during the Gang of Four period, were simply reinstated by commune authorities from mid-1977 on (elections were not mentioned) (in JPRS 73067 [March 23, 1979]: 6–7).

124. In another case, however, a brigade official was elected in spite of commune opposition. This probably was not the norm. See He Nong, "Zhongguo yi ge nongcun gongshe xuanju yinqi de fengbo" [Disturbances in a rural commune election in China], *Fengfan* (Taiyuan, 1980), reprinted in *Zhongguo Minzhu Yundong* (Hong Kong) 1, no. 3 (March 1981): 10.

125. *NFRB,* Feb. 24, 1980. See also "Branch Committee Election Held Without Any Restrictive Framework Imposed," *Beijing Ribao,* Jan. 15, 1979, in JPRS 73201 (April 11, 1979): 6–7.

126. Interview File NKP2 (Fujian) (8.8.82).

127. While these labels are not strictly accurate, they convey the sense of division that characterized the time. The labels were misleading because they ignored the extent to which local issues and relationships were as important or more important in explaining the conflict. Administration at the local level was divided on

policy and personal issues between groups associated at county and provincial level with Gang of Four and "Deng" supporters, mirroring divisions further up the hierarchy. Central authorities by 1978, when this episode took place, had not affected a thoroughgoing purge of all Gang of Four supporters throughout the country.

128. For a description of the campaign, linking it to the campaign to criticize the Gang of Four, see *RMRB*, Nov. 5, 1978.

129. In another case, a lineage that defied a Shanxi commune party secretary by deposing his favorite (from another lineage) in an election for brigade head found that the commune official became unresponsive to their problems. Had they bowed to the commune secretary's wishes, he might have been more forthcoming. See He Nong, "Zhongguo yi ge nongcun gongshe xuanju yinqi de fengbo."

130. *NFRB*, Feb. 14, 1979. There was no reply.

131. "Zhongguo gongchandang nongcun zhibu gongzuo tiaoli (shixing caoan)" [Work regulations for rural Chinese Communist party branches (Draft for trial use)], arts. 10, 14 (Beijing: Zhonggong zuzhibu, 1981), in *Zhonggong Yanjiu* (Taibei) 16, no. 9 (Sept. 15, 1982): 139, 143.

132. *NFRB*, March 7, 1979. See also *Beijing Ribao*, Jan. 15, 1979, in JPRS 73201 (April 11, 1979): 6–7.

133. "Zhongguo Pingba xianwei zhengdun, gaixuan dadui dang zhibu de qingkuang baogao" [Report on the rectification and election of Pingba County committee's brigade party branches] (Guizhou), June 14, 1982, in *Zhonggong Yanjiu* 195 (March 15, 1983): 137–46.

134. Radio Chengdu, Nov. 25, 1979, in FBIS 229 (Nov. 27, 1979): Q3.

135. Interview File NKP2 (Fujian) (15.8.82).

136. Radio Xi'an, Nov. 1, 1980, in FBIS 220 (Nov. 12, 1980): T2.

137. *Sichuan Ribao*, Nov. 19, 1980.

138. See Interview File NKP2 (Fujian) (15.8.82) for a report of the election of a commune management committee in his commune. Commune party authorities nominated the candidates, but delegates gave many fewer votes than expected to an unpopular commune favorite.

139. Alex Pravda, "Elections in Communist Party States," in Guy Hermet et al., eds., *Elections Without Choice* (London: Macmillan, 1978), pp. 186–92.

140. Zhang Qingfu and Pi Chunxie, "Revise the Electoral Laws to Institutionalize Democracy," *RMRB*, May 22, 1979, in FBIS 103 (May 25, 1979): L5–L8.

141. See, e.g., *RMRB*, April 17, 1978.

142. One of the "three fears" (*san pa*) identified in *RMRB*, Feb. 26, 1979. (The other fears were that "commune members' opinions would be divided, resulting in disorder in the elections" and that "those elected by the masses would be incompetent.") See also *RMRB*, Jan. 21, 1979; and *Zhejiang Ribao*, Dec. 11, 1980.

Chapter 6

1. Ezra Vogel, "Land Reform in Kwangtung: 1951–1953," *CQ* 38 (April–June 1969): 46.

2. See William Parish, "China—Team, Brigade, or Commune," *Problems of Communism* 25, no. 2 (March–April 1976): 51–65.

3. Jean C. Oi, "Communism and Clientelism," *World Politics* 37, no. 2 (Jan. 1985): 238–66.

4. For a general discussion of factions in Chinese politics, see Lucian Pye, *The Dynamics of Chinese Politics* (Cambridge: Oelgeschlager, Gunn, and Hain, 1981). The importance of personal relations (*guanxi*) in Chinese politics is discussed in J. Bruce Jacobs, *Local Politics in a Rural Chinese Cultural Setting* (Canberra: Australian National University, 1981). For evidence of factions in rural politics, see Interview Files NKP2 (Fujian) (15.8.82); NM3 (Shanghai) (15.7.82). Secondary accounts of village politics in North China also indicate that factions were significant. See Isabel and David Crook, *Ten Mile Inn* (New York: Pantheon Books, 1979), chap. 8; and William Hinton, *Shenfan* (New York: Random House, 1983). For the importance of patronage politics in South China, see Chan, Madsen, and Unger, *Chen Village*.

5. Oi, "Communism and Clientelism," p. 265.

6. See Jurgen Domes, "New Policies in the Communes," *JAS* 41, no. 2 (Feb. 1982): 256.

7. Potter, "The Economic and Social Consequences," p. 36.

8. Chester J. Cheng, ed., *The Politics of the Chinese Red Army* (Stanford: Hoover Institution, 1966), pp. 11–14, 200, 234, 284, 320, 475, 613–14.

9. Interview File NM3B-5 (Guangdong).

10. Interview File CN5K-9-11 (Guangdong). Press reports also indicate that villagers used personal ties to enable them to leave the countryside to work at more lucrative city jobs. See Radio Changsha, May 11, 1980, in FBIS 95 (May 14, 1980): P6; also Interview Files NKP2 (Fujian) (20.9.82); CN5H-8, 9 (Guangdong); CN5F-16 (Guangdong); and CN5K-16 (Guangdong).

11. Interview File NM4D-7 (Guangdong). Many cases of bribery to obtain these materials were revealed in the press from 1979 to 1982. Here, however, I am concerned only with the use of personal ties to obtain the material. Local cadres probably often used these channels, but I am concerned with the behavior of ordinary peasants.

12. Interview File NKP2 (Fujian) (3.9.82).

13. Mao Zedong, "Oppose Book Worship," *Selected Readings from the Works of Mao Tse-tung* (Beijing: Foreign Languages Press, 1967), pp. 33–41.

14. Ibid., p. 40.

15. See Mao Zedong, "On the Question of Agricultural Co-operation," *Selected Readings from the Works of Mao Tse-tung*, p. 321, for the importance of "checking up" on local levels.

16. See Letter to the Editor, "Gongzuodui gaiwei diaochazu hao" [Turning work teams into investigation teams is good], *RMRB,* March 27, 1979. The author of the letter, a county official from Hubei, distinguished work teams from investigation teams by their large size and their work methods. Work teams tended to take over the management of units they were investigating.

17. See *NFRB,* June 7, 1973, in Union Research Service 72, no. 10 (Aug. 3, 1973): 132; Radio Nanchang, March 15, 1964, in *NPCRS* 49 (March 19, 1964): 1; Radio Guiyang, May 17, 1966, in *NPCRS* 159 (May 26, 1966): 28; Interview Files NM11G-11 (Guangdong); and CN5J-24 (Guangdong).

18. Lianjiang Documents, pp. 105–6.

19. For examples of 1979 and 1980 investigation teams, see Xinhua, Jan. 14, 1979, in FBIS 11 (Jan. 16, 1979): J1–J2; Radio Changchun, Feb. 16, 1979, in FBIS 37 (Feb. 22, 1979): L1–L2; Xinhua, Feb. 24, 1979, in FBIS 40 (Feb. 27, 1979): G8; Xinhua, May 9, 1980, in FBIS 93 (May 12, 1980): L7–L8; Radio Haikou, June 24, 1980, in FBIS 128 (July 1, 1980): P4; Radio Hefei, July 5, 1980, in FBIS 132 (July 8, 1980): O1; Xinhua, July 12, 1980, in FBIS 138 (July 16, 1980): Q3–Q4; Radio Changsha, Aug. 6, 1980, in FBIS 155 (Aug. 8, 1980): P5; and Radio Wuhan, Dec. 20, 1980, in FBIS 249 (Dec. 24, 1980): P4.

20. See Xinhua May 21, 1981, in FBIS 99 (May 22, 1981): K1–K2.

21. Radio Zhengzhou, Feb. 19, 1981, in FBIS 50 (March 16, 1981): P9; Radio Nanjing, Feb. 25, 1981, in FBIS 38 (Feb. 26, 1981): O5–O6; Radio Hangzhou, March 1, 1981, in FBIS 41 (March 3, 1981): O6; Radio Lanzhou, April 7, 1981, in FBIS 68 (April 9, 1981): T1; Xinhua, April 15, 1981, in FBIS 73 (April 16, 1981): R3–R4; Radio Hefei, April 23, 1981, in FBIS 79 (April 24, 1981): O1; Radio Changchun, May 7, 1981, in FBIS 89 (May 8, 1981): S1–S2; Radio Nanchang, May 11, 1981, in FBIS 91 (May 12, 1981): O1; Xinhua, July 21, 1981, in FBIS 141 (July 23, 1981): K3; and Xinhua, Aug. 27, 1981, in FBIS 168 (Aug. 31, 1981): O1.

22. See Radio Guangzhou, Jan. 24, 1973, in FBIS 18 (Jan. 26, 1973): D3; and Interview File NKP 4 (Fujian) (16.4.82). See also Jack Chen, *A Year in Upper Felicity* (New York: Random House, 1975); and Ezra Vogel, *Canton Under Communism* (New York: Harper and Row, 1969), pp. 223–24.

23. Radio Zhengzhou, June 20, 1980, in FBIS 126 (June 27, 1980): P4–P5.

24. Interview File NM11I-8 (Guangdong).

25. For accounts of the media in China, see Frederick T. C. Yu, *Mass Persuasion in Communist China* (New York: Praeger, 1964); Alan P. L. Liu, *Communications and National Integration in Communist China* (Berkeley and Los Angeles: University of California Press, 1971); Godwin C. Chu, *Radical Change Through Communication in Mao's China* (Honolulu: University of Hawaii Press, 1977); Jorg-Meinhard Rudolph, "China's Media," *Problems of Communism* 33 (July–Aug. 1984): 58–67; and Andrew J. Nathan, *Chinese Democracy,* chap. 8. On the local and provincial media, see Lynn T. White, "Local Newspapers and Community Change," in Godwin Chu and Francis L. K. Hsu, eds., *Moving a Mountain* (Hono-

lulu: University of Hawaii Press, 1979), pp. 76–112; and Vivienne Shue, "China's Local News Media," *CQ* 86 (June 1981): 322–31.

26. See the reportage of Liu Binyan, in Perry Link, ed., *People or Monsters?* (Bloomington: Indiana University Press, 1983).

27. "Bu zhun ziliudi shucai shangshi" [Not permitting vegetables from private plots in the market], *NFRB*, July 16, 1980.

28. "Jieshou piping, quxiao cuowu jueding" [Accepts criticism, abolishes incorrect decision], *NFRB*, Aug. 6, 1980.

29. Radio Guangzhou, Jan. 12, 1979, in FBIS 10 (Jan. 15, 1979): H4–H5.

30. "Criticize the Sixth Brigade of Dongwang Commune for Its Thwarting the Implementation of the Policy Governing Private Plots," *RMRB*, Oct. 14, 1979, in JPRS 74800 (Dec. 20, 1979): 51–53.

31. By 1975, 93 percent of production teams and 70 percent of rural households were linked to wired broadcasting, with 106 million loudspeakers in rural areas. See *NCNA*, Sept. 14, 1975, in *China News Summary* (Hong Kong) 584 (Sept. 24, 1975). For the extent of local broadcasting systems in some provinces, see Radio Changsha, Nov. 7, 1979, in FBIS 223 (Nov. 16, 1979): P1–P2, which indicates that 91 percent of Hunan production teams received these broadcasts; Radio Xi'an, April 14, 1981, in FBIS 74 (April 17, 1981): T2, which indicates that 80 percent of peasant households in Shaanxi received these broadcasts; and Radio Chengdu, Dec. 26, 1980, in FBIS 253 (Dec. 31, 1980): Q3. See also Nathan, *Chinese Democracy*, p. 164.

32. I am grateful to David Zweig for drawing this to my attention.

33. See Lowell Dittmer, *Liu Shao-ch'i and the Cultural Revolution* (Berkeley and Los Angeles: University of California Press, 1974), pp. 123–26. For a discussion of work teams in the Four Clean-ups, see Richard Baum, *Prelude to Revolution*.

34. See Dittmer, *Liu Shao-ch'i*, p. 80, for Mao's lukewarm endorsement of the dispatch of work teams in 1956: "Work teams must be sent, but it must be stated very clearly that they are being sent to help local party organizations, not to replace them."

35. Mao Zedong, "Talk on the Four Clean-ups Movement," in JPRS, *Miscellany of Mao Tse-tung Thought* (Feb. 20, 1974), p. 443 (orig. pub. in *Mao Zedong sixiang wansui*).

36. Dittmer, *Liu Shao-ch'i*, pp. 79–80.

37. "Bu yao luan pai gongzuodui" [Do not wastefully dispatch work teams], *RMRB*, Feb. 5, 1979.

38. Ibid., and Nan Zhenzhong, "Is It Still Necessary to Send Work Teams to the Countryside?" Xinhua, Jan. 27, 1979, in FBIS 23 (Feb. 1, 1979): E16.

39. *RMRB*, Feb. 5, 1979; and Xinhua, Jan. 27, 1979.

40. *RMRB*, Feb. 8, 1979; and ibid.

41. *RMRB*, Aug. 11, 1979; *Fujian Ribao*, Feb. 5, 1981; *RMRB*, May 9, 1979.

42. *RMRB*, Aug. 11, 1979. See also *Fujian Ribao*, Feb. 5, 1981.

43. *RMRB,* May 9, 1979.

44. *Fujian Ribao,* May 2, 1981.

45. *Fujian Ribao,* Jan. 24, 1981.

46. *RMRB,* Feb. 5, 1979, and Xinhua, Jan. 27, 1979.

47. "Gongshe ganbu changnian baodui de fangfa gaijin" [We must change the method of commune cadres guaranteeing brigades for a long time], *RMRB,* March 27, 1979; "Gongshe ganbu baodui shi yi hao banfa" [Commune cadres guaranteeing brigades is a good method], *RMRB,* May 9, 1979.

48. *RMRB,* Feb. 5, 1979.

49. Interview File NKP2 (Fujian) (8.8.82).

50. "Gongzuodui gaiwai diaochazu hao" [Work teams should be changed into investigation teams], *RMRB,* March 27, 1979.

51. "Nongcun gongzuodui bu neng jiandan fouding" [Rural work teams cannot be simply abolished], *RMRB,* March 27, 1979; "Ganbu haishi yao xia jiceng" [Cadres still must go to basic levels], *RMRB,* March 27, 1979; and "Gongshe ganbu baodui shi yi hao banfa," *RMRB,* May 9, 1979; "Gongzuodui haishi yao pai de" [Work teams still should be dispatched], *RMRB,* April 12, 1979.

52. On May 6, 1979, a *RMRB* commentator acknowledged the problems with work teams but endorsed their continued usefulness (in FBIS 92 [May 10, 1979]:L9–L10).

53. Interview File CN3A, B, C (Shanghai).

54. Detailed general accounts of the Four Clean-ups Campaign are available in Baum, *Prelude to Revolution;* and Ahn, *Chinese Politics and the Cultural Revolution,* pp. 89–122. Detailed case studies of Four Clean-ups work teams appear in Chan, Madsen, and Unger, *Chen Village,* chap. 2; and Hinton, *Shenfan,* pp. 351–69.

55. Madsen argues that the Four Clean-ups work teams must have created quite a spectacle, because of their harsh denunciation of the "traditional" way of doing things. Petty corruption, widespread in the countryside, was generally accepted as grease for the patronage mill that linked village leaders to their supporters. See Madsen, *Morality and Power in a Chinese Village.* For an indication of the scope of corruption in one Fujian area, see the Lianjiang Documents, pp. 196–97.

56. This was not an idle fear. See Baum, *Prelude to Revolution,* pp. 112–17; and Radio Xi'an, Dec. 3, 1964, in *NPCRS* 86 (Dec. 10, 1964): 33–34, for cases of cadre retaliation.

57. Interview File CN5K (Guangdong).

58. Interview File CN5K-7 (Guangdong).

59. "Ruhe kandai nongcun jieji douzheng wenti?" [How should we view the problem of rural class struggle?], *RMRB,* Sept. 1, 1979.

60. See *Fujian Ribao,* April 23, 1982, and July 7, 1982.

61. *RMRB,* March 7, 1979; *NFRB,* Feb. 13, 1979.

62. Interview File CN11 A,B,C (Guangdong).

63. Interview File CN11D-3 (Guangdong).

64. *NFRB,* March 3, 1963.

65. Radio Jinan, May 16, 1972, in FBIS 99 (May 1972): C7.

66. Interview File NKP1 (Fujian) (30.6.82).

67. *San zi yi bao* means the "three freedoms and one guarantee," a policy associated with Liu Shaoqi and criticized during the Cultural Revolution as "capitalist" and "revisionist."

68. Interview File NKP1 (Fujian) (30.6.82).

69. For an example of a 1978 work team that criticized peasants for "capitalist tendencies" that the center subsequently approved of in 1980, see *Fujian Ribao*, Feb. 22, 1981.

70. See *Fujian Ribao*, May 5, 1981, for an example of a work team criticizing a production team for practicing household contracting.

Chapter 7

1. Although all of the People's Republic's four state constitutions include provisions for freedom of speech, only the 1954, 1978, and 1982 constitutions include the right to bring complaints against state officials. See the 1954 state constitution, art. 97; the 1978 state constitution, art. 55; and the 1982 state constitution, art. 41. The 1982 constitution extended the people's right to criticize both government officials and state offices.

2. Writing posters is a traditional means of political expression in China. The 1975 and 1978 constitutions gave citizens the right to post big-character posters (1975 state constitution, art. 13; 1978 state constitution, art. 45). The 1978 constitution was amended in 1980 to withdraw this right.

3. The "Letters from Our Readers" column of *Renmin Ribao* was abolished during the Cultural Revolution and not restored until Sept. 1977 (Xinhua, Dec. 14, 1979, in FBIS 242 [Dec. 14, 1979]:L6).

4. *RMRB*, Feb. 24, 1978.

5. Xinhua, Dec. 14, 1979, in FBIS 242 (Dec. 14, 1979): L6–L7. The number of letters declined to 500,000 in 1979.

6. *RMRB*, July 11, 1979, in FBIS 139 (July 18, 1979): L4.

7. "Kaifeng diqu xinfang gongzuo jianjie" [Brief introduction to the letters and visits work of Kaifeng district], *RMRB*, July 27, 1979.

8. "Xinfang gongzuozhe de husheng" [The outcry of the letters and visits workers], *RMRB*, July 27, 1979.

9. Radio Hefei, Sept. 25, 1979, in FBIS 189 (Sept. 27, 1979): O1.

10. *NFRB*, March 7, 1979.

11. *Guizhou Ribao*, Nov. 20, 1979, in FBIS 239 (Dec. 10, 1980): Q1–Q2.

12. *NFRB*, Jan. 7, 1979.

13. "Tantan baozhi kaizhan piping de 'sannan'" [A discussion of the "three difficulties" of newspapers launching criticism], *Jiefang Ribao*, Nov. 18, 1980.

14. *NFRB*, May 25, 1980.

15. Godwin C. Chu and Leonard L. Chu, "Parties in Conflict," *Journal of Com-*

munication 31, no. 4 (Autumn 1981): 78. See also Godwin C. Chu, *Radical Change Through Communication in Mao's China* (Honolulu: University of Hawaii Press, 1977), p. 238.

16. The letters can be found in *NFRB* from 1979 to 1981; *Sichuan Ribao,* 1981; *Fujian Ribao,* 1981; *Zhejiang Ribao,* 1981; and *Xinhua Ribao,* 1981. These were supplemented by letters from the following sources: *Gansu Ribao,* Oct. 11, 1979, in JPRS 74468 (Oct. 29, 1979): 25–26; *Zhongguo Nongmin Bao,* March 19, 1981, in Zhongguo renmin daxue shubao cailiao she, *Nongye Jingji* 7 (1981): 64; *Nei Menggu Ribao,* Feb. 8, 1979, in FBIS 32 (Feb. 14, 1979): K1; *Hunan Ribao,* May 11, 1980, in FBIS 95 (May 14, 1980): P6; *Hunan Ribao,* Sept. 26, 1980, in FBIS 188 (Sept. 29, 1981): P7; *Shanxi Ribao,* July 22, 1981, in FBIS 161 (Aug. 20, 1981): R1–R6; *Shanxi Ribao,* Oct. 13, 1982, in *Ming Bao* (Hong Kong), March 21, 1983; *Sichuan Ribao,* June 18, 1982, in FBIS 128 (July 2, 1982): Q3; *Guizhou Ribao,* Feb. 2, 1979, in FBIS (Feb. 5, 1979): J1; *Sichuan Ribao,* Jan. 14, 1979, in FBIS (Jan. 15, 1979): J1–J2.

17. *NFRB,* March 7, 1979.

18. *NFRB,* Feb. 14, 1979.

19. *NFRB,* Jan. 10, 1979.

20. *Fujian Ribao,* Oct. 25, 1982.

21. *Hunan Ribao,* Sept. 26, 1981, in FBIS 188 (Sept. 29, 1981): P7.

22. *NFRB,* Nov. 18, 1979, and *NFRB,* Feb. 6, 1979.

23. *Gansu Ribao,* Oct. 11, 1979, in JPRS 74468 (Oct. 29, 1979): 25–26.

24. *Zhongguo Nongmin Bao,* March 19, 1981, in Zhongguo renmin daxue shubao cailiao she, *Nongye Jingji* 7 (1981): 64.

25. *RMRB,* Jan. 4, 1979, and *Shaanxi Ribao,* Jan. 10, 1979, in FBIS 12 (Jan. 17, 1979): M4–M7; *Nei Menggu Ribao,* Feb. 8, 1979, in FBIS 32 (Feb. 14, 1979): K1–K2.

26. See, e.g., *Hunan Ribao,* May 11, 1980, in FBIS 95 (May 14, 1980): P6.

27. *Sichuan Ribao,* Jan. 14, 1979, in FBIS 10 (Jan. 15, 1979): J1–J2.

28. *Zhejiang Ribao,* Nov. 7, 1980.

29. *NFRB,* March 21, 1981.

30. *Sichuan Ribao,* June 18, 1982, in FBIS 128 (July 2, 1982): Q3.

31. Chu and Chu, "Parties in Conflict," pp. 81–85.

32. *NFRB,* Nov. 5, 1979.

33. *NFRB,* Nov. 18, 1979.

34. *Gansu Ribao,* Oct. 11, 1979, in JPRS 74468 (Oct. 29, 1979): 25–26.

35. *NFRB,* Feb. 14, 1979. Usually in such cases, the newspaper issues or obtains a ruling from authorities.

36. Chu and Chu, "Parties in Conflict," p. 87.

37. See, e.g., *NFRB,* Jan. 8, 1965.

38. See *NFRB,* July 26, 1962; *NFRB,* Aug. 23, 1962, in *SCMP* 2826 (Sept. 26, 1962), p. 10.

39. *RMRB,* April 24, 1981, in FBIS 83 (April 30, 1981): K9–K11. In 1964

two Hunan counties reported that they had received 900 letters or visits from peasants during the year (Radio Hunan, Dec. 27, 1964, in *NPCRS* 88 [Dec. 30, 1964]: 17). See also Du Jian, "Attention Must Be Paid to Letters and Visits by the People," *Hongqi* 11 (Oct. 1971), in Chu, *Radical Change,* p. 241.

40. *RMRB,* June 22, 1962, in *SCMP* 2777 (July 13, 1962): 3–7.

41. Baum, *Prelude to Revolution,* pp. 114–15.

42. Radio Guangzhou, April 5, 1980, in FBIS 75 (April 16, 1980): P1; and Radio Guangzhou, Jan. 8, 1979, in FBIS 8 (Jan. 11, 1979): H1–H2.

43. Radio Shijiazhuang, Oct. 16, 1980, in FBIS 209 (Oct. 27, 1980): R4–R5; Radio Beijing, May 28, 1980, in FBIS 108 (June 3, 1980): L9–L10; and Radio Wuhan, May 21, 1982, in FBIS 100 (May 24, 1982): P2.

44. *China Daily* (Beijing), Dec. 25, 1983; and Fei Xiaotong, "Speech to the Chinese People's Political Consultative Conference," June 22, 1983, *Da Gong Bao* (Hong Kong), June 25, 1983.

45. Interview File NCN1 (Yunnan) (6.7.82).

46. See the 1954 state constitution, art. 97; the 1978 state constitution, art. 55; and the 1982 state constitution, art. 41. This right was omitted from the 1975 state constitution. Petition here means written petition.

47. See Xinhua, Sept. 17, 1979, in FBIS 182 (Sept. 18, 1979): L7–L10; Xinhua, Oct. 21, 1979, in FBIS 205 (Oct. 22, 1979): L1–L4; and Radio Kunming, Oct. 13, 1979, in FBIS 201 (Oct. 16, 1979): Q1–Q2. See also Roger Garside, *Coming Alive* (New York: McGraw Hill, 1981), pp. 231–32.

48. Radio Jinan, Sept. 18, 1980, in FBIS 187 (Sept. 24, 1980): O4–O5.

49. Interview File NM1C-1, 2 (Guangdong).

50. Interview File NM4E-2 (Guangdong).

51. See Zweig, "Limits to Agrarian Radicalism in China," p. 9, who points out that the policy of amalgamating teams was never approved by the center. Some officials in Beijing and the provinces approved of it, however, and sought to implement it throughout the 1970s.

52. "Report on the Work of the Government," delivered at the First Session of the Second National People's Congress on April 18, 1959 (Beijing, 1959), p. 45, in Townsend, *Political Participation,* p. 98.

53. Mao Zedong, "Sixteen Points," point 7.

54. Chan, Madsen, and Unger, *Chen Village,* pp. 114–16, 124, 131; Hinton, *Shenfan,* pp. 509–45.

55. Chan, Madsen, and Unger, *Chen Village,* p. 116.

56. Ibid., p. 124.

57. Li Yizhe, "Concerning Socialist Democracy and Legal System," in *The Revolution is Dead, Long Live the Revolution* (Hong Kong: The Seventies), pp. 249–83. For an analysis of the poster, see Susan Shirk, "Going Against the Tide," *Survey* 24, no. 1 (Winter 1979): 82–114.

58. In the Li Yizhe poster, the authors pointed out that the right to post bigcharacter posters was suppressed in Guangzhou in 1973–1974 by "City Political Appearance Cleaning and Sweeping Teams," organized by the Guangzhou Muni-

cipal Party Committee and equipped with water hoses and brooms to remove big-character posters appearing on any street or alley. Mao Zedong then issued "Document 18" giving legitimacy to the use of big-character posters.

59. The 1975 state constitution, art. 13, states: "Speaking out freely, airing views fully, holding great debates, and writing big-character posters [the four great freedoms] are new forms of carrying on socialist revolution created by the masses of the people. The State shall ensure to the masses the right to use these forms to create a political situation in which there are both centralism and democracy, both discipline and freedom, both unity of will and personal ease of mind and liveliness, and so help consolidate the leadership of the Communist Party of China over the State and consolidate the dictatorship of the proletariat."

60. 1978 state constitution, art. 45.

61. See Roger Garside, *Coming Alive*, pp. 195–278, for an account of these posters.

62. See Stanley Rosen, "Guangzhou's Democracy Movement in Cultural Revolution Perspective," *CQ* 101 (March 1985): 1–31, for an account of the interaction between the democracy movement and official policy.

63. Radio Shenyang, May 4, 1979, in FBIS 89 (May 7, 1979): S1–S2; "Bu zhun liyong dazibao wuxian hao ren" [Do not permit the use of big-character posters to slander good people], *RMRB*, May 11, 1979.

64. Ibid.

65. Radio Shenyang, May 4, 1979, in FBIS 89 (May 7, 1979): S1.

66. Ibid.: S1–S3; and *RMRB*, May 11, 1979.

67. Xinhua, June 29, 1979, in FBIS 127 (June 29, 1979): L3–L4.

68. See *Beijing Review* 40 (Oct. 6, 1980): 22–28. See also Xinhua, April 16, 1980, in FBIS 75 (April 16, 1980): L5; and *Beijing Ribao*, Feb. 1, 1980, in FBIS 28 (Feb. 8, 1980): L5–L6.

69. See Rosen, "Guangzhou's Democracy Movement," p. 21.

70. *RMRB*, May 20, 1979.

71. Interview File NT1 (Fujian) (6.7.82).

72. See, e.g., Interview Files NCN1 (Yunnan) (6.7.82); NKP1 (Fujian) (5.7.82); NCN3 (Fujian) (29.7.82).

73. Interview File NKP1 (Fujian) (5.7.82). See also NCN3 (Fujian) (29.7.82).

74. Interview File CN8A-11 (Guangdong).

75. Interview File CN4D (Guangdong); see also CN8A-11 (Guangdong); NKP1 (Fujian) (5.7.82); and NCN3 (Shanghai) (29.7.82).

76. Interview File NT3 (Fujian) (2.8.82).

Chapter 8

1. See the 1975 state constitution, art. 28; and the 1978 state constitution, art. 45. Neither the 1954 nor the 1982 constitutions included this provision. In 1982, after authorities decided to delete the right to strike from the new constitution, trade union officials pointed out that workers could use channels other than strikes

to protect their interests. In any case, they argued, the long-term interests of the working class and the state coincided. Although the right has been abolished, this "does not mean that there exists a prohibition against strikes nor does it mean that all strikes are illegal." See NCNA, Aug. 26, 1982, in *SWB* FE/7116/BII/1 (Aug. 28, 1982).

2. See the 1954 state constitution, art. 87; the 1975 state constitution, art. 28; the 1978 state constitution, art. 45; and the 1982 state constitution, art. 35.

3. See *RMRB,* Aug. 7, 1981, in FBIS 159 (Aug. 18, 1981): K5.

4. *Da Gong Bao* (Hong Kong), Feb. 11, 1982, p. 4.

5. For an example of such regulations, see "Provisional Methods for Rewards and Penalties for State Organ Work Personnel," *Shanxi Ribao,* Nov. 30, 1981, in FBIS 238 (Dec. 11, 1981): R1–R2.

6. See Baum, *Prelude to Revolution,* pp. 103–33; and Chan, Madsen, and Unger, *Chen Village,* chap. 2.

7. See "Zhejiang jiehe jiepi sirenbang kaizhan shuangda douzheng" [Zhejiang Province combines the struggle to expose and criticize the Gang of Four with the start of the Double Hits], *RMRB,* Nov. 5, 1978; Interview File NKP2 (Fujian) (8.8.82).

8. "Criminal Law of the People's Republic of China," July 1, 1979, art. 155, in FBIS 146 (July 27, 1979), Supplement 19: 57.

9. *Da Gong Bao* (Hong Kong), March 11, 1982.

10. *RMRB,* March 1, 1954, in Shue, *Peasant China in Transition,* p. 215.

11. See the 1953 Election Law, art. 62; and the 1979 Election Law, art. 43.

12. See the 1979 Criminal Law, arts. 158, 159, 160. For a comparison of the use of violence in the 1950s and again since 1979, see Elizabeth J. Perry, "Rural Violence in Socialist China," *CQ* 103 (Sept. 1985): 414–40, and Perry, "Rural Collective Violence," in Perry and Wong, eds., *The Political Economy of Reform,* pp. 175–94. See also Jim Scott, "Everyday Forms of Peasant Resistance" (unpublished).

13. See, e.g., Interview File NM3A-5 (Guangdong); and Jean C. Oi, "Communism and Clientelism," *World Politics* 37, no. 2 (Jan. 1985): 260.

14. Interview File NKP2 (Fujian) (3.8.82).

15. Nong He, "Zhongguo yige nongcun gongshe xuanju yinqide fengbo," p. 10.

16. Interview File NT3 (Shanghai) (2.8.82).

17. Interview File CN11 A, B, C (Guangdong).

18. See, e.g., Hinton, *Shenfan,* p. 381.

19. Lianjiang Documents, p. 192.

20. "Gao Guilin pohuai minzhu xuanju shoudao falü zhicai" [Gao Guilin sabotages democratic elections and receives punishment according to law], *Xinhua Ribao,* July 7, 1980.

21. Interview File NKP2 (Fujian) (7.9.82).

22. Villagers evaded taxes, hid grain, and withheld labor before 1962, indicating long-term use of these strategies in the Chinese countryside. See Vivienne Shue, *Transition of Chinese Peasants to Socialism,* pp. 126–43; and John P. Burns,

"Chinese Peasant Interest Articulation, 1949–1974" (Ph.D. dissertation, Columbia University, 1979).

23. Radio Nanchang, Jan. 1, 1967, in *NPCRS* 193 (Feb. 2, 1967); Radio Nanchang, Jan. 25, 1964, in *NPCRS* 43 (Jan. 30, 1964); Radio Beijing, Aug. 24, 1972, in FBIS 168 (Aug. 28, 1972): B5; *Guangming Ribao,* Aug. 22, 1971, in *SCMP* 4969 (Sept. 7, 1971): 1; Interview Files NM4D-8 (Guangdong); NKP2 (Fujian) (20.9.82); and NT3 (Shanghai) (2.8.82).

24. Interview Files NKP4 (Fujian) (22.9.82); and NCN1 (Yunnan) (15.7.82).

25. Interview File NT1 (Fujian) (12.7.82).

26. Interview Files NT3 (Shanghai) (2.8.82). For similar cases, see Interview Files NKP2 (Fujian) (20.9.82); NCN1 (Yunnan) (15.7.82); and NKP4 (Fujian) (22.9.82).

27. *NFRB,* March 20, 1963; *Baoan Bulletin,* p. 128; *RMRB,* May 10, 1962; Intrview Files NM6H-10 (Guangdong); and NT1 (Fujian) (12.7.82).

28. Interview Files CN5K-16 (Guangdong) and NM6H-10 (Guangdong). See also CN4B-6 (Guangdong).

29. See Anita Chan and Jonathan Unger, "Grey and Black," *Pacific Affairs* 55 (1983): 452–71; and John P. Burns, "Rural Guangdong's 'Second Economy,' 1962–1974," *CQ* 88 (Dec. 1981): 629–43. For a discussion of the politics of grain procurement in China, see Jean C. Oi, "State and Peasants in Contemporary China," (Ph.D. dissertation, University of Michigan, 1983).

30. Wan Li, "Speech at a Joint Session of the Conference of Agricultural Secretaries and Conference on Rural Ideological and Political Work," Nov. 5, 1982, in *RMRB,* Dec. 23, 1982, in FBIS 2 (Jan. 4, 1983): K4. (Italics added.)

31. Authorities discovered widespread corruption among cadres during the early and mid-1960s and again from 1978 to 1982. The Four Clean-ups and the Double Hits campaigns were specifically aimed at reducing rural corruption. For evidence of the extent of corrupt activities in Fujian during the early 1960s, see the Lianjiang Documents, pp. 196–98, 218, 229, 231, and 233–34.

32. See Radio Xi'an, Jan. 14, 1964, in *NPCRS* 91 (Jan. 21, 1965): 37–38; *RMRB,* June 23, 1975, in *SCMP* 5901 (July 24, 1975): 142; and Interview Files NCN3 (Fujian) (29.7.82); NKP2 (Fujian) (20.9.82); NCN1 (Yunnan) (15.7.82); and NT3 (Shanghai) (2.8.82).

33. Interview Files NKP2 (Fujian) (20.9.82); NCN1 (Yunnan) (15.7.82); NT3 (Shanghai) (2.8.82); NCN3 (Fujian) (29.7.82).

34. Interview File NCN3 (Fujian) (29.7.82).

35. Peasants in rural Guangdong and Fujian reportedly paid thousands of dollars to speed up the processing of exit permits to allow relatives to emigrate to Hong Kong. See *NFRB,* Sept. 30, 1980; and *NFRB,* Dec. 15, 1980.

36. "Xianren houji de dang zhishu" [The impartial party branch secretary], *NFRB,* June 6, 1981.

37. "Jujue huilu de hao tuanyuan" [The good youth league member who refused bribes], *Zhejiang Ribao,* Jan. 15, 1981.

38. Radio Xi'an, Jan. 14, 1964, in *NPCRS* 91 (Jan. 21, 1965): 37–38.

39. For an account of the demonstration, see Roger Garside, *Coming Alive,* pp. 221–43.

40. See reports of demonstrations of 70,000 sent-down youth in Xinjiang in Nov. 1980, which were followed by several days of rioting in Shanghai and Hangzhou. In Agence France Presse, Feb. 2, 1981, in FBIS 21 (Feb. 2, 1981): O10; Radio Hangzhou, Feb. 12, 1979, in FBIS 30 (Feb. 12, 1979): G1; and Radio Shanghai, Feb. 11, 1979, in FBIS 30 (Feb. 12, 1979): G1–3.

41. Radio Changsha, April 5, 1981, in FBIS 67 (April 8, 1981): P14–P15; Radio Haikou (Hainan Island), Oct. 19, 1981, in FBIS 205 (Oct. 23, 1981): P1–P2; and Xinhua, July 11, 1982, in FBIS 133 (July 12, 1982): K5–K6. See also Interview File NT1 (Fujian) (12.7.82).

42. Radio Guangzhou, Oct. 26, 1980, in FBIS 209 (Oct. 27, 1980): P2.

43. "Cadres of Xingtai County People's Court Violate Law and Discipline, Arouse Popular Indignation," *RMRB,* Sept. 3, 1980, in JPRS 76736 (Oct. 31, 1980): 56–58. For a similar case, see Interview File NKP4 (Fujian) (22.9.82).

44. *NFRB,* July 22, 1983.

45. Interview File CN5K-12-14 (Guangdong).

46. Radio Changsha, Dec. 14, 1981, in FBIS 242 (Dec. 17, 1981): K16.

47. Radio Changsha, Aug. 1, 1982, in *SWB* FE/7098/BII/19 (Aug. 7, 1982).

48. Radio Jinan, Sept. 18, 1980, in FBIS 187 (Sept. 24, 1980): O4–O5.

49. See, e.g., Interview File NT1 (Fujian) (12.7.82).

50. Radio Guangzhou, Aug. 17, 1979, in FBIS 164 (Aug. 22, 1979): P1.

51. See *Qinghai Ribao,* Dec. 24, 1954; *Xin Hunan Bao,* Aug. 22, 1957; *Nongcun Gongzuo Tongxun,* Aug. 20, 1957; *NFRB,* Aug. 30, 1957; *Guangxi Ribao,* Sept. 15, 1957; *Shenyang Ribao,* Sept. 9, 1957; *Jiangxi Ribao,* Sept. 15, 1957; *Fujian Ribao,* Oct. 28, 1957; *RMRB,* Sept. 4, 1957; *Xinjiang Ribao,* Oct. 29, 1957; *Anhui Ribao,* Aug. 16, 1957; *Da Gong Bao* (Beijing), Sept. 22, 1957; *Fujian Ribao,* Dec. 28, 1957; *Guangxi Ribao,* Aug. 14, 1957. See also Thomas Bernstein, "Cadre and Peasant Behavior Under Conditions of Insecurity and Deprivation," in A. Doak Barnett, *Chinese Communist Politics in Action* (Seattle: University of Washington Press, 1969), pp. 378–85; and Elizabeth J. Perry, "Rural Violence in Socialist China," *CQ* 103 (Sept. 1985): 426. For the early 1950s, Vivienne Shue is skeptical of official reports that blamed illegal activities exclusively on the "bad" classes (*Peasant China in Transition,* p. 127): "Although the authorities liked to say that landlords and rich peasants were the ones primarily guilty of concealing land and that the great majority of poorer peasants were eager to pay their taxes to support the revolutionary government [in 1950–1952], they were in fact well aware that tax evasion was extremely widespread, even of epidemic proportions, and that it crossed all class lines."

Chapter 9

1. See, e.g., Huntington, "Social and Institutional Dynamics of One Party Systems"; Weiner, "Political Participation"; Schulz, "On the Nature and Function of

Participation in Communist Systems"; and Huntington and Nelson, *No Easy Choice,* chap. 3.

2. Huntington, "Social and Institutional Dynamics of One-Party Systems," pp. 25–40.

3. Ibid., p. 33.

4. Schulz, "On the Nature and Function of Participation," pp. 30–31.

5. Huntington and Nelson, *No Easy Choice,* p. 166.

6. Huntington, "Social and Institutional Dynamics of One-Party Systems," p. 36.

7. Huntington and Nelson, *No Easy Choice,* p. 166.

8. Huntington, "Social and Institutional Dynamics of One-Party Systems," p. 4.

9. Huntington and Nelson, *No Easy Choice,* p. 45.

10. Ibid., pp. 48–53.

11. Ibid., p. 28.

12. Ibid., p. 53.

13. H. Gordon Skilling, "Groups in Soviet Politics," in Skilling and Franklyn Griffiths, eds., *Interest Groups in Soviet Politics* (Princeton: Princeton University Press, 1971), p. 24. See Skilling's recent assessment (with an extensive bibliography) of the imapct of *Interest Groups in Soviet Politics* in "Interest Groups and Communist Politics Revisited," *World Politics* 35 (1983): 1–27.

14. Skilling, "Groups in Soviet Politics," pp. 24–25.

15. Ibid., p. 36.

16. Ibid., p. 37.

17. Ibid.

18. See Michel Oksenberg, "Occupational Groups in Chinese Society and the Cultural Revolution," in *The Cultural Revolution* (Ann Arbor: Michigan Papers in Chinese Studies, no. 2, 1968); David S. G. Goodman, ed., *Groups and Politics in the People's Republic of China* (Armonk, N.Y.: M. E. Sharpe, 1984); and Victor C. Falkenheim, ed., *Citizens and Groups in Contemporary China* (Ann Arbor: Michigan Monographs in Chinese Studies, no. 56, 1987).

19. See, e.g., chapters by Barbara Krug, Gerald Segal, and James Cotton, in Goodman, ed., *Groups and Politics,* pp. 57, 97, and 176, who argue that neither economists, the PLA, nor intellectuals form "interest groups" in Chinese politics. These groups are internally divided and lack autonomy from the party.

20. Parish and Whyte, *Village and Family,* pp. 100, 105.

21. *RMRB,* April 9, 1980, reports that 200 million peasants still lived in poverty, earning less than 50 yuan per capita per year, in David Zweig, "Economic Development and Social Conflict" (paper prepared for the 1984 Annual Meeting of the Association of Asian Studies, Washington Hilton Hotel, Washington, D.C., March 23–25, 1984), p. 1.

22. Liao Gailong, "The 1980 Reform Program of China" (Part Four), in FBIS 50 (March 16, 1981): U11.

23. *Beijing Review* 8 (Feb. 20, 1984).

24. *RMRB,* June 15, 1982, in FBIS 11 (June 21, 1982): K14.

25. See, e.g., "Reqing xishou 'lianghu' zhong xianjin fenzi ru dang" [Enthusiastically recruit into the party progressive persons from among "the two households"], *RMRB,* April 6, 1984, p. 1.

26. Schulz, "On the Nature and Function of Participation," pp. 30–31.

27. Huntington and Nelson, *No Easy Choice,* p. 166.

28. See the "Organizational Rules of Poor and Lower-Middle Peasant Associations (Draft)," in Baum and Teiwes, *Ssu-ch'ing.*

29. Kay Johnson, *Women, the Family, and Peasant Revolution in China* (Chicago: University of Chicago Press, 1983), pp. 194–95.

30. Cheng Zihua, "Summary Report on the Work of the Nationwide County-Level Direct Elections," *RMRB,* Sept. 12, 1981, in FBIS 177 (Sept. 14, 1981): K6.

31. Townsend, *Political Participation,* p. 119.

32. Popkin, *The Rational Peasant,* p. 258. See also Migdal, *Peasants, Politics, and Revolution,* pp. 214–29.

33. See Popkin, *The Rational Peasant,* pp. 27–31, 72–78.

34. See Oi, "Communism and Clientelism," pp. 238–66.

35. See Madsen, *Morality and Power,* chap. 3.

36. Chan, Madsen, and Unger, *Chen Village,* pp. 61–64. See also Hinton, *Fanshen,* for the earlier period.

37. See, e.g., *RMRB,* June 9, 1984.

38. For the social composition of the Guomindang, see Hung-mao Tien, *Government and Politics in Kuomintang China, 1927–1937* (Stanford: Stanford University Press, 1972), chap. 8; Chi Shisheng, *Nationalist China at War* (Ann Arbor: University of Michigan Press, 1982), chaps. 1–2; Geisert, "Power and Society," pp. 18–25; and Barkan, "Nationalists, Communists, and Rural Leaders," pp. 159–62, 449–52.

39. John Lewis, *Leadership in Communist China,* p. 108. In 1956, there were 7.4 million party members of "peasant status" (*nongmin chengfen*). See also Thomas Bernstein, "Leadership and Mobilization in the Collectivization of Agriculture in China and Russia" (Ph.D. dissertation, Columbia University, 1970), p. 273.

40. Xinhua, in *China Daily* (Beijing), July 2, 1984. The party has recruited heavily from among intellectuals. This group could, however, contain persons of peasant origin. These figures confuse origin (father's occupation) with current occupation.

41. Lewis, *Leadership in Communist China,* p. 123.

42. See James C. F. Wang, *Contemporary Chinese Politics* (Englewood Cliffs, N.J.: Prentice Hall, 1981), pp. 71, 117. The number of senior party cadres of peasant origin, however, must be much higher. They are now included in the more general categories "party or government cadres" or "PLA representatives" in the figures issued for the Central Committee elected by the Twelfth Party Congress. See *Issues and Studies* 18, no. 11 (Nov. 1982): 22.

43. Wang, *Contemporary Chinese Politics,* p. 100. In the Fourth National People's

Congress (1975), "workers, peasants, and soldiers" formed 72 percent of the delegates ("Quarterly Chronicle and Documentation," *CQ* 62 [June 1975] : 340). Figures for the peasant component of the Third National People's Congress (1965) were not available.

44. *Beijing Review* 22 (May 30, 1983): 5.

45. Richard Solomon, "On Activism and Activists," *CQ* 39 (July–Sept. 1969) : 76–114.

46. See Chan, Madsen, and Unger, *Chen Village,* for a discussion of the role of sent-down youth activists during the 1960s and early 1970s.

47. See Madsen, *Morality and Power,* pp. 255–57.

48. See *Jingji Ribao,* Jan. 28, 1984, for the results of a 10 percent sample survey of the 1982 census. Illiteracy was found to be the lowest in Beijing (10.39 percent), rising to 22.35 percent in the suburbs. But 50 percent of some mostly rural provinces were found to be "illiterate or semi-literate" (unable to read up to 1,500 characters).

49. See Falkenheim, "Political Participation in China," p. 22, who found that "respondents for the most part regarded political involvement as time-consuming, competitive with attention to their professional interests, false, empty, and most often potentially dangerous. Significantly, though, the general lack of concern with politics expressed did not translate into apathy or passivity. Instead, it went hand in hand with relatively high levels of attention to media coverage and rituals of support."

SELECT BIBLIOGRAPHY

Frequently Cited Periodicals

Beijing Review (called *Peking Review* before 1979).
Beijing Ribao [Beijing Daily].
China Daily. Beijing.
Fujian Ribao [Fujian Daily].
Guangming Ribao [Guangming Daily].
Hebei Ribao [Hebei Daily].
Heilongjiang Ribao [Heilongjiang Daily].
Hongqi [Red Flag]. Beijing.
Jiefang Ribao [Liberation Daily]. Shanghai.
Jingji Guanli [Economic Management]. Beijing.
Liaowang [Outlook]. Beijing.
Nanfang Ribao (*NFRB*) [Southern Daily]. Guangzhou.
Ningxia Ribao [Ningxia Daily].
Nongye Jingji [Agricultural Economics]. Edited by Zhongguo renmin daxue shu-
    bao cailiao she [Chinese People's University Book and Newspaper Materials So-
    ciety, Beijing].
Renmin Ribao (*RMRB*) [People's Daily]. Beijing.
Shanxi Nongmin Bao [Shanxi Peasant News].
Shanxi Ribao [Shanxi Daily].
Sichuan Ribao [Sichuan Daily].
Tianjin Ribao [Tianjin Daily].
Xinhua Ribao [New China Daily]. Jiangsu.
Yangcheng Wanbao [Yangcheng Evening News]. Guangzhou.
Zhejiang Ribao [Zhejiang Daily].
Zhonggong Yanjiu [Studies on Chinese Communism]. Taibei.

Books and Articles in Chinese

"Baodui ganbu bu ying baoban xuanju" [Guarantee cadres should not "guarantee"
    elections]. *RMRB,* Dec. 1, 1978.
Beijing Shi Difangxing Fagui Huibian: 1980–1985 [Selection of Beijing municipal
    local laws: 1980–1985]. Beijing: Zhongguo zhengfa daxue chubanshe, 1986.

"Bu yao luan pai gongzuodui" [Do not wastefully dispatch work teams]. *RMRB*, Feb. 5, 1979.

"Bu zhun liyong dazibao wuxian hao ren" [Do not permit the use of big-character posters to slander good people]. *RMRB*, May 11, 1979.

"Bu zhun ziliudi shucai shangshi" [Not permitting vegetables from private plots in the market]. *NFRB*, July 16, 1980.

"Caiqu duo zhong banfa xuanba peiyang zhong- qingnian ganbu" [Use many methods for selecting and cultivating young and middle-aged cadres]. *Sichuan Ribao*, Sept. 22, 1980.

"Cong xuanju bu xuan xiao tanqi" [Talking about elections being overruled]. *NFRB*, March 15, 1979.

"Cong xuanju daibiao tanqi [Talking about electing representatives]. *RMRB*, Oct. 9, 1978.

"Dalemu cun minzhu xuanju cunzhang de diaocha" [Investigation of the democratic election of the village head of Dalemu village]. *Nongye Jingji Wenti* [Problems of Rural Economics] 8 (1982): 38–39.

Dalu Dixia Kanwu Huibian [Collection of underground publications from the Chinese mainland]. Taibei: Institute for the Study of Chinese Communist Problems, 1980.

Ding Zhengquan. "Jiandou" [Gathering beans]. *Yuhua* [Rain and Flowers] (Beijing) 3 (March 1980): 4–12.

Du Runsheng. "Nongcun gongzuo de lishixing zhuanbian" [Critical turning point in the history of rural work]. *RMRB*, Sept. 16, 1982.

"Ganbu haishi yao xia jiceng" [Cadres still must go to basic levels]. *RMRB*, March 27, 1979.

"Gao Guilin pohuai minzhu xuanju shoudao falü zhicai" [Gao Guilin sabotages democratic elections and receives punishment according to law]. *Xinhua Ribao*, July 7, 1980.

"Gongshe ganbu baodui shi yi hao banfa" [Commune cadres guaranteeing brigades is a good method]. *RMRB*, May 9, 1979.

"Gongshe ganbu changnian baoduide fangfa gaijin" [We must improve the method of commune cadres guaranteeing brigades for a long time]. *RMRB*, March 27, 1979.

"Gongzuodui gaiwei diaochazu hao" [Work teams should be changed into investigation teams]. *RMRB*, March 27, 1979.

"Gongzuodui haishi yao pai de" [Work teams still should be dispatched]. *RMRB*, April 12, 1979.

Guangdong sheng xuanju gongzuo bangongshi [Guandong Province Election Work Office]. "Zhijie xuanju xuanchuan tigang" [Direct election propaganda outline]. Dec. 29, 1983.

Guangzhou shi jiaoqu xuanju weiyuanhui bangongshi [Guangzhou City Suburban Election Committee Office]. "Guangzhou shi, jiaoqu, zhen, xiang dibajie renda daibiao xuanju xuanchuan cailiao" [Guangzhou city, suburb, town, and township propaganda materials for the election of delegates to the Eighth People's Congress]. Jan. 9, 1984.

"Guanyu jinyibu jiaqiang he wanshan nongye shengchan zerenzhi de jige wenti" [Concerning further strengthening and perfecting the system of job responsibility for agricultural production]. *Zhongfa* (1980) no. 75, in *Zhonggong Yanjiu* (Taibei) 171 (March 15, 1981): 110–18.

He Nong. "Zhongguo yi ge nongcun gongshe xuanju yinqi de fengbo" [Disturbances in a rural commune election in China]. *Fengfan* [Full Sail] (Taiyuan, 1980). Reprinted in *Zhongguo Minzhu Yundong* (Hong Kong) 1, no. 3 (March 1981): 10.

"Hui mai mou shijian shuoming le shenme?" [What is the explanation for destroying the wheatfield?). In Zhongguo renmin daxue shubao cailiao she [Chinese People's University Books and Newspapers Materials Society], *Nongye Jingji* F2 10 (1981): 87–89.

"Jianli zerenzhi yao ying dui zhiyi" [Establish responsibility systems suitable to the brigade]. *Sichuan Ribao*, Sept. 13, 1981.

"Jieshou piping, quxiao cuowu jueding" [Accepts criticism, abolishes incorrect decision]. *NFRB*, Aug. 6, 1980.

Jilin sheng nongye weiyuanhui, ed. [Jilin Province Rural Committee]. "Jilin sheng nongcun renmin gongshe nongye shengchan zerenzhi shixing banfa" [Trial methods for implementing the rural production responsibility system in Jilin Province's rural people's communes]. *Jilin Ribao*, Dec. 19. 1981, in Zhongguo renmin daxue shubao cailiao she, *Nongye Jingji* F2 1 (1982): 69.

"Jingjian shedui fei shengchan renyuan jianjing nongmin fudan" [Simplify (the numbers of) commune and brigade nonproductive personnel, reduce the peasants' burden]. *Jingji Guanli*, Jan. 1982, p. 59.

"Jujue huilu de hao tuanyuan" [The good youth league member who refused bribes]. *Zhejiang Ribao*, Jan. 15, 1981.

"Kaifeng diqu xinfang gongzuo jianjie" [Brief introduction to the letters and visits work of Kaifeng district]. *RMRB*, July 27, 1979.

"Kuaiji duiwu xiangdui wending hao" [Relative stability of team accountants is good]. *Zhejiang Ribao*, July 25, 1980.

Lin Tian. "Guanyu renmin gongshe tizhi wenti de shentao" [Discussion of the problem of the people's commune system]. *Jingji Guanli*, Jan. 1981, pp. 10–13.

"Lingdao banzi bian yi nian da bianhua" [Leadership group change, in one year a big change]. *Xinhua Ribao*, May 14, 1980.

Liu Cheng and Chen Wuyuan. "Nongcun guanli tizhi gaige de chubu shi" [Preliminary experiment in the reform of the rural management system]. *Jingji Guanli*, April 1981, pp. 37–41.

Liu Jianzheng, "Nongye shengchan zerenzhi cujin le nongcun de minzhu jianshe" [Implementing the agricultural responsibility system results in building village democracy]. *Guangming Ribao*, Dec. 27, 1982.

Liu Xumao. "Woguo nongcun xianxing de ji zhong zhuyao shengchan zerenzhi jianjie" [Introduction to several important production responsibility systems implemented in China's countryside]. *Jingji Guanli,* Sept. 1981, pp. 12–14.

Long Chun. "Guanyu nongye shengchan zerenzhi de jige wenti" [Several problems regarding the agricultural production responsibility system]. *Jingji Wenti Tansuo* [Exploration of Economic Problems] 1 (1982), in Zhongguo renmin daxue shubao cailiao she, *Nongye Jingji* F2 (1982) 4:65–68.

Ma Biao. "Anhui nongcun baochan daohu qingkuang kaocha" [Examination of the situation of contracting output to households in rural Anhui]. *Jingji Guanli,* Feb. 1981, pp. 19–22.

Ma Renping. "Nongcun shixing shengchan zerenzhi hou chuxian de xin wenti" [New problems that have emerged after the implementation of the rural production responsibility system]. *Jingji Guanli,* Aug. 1981, pp. 3–8.

"Minzhu xuanchu chengxin dangjiaren" [Democratically select appropriate masters]. *NFRB,* Feb. 24, 1980.

"Nongcun diaocha baogao" [Rural investigation report]. *Guangxi Daxue Xuebao* 2 (1981), in Zhongguo renmin daxue shubao cailiao she, *Nongye Jingji* F2 (1982) 2:55–59.

"Nongcun gongzuodui bu neng jiandan fouding" [Rural work teams cannot be simply abolished]. *RMRB,* March 27, 1979.

Pan Naiyue. "Nongcun shedui jingying guanli de huigu he gaige weiyi" [Management of rural communes and brigades in retrospect with suggestions for reform]. *Nongye Jingji Wenti* 4 (1981), in Zhongguo renmin daxue shubao cailiao she, *Nongye Jingji* F2 (1981) 9:100–2.

"Quanding dake bubi" [Fixing is not necessary]. *NFRB,* March 14, 1979.

"Qunzhong xuanju ziji xinren de ganbu haochu duo" [The many advantages of the masses electing their own trusted cadres]. *NFRB,* Jan. 20, 1980.

"Renmin zui zhongyao de quanli shi xuanju quanli" [The people's most important power is the right of election]. *NFRB,* Jan. 16, 1979.

"Renyang gongshe yu lingdao de minzhu xuanju shengchan duizhang" [Renyang commune leads the democratic election of production team leaders]. *Xinhua Ribao,* Dec. 1, 1980.

"Reqing xishou 'lianghu' zhong xianjin fenzi ru dang" [Enthusiastically recruit into the party progressive persons from among the "two households"]. *RMRB,* April 6, 1984.

"Ruhe kandai nongcun jieji douzheng wenti?" [How should we view the problem of rural class struggle?]. *RMRB,* Sept. 1, 1979.

"Shangmian quanding duizhang jiushi bu minzhu" [Upper levels choosing team leaders is not democratic]. *NFRB,* Feb. 14, 1979.

"Shanxi sheng geji renmin daibiao dahui xuanju shishi xize" [Bylaws for the implementation of various levels of people's congress elections in Shanxi Province]. In Shanxi sheng renmin dachanghui bangongshi, ed. [Office of the Standing Committee of the People's Congress of Shanxi Province]. *Difang Renda Gongzuo*

Shouce [Handbook for local people's congresses' work], vol. 1. Taiyuan, 1984.

"Shei shi zhenzheng de Baili?" [Who is the real Baili?]. *Sichuan Ribao,* July 10, 1980.

"Shengchandui ganbu bixu minzhu xuanju" [Production team cadres should be democratically elected]. *NFRB,* Jan. 10, 1979.

"Tantan baozhi kaizhan piping de 'sannan'" [A discussion of the "three difficulties" of newspapers launching criticism]. *Jiefang Ribao,* Nov. 18, 1980.

"Taopi gongshe minzhu xuanju shengchan duizhang" [Taopi commune democratically elects team leaders]. *RMRB,* Jan. 21, 1979.

"Tuanjie 'wailaihu'" [Unite with "outsider households"]. *Fujian Ribao,* April 4, 1982.

Wang Shuheng and Chen Quanyi. "Guanyu wanshan nongye shengchan zerenzhi de jige wenti" [Several questions on the perfection of the rural production responsibility system]. *Jiangxi Shehui Kexue* 5–6 (1981), in Zhongguo renmin daxue shubao cailiao she, *Nongye Jingji* 1 (1982): 75–82.

"Wei shenme chuxian fendui xianxiang?" [Why has the phenomenon of splitting up the team emerged?]. *RMRB,* May 5, 1979.

"Wei xuan shengchan duizhang shuo ji ju hua" [A few words on the election of production team leaders]. *Zhejiang Ribao,* Nov. 6, 1981.

"Xianren houji de dang zhishu" [The impartial party branch secretary]. *NFRB,* June 6, 1981.

"Xinfang gongzuozhe de husheng" [The outcry of the letters and visits workers]. *RMRB,* July 27, 1979.

Xu Chongde and Pi Chunxie. *Xuanju Zhidu Wenda* [Questions and answers on the election system]. Beijing: Qunzhong chubanshe, 1980.

"Xuan hao dangjiaren" [Elect the masters well]. *NFRB,* March 15, 1979.

"Xuanju neng lingdao qun zengchan de ren dang duizhang" [Elect those who can lead the masses to raise production to be team leaders]. *RMRB,* Feb. 20, 1979.

Yan Jiaji. "Minzhu shi yi zhong guojia xingshi" [Democracy is a state form]. In *Minzhu Wenti Jianghua.* Beijing: Qunzhong chubanshe, 1980.

"Yao jiena sheyuan de zhengque yijian" [(We) must accept commune members' correct opinions]. *NFRB,* Feb. 19, 1979.

"Yiyuanhua lingdao bu shi yi ge ren lingdao" [United leadership is not one-man leadership]. *Zhejiang Ribao,* Dec. 18, 1980.

"Zhejiang jiehe jiepi sirenbang kaizhan shuangda douzheng" [Zhejiang combines the struggle to expose and criticize the Gang of Four with the start of the Double Hits]. *RMRB,* Nov. 5, 1978.

"Zhengzhi zhidaoyuan haiyou gongzuo kezuo ma?" [Do political thought cadres still have work to do?]. *RMRB,* April 27, 1979.

"Zhezhong quanding shi biyao de" [This sort of choosing is necessary]. *NFRB,* Feb. 21, 1979.

"Zhonggong Pingba xianwei zhengdun, gaixuan dadui dang zhibu de qingkuang baogao" [Report on the rectification and reelection of the branch of the CCP committee of Pingba County]. *Zhonggong Yanjiu* (Taibei) 195 (March 15, 1983): 137–46.

"Zhonggong zhongyang guanyu jiakuai nongye fazhan ruogan wenti de jueding (caoan)" [Decisions on some questions concerning the acceleration of agricultural development (Draft)]. *Zhonggong Yanjiu* 13, no. 5 (May 15, 1979): 150–62.

"Zhonggong zhongyang guanyu yi-jiu-ba-si nian nongcun gongzuo de tongzhi" [Party central notice on 1984 agricultural work]. *RMRB*, June 12, 1984.

"Zhongguo gongchandang nongcun dang zhibu gongzuo tiaoli (shixing caoan)" [CCP rural party branch regulations (Draft for trial use)]. Beijing: Zhonggong zuzhibu, Dec. 1981, in *Zhonggong Yanjiu* 16, no. 9 (Sept. 15, 1982): 131–50.

Zhongguo nongcun fazhan yanjiu zhongxin cailiao she [China Rural Development Research Center Materials Society], ed. *Nongcun Zhuanyehu Qin Lao Zhi Fu Yibai Li* [One hundred examples of rural specialized households becoming rich through labor]. Beijing: Renmin chubanshe, 1983.

Zhou Cheng. "Lun baochan dao hu" [On contracting output to households]. *Jingji Lilun yu Jingji Guanli* 2 (1981), in Zhongguo renmin daxue shubao cailiao she, *Nongye Jingji* F2 (1981): 83–89.

Books and Articles in English

Ahn, Byung-joon. *Chinese Politics and the Cultural Revolution: The Dynamics of Policy Processes*. Seattle: University of Washington Press, 1976.

Aird, John S. "Population Studies and Population Policy in China." *Population and Development Review* 8, no. 2 (June 1982): 267–97.

Alitto, Guy S. "Rural Elites in Transition: China's Cultural Crisis and the Problem of Legitimacy." In Susan Mann Jones, ed., *Select Papers from the Center for Far Eastern Studies, 1978–1979*, no. 3, pp. 218–75. Chicago: University of Chicago, 1979.

"All Power Belongs to the People." *RMRB*, Jan. 6, 1983, in FBIS 5 (Jan. 7, 1983): K2.

Andors, Stephen. *China's Industrial Revolution: Politics, Planning, and Management, 1949 to the Present*. New York: Pantheon Books, 1977.

Banister, Judith. *China's Changing Population*. Stanford: Stanford University Press, 1985.

Baoan Bulletin. Trans. in Union Research Service, vol. 27, nos. 7, 8, and 9 (April 24, April 27, and May 1, 1962). Hong Kong: Union Research Institute.

Barkan, Lenore. "Nationalists, Communists, and Rural Leaders: Political Dynamics in a Chinese County, 1927–1937." Ph.D. dissertation, University of Washington, 1983.

Barker, Randolph, and Radha Sinha, eds. *The Chinese Agricultural Economy*. Boulder: Westview Press, 1982.

Barnett, A. Doak. *Cadres, Bureaucracy, and Political Power.* New York: Columbia University Press, 1967.

Baum, Richard. "The Cultural Revolution in the Countryside: Anatomy of a Limited Rebellion." In Thomas W. Robinson, ed., *The Cultural Revolution in China*, pp. 367–477. Berkeley and Los Angeles: University of California Press, 1971.

———. *Prelude to Revolution: Mao, the Party, and the Peasant Question, 1962–1966.* New York: Columbia University Press, 1975.

Baum, Richard, and Frederick Teiwes. *Ssu-ch'ing: The Socialist Education Movement of 1962–1966.* Berkeley: Center for Chinese Studies, Monograph Series, University of California, 1968.

Bedeski, Robert E. *State-Building in Modern China: The Kuomintang in the Pre-War Period.* Berkeley: University of California China Research Monograph, 1981.

Bennett, Gordon. "Huadong People's Commune, 1980: A Second Look After Seven Years," *Asian Survey* 22, no. 8 (Aug. 1982): 745–56.

———. *Huadong: The Story of a Chinese People's Commune.* Boulder: Westview Press, 1978.

Bernstein, Thomas P. "Cadre and Peasant Behavior under Conditions of Insecurity and Deprivation: The Grain Supply Crisis of the Spring of 1955." In A. Doak Barnett, *Chinese Communist Politics in Action*, pp. 365–99. Seattle: University of Washington Press, 1969.

———. "Leadership and Mobilization in the Collectivization of Agriculture in China and Russia: A Comparison." Ph.D. dissertation, Columbia University, 1970.

———. *Up to the Mountains and Down to the Villages: The Transfer of Youth from Urban to Rural China.* New Haven: Yale University Press, 1977.

Blecher, Marc. "Consensual Politics in Rural Chinese Communities: The Mass Line in Theory and Practice." *Modern China* 5, no. 1 (Jan. 1979): 105–26.

———. "Income Distribution in Small Rural Chinese Communities." *CQ* 68 (Dec. 1976): 797–816.

———. "Leader-Mass Relations in Rural Chinese Communities: Local Politics in a Revolutionary Society." Ph.D. dissertation, University of Chicago, 1978.

Booth, John A. "Political Participation in Latin America: Levels, Structure, Context, Concentration and Rationality." *Latin American Research Review* 14, no. 3 (1979): 29–60.

"Branch Committee Election Held Without Any Restrictive Framework Imposed." *Beijing Ribao,* Jan. 15, 1979, in JPRS 73201 (April 11, 1979): 6–7.

Brodsgaard, Kjeld Erick. "The Democracy Movement in China, 1978–1979: Opposition Movements, Wall Poster Campaigns, and Underground Journals." *Asian Survey* 21, no. 7 (July 1981): 742–74.

Brown, H. O. "Recent Policy Towards Rural Education in the People's Republic of China." *Hong Kong Journal of Public Administration* 3, no. 2 (Dec. 1981): 168–88.

Brugger, William. *Democracy and Organization in the Chinese Industrial Enterprise, 1948–53.* Cambridge: Cambridge University Press, 1976.

Burns, John P. "Chinese Peasant Interest Articulation, 1949–1974." Ph.D. dissertation, Columbia University, 1979.

———. "The Election of Production Team Leaders in Rural China, 1958–74." *CQ* 74 (June 1978): 273–96.

———. "Local Cadre Accommodation to the 'Responsibility System' in Rural China." *Pacific Affairs* 58, no. 4 (Winter 1985–86): 607–25.

———. "Peasant Interest Articulation and Work Teams in Rural China: 1962–1974." In Godwin C. Chu and Francis L. K. Hsu, eds., *China's New Social Fabric,* pp. 147–55. London: Kegan, Paul International, 1984.

———. "Rural Guangdong's 'Second Economy,' 1962–1974." *CQ* 88 (Dec. 1981): 629–43.

Butler, Steven. *Agricultural Mechanization in China: The Administrative Impact.* New York: East Asian Institute, Columbia University, 1978.

"Cadres of Xingtai County People's Court Violate Law and Discipline, Arouse Popular Indignation." *RMRB,* Sept. 3, 1980, in JPRS 76736 (Oct. 31, 1980): 56–58.

Cao Ruitian. "A Talk About Poverty and Wealth." *RMRB,* May 18, 1982, in FBIS 99 (May 21, 1982): K2–K3.

"CCP Central Committee Directive Concerning the Question of Distribution in Rural People's Communes." *Zhongfa* (1971) 82, in *Issues and Studies* 9, no. 2 (Nov. 1972): 92–95.

CCP Ssumao District Committee. "Ssumao District Party Committee's Opinion About the Implementation of the CCP Central Committee Directive Concerning the Question of Distribution in the Rural People's Commune." *Sidongfa* (1972) 22, in *Issues and Studies* 9, no. 6 (March 1973): 91–97.

"Certain Regulations by the National People's Congress Standing Committee Concerning the Direct Election of Deputies to People's Congresses at the County Level and Below." Xinhua, March 7, 1983, in FBIS 46 (March 8, 1983): K1–K3.

Chan, Anita, and Jonathan Unger. "Grey and Black: The Hidden Economy of Rural China." *Pacific Affairs* 55 (1983): 452–71.

Chan, Anita, Richard Madsen, and Jonathan Unger. *Chen Village: The Recent History of a Peasant Community in Mao's China.* Berkeley and Los Angeles: University of California Press, 1984.

Chen, C. S., and Charles Price Ridley, eds. (Lianjiang Documents). *Rural People's Communes in Lien-chiang.* Stanford: Hoover Institution, 1969.

Chen, Jack. *A Year in Upper Felicity.* New York: Random House, 1975.

Chen Ruoxi. *Democracy Wall and the Unofficial Journals.* Berkeley: Center for Chinese Studies, Studies in Chinese Terminology No. 20, 1982.

Chen, Theodore H. E., ed. *The Chinese Communist Regime: Documents and Commentary.* New York: Praeger, 1967.

Chen Yung-fa. *Making Revolution: The Communist Movement in Eastern and Central China, 1937–45*. Berkeley and Los Angeles: University of California Press, 1986.

———. "Rural Elections in Wartime Central China: Democratization of Sub-bureaucracy." *Modern China* 6, no. 3 (July 1980): 267–310.

Ch'en Ting-chung. "The Prospects of the People's Commune: The 'Three Freedoms and One Contract.'" *Issues and Studies* 18, no. 5 (May 1982): 39.

Cheng, Chester J., ed. *The Politics of the Chinese Red Army: A Translation of the "Bulletin of Activities" of the People's Liberation Army*. Stanford: Hoover Institution, 1966.

Cheng Zihua. "Summing Up Report on the National Direct Election at the County Level." Sept. 3, 1981, in FBIS 177 (Sept. 14, 1981): K2–K10.

Chi Shisheng. *Nationalist China at War: Military Defeat and Political Collapse*. Ann Arbor: University of Michigan Press, 1982.

Ch'ien Tuan-sheng. *The Government and Politics of China, 1912–1949*. Stanford: Stanford University Press, 1970.

Chinese Ministry of Information. *China Handbook, 1937–1945*. New York: Macmillan, 1947.

Chu, David S. K., ed. *Sociology and Society in Contemporary China: 1979–1983*. Armonk: M. E. Sharpe, 1984.

Chu, Godwin C. *Radical Change Through Communication in Mao's China*. Honolulu: University of Hawaii Press, 1977.

Chu, Godwin C., and Leonard L. Chu. "Parties in Conflict: Letters to the Editor of the *People's Daily*." *Journal of Communication* 31, no. 4 (Autumn 1981): 74–91.

Chu Li and Tian Jieyuan. *Inside a People's Commune*. Beijing: Foreign Languages Press, 1974.

Ch'u T'ung-tsu. *Local Government in China Under the Ch'ing*. Stanford: Stanford University Press, 1969.

"Communique of the Third Plenary Session of the 11th Central Committee of the Communist Party of China." Dec. 22, 1978, in FBIS 248 (Dec. 26, 1978): E4–E13.

"Consciously Carry out the Party's Rural Policies." *RMRB*, Jan. 26, 1979, in FBIS 22 (Jan. 31, 1979): E19–20.

"Constitution of the People's Republic of China" (1954). In Theodore H. E. Chen, ed., *The Chinese Communist Regime: Documents and Commentary*, pp. 75–91. New York: Praeger, 1967.

"Constitution of the People's Republic of China" (1975). *Peking Review* 4 (Jan. 24, 1975): 12–17.

"Constitution of the People's Republic of China" (1978). *Peking Review* 11 (March 17, 1978): 5–14.

"Constitution of the People's Republic of China" (1982). FBIS 235 (Dec. 7, 1982): K1–K28.

"Criminal Law of the People's Republic of China." July 1, 1979, in FBIS 146 (July 27, 1979), Supplement 19, pp. 33–62.

"Criticize the Sixth Brigade of Dongwang Commune for Its Thwarting the Implementation of the Policy Governing Private Plots." *RMRB*, Oct. 14, 1979, in JPRS 74800 (Dec. 20, 1979): 51–53.

Crook, Frederick. "The *Baogan Daohu* Incentive System: Translation and Analysis of a Model Contract." *CQ* 102 (June 1985): 291–303.

———. "The Commune System in the People's Republic of China, 1963–1974." In Joint Economic Committee, 94th U.S. Congress, eds., *China: A Reassessment of the Economy*, pp. 366–408. Washington, D.C.: U.S. Government Printing Office, 1975.

Crook, Isabel, and David Crook. *Ten Mile Inn: Mass Movement in a Chinese Village.* New York: Pantheon, 1979.

Dai Qingqi and Yu Zhan. "Study Comrade Deng Zihui's Viewpoint on the Agricultural Production Responsibility System." *RMRB*, Feb. 23, 1982, in FBIS 44 (March 5, 1982): K16–K20.

"Decision of the Central Committee of the Chinese Communist Party Concerning the Great Proletarian Cultural Revolution." Aug. 8, 1966, in *Peking Review* 33 (Aug. 12, 1966): 6–11.

Deng Xiaoping. "Speech to the Enlarged Meeting of the Politburo." Aug. 18, 1980, in FBIS 77 (April 22, 1981): W1–W14.

Diamond, Norma. "Taitou Revisited: State Policies and Social Change." In William Parish, ed., *Chinese Rural Development: The Great Transformation*, pp. 246–70. Armonk: M. E. Sharpe, 1985.

Dittmer, Lowell. "'Line Struggle' in Theory and Practice: The Origins of the Cultural Revolution Reconsidered." *CQ* 72 (Dec. 1977): 675–712.

———. *Liu Shao-ch'i and the Chinese Cultural Revolution: The Politics of Mass Criticism.* Berkeley and Los Angeles: University of California Press, 1974.

Dixon, John. *The Chinese Welfare System, 1949–1979.* New York: Praeger, 1981.

Domes, Jurgen. *The Internal Politics of China, 1949–1972.* New York: Praeger, 1973.

———. "New Policies in the Communes: Notes on Rural Societal Structures in China, 1976–1981." *JAS* 41, no. 2 (Feb. 1982): 253–68.

Eastman, Lloyd E. *The Abortive Revolution: China Under Nationalist Rule, 1927–1937.* Cambridge, Mass.: Harvard University Press, 1974.

———. *Seeds of Destruction: Nationalist China in War and Revolution, 1937–1949.* Stanford: Stanford University Press, 1984.

Editor. "Sources of Labor Discontent in China: The Worker-Peasant System." *Current Scene* 5 (March 15, 1968).

"The Electoral Law of the National Peoples' Congress and Local Peoples' Congresses of the People's Republic of China." July 1, 1979, amended on Dec. 10, 1982. The amended version appears in FBIS 243 (Dec. 17, 1982): K14–K21.

"The Electoral Law of the People's Republic of China" (1953). In Theodore H. E.

Chen, ed., *The Chinese Communist Regime: Documents and Commentary*, pp. 65–75. New York: Praeger, 1967.

"Eliminate Factionalist Interference and Uphold the Principle of Party Spirit." *Shanxi Ribao*, Sept. 8, 1981, in FBIS 193 (Oct. 6, 1981): R7–R8.

"Enthusiastically Assist Poverty-Stricken Communes, and Production Brigades and Teams." *RMRB*, May 18, 1982, in FBIS 98 (May 20, 1982): K1–K2.

Fairbank, John K., and Albert Feuerwerker, eds. *The Cambridge History of China: Republican China, 1912–1949*. Vol. 13, part 2. Cambridge: Cambridge University Press, 1986.

Falkenheim, Victor C. "Political Participation in China." *Problems of Communism* 27 (May–June 1978): 18–32.

Falkenheim, Victor C., ed. *Citizens and Groups in Contemporary China*. Ann Arbor: Michigan Monographs in Chinese Studies, no. 56, 1987.

Fei Xiaotong. *Peasant Life in China: A Field Study of Country Life in the Yangtze Valley*. New York: Dutton, 1939.

Fincher, John. *Chinese Democracy: The Self-Government Movement in Local Provincial and National Politics, 1905–1914*. London: Croom Helm, 1981.

Freedman, Maurice. *Chinese Lineage and Society: Fukien and Kwangtung*. London: Athlone Press, 1971.

Fried, Morton. *Fabric of Chinese Society*. New York: Octagon Books, 1969.

Friedgut, Theodore H. *Political Participation in the USSR*. Princeton: Princeton University Press, 1979.

Fu Po-shek. "The 'Unacknowledged Phase' of the Chinese Democratic Movement, 1980–1981." Unpublished paper, 1982.

Gamble, Sidney D. *North China Villages: Social, Political, and Economic Activities Before 1933*. Berkeley and Los Angeles: University of California Press, 1963.

———. *Ting Hsien: A North China Rural Community*. Stanford: Stanford University Press, 1968.

Gardner, John. "Political Participation and Chinese Communism." In Geraint Parry, ed., *Participation in Politics*, pp. 218–45. Manchester: University of Manchester Press, 1972.

Garside, Roger. *Coming Alive: China After Mao*. New York: McGraw Hill, 1981.

Geisert, Bradley K. "Power and Society: The Kuomintang and Local Elites in Kiangsu Province, China, 1924–1937." Ph.D. dissertation, University of Virginia, 1979.

"Give Play to the Leadership Role of Rural Basic Level Organizations." *RMRB*, Feb. 19, 1982, in FBIS 41 (March 2, 1982): K8–K11.

Goodman, David S. G., ed. *Groups and Politics in the People's Republic of China*. Armonk: M. E. Sharpe, 1984.

Goodstadt, Leo. "Taxation and Economic Modernization in Contemporary China." *Development and Change* 10 (1979): 403–21.

Grindle, Merilee S., ed. *Politics and Policy Implementation in the Third World*. Princeton: Princeton University Press, 1980.

Harding, Harry. "Maoist Theories of Policy-Making and Organization." In Thomas W. Robinson, ed., *The Cultural Revolution in China*, pp. 117–42. Berkeley and Los Angeles: University of California Press, 1971.

Hinton, William. *Fanshen: A Documentary of Revolution in a Chinese Village*. New York: Vintage Books, 1966.

———. *Shenfan: The Continuing Revolution in a Chinese Village*. New York: Random House, 1983.

Hoffmann, Charles. "Worker Participation in Chinese Factories." *Modern China* 3 (July 1977): 291–320.

Hofheinz, Roy. *The Broken Wave: The Chinese Communist Peasant Movement, 1922–1928*. Cambridge, Mass.: Harvard University Press, 1977.

Hsiao Kung-chuan. *Rural China: Imperial Control in the Nineteenth Century*. Seattle: University of Washington Press, 1972.

Hsiao Tso-liang. *The Land Revolution in China, 1930–1934*. Seattle: University of Washington Press, 1969.

Hu Jian, "Wealth of the People and Wealth of the Nation." *RMRB*, Feb. 1, 1983, in FBIS 25 (Feb. 4, 1983): K2–K3.

Huang, Philip. *The Peasant Economy and Social Change in North China*. Stanford: Stanford University Press, 1985.

Hunan Provincial Proletarian Revolutionary Great Alliance Committee (Sheng wu lian). "Whither China?" In *The Revolution is Dead, Long Live the Revolution*, pp. 180–200. Hong Kong: The Seventies, n.d.

Huntington, Samuel P. *Political Order in Changing Societies*. New Haven: Yale University Press, 1971.

———. "Social and Institutional Dynamics of One-Party Systems." In Samuel P. Huntington and Clement H. Moore, eds., *Authoritarian Politics in Modern Society: The Dynamics of Established One Party Systems*, pp. 3–47. New York: Basic Books, 1970.

Huntington, Samuel P., and Joan Nelson. *No Easy Choice: Political Participation in Developing Countries*. Cambridge, Mass.: Harvard University Press, 1976.

Huo Shilian. "Much Can Be Accomplished by Peasant Households Which Have Become Rich Through Labor." *RMRB*, June 15, 1982, in FBIS 119 (June 21, 1982): K13–K18.

Jacobs, J. Bruce. *Local Politics in a Rural Chinese Cultural Setting: A Field Study of Mazu Township, Taiwan*. Canberra: Australian National University, 1981.

Johnson, Graham E. "The Production Responsibility System in Chinese Agriculture: Some Examples from Guangdong." *Pacific Affairs* 55 (1983): 430–51.

Johnson, Kay Ann. *Women, the Family, and Peasant Revolution in China*. Chicago: University of Chicago Press, 1983.

Ken Ling. *The Revenge of Heaven: The Journal of a Young Chinese*. New York: G. P. Putnam and Sons, 1972.

Kraus, Richard. *Class Conflict in Chinese Socialism*. New York: Columbia University Press, 1981.

Kuhn, Philip. "Local Self-Government Under the Republic: Problems of Control, Autonomy, and Mobilization." In Frederic Wakeman, Jr., and Carolyn Grant, eds., *Conflict and Control in Late Imperial China,* pp. 257–97. Berkeley and Los Angeles: University of California Press, 1975.

———. *Rebellion and Its Enemies in Late Imperial China: Militarization and Social Structure, 1796–1864.* Cambridge: Cambridge University Press, 1970.

Lampton, David M., ed. *Policy Implementation in Post-Mao China.* Berkeley and Los Angeles: University of California Press, 1987.

Lardy, Nicholas R. *Agriculture in China's Modern Economic Development.* Cambridge: Cambridge University Press, 1983.

Lee, Hong Yung. *The Politics of the Chinese Cultural Revolution.* Berkeley and Los Angeles: University of California Press, 1978.

Lewis, John. "Commerce, Education, and Political Development in Tangshan: 1956–69." In Lewis, ed., *The City in Communist China,* pp. 153–79. Stanford: Stanford University Press, 1971.

———. *Leadership in Communist China.* Ithaca: Cornell University Press, 1963.

Li Qiming. "Uproot Factionalism, Guarantee Reform." *RMRB,* March 21, 1983, in FBIS 56 (March 22, 1983): K1–K3.

Li Yizhe. "Concerning Socialist Democracy and Legal System." In *The Revolution is Dead, Long Live the Revolution,* pp. 249–83. Hong Kong: The Seventies, n.d. (Also in *Issues and Studies* 12, no. 1 [Jan. 1976]: 110–49.)

Li Yuning. *The Introduction of Socialism Into China.* New York: Columbia University Press, 1971.

Li Zaizao and Chen Jinluo. "A Talk on the Fundamental Spirit of Election Laws and the Significance of Direct Election of People's Congresses at the County Level." *Faxue Yanjiu* 2 (April 23, 1980), in JPRS 76527 (Oct. 2, 1980): 6–13.

Liao Gailong. "The 1980 Reform Program of China" (Part Four). In FBIS 50 (March 16, 1981): U1–U19.

Lin Chen. "The Commune System: Survival or Extension." *Issues and Studies* 18, no. 2 (Feb. 1982): 18–30.

Lin Zeng. "Rural Workers Must Not Be Hired Indiscriminately." *Yangcheng Wanbao,* Aug. 3, 1982, in *SWB,* FE/7098/BII/18 (Aug. 7, 1982).

Lippitt, Victor. "The People's Communes and China's New Development Strategy." *Bulletin of Concerned Asian Scholars* 13, no. 3 (July–Sept. 1981): 19–30.

Little, D. Richard. "Mass Political Participation in the U.S. and the U.S.S.R." *Comparative Political Studies* 8, no. 4 (Jan. 1976): 449–51.

Liu, Alan P. L. *Communications and National Integration in Communist China.* Berkeley and Los Angeles: University of California Press, 1971.

Liu Binyan. *People or Monsters? And Other Stories and Reportage from China After Mao.* Edited by Perry Link. Bloomington: Indiana University Press, 1983.

Liu Qing. "Prison Notes." Trans. in *Speahrhead* 14/15 (Summer/Autumn 1982): 8–58.

Lockett, Martin, and Craig R. Littler. "Trends in Enterprise Management, 1978–

82." Paper prepared for the Conference on China in Transition, Queen Elizabeth House, Oxford, Sept. 7–10, 1982.

Madsen, Richard. *Morality and Power in a Chinese Village.* Berkeley and Los Angeles: University of California Press, 1984.

Mao Zedong. "Analysis of the Classes in Chinese Society." *Selected Readings from the Works of Mao Tse-tung,* pp. 11–20. Beijing: Foreign Languages Press, 1967.

————. "On the Correct Handling of Contradictions Among the People." *Selected Readings from the Works of Mao Tse-tung,* pp. 350–85. Beijing: Foreign Languages Press, 1967.

————. "On the Question of Agricultural Cooperation." *Selected Readings from the Works of Mao Tse-tung,* pp. 316–40. Beijing: Foreign Languages Press, 1967.

————. "Oppose Book Worship." *Selected Readings from the Works of Mao Tse-tung,* pp. 33–41. Beijing: Foreign Languages Press, 1967.

————. "Some Questions Concerning Methods of Leadership." *Selected Readings from the Works of Mao Tse-tung,* pp. 234–39. Beijing: Foreign Languages Press, 1967.

————. "Talk at an Enlarged Working Conference Convened by the Central Committee of the Communist Party of China, January 30, 1962." In Qi Xin et al., eds., *China's New Democracy,* pp. 247–78. Hong Kong: Cosmos Books, 1979.

————. "Talk on the Four Clean-ups Movement." In JPRS 61269-2, *Miscellany of Mao Tse-tung Thought* (Feb. 20, 1974), p. 443.

McClosky, Herbert. "Political Participation." *International Encyclopedia of the Social Sciences.* Vol. 11, pp. 252–65. New York: Macmillan, 1968.

McCormick, Barrett L. "Election Campaign in Nanjing: The Center, Local Cadres, and the People." Paper prepared for the 33rd Annual Meeting of the Association of Asian Studies, San Francisco, March 1983.

————. "Reforming the People's Congress System: A Case Study of the Implementation of 'Strengthening Socialist Law and Socialist Democracy' in Post-Mao China." In David M. Lampton, ed., *Policy Implementation in Post-Mao China.* Berkeley and Los Angeles: University of California Press, 1987.

Migdal, Joel. *Peasants, Politics, and Revolution: Pressures Toward Political and Social Change in the Third World.* Princeton: Princeton University Press, 1974.

Mosher, Steven W. *Broken Earth: The Rural Chinese.* New York: Free Press, 1983.

Nan Zhenzhong. "Is It Still Necessary to Send Work Teams to the Countryside?" Xinhua, Jan. 27, 1979, in FBIS 23 (Feb. 1, 1979): E15–E17.

Nathan, Andrew J. *Chinese Democracy.* New York: Alfred Knopf, 1985.

Oi, Jean C. "Communism and Clientelism: Rural Policies in China." *World Politics* 37, no. 2 (Jan. 1985): 238–66.

————. "State and Peasants in Contemporary China: the Politics of Grain Procurement." Ph.D. dissertation, University of Michigan, 1983.

Oksenberg, Michel. "Local Leaders in Rural China, 1962–1965: Individual Attributes, Bureaucratic Positions, and Political Recruitment." In A. Doak Barnett, ed., *Chinese Communist Politics in Action,* pp. 155–215.

———. "Occupational Groups in Chinese Society and the Cultural Revolution." In *The Cultural Revolution: 1967 in Review,* pp. 1–44. Ann Arbor: Michigan Papers in Chinese Studies, no. 2, 1968.

O'Leary, Greg, and Andrew Watson. "The Production Responsibility System and the Future of Collective Farming." *Australian Journal of Chinese Affairs* 8 (1982): 1–34.

"The Organic Law for the Local People's Congresses and Local People's Governments of the People's Republic of China." July 1, 1979, amended Dec. 10, 1982, in FBIS 244 (Dec. 20, 1982): K43–K54.

Parish, William. "China—Team, Brigade, or Commune?" *Problems of Communism* 25, no. 2 (March–April 1976): 51–65.

———. "Egalitarianism in Chinese Society." *Problems of Communism* 30 (Jan.–Feb. 1981): 37–53.

Parish, William, and Martin King Whyte. *Village and Family in Contemporary China.* Chicago: University of Chicago Press, 1978.

Pelzel, John. "Economic Management of a Production Brigade in Post-Leap China." In W. E. Willmott, ed., *Economic Organization in Chinese Society,* pp. 387–414. Stanford: Stanford University Press, 1972.

Pepper, Suzanne. "Chinese Education After Mao: Two Steps Forward, Two Steps Back and Begin Again." *CQ* 81 (March 1980): 1–65.

Perry, Elizabeth J. *Rebels and Revolutionaries in North China, 1845–1945.* Stanford: Stanford University Press, 1980.

———. "Rural Violence in Socialist China." *CQ* 103 (Sept. 1985): 414–40.

Perry, Elizabeth J., and Christine Wong, eds. *The Political Economy of Reform in Post-Mao China.* Cambridge, Mass.: Harvard University Press, 1985.

Popkin, Samuel L. *The Rational Peasant: The Political Economy of Rural Society in Vietnam.* Berkeley and Los Angeles: University of California Press, 1979.

Potter, Jack. "The Economic and Social Consequences of Changes in China's Rural Economic Policies, 1978–1981." Unpublished paper.

———. "Land and Lineage in Traditional China." In Maurice Freedman, ed., *Family and Kinship in Chinese Society,* pp. 121–38. Stanford: Stanford University Press, 1970.

Potter, Sulamith H. "The Position of Peasants in Modern China's Social Order." *Modern China* 9, no. 4 (Oct. 1983): 465–99.

Pravda, Alex. "Elections in Communist Party States." In Guy Hermet et al., eds., *Elections Without Choice,* pp. 169–95. London: Macmillan, 1978.

"Protect Peasants Who Get Rich Through Hard Work." *RMRB,* May 20, 1981, in FBIS 101 (May 25, 1981): K16–K18.

"Provisional Methods for Rewards and Penalties for State Organ Work Personnel." *Shanxi Ribao,* Nov. 30, 1981, in FBIS 238 (Dec. 11, 1981): R1–R2.

Pye, Lucian. *The Dynamics of Chinese Politics*. Cambridge, Mass.: Oelgeschlager, Gunn and Hain, 1981.

———. "Mass Participation in Communist China: Its Limitations and the Continuity of Culture." In John Lindbeck, ed., *China: Management of a Revolutionary Society,* pp. 3–33. Seattle: University of Washington Press, 1971.

Rawksi, Evelyn S. *Education and Popular Literacy in Ch'ing China*. Ann Arbor: University of Michigan Press, 1979.

"Regulations on the Work of the Rural People's Communes." Revised Draft, Sept. 1962. In Union Research Service, ed., *Documents of the Chinese Communist Party Central Committee, September 1956–April 1969,* vol. 1, pp. 695–725. Hong Kong: Union Research Institute, 1971.

"Regulations on the Work in Rural People's Communes (Draft for Trial Use)." Trans. in *Issues and Studies* 15, no. 8 (Aug. 1979): 100–12 and 15, no. 9 (Sept. 1979): 104–15.

"Resolution on Certain Questions in the History of Our Party Since the Founding of the People's Republic of China." *Beijing Review* 27 (July 6, 1981): 10–39.

Rosen, Stanley. "Education and Political Socialization of Chinese Youths." In John N. Hawkins, ed., *Education and Social Change in the People's Republic of China,* pp. 97–133. New York: Praeger, 1983.

———. "Guangzhou's Democracy Movement in Cultural Revolution Perspective." *CQ* 101 (March 1985): 1–31.

Rudolph, Jorg-Meinhard. "China's Media: Fitting News to Print." *Problems of Communism* 33 (July–August 1984): 58–67.

Salisbury, Robert H. "Research on Political Participation." *American Journal of Political Science* 19, no. 2 (1975): 323–41.

Schran, Peter. *The Development of Chinese Agriculture, 1950–1959*. Urbana, Ill.: University of Illinois Press, 1969.

Schulz, Donald E. "On the Nature and Function of Participation in Communist Systems: A Developmental Analysis." In Schulz and Jan S. Adams, eds., *Political Participation in Communist Systems,* pp. 26–78. New York: Pergamon Press, 1981.

———. "Political Participation in Communist Systems: The Conceptual Frontier." In Schulz and Jan S. Adams, eds., *Political Participation in Communist Systems,* pp. 1–25. New York: Pergamon Press, 1981.

Scott, Jim. "Everyday Forms of Peasant Resistance." Unpublished paper.

Selden, Mark. "Income Inequality and the State." In William L. Parish, ed., *Chinese Rural Development: The Great Transformation,* pp. 194–203. Armonk: M. E. Sharpe, 1985.

———. *The Yenan Way in Revolutionary China*. Cambridge, Mass.: Harvard University Press, 1971.

Selden, Mark, ed., *The People's Republic of China: A Documentary History of Revolutionary Change*. New York: Monthly Review Press, 1979.

Seymour, James., ed. *The Fifth Modernization: China's Human Rights Movement,*

1978–1979. Stanfordville, N.Y.: Human Rights Publishing Group, 1980.

Sharlet, Robert S. "Concept Formation in Political Science and Communist Studies: Conceptualizing Political Participation." In Frederic J. Fleron, ed., *Communist Studies and the Social Sciences*, pp. 244–53. Chicago: Rand McNally, 1969.

Shirk, Susan L. "Going Against the Tide: Political Dissent in China." *Survey* 24, no. 1 (Winter 1979): 82–97.

Shue, Vivienne. "China's Local News Media." *CQ* 86 (June 1981): 322–31.

———. "The Fate of the Commune." *Modern China* 10, no. 3 (July 1984): 259–83.

———. *Peasant China in Transition: The Dynamics of Development Toward Socialism, 1949–1956*. Berkeley and Los Angeles: University of California Press, 1980.

———. "Peasant Culture and Socialist Culture in China: On the Dynamics of Structure, Behavior, and Value Change in Socialist Systems." In Godwin Chu and Francis L. K. Hsu, eds., *Moving a Mountain: Cultural Change in China*, pp. 305–40. Honolulu: University of Hawaii Press, 1979.

Siu, Helen. "The Nature of Encapsulation: An Evaluation of Receptivity to Production Responsibility Systems by Two Brigades in Southern China." Paper prepared for the Workshop on Recent Reforms in China: Economic, Political, and Social Implications, Harvard University, April 30, 1983.

Skilling, H. Gordon. "Interest Groups and Communist Politics Revisited." *World Politics* 35 (1983): 1–27.

Skilling, H. Gordon, and Franklyn Griffiths, eds. *Interest Groups in Soviet Politics*. Princeton: Princeton University Press, 1971.

Skinner, G. William. "Chinese Peasants and the Closed Community: An Open and Shut Case." *Comparative Studies in Society and History* 13 (1971): 270–381.

———. "Marketing and Social Structure in Rural China." *JAS* 24 (1964): 3–43 and 24 (1965): 195–228.

Smith, Arthur. *Village Life in China*. Boston: Little, Brown, 1970.

Solomon, Richard. *Mao's Revolution and the Chinese Political Culture*. Berkeley and Los Angeles: University of California Press, 1971.

———. "On Activism and Activists: Maoist Conceptions of Motivation and Political Roles Linking State to Society." *CQ* 39 (July–Sept. 1969): 76–114.

Starr, John Bryan. *Continuing the Revolution: The Political Thought of Mao*. Princeton: Princeton University Press, 1979.

"State Council Report on the Use of Farmland for Housing Construction" (Oct. 29, 1982). Xinhua, Nov. 5, 1982, in FBIS 216 (Nov. 8, 1982): K16–K18.

State Economic Commission. "Report on Doing a Better Job in Engaging in Agricultural Sideline Production by Industrial and Mining Enterprises." Transmitted by the State Council, Oct. 7, 1981. Xinhua, Oct. 15, 1981, in FBIS 201 (Oct. 19, 1981): K3–K4.

Stavis, Benedict. *People's Communes and Rural Development in China*. Ithaca, N.Y.: Rural Development Committee, Cornell University, 1974.

Strand, David G. "Reform of Political Participation." Paper prepared for the Conference on Reform of the Chinese Political Order, Harwichport, Mass., June 18–23, 1984.

Sun Qimeng. "Carry Out Two Kinds of Supervision of Different Natures." *RMRB*, July 1, 1982, in FBIS 131 (July 8, 1982): K1–K4.

"Ten Major Crimes of Private Plots." *China News Service* (Hong Kong) 146 (Nov. 17, 1966): 2.

Tien, H. Yuan. *China's Population Struggle: Demographic Decision of the People's Republic of China*. Columbus: Ohio State University Press, 1973.

Tien Hung-mao. *Government and Politics in Kuomintang China, 1927–1937*. Stanford: Stanford University Press, 1972.

Townsend, James R. *Political Participation in Communist China*. Berkeley and Los Angeles: University of California Press, 1969.

Tsou Tang, Marc Blecher, and Mitch Meisner. "National Agricultural Policy: The Dazhai Model and Local Change in the Post-Mao Era." In Mark Selden and Victor Lippitt, eds., *The Transition to Socialism in China*, pp. 266–99. Armonk: M. E. Sharpe, 1982.

———, ———, and ———. "The Responsibility System in Agriculture: Its Implementation in Xiyang and Dazhai." *Modern China* 8, no. 1 (Jan. 1982): 41–103.

Unger, Jonathan. *Education Under Mao: Class and Competition in Canton Schools, 1960–1980*. New York: Columbia University Press, 1982.

———. "Incentives, Ideology, and Peasant Interests in a Chinese Village, 1960–1980." In William L. Parish, ed., *Chinese Rural Development: The Great Transformation*, pp. 117–40. Armonk: M. E. Sharpe, 1985.

Verba, Sidney, and Norman H. Nie. *Participation in America: Political Democracy and Social Equality*. New York: Harper and Row, 1977.

Vogel, Ezra. *Canton Under Communism: Programs and Politics in a Provincial Capital*. New York: Harper and Row, 1969.

———. "Land Reform in Kwangtung: 1951–1953." *CQ* 38 (April–June, 1969): 27–62.

Walder, Andrew. "Participative Management and Worker Control in China." *Sociology of Work and Occupations* 8, no. 2 (May 1981): 224–52.

———. "Some Ironies of the Maoist Legacy in Industry." In Mark Selden and Victor Lippitt, eds., *The Transition to Socialism in China*, pp. 215–37. Armonk: M. E. Sharpe, 1982.

Walker, Kenneth R. *Planning in Chinese Agriculture: Socialization and the Private Sector, 1956–62*. Chicago: Aldine Press, 1965.

Wan Li. "Speech at a Joint Session of the Conference of Agricultural Secretaries and Conference on Rural Ideological and Political Work." Nov. 5, 1982, in *RMRB*, Dec. 23, 1982, in FBIS 2 (Jan. 4, 1983): K2–K20.

Wang, James C. F. *Contemporary Chinese Politics: An Introduction*. Englewood Cliffs, N.J.: Prentice Hall, 1981.

Wang Xizhe. *Mao Zedong and the Cultural Revolution.* Hong Kong: Plough Publications, 1981.

Watson, Andrew. "Industrial Management—Experiments in Mass Participation." In Bill Brugger, ed., *China: The Impact of the Cultural Revolution,* pp. 171– 202. London: Croom-Helm, 1978.

Weiner, Myron. "Political Participation: Crisis of the Political Process." In Leonard Binder et al., eds., *Crises and Sequences in Political Development,* pp. 159– 204. Princeton: Princeton University Press, 1971.

White, Gordon. *The Politics of Class and Class Origin: The Case of the Cultural Revolution.* Canberra: Australian National University, 1976.

White, Lynn T. *Careers in Shanghai.* Berkeley and Los Angeles: University of California Press, 1978.

———. "Local Newspapers and Community Change: 1949–1969." In Godwin Chu and Francis L. K. Hsu, eds., *Moving a Mountain: Cultural Change in China,* pp. 76–112. Honolulu: University of Hawaii Press, 1979.

Whyte, Martin King. "Inequality and Stratification in China." *CQ* 64 (Dec. 1975): 684–711.

Womack, Brantly. *The Foundations of Mao Zedong's Political Thought, 1917–1935.* Honolulu: University of Hawaii Press, 1982.

———. "The 1980 County-Level Elections in China: Experiment in Democratic Modernization." *Asian Survey* 22, no. 3 (March 1982): 261–77.

Womack, Brantly, ed. "Electoral Reform in China." *Chinese Law and Government* 15, nos. 3–4 (Fall–Winter 1982–83).

Wong Siu-lun. "Consequences of China's New Population Policy." *CQ* 98 (June 1984): 220–40.

Woodhead, H. G. W., ed. *The China Yearbook, 1929–1930.* Tianjin: Tianjin Press, 1930.

Woodward, Dennis. "'Two Line Struggle' in Agriculture." In Bill Brugger, ed., *China: The Impact of the Cultural Revolution,* pp. 153–70. London: Croom-Helm, 1978.

The World Bank. *China: Socialist Economic Development.* Annex C, Agricultural Development. Report no. 3391-CHA, June 1, 1981.

Wu Min. "From Integration to Separation of Government Administration and Commune Management." *Shanxi Ribao,* June 7, 1982, in FBIS 121 (June 23, 1982): R5–R7.

Wylie, Ray. "The Great Debate." *Far Eastern Economic Review,* Sept. 14, 1967, p. 11.

Yang, C. K. *A Chinese Village in Early Communist Transition.* Boston: MIT Press, 1968.

Yang, Martin C. *A Chinese Village: Taitou, Shantung Province.* New York: Columbia University Press, 1965.

Yu, Frederick T. C. *Mass Persuasion in Communist China.* New York: Praeger, 1964.

Yu Guoyao. "A Brief Discussion of Rural Specialized Households." *RMRB,* June 14, 1982, in FBIS 121 (June 23, 1982): K8–K10.

Zhao Baoxu. "China's Agricultural Policies, Past and Present." Paper presented at the Center for Chinese Studies, University of California, Berkeley, Dec. 1982.

Zhang Chunsheng and Song Dahan. "Separation of Government Administration from Commune Administration Required by the Development of the Rural Economy and the Building of State Power." *RMRB*, July 30, 1982, in *SWB* FE/7098/BII/10 (Aug. 7, 1982).

Zhang Huanguang. "What is Meant by Direct Elections at the County Level?" *RMRB*, Aug. 20, 1980, in JPRS 76547 (Oct. 3, 1980): 30–31.

Zhang Qingfu and Pi Chunxie. "Revise the Electoral Laws to Institutionalize Democracy." *RMRB*, May 22, 1979, in FBIS 103 (May 25, 1979): L5–L8.

Zhu Tong. "Commenting on a Viewpoint of Democracy." *Beijing Ribao*, April 23, 1982, in FBIS 86 (May 4, 1982): K14–K19.

Zweig, David. "Agrarian Radicalism in China, 1968–1978: The Search for a Social Base." Ph.D. dissertation, University of Michigan, 1983.

———. "Context and Content in Policy Implementation: Household Contracts in China, 1977–1983." In David M. Lampton, ed., *Policy Implementation in Post-Mao China*, forthcoming. Berkeley and Los Angeles: University of California Press, 1987.

———. "Economic Development and Social Conflict: The Politics of Prosperity in Rural China." Paper prepared for the 1984 Annual Meeting of the Association of Asian Studies, Washington Hilton Hotel, Washington, D.C., March 23–25, 1984.

———. "Limits to Agrarian Radicalism in China: Local Interests and Opposition to Institutional Transformation in the Chinese Countryside, 1968–1977." Paper presented to the Canadian Political Science Association, Ottawa, Ontario, June 1982.

———. "Opposition to Change in Rural China: The System of Responsibility and People's Communes." *Asian Survey* 23, no. 7 (July 1983): 879–900.

———. "Peasants and the New Incentive System: A Comparison of Three Brigades in Jiangsu Province, 1978–1981." In William Parish, ed., *Chinese Rural Development: The Great Transformation*, pp. 141–63. Armonk: M. E. Sharpe, 1985.

Index

Compositor: G & S Typesetters, Inc.
Text: 10/13 Galliard
Display: Friz Quadrata
Printer: Braun-Brumfield, Inc.
Binder: Braun-Brumfield, Inc.